D De Kee & P N Kaloni (Editors)
University of Windsor, Canada

Recent developments in structured continua

Longman Scientific & Technical
Copublished in the United States with
John Wiley & Sons, Inc., New York

Longman Scientific & Technical
Longman Group UK Limited
Longman House, Burnt Mill, Harlow
Essex CM20 2JE, England
and Associated Companies throughout the world.

Copublished in the United States with
John Wiley & Sons, Inc., 605 Third Avenue, New York, NY 10158

First published 1986

AMS Subject Classifications: 76A, 76D, 76L, 76T, 76Z, 70D, 73B, 73F

ISSN 0269-3674

British Library Cataloguing in Publication Data
Recent developments in structured continua.
—(Pitman research notes in
mathematics series, ISSN 0269-3674; 143)
1. Fluid mechanics—Mathematics
I. De Kee, Daniel II. Kaloni, Purna
532′.001′51 QC145.2

ISBN 0-582-98895-0

Library of Congress Cataloging-in-Publication Data
Recent developments in structured continua.
(Pitman research notes in
mathematics series, ISSN 0269-3674; 143)
Includes bibliographies and indexes.
1. Fluid dynamics. 2. Transport theory.
I. De Kee, Daniel. II. Kaloni, Purna. III. Series:
Pitman research notes in mathematics; 143.
QA911.R4 1986 532′.05 86-13264
ISBN 0-470-20364-1 (USA only)

Printed and bound in Great Britain by
Biddles Ltd, Guildford and King's Lynn

Pitman Research Notes in Mathematics Series

Submission of proposals for consideration
Suggestions for publication, in the form of outlines and representative samples, are invited by the Editorial Board for assessment. Intending authors should approach one of the main editors or another member of the Editorial Board, citing the relevant AMS subject classifications. Alternatively, outlines may be sent directly to the publisher's offices. Refereeing is by members of the board and other mathematical authorities in the topic concerned, throughout the world.

Preparation of accepted manuscripts
On acceptance of a proposal, the publisher will supply full instructions for the preparation of manuscripts in a form suitable for direct photo-lithographic reproduction. Specially printed grid sheets are provided and a contribution is offered by the publisher towards the cost of typing. Word processor output, subject to the publisher's approval, is also acceptable.

Illustrations should be prepared by the authors, ready for direct reproduction without further improvement. The use of hand-drawn symbols should be avoided wherever possible, in order to maintain maximum clarity of the text.

The publisher will be pleased to give any guidance necessary during the preparation of a typescript, and will be happy to answer any queries.

Important note
In order to avoid later retyping, intending authors are strongly urged not to begin final preparation of a typescript before receiving the publisher's guidelines and special paper. In this way it is hoped to preserve the uniform appearance of the series.

Longman Scientific & Technical
Longman House
Burnt Mill
Harlow, Essex, UK
(tel (0279) 26721)

Titles in this series

1 Improperly posed boundary value problems
A Carasso and A P Stone
2 Lie algebras generated by finite dimensional ideals
I N Stewart
3 Bifurcation problems in nonlinear elasticity
R W Dickey
4 Partial differential equations in the complex domain
D L Colton
5 Quasilinear hyperbolic systems and waves
A Jeffrey
6 Solution of boundary value problems by the method of integral operators
D L Colton
7 Taylor expansions and catastrophes
T Poston and I N Stewart
8 Function theoretic methods in differential equations
R P Gilbert and R J Weinacht
9 Differential topology with a view to applications
D R J Chillingworth
10 Characteristic classes of foliations
H V Pittie
11 Stochastic integration and generalized martingales
A U Kussmaul
12 Zeta-functions: An introduction to algebraic geometry
A D Thomas
13 Explicit *a priori* inequalities with applications to boundary value problems
V G Sigillito
14 Nonlinear diffusion
W E Fitzgibbon III and H F Walker
15 Unsolved problems concerning lattice points
J Hammer
16 Edge-colourings of graphs
S Fiorini and R J Wilson
17 Nonlinear analysis and mechanics: Heriot-Watt Symposium Volume I
R J Knops
18 Actions of fine abelian groups
C Kosniowski
19 Closed graph theorems and webbed spaces
M De Wilde
20 Singular perturbation techniques applied to integro-differential equations
H Grabmüller
21 Retarded functional differential equations: A global point of view
S E A Mohammed
22 Multiparameter spectral theory in Hilbert space
B D Sleeman
24 Mathematical modelling techniques
R Aris
25 Singular points of smooth mappings
C G Gibson
26 Nonlinear evolution equations solvable by the spectral transform
F Calogero
27 Nonlinear analysis and mechanics: Heriot-Watt Symposium Volume II
R J Knops
28 Constructive functional analysis
D S Bridges
29 Elongational flows: Aspects of the behaviour of model elasticoviscous fluids
C J S Petrie
30 Nonlinear analysis and mechanics: Heriot-Watt Symposium Volume III
R J Knops
31 Fractional calculus and integral transforms of generalized functions
A C McBride
32 Complex manifold techniques in theoretical physics
D E Lerner and P D Sommers
33 Hilbert's third problem: scissors congruence
C-H Sah
34 Graph theory and combinatorics
R J Wilson
35 The Tricomi equation with applications to the theory of plane transonic flow
A R Manwell
36 Abstract differential equations
S D Zaidman
37 Advances in twistor theory
L P Hughston and R S Ward
38 Operator theory and functional analysis
I Erdelyi
39 Nonlinear analysis and mechanics: Heriot-Watt Symposium Volume IV
R J Knops
40 Singular systems of differential equations
S L Campbell
41 N-dimensional crystallography
R L E Schwarzenberger
42 Nonlinear partial differential equations in physical problems
D Graffi
43 Shifts and periodicity for right invertible operators
D Przeworska-Rolewicz
44 Rings with chain conditions
A W Chatters and C R Hajarnavis
45 Moduli, deformations and classifications of compact complex manifolds
D Sundararaman
46 Nonlinear problems of analysis in geometry and mechanics
M Atteia, D Bancel and I Gumowski
47 Algorithmic methods in optimal control
W A Gruver and E Sachs
48 Abstract Cauchy problems and functional differential equations
F Kappel and W Schappacher
49 Sequence spaces
W H Ruckle
50 Recent contributions to nonlinear partial differential equations
H Berestycki and H Brezis
51 Subnormal operators
J B Conway
52 Wave propagation in viscoelastic media
F Mainardi
53 Nonlinear partial differential equations and their applications: Collège de France Seminar. Volume I
H Brezis and J L Lions

54 Geometry of Coxeter groups
H Hiller
55 Cusps of Gauss mappings
T Banchoff, T Gaffney and C McCrory
56 An approach to algebraic K-theory
A J Berrick
57 Convex analysis and optimization
J-P Aubin and R B Vintner
58 Convex analysis with applications in the differentiation of convex functions
J R Giles
59 Weak and variational methods for moving boundary problems
C M Elliott and J R Ockendon
60 Nonlinear partial differential equations and their applications: Collège de France Seminar. Volume II
H Brezis and J L Lions
61 Singular systems of differential equations II
S L Campbell
62 Rates of convergence in the central limit theorem
Peter Hall
63 Solution of differential equations by means of one-parameter groups
J M Hill
64 Hankel operators on Hilbert space
S C Power
65 Schrödinger-type operators with continuous spectra
M S P Eastham and H Kalf
66 Recent applications of generalized inverses
S L Campbell
67 Riesz and Fredholm theory in Banach algebra
B A Barnes, G J Murphy, M R F Smyth and T T West
68 Evolution equations and their applications
F Kappel and W Schappacher
69 Generalized solutions of Hamilton-Jacobi equations
P L Lions
70 Nonlinear partial differential equations and their applications: Collège de France Seminar. Volume III
H Brezis and J L Lions
71 Spectral theory and wave operators for the Schrödinger equation
A M Berthier
72 Approximation of Hilbert space operators I
D A Herrero
73 Vector valued Nevanlinna Theory
H J W Ziegler
74 Instability, nonexistence and weighted energy methods in fluid dynamics and related theories
B Straughan
75 Local bifurcation and symmetry
A Vanderbauwhede
76 Clifford analysis
F Brackx, R Delanghe and F Sommen
77 Nonlinear equivalence, reduction of PDEs to ODEs and fast convergent numerical methods
E E Rosinger
78 Free boundary problems, theory and applications. Volume I
A Fasano and M Primicerio
79 Free boundary problems, theory and applications. Volume II
A Fasano and M Primicerio
80 Symplectic geometry
A Crumeyrolle and J Grifone
81 An algorithmic analysis of a communication model with retransmission of flawed messages
D M Lucantoni
82 Geometric games and their applications
W H Ruckle
83 Additive groups of rings
S Feigelstock
84 Nonlinear partial differential equations and their applications: Collège de France Seminar. Volume IV
H Brezis and J L Lions
85 Multiplicative functionals on topological algebras
T Husain
86 Hamilton-Jacobi equations in Hilbert spaces
V Barbu and G Da Prato
87 Harmonic maps with symmetry, harmonic morphisms and deformations of metrics
P Baird
88 Similarity solutions of nonlinear partial differential equations
L Dresner
89 Contributions to nonlinear partial differential equations
C Bardos, A Damlamian, J I Díaz and J Hernández
90 Banach and Hilbert spaces of vector-valued functions
J Burbea and P Masani
91 Control and observation of neutral systems
D Salamon
92 Banach bundles, Banach modules and automorphisms of C*-algebras
M J Dupré and R M Gillette
93 Nonlinear partial differential equations and their applications: Collège de France Seminar. Volume V
H Brezis and J L Lions
94 Computer algebra in applied mathematics: an introduction to MACSYMA
R H Rand
95 Advances in nonlinear waves. Volume I
L Debnath
96 FC-groups
M J Tomkinson
97 Topics in relaxation and ellipsoidal methods
M Akgül
98 Analogue of the group algebra for topological semigroups
H Dzinotyiweyi
99 Stochastic functional differential equations
S E A Mohammed
100 Optimal control of variational inequalities
V Barbu
101 Partial differential equations and dynamical systems
W E Fitzgibbon III
102 Approximation of Hilbert space operators. Volume II
C Apostol, L A Fialkow, D A Herrero and D Voiculescu
103 Nondiscrete induction and iterative processes
V Ptak and F-A Potra

104 Analytic functions – growth aspects
O P Juneja and G P Kapoor
105 Theory of Tikhonov regularization for Fredholm equations of the first kind
C W Groetsch
106 Nonlinear partial differential equations and free boundaries. Volume I
J I Díaz
107 Tight and taut immersions of manifolds
T E Cecil and P J Ryan
108 A layering method for viscous, incompressible L_p flows occupying R^n
A Douglis and E B Fabes
109 Nonlinear partial differential equations and their applications: Collège de France Seminar. Volume VI
H Brezis and J L Lions
110 Finite generalized quadrangles
S E Payne and J A Thas
111 Advances in nonlinear waves. Volume II
L Debnath
112 Topics in several complex variables
E Ramírez de Arellano and D Sundararaman
113 Differential equations, flow invariance and applications
N H Pavel
114 Geometrical combinatorics
F C Holroyd and R J Wilson
115 Generators of strongly continuous semigroups
J A van Casteren
116 Growth of algebras and Gelfand–Kirillov dimension
G R Krause and T H Lenagan
117 Theory of bases and cones
P K Kamthan and M Gupta
118 Linear groups and permutations
A R Camina and E A Whelan
119 General Wiener–Hopf factorization methods
F-O Speck
120 Free boundary problems: applications and theory, Volume III
A Bossavit, A Damlamian and M Fremond
121 Free boundary problems: applications and theory, Volume IV
A Bossavit, A Damlamian and M Fremond
122 Nonlinear partial differential equations and their applications: Collège de France Seminar. Volume VII
H Brezis and J L Lions
123 Geometric methods in operator algebras
H Araki and E G Effros
124 Infinite dimensional analysis–stochastic processes
S Albeverio
125 Ennio de Giorgi Colloquium
P Krée
126 Almost-periodic functions in abstract spaces
S Zaidman
127 Nonlinear variational problems
A Marino, L Modica, S Spagnolo and M Degiovanni
128 Second-order systems of partial differential equations in the plane
L K Hua, W Lin and C-Q Wu
129 Asymptotics of high-order ordinary differential equations
R B Paris and A D Wood
130 Stochastic differential equations
R Wu
131 Differential geometry
L A Cordero
132 Nonlinear differential equations
J K Hale and P Martinez-Amores
133 Approximation theory and applications
S P Singh
134 Near-rings and their links with groups
J D P Meldrum
135 Estimating eigenvalues with *a posteriori/a priori* inequalities
J R Kuttler and V G Sigillito
136 Regular semigroups as extensions
F J Pastijn and M Petrich
137 Representations of rank one Lie groups
D H Collingwood
138 Fractional calculus
G F Roach and A C McBride
139 Hamilton's principle in continuum mechanics
A Bedford
140 Numerical analysis
D F Griffiths and G A Watson
141 Semigroups, theory and applications. Volume I
H Brezis, M G Crandall and F Kappel
142 Distribution theorems of L-functions
D Joyner
143 Recent developments in structured continua
D De Kee and P Kaloni
144 Functional analysis and two-point differential operators
J Locker
145 Numerical methods for partial differential equations
S I Hariharan and T H Moulden
146 Completely bounded maps and dilations
V I Paulsen
147 Harmonic analysis on the Heisenberg nilpotent Lie group
W Schempp
148 Contributions to modern calculus of variations
L Cesari
149 Nonlinear parabolic equations: qualitative properties of solutions
L Boccardo and A Tesei
150 From local times to global geometry, control and physics
K D Elworthy
151 A stochastic maximum principle for optimal control of diffusions
U G Haussmann
152 Semigroups, theory and applications. Volume II
H Brezis, M G Crandall and F Kappel

Recent developments in structured continua

Contents

Page

CHAPTER 5

CHAPTER 6

CHAPTER 7

Preface

This collection of papers contains the full text of the invited lectures presented at the Conference on "Recent Developments in Structured Continua", held at the University of Windsor, May 29-31, 1985. Recent rapid advances in the fields of transport phenomena, polymer mechanics, flow properties of biological fluids and the structured fluid theories clearly indicated that such a meeting was desirable and timely. While we could not avail the services of various other experts, we hope that the present collection makes a significant contribution in the areas mentioned above.

The technical content of the papers is also roughly divided into the four broad categories stated above. In Chapter 1, Adler discusses the transport processes in fractals and reports several new contributions in this fascinating but relatively new field of research. In Chapter 2, Haber and Brenner generalize the important Taylor-Aris dispersion problem by deriving the formula for the molecular diffusivity of a deformable chain, under quite general circumstances. In the next chapter Brunn treats the suspension problem in tube flow and proposes a classification scheme to analyze various rheological regimes. In Chapter 4, Carreau and Grmela discuss theories, proposed through molecular considerations, to describe the behaviour of polymeric materials. They also discuss the advantages and limitations of such theories as they relate to several observed phenomena dealing with polymeric fluids. In Chapter 5, De Kee presents a critique of the equations of state, which have been inspired by the network theories, and discusses the use of newly developed tests for discriminating various rheological models. In the next chapter, Goddard addresses the celebrated question of deriving the continuum stress fields from the statistical mechanics approach and raises several interesting unresolved issues. In Chapter 7, Goldsmith et al. discuss some of their recent results regarding the cellular interactions in human blood subjected to flow in tubes. In the last chapter, Niefer and Kaloni present a general Cartesian tensor solution of the polar fluid equations and use the results to present the solution of some standard suspension problems in polar fluids.

Our thanks go to the invited speakers for their cooperation in submitting the material for this volume. We would like to acknowledge the financial support received from the NSERC of Canada, the President and Deans of the faculties of Science and Engineering of the University of Windsor. Finally, we wish to record our special thanks to Mrs. Linda Breschuk for excellent typing.

D. De Kee

P.N. Kaloni

November, 1985

ACKNOWLEDGEMENTS

Thanks are due to the following for permission to reproduce material from their publications:

Academic Press
The Canadian Journal of Chemical Engineering
New York Academy of Sciences
Pergamon Press
The Society of Rheology Inc.

List of contributors

Dr. P.M. Adler
C.N.R.S.
Meudon, France

Mr. D.N. Bell
McGill University
Montreal, Canada

Professor H. Brenner
W.H. Dow Professor of Chemical Engineering
Massachusetts Institute of Technology
Cambridge, U.S.A.

Dr. P.O. Brunn
Department of Chemical Engineering and Applied Chemistry
Columbia University
New York, U.S.A.

Professor P.J. Carreau
Department of Chemical Engineering
Ecole Polytechnique
Montreal, Canada

Professor D. De Kee
Department of Chemical Engineering and Fluid Dynamics Research Institute
University of Windsor
Windsor, Canada

Professor J.D. Goddard
R.J. Fluor Professor of Chemical Engineering
University of Southern California
Los Angeles, U.S.A.

Professor H.L. Goldsmith
Montreal General Hospital
McGill University
Montreal, Canada

Dr. M. Grmela
Ecole Polytechnique
Montreal, Canada

Dr. S. Haber
Faculty of Mechanical Engineering
Technion - Israel Institute of Technology
Haifa, Israel

Professor P.N. Kaloni
Department of Mathematics and Fluid Dynamics Research Institute
University of Windsor
Windsor, Canada

Dr. R. Niefer
Memorial University
Newfoundland, Canada

Mrs. S. Spain
McGill University
Montreal, Canada

Dr. S.P. Tha
McGill University
Montreal, Canada

P M ADLER

Transport processes in fractals

1. INTRODUCTION

The determination of the transport properties of dispersed systems, such as suspensions, porous media... is a problem of fundamental interest and of great practical utility. Though a very large number of papers, reviews and books has been published on the subject over the years, it has not been satisfactorily solved yet.

Dispersed systems are characterized by the existence of various length scales. Classically, two classes of length scales are distinguished. These are : (i) the interval of scales (a_{min}, a_{max}) of the particles over which the local, interstitial fields vary ; (ii) the length scale L over which the mean or average fields vary sensibly. Typically, L corresponds to a characteristic linear dimension of the external boundaries of the system. Since L is usually much larger than a_{max}, it is standard to introduce an intermediate length scale $\mathcal{L}$, such that $L \gg \mathcal{L} \gg a_{max}$; $\mathcal{L}$ corresponds to the existence of a translational symmetry in the dispersed system.

So far, no hypothesis has been made on the local structures, symbolized by the interval (a_{min}, a_{max}). These structures may be very simple such as a regular array of equal solid spheres ; the limits a_{min} and a_{max} coalesce into a single scale, say a, the radius of the sphere. In this situation, no further information can be gained without solving the whole problem.

However, recently new structures of high interest have been introduced when dispersed media possess a dilational invariance, which implies a whole spectrum of length scales between a_{min} and a_{max}. A loose definition of such objects is that they look the same, whatever the observation scale ; a classical example is the Sierpinski gasket which will be described below. Such objects which are called fractals were first introduced by Mandelbrot ; his most recent book [14] is a fascinating recollection of his major works. The development of this new field is spurred by a large range of applications, which include heterogeneous porous media. Note that the fractal character may be a consequence of the existence of many predetermined length scales in the medium, such as a very heterogeneous sand. It may also be a consequence of the statistical construction of the material (cf. percolation networks and Witten-Sanders aggregates [19,22] ; in these examples, there is only one size of the network or of the particles, but a whole spectrum of length scales is obtained through the statistical generation of the material.

This close connection between randomly generated objects and fractals explains why the field of potential applications is so wide, such as polymer coils, polymers adsorbed on a solid surface [8], clouds [10], dielectric breakdown [16], fracture surfaces of metals [15], aggregates of colloids [21], fluid-fluid interfaces in porous media [12], and so on.

In view of these numerous applications, a systematic study of transport properties in these fractal media was undertaken. The purpose of this paper is to briefly introduce fractals, to survey our own contributions and to indicate the major extensions which will be done in a near future.

This paper is organized as follows. Generalities are gathered in section 2 ; fractals are defined as well as the important concept of fractal dimension ; some useful examples are given ; the various transport processes of interest are briefly recalled. Fractal capillary networks are studied in section 3 ; we restricted ourselves to homogeneous fractals ; flows of Newtonian and non-Newtonian fluids are calculated by means of transfer matrices ; power laws are obtained, the exponent of which is independent of the elementary graphs ; Taylor dispersion is then briefly analysed in a tree and a Sierpinski carpet.

Continuous structures are gathered in section 4 ; here, fluids are flowing around solid objects of finite dimensions. So far, only two-dimensional geometries have been studied. Transversal properties of Leibniz packings are calculated in the lubrication limit ; power laws are obtained for conductivity and permeability ; in the former process, an interesting phenomenon called isotropisation is obtained. The longitudinal permeability of Sierpinski carpet is shown to have the same scaling as the classical Carman-Kozeny law, in the limit of large fractal generation ; this result could be of a very large general interest. Finally, transport properties along a particular sort of fractal that we have called the Cantor-Taylor brush are shown to become very rapidly constant with the fractal generation ; this may prove to be important in several areas such as the classical problem of the boundary condition at the surface of a porous medium.

Some general concluding remarks are offered in section 5, as well as various extensions of the previous topics, such as three dimensional and random structures, nonlinear and time dependent phenomena.

2. GENERAL

The easiest way to introduce fractals is to quote Mandelbrot (1982). He noticed that he was spurred by the "existence of irregular and fragmented patterns in Nature, such as clouds, mountains, coastlines or trees". Also the most remarkable feature of these shapes is that "they tend to be scaling, implying that the degree of their irregularity and/or fragmentation is identical at all length scales". An important aspect which is left out in this paper is the random character of these shapes ; note that the two concepts are closely related since Brownian paths are fractal.

Basic definition

A useful way to technically introduce fractals was given by Hutchinson [11]. He defined an invariant compact set $K \subseteq R^n$ as a set such that

$$K = \bigcup_{\alpha=1}^{M} S_\alpha K \qquad (2.1)$$

where $\{S_\alpha \; ; \alpha = 1, \ldots, M\}$ is a finite family of contraction maps on R^n. Often, but not always the S_α are similitudes. It should be noted that such a set usually possesses no inferior limit to its scales, which is not actually what happens in nature.

This definition may be used as a tool to generate fractals. Different construction processes with an initiator and a generator are given by Mandelbrot [14], but (2.1) is certainly very versatile. Let us start with an elementary set K_0 (such as a graph or a geometrical shape). Then, a finite family of transformations S_α is applied to K_0 ; M sets $S_\alpha K_0$ are obtained and unionized ; this yields K_1. Such a process may be repeated as many times as desired and is expressed by the recursion relation

$$K_N = \bigcup_{\alpha=1}^{M} S_\alpha K_{N-1} \qquad (2.2)$$

The index N is called the generation or the construction stage. The set K is obtained in the limit where N tends towards infinity.

The most classical examples of fractals, due to Sierpinski, are shown in Figure 2.1. Many other ones are given in Mandelbrot [14].

A basic concept is the fractal dimension of such sets (which may provide an other way to define fractals). The only sharp concept is the so-called Hausdorff dimension, but it turns out in most cases to be extremely difficult to use. Another notion is the similarity dimension ; let r_α be the ratio of

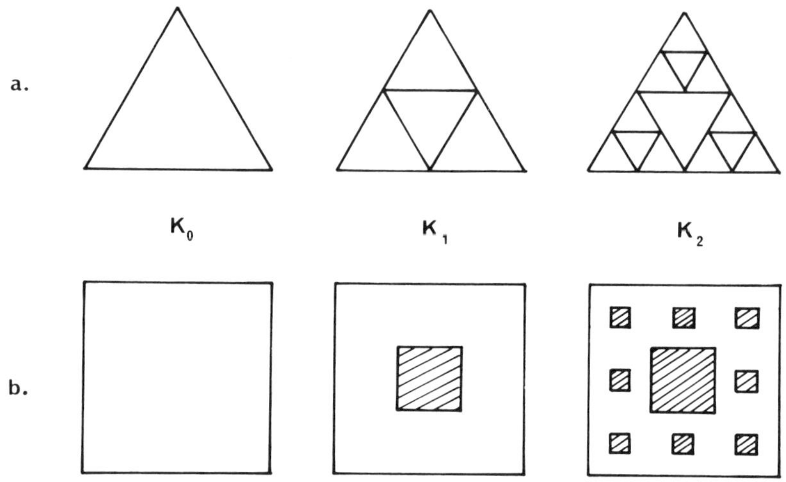

Fig. 2.1 - Two classical examples of fractals.
(a) : Sierpinski gasket ; the basic set is a triangle ; three such triangles reduced by a ratio 2 are assembled.
(b) : Sierpinski carpet ; the basic set is a square whose centre has been removed ; eight such sets reduced by a ratio 3 are assembled.

the similarity S_α ; then, the similarity dimension is defined as the unique positive number such that

$$\sum_{\alpha=1}^{M} r_i^D = 1 \qquad (2.3)$$

In most cases, the similarity dimension is identical to the Hausdorff dimension (cf. [11]). When the M similarities S_α are the same, with a common ratio r, D is deduced from (2.3) to be

$$D = \frac{\text{Log } M}{\text{Log } 1/r} \qquad (2.4)$$

Note that for ordinary objects, the standard Euclidean dimension is obtained: a segment of length 1 may be divided in M = b parts of length 1/M ; hence 1/r = M and (2.4) obviously yields D = 1.

The examples of Figure 2.1 have the following fractal dimensions. A Sierpinski gasket is composed of M = 3 gaskets reduced by a factor r = 1/2 ; its dimension is thus D = Log 3/Log 2 = 1.5849... Likewise a Sierpinski carpet is composed of M = 8 carpets reduced by a factor r = 1/3 ; its dimension is thus D = Log 8/Log 3 = 1.8927...

Transport processes

Our major purpose is the calculation of some of the most usual transport processes in an around simple and typical fractals. These processes may be classified as follows.

Let us first consider conduction-type transport phenomena, which include molecular diffusion of matter, heat conduction and flow of electric current via conduction. When the terminology of heat conduction is used, they are governed at the microscopic level by Fourier's law in addition to the conservation of energy ; they may be expressed as

$$\underset{\sim}{j} = -k \nabla T \quad ; \qquad \nabla . \underset{\sim}{j} = 0 \qquad (2.5)$$

where $\underset{\sim}{j}$ is the local heat flux, k the conductivity, T the temperature. To these equations are associated various boundary conditions such as the continuity of $\underset{\sim}{j}$ across any solid surface and the like. Usually, one wants to determine a macroscopic conductivity tensor.

The second basic transport process consists of the flow of a Newtonian fluid through a porous medium, at low Reynolds number ; the fluid velocity $\underset{\sim}{v}$ and the pressure obey to the classical Stokes equations

$$\nabla p = \mu \nabla^2 \underset{\sim}{v} \; ; \quad \nabla . \underset{\sim}{v} = 0 \tag{2.6}$$

together with the adherence condition at the surface of solid particles. μ is the viscosity of the fluid. Here, a macroscopic permeability tensor is generally calculated.

Next, the flow of non-Newtonian fluids can be considered. The simplest case of such fluids are the so-called power-law fluids. They are characterized by a shear rate-dependent scalar viscosity function

$$\mu = K\,(2\underset{\sim}{\underset{\sim}{S}}:\underset{\sim}{\underset{\sim}{S}})^{n-1} \tag{2.7}$$

where n and K are the power-law index and consistency of the fluid, respectively. $\underset{\sim}{\underset{\sim}{S}}$ is the rate-of-strain dyadic. A macroscopic transfer function may be deduced.

Finally, Taylor dispersion is of great theoretical and practical importance. It is concerned with the asymptotic time-dependent, spatial distribution of a Brownian particle when introduced into a fluid flowing through a porous medium. The probability P is locally governed by a convective-diffusion equation

$$\frac{\partial P}{\partial t} = - \nabla . (\underset{\sim}{v} P) + D \nabla^2 P \tag{2.8}$$

where D is the molecular diffusivity of the tracer. Usually, the asymptotic behaviour for large times of the first moments of P is analysed.

These may be considered as the major transport processes which are usually encountered. Note that the processes may occur inside a given fractal or around it. Both cases will be studied here, and the specific applications will be mentionned.

Generally speaking, to a given transport process is associated a macroscopic quantity of interest such as a macroscopic conductivity or permeability tensor. According to our results relative to the configuations that we have studied such as Leibniz packings, fractal networks and others, it is always true that these macroscopic quantities generically denoted by $\overline{K}_N$ asymptotically behave as

$$\overline{K}_N \sim k_1 . \ \alpha_1^N , \quad \text{for large } N \tag{2.9.a}$$

$$\sim k . \ N_n^{\alpha} , \quad \text{equivalently} \tag{2.9.b}$$

where k, k_1, α, α_1 are constant. N_n denotes the number of sets K_o in the fractal; it is thus equal to M^N. Usually, the form (2.9.b) is preferred. It is generally believed that the constant k depends upon the detailed features of the configuration, while the exponent α is independent of those details and depends only upon the gross features. Let us illustrate these comments as follows ; in Sierpinski carpets, the removed squares may be replaced by disks whose diameter is equal to the sides of the corresponding squares. The general belief is that k depends upon the shape, disks or squares, but that α is the same for both.

It is now possible to restate our major goal. For a series of characteristic configurations, we wish to determine the exponent α of the asymptotic power law (2.9.b), and when possible, the constant k. For this purpose, it is sometimes necessary to forge new methods.

The rest of this paper is devoted to specific situations. Capillary networks are addressed in Section 3, and continuous structures in Section 4.

3. FRACTAL CAPILLARY NETWORKS

The study of this particular class of fractals is motivated by several reasons. First, natural porous media are often schematized by consolidated arrays of interconnected capillary networks ; the fractal structure is thus a convenient idealization of the heterogeneous character of these media, with the proeminent example of the percolation network (see [19]). Second, it is much easier to solve the discrete system of equations which describes the process in networks than the partial differential equations relative to the same process in continuous systems. Third, it will be seen in Section 4 that transport processes in continuous structures are not amenable so far to analytical calculations ; hence, they must be solved by using finite element methods, which yield discretized systems very close to the networks studied here.

After a brief description of the construction process, the permeability for Stokes flow of these networks is derived by means of transfer matrices ;

non linear flow problems are addressed and some comments are made on Taylor dispersion in these structures.

Construction

Of course, a capillary network may be schematized by a graph, when a clear distinction exists between the junctions themselves and the capillaries connecting them. In place of the physical terms "junctions" and "capillaries", we shall employ the graph terms "vertices" and "edges", respectively (cf. [3] which is hereafter referred to as II).

The fractal capillary network may be constructed in a way which is readily deduced from (2.2), where the compact sets K_N are replaced by finite graphs. The starting point is an elementary graph Γ_0 called the basic graph ; then, the successive fractal graphs Γ_N are obtained by application of the recursion relation

$$\Gamma_N = \bigcup_{\alpha=1}^{M} S_\alpha \Gamma_{N-1} \quad ; \quad N > 1 \tag{3.1}$$

This construction process may be decomposed in the two major steps illustrated in Figure 3.1 for N = 1. First, the graph Γ_1' is defined as the juxtaposition of the graphs $S_\alpha \Gamma_0$; at this stage, there is no interconnection between the external vertices of the graphs $S_\alpha \Gamma_0$. Second, these external vertices are connected one to the other one in a specified way.

Let us assume that Γ_0 possesses n_e external vertices and that the interconnections are defined in such a way as to leave n_e external vertices to the graph Γ_1. Then, the construction process can be indefinitely continued. This restriction is a major one, since the number of common vertices between two successive generations is always equal to n_e ; in the terminology of Leyvraz and Stanley [13], such a fractal is called non-homogeneous ; this refers to the small number of vertices, or "bottlenecks", between successive generations ; when the number of common vertices goes to infinity (cf. the percolation network), the fractal is called homogeneous, and several examples are offered in the next section.

Other restrictions are imposed on this construction process ; they are more technical in character and can be found in II with the relevant details; they may be summed up as follows. Connections between external and internal vertices of different subgraphs are forbidden ; an external vertex or $S_\alpha \Gamma_0$

cannot be left dangling ; multiple connections between three or more external vertices are not allowed.

Finally, the construction can be algebraically described by a few finite matrices which will be introduced later. Now, let us analyse and solve three usual transport processes in these homogeneous capillary networks.

Stokes flow

Flow of a Newtonian fluid at low Reynolds number in a capillary network is characterized by two laws, which are readily deduced from (2.6). The pressure difference between two adjacent vertices i and i' is proportional to the flow rate J(j) between these vertices.
Explicitly,

$$p(i) - p(i') = \mu\, s(j)\, J(j) \tag{3.2}$$

where j denotes the oriented edge {i,i'}. s(j) is the "pressure drop-flow rate conductivity" coefficient along the edge j. When the capillary j is a cylinder of radius R(j) and length L(j), Poiseuille law applies and s(j) can be expressed as

$$s(j) = \frac{8}{\pi} \cdot \frac{L(j)}{R^4(j)} \tag{3.3}$$

The second law is the conservation of the total flow rate at each vertex i ; it may be expressed as

$$\sum_{j \in \Omega^+(i)} J(j) - \sum_{j \in \Omega^-(i)} J(j) = 0 \tag{3.4}$$

where $\Omega^+(i)$ is the set of the edges j incident to the vertex i, while $\Omega^-(i)$ is the set of the edges j going out of the vertex i.

These two laws govern the flow inside any capillary network. Now, let us consider the fractal network Γ_N. A priori, we are only interested by the relation between the flow rates going in and out of the network, and the pressures imposed at the external vertices. Hence, to each external vertex of Γ_N can be associated a pressure and a flow rate, with the arbitrary convention that the flow rate is positive when it goes out of Γ_N. The n_e pressures and flow rates can be represented by the vectors $\underset{\sim}{P}_N^{(e)}$ and $\underset{\sim}{J}_N^{(e)}$, whose i^{th} elements are the pressure and flow rates at the ith external vertex of Γ_N. As a consequence of the linearity of (3.2) and (3.4), a linear relation exists between these two vectors, which may be expressed as

$$\underset{\sim}{J}_N^{(e)} = \frac{1}{\mu} \cdot \underset{\approx}{A}_N \cdot \underset{\sim}{P}_N^{(e)} \tag{3.5}$$

where $\underset{\approx}{A}_N$ is a $n_e x n_e$ matrix, called the transfer matrix of the graph Γ_N.

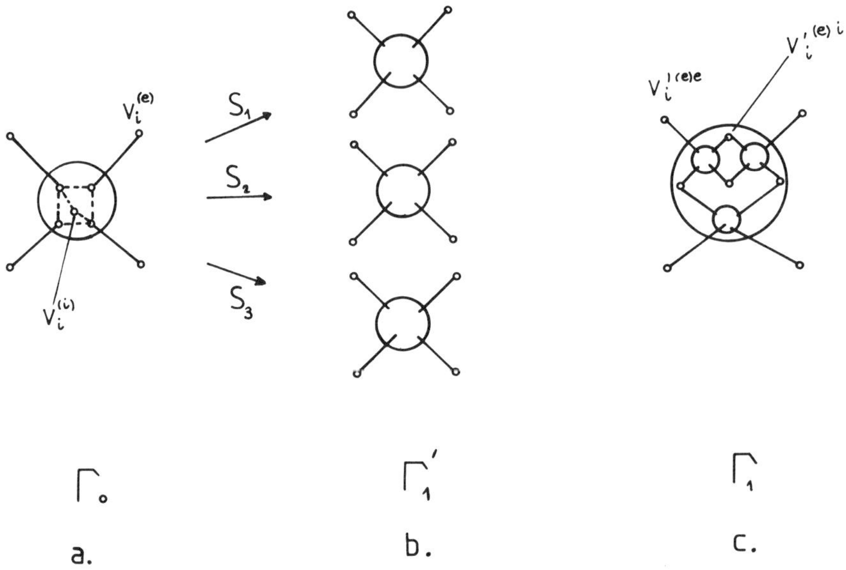

Fig. 3.1 - Construction of a fractal.
(a) : The basic graph Γ_o with its n_e external vertices $v_i^{(e)}$ and its $n-n_e$ internal vertices $v_i^{(i)}$.
(b) : The transformations S_α (α=1,...,M) yield the graph Γ'_1 made of the juxtaposition of M transformed graphs $S_\alpha\ \Gamma_o$.
(c) : These graphs are then interconnected in a specified way to form the graph Γ_1. Note the distinction between the external vertices $v_i^{'(e)i}$ of Γ'_1 which become internal vertices of Γ_1, and the external vertices $v_i^{'(e)e}$ of Γ'_1 which become external vertices of Γ_1.

$\underset{\approx}{A}_N$ is symmetric, but non-invertible. Rather, the flow rates do not vary when an arbitrary constant is added to the pressures ; hence

$$\underset{\approx}{A}_N \cdot \underset{\sim}{1} = 0 \tag{3.6}$$

where $\underset{\sim}{1}$ denotes the vector $(\overbrace{1 \ldots 1}^{n_e})^t$. Equivalently, there exists a transposed relation of (3.6) which may be interpreted as the fact that the sum of the outgoing flow rates is equal to 0.

One of the major purposes of the analysis of Stokes flow in fractal networks is to derive the asymptotic behaviour of the transfer matrix $\underset{\approx}{A}_N$, when N is large. The easiest way to obtain it consists in the derivation of a recursion relation between successive generations. In II, such a relation is derived with many technical details. It may be expressed as

$$\underset{\approx}{A}_N = \underset{\approx}{F}(\underset{\approx}{A}_{N-1}) = -(\underset{\approx}{S}_2 . \underset{\approx\approx}{E}_1 : \underset{\approx}{A}_{N-1}) \cdot \underset{\approx}{L}^+ \cdot [\underset{\approx}{L} . (\underset{\approx}{S}_1 . \underset{\approx\approx}{E}_1 : \underset{\approx}{A}_{N-1}) \cdot \underset{\approx}{L}^+]^{-1} .$$

$$(\underset{\approx}{L} . \underset{\approx}{S}_1 . \underset{\approx\approx}{E}_2 : \underset{\approx}{A}_{N-1}) + \underset{\approx}{S}_2 . \underset{\approx\approx}{E}_2 : \underset{\approx}{A}_{N-1} \tag{3.7}$$

which is nonlinear. The ingredients present in the construction process may be recognized in this formula. The replications of the M subgraphs is performed by the fourth-order tensors $\underset{\approx\approx}{E}_1$ and $\underset{\approx\approx}{E}_2$; the similarity transformations $S_\alpha(\alpha=1,\ldots,M)$ are symbolized by the second-order tensors $\underset{\approx}{S}_1$ and $\underset{\approx}{S}_2$. The indices 1 and 2 are related to the external vertices of the graphs $S_\alpha \Gamma_{N-1}$ which become either internal or external vertices at the generation N. The second-order tensor $\underset{\approx}{L}$ algebraically describes the connections between the various subgraphs. Finally, (3.7) is derived by writing that, at external connected vertices, pressures are equal and flow rates equal and opposite.

An important simplification occurs when the relation (3.7) can be linearized and written as

$$\underset{\approx}{A}_N = \underset{\approx\approx}{\mathfrak{F}} : \underset{\approx}{A}_{N-1} \tag{3.8}$$

where $\underset{\approx\approx}{\mathfrak{F}}$ is a fourth-order tensor that we called the fractal tensor.

Such a relation can be obtained when $\underset{\approx}{F}$ has a fixed point $\underset{\approx}{A}_\infty$, i.e.

$$\underset{\approx}{A}_\infty = \underset{\approx}{F}(\underset{\approx}{A}_\infty) \tag{3.9}$$

which is in many cases located at the origin, i.e. $\underset{\approx}{A}_\infty = 0$. When $\underset{\approx}{F}$ is differentiable near $\underset{\approx}{A}_{\infty}$, it is an easy matter to realize that the fractal tensor $\underset{\approx}{\mathcal{F}}$ may be expressed as

$$\underset{\approx}{\mathcal{F}} = \left. \frac{\partial \underset{\approx}{F}}{\partial \underset{\approx}{A}} \right|_{\underset{\approx}{A}_{\infty}} \tag{3.10}$$

The relation (3.7) has a remarkable feature which was not fully realized and thus discussed in II. $\underset{\approx}{A}_o$ is nowhere present in (3.7) ; $\underset{\approx}{A}_o$ only provides the initial conditions to the recursion relation (3.7). Hence, it can be stated that the final fractal relation does not depend upon the structure of the initial graph, or equivalently upon the details of the basic graphs.

This may not always be true and serious problems may arise in connection with the unicity of the fixed points of $\underset{\approx}{F}(\underset{\approx}{A})$. $\underset{\approx}{A}_N$ may tend towards various fixed points, depending upon the region where $\underset{\approx}{A}_o$ is initially located. This technical matter will not be addressed further in this paper, since we could not exhibit yet such pathological structures of practical interest.

As a direct consequence, the fractal tensor (3.10) may be considered as generally independent upon $\underset{\approx}{A}_o$. It shows that the exponent α of the power law (2.9) is also independent of $\underset{\approx}{A}_o$ and thus of the detailed structure of the basic graph, as it was stated in the previous section.

Another important relation is that the pressure and flow rate vectors $\underset{\sim}{P}_N^{(e)}$ and $\underset{\sim}{J}_N^{(e)}$ are themselves fractal in the limit of large N. Let $\underset{\sim}{P}'^{(e)}_{N-1}$ and $\underset{\sim}{J}'^{(e)}_{N-1}$ denote the pressure and flow rate vectors at the external vertices of the juxtaposed graph Γ'_{N-1}. We could show in II that

$$\underset{\sim}{P}'^{(e)}_{N-1} \simeq \underset{\approx}{G} \cdot \underset{\sim}{P}_N^{(e)} \quad , \quad N \to \infty \tag{3.11.a}$$

$$\underset{\sim}{J}'^{(e)}_{N-1} \simeq \underset{\approx}{H} \cdot \underset{\sim}{J}_N^{(e)} \quad , \quad N \to \infty \tag{3.11.b}$$

where $\underset{\approx}{G}$ and $\underset{\approx}{H}$ are $Mn_e \times n_e$ matrices.

These developments may be illustrated by the Sierpinski gasket displayed in Fig. 2.1.a. It is easily shown that the recursion relation (3.7) simplifies into

$$\underset{\approx}{A}_N = \frac{3}{5} \cdot \underset{\approx}{A}_{N-1} \tag{3.12}$$

Note that such a relation can be readily derived by an application of the classical star-triangle transformation.

Extension to nonlinear flow problems

The previous methods were generalized in Adler [4] (1985.b), hereafter referred to as IV, to non-Newtonian fluids flowing through a fractal capillary network.

Let us start with power law fluids. These are the inelastic fluids described by (2.7). The pressure drop along a given edge j is concisely summarized by

$$p(i) - p(i') = K.s(j).|J(j)|^{n-1}.J(j) \tag{3.13}$$

where s(j) is the "conductance" of the edge j = {i,i'}. It depends, inter alia, upon the geometrical characteristics of j.

Note that it is necessary to keep track of the algebraic sign of J(j) in the application of (3.13).

The conservation of the total flow rate at each vertex i may still be expressed by (3.4).

The relation (3.5) between flow rates and pressures at the external vertices of the basic graph Γ_0 may be generalized as

$$\underset{\sim}{J}_N^{(e)} = \underset{\sim}{A}_N\ (\underset{\sim}{P}_N^{(e)}) \tag{3.14}$$

where $\underset{\sim}{A}_N$ is a nonlinear vectorial function with n_e components. It may be called the nonlinear transfer function of the graph Γ_N. Again, one of the purposes of the calculations is to derive these functions $\underset{\sim}{A}_N$. Actually, it is easier to obtain iteration formulae which can be expressed as

$$\underset{\sim}{A}_N = \underset{\sim}{F}\ (\underset{\sim}{A}_{N-1}) \tag{3.15}$$

General methods are given in IV in order to derive these recursion formulae. Though they are deduced in a way which is reminiscent of the method set up for linear problems, explicit expressions cannot be furnished, because of the nonlinearities which are involved ; again, the equations follow from the equality at the external vertices of the graphs of the pressures and of the flow rates (within a sign change).

Let us use again a Sierpinski gasket in which a power law fluid flows. In the limit of large N, it was numerically shown that

$$\underset{\sim}{A}_N \simeq \alpha(n) \cdot \underset{\sim}{A}_{N-1} \tag{3.16}$$

where $\alpha(n)$ is a constant which only depends upon the fluid index n. The function $\alpha(n)$ was then systematically determined. Results are displayed in Fig. 3.2. For n = 1, i.e. for a Newtonian fluid, the classical constant 3/5 is again obtained (cf. (3.12)), and this serves as a useful check. When n is small, the fluid is shear-thinning, and $\alpha(n)$ tends towards 0. When n is large, the fluid is shear-thickening and $\alpha(n)$ towards 1. So far, we have not been able to derive the constant $\alpha(n)$ on simple grounds, mainly because the star-triangle transformation is not valid anymore.

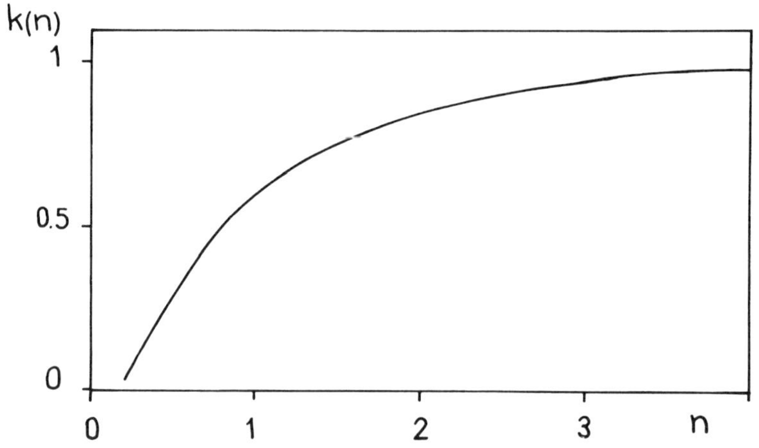

Fig. 3.2 - The fractal constant $\alpha(n)$ for a Sierpinski gasket as a function of the fluid index n.

This way of reasonning may be extended to fluids for which the pressure drop-flow rate relationship along an edge can be inverted. More precisely, in lieu of (3.13), one could obviously cope with the more general functional relationship

$$p(i) - p(i') = f[J(j)] \tag{3.17}$$

Hence, a very large class of fluids is concerned by this extension.

A somewhat different class of fluids consists of Bingham fluids, which start flowing when a threshold is overcome. Then, the first problem consists in the determination of the condition at which such a fluid will start flowing as a function of the pressures imposed at the external vertices of the fractal capillary network ; a general method is given in IV, in terms of the shortest routes existing between the external vertices of the graph.

Taylor dispersion

Taylor dispersion is an important transfer process, whose study is motivated by various reasons which can be found in our papers dealing with this subject (Adler [1] and Brenner, 1984.a ; Adler [5], 1985.c hereafter referred to as III). Note that Taylor dispersion is also closely related to the so-called oriented conduction (cf. Odagaki and Las, 1980 [17]).

Let us recall first how the continuous equation (2.8) may be discretized here. Imagine a tracer particle initially introduced at time t = 0 into the network at vertex i'. The probability of finding this particle within any capillary is assumed to be negligible owing to the relatively small volume assumed for the capillaries compared with the vertices. The probability density of finding this tracer particle at vertex i at time t is denoted by

$$P(i,t|i') \tag{3.18}$$

When the capillary walls are assumed to be impermeable to solute permeation, the probability density at each vertex i obeys the first order differential equation

$$v(i).\frac{dP}{dt}(i,t|i') = \delta(i,i').\,\delta(t) + \sum_{\substack{j\in\Omega^+(i)\\ j=\{i'',i\}}} J(j)\, P(i'',t|i') - \left(\sum_{j\in\Omega^-(i)} J(j)\right).\, P(i,t|i') \tag{3.19}$$

where $\delta(i,i')$ is a Kronecker delta, and $\delta(t)$ is a Dirac's delta function. $v(i)$ is the volume of vertex i. This equation has already been commented by Adler and Brenner (1984) [1]. The probability also satisfies the usual unit normalization condition

$$\sum_{i\in\Gamma} P(i,t|i')\, v(i) = 1 \quad , \quad t > 0 \tag{3.20}$$

The m-adic global moments of the probability density are defined by the expressions

$$\underset{\sim}{M}_m(t|i') = \sum_{i\in\Gamma} v(i)\,[\underset{\sim}{R}(i) - \underset{\sim}{R}(i')]^m\, P(i,t|i') \tag{3.21}$$

where, generically, for any vector $\underset{\sim}{V}$, $\underset{\sim}{V}^m$ is the m-adic $\underset{\sim}{V}\ldots\underset{\sim}{V}$ (m times). Usually, only the two first moments are evaluated ; the first one is related to the average translation of the tracer and the second one to its dispersion. In spatially periodic networks, in the asymptotic limit of long times, their time derivatives were found to be equivalent to

$$\frac{d}{dt}\underset{\sim}{M}_1(t|i') \simeq \overline{\underset{\sim}{v}}^* \tag{3.22a}$$

$$\frac{d}{dt}[\underset{\approx}{M}_2(t|i') - \underset{\sim}{M}_1(t|i')\,\underset{\sim}{M}_1(t|i')] \simeq 2\,\overline{\underset{\approx}{D}}^* \tag{3.22b}$$

where $\overline{\underset{\sim}{v}}^*$ is equal to the interstitial velocity and $\overline{\underset{\approx}{D}}^*$ is the dispersivity dyadic [1].

Thus, our general purpose is to derive the asymptotic behaviour of various moments in fractal networks. So far, we could not derive a general theory and we restricted ourselves to two basic examples of fractal graphs, namely a tree and a Sierpinski gasket.

Generally speaking, a tree is a graph without any cycles. Let us consider here an infinite tree in which each vertex has the same degree 3 (see Fig. 3.3). Thus, at step N, there are 2^N vertices ; the abscissa x_N of these 2^N vertices is equal to N

$$x_N = N \tag{3.23}$$

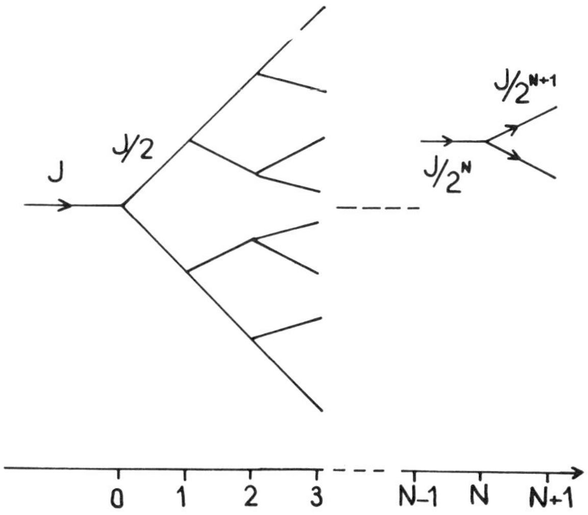

Fig. 3.3 - An infinite tree of degree 3.

Moreover, the 2^N vertices are assumed to have the same volume v(N), which may be expressed as

$$v(N) = \left(\frac{s}{2}\right)^N \tag{3.24}$$

in dimensionless units. s is a positive arbitrary constant.

The resistance to the flow is assumed to be the same for all the edges of the tree. Hence, starting at step N = 0 with a flow rate equal to J, the flow rate is equal to $J/2^N$ after N subdivisions, as it is shown in Fig. 3.3.

Let us work with dimensionless quantities, for sake of simplicity. In application of (3.19), the probability density P(N,t) of any vertex of abscissa $N > 0$ verifies the differential equation

$$\frac{s^N}{J} \cdot \frac{dP(N,t)}{dt} = P(N-1,t) - P(N,t), \quad N \neq 0 \tag{3.24a}$$

$$\frac{1}{J} \cdot \frac{dP(0,t)}{dt} = - P(0,t), \qquad N = 0 \tag{3.24b}$$

together with the initial conditions

$$P(0,t=0) = 1 \quad ; \quad P(N,t=0) = 0, \qquad N \neq 0 \tag{3.24c}$$

The general solution of this system can be analytically derived (cf.III). Though it is very simple, the system (3.24) can display very different asymptotic time behaviours, depending upon the value of the parameter s, that we shall briefly expose.

When s is strictly larger than 1, the total space offered to the tracer particle is larger and larger ; thus, the tracer moves more and more slowly along the tree. Actually, it can be shown that, for long time, the first moment has a logarithmic behaviour,

$$\underset{\sim}{M}_1 \simeq \frac{\text{Log (Jt Log s)}}{\text{Log s}} \tag{3.25}$$

while the mean-square displacement $\underset{\approx}{M}_2(t|0) - [\underset{\sim}{M}_1(t|0)]^2$ tends towards a constant.

When s is strictly smaller than 1, a completely different behaviour occurs, since less and less space is available to the tracer particle, as it proceeds in the tree. In this case, the particle reaches infinity in a finite time interval. After it, the total amount of solute contained in the network at finite distances is smaller than 1, in contradiction with (3.20). In the long time limit, the various moments vary as

$$M_m(t|0) \simeq \mathcal{M}_m . e^{-Jt} \tag{3.26}$$

where the coefficients $\mathcal{M}_m$ only depend upon s.

Finally, when α is equal to 1, the space available to the tracer particle is constant and the classical behaviour of Taylor dispersion in spatially periodic media is recovered (cf. (3.22)).

As previously stated, three different behaviours can be displayed by this system, which is very simple indeed, as it does not contain any cycle, but has the decisive advantage of being analytically handled.

A more complicated situation was thus selected, namely the classical Sierpinski gasket. All the edges are assumed to have the same resistance per unit length ; the corresponding flow rates can be calculated as described previously. The external vertices of Γ_N are denoted by the index 1, 2 or 3 (cf. Fig. 2.1a). The flow rates, which are arbitrarily assumed to be positive when the flow goes out of Γ_N, may be expressed as

$$J_N^{(e)1} = -1 \; ; \quad J_N^{(e)2} = \frac{1}{1+\lambda} \quad ; \quad J_N^{(e)3} = \frac{\lambda}{1+\lambda} \qquad (3.27)$$

where λ is a dimensionless parameter ranging from 1 to 0.

The most remarkable feature which occurs is a phenomenon that we have called isotropisation in III. When N is large, the flow rates near the inlet 1 of the gasket do not depend anymore upon the parameter λ. In consequence of this fact, Taylor dispersion is expected not to depend too much upon λ.

This is numerically investigated in III, since the differential system (3.19) cannot be solved analytically. No obvious scaling could be deduced from the numerical data. Note that, when compared to a tree, the Sierpinski gasket is characterized by an increasing volume offered to the tracer and by the regular presence of bottle necks which connect two successive generations.

This terminates the review of our works dealing with fractal networks. If linear and nonlinear phenomena are in pretty good shape when they are not time-dependent, obviously some additional efforts should be done to develop a general theory of Taylor dispersion in fractals.

4 CONTINUOUS FRACTAL STRUCTURES

In this section, solid fractal objects with finite dimensions are presented. In most cases, Stokes flow of Newtonian fluids is studied in or along these structures.

There are three different ways to pave the Euclidean plane with regular polygons, namely with equilateral triangles, squares or hexagons. Actually, since hexagons may be viewed as equivalent to triangles, there are basically two ways left, to which correspond the two structures, which are going to be studied at the beginning of this section, i.e. Leibniz packings and Sierpinski carpets.

Transversal properties of Leibniz packings

Such packings are constructed as follows [2] (hereafter referred to as I, where the relevant references and further details are given). This is illustrated in Fig. 4.1. Let us draw three disks tangent to

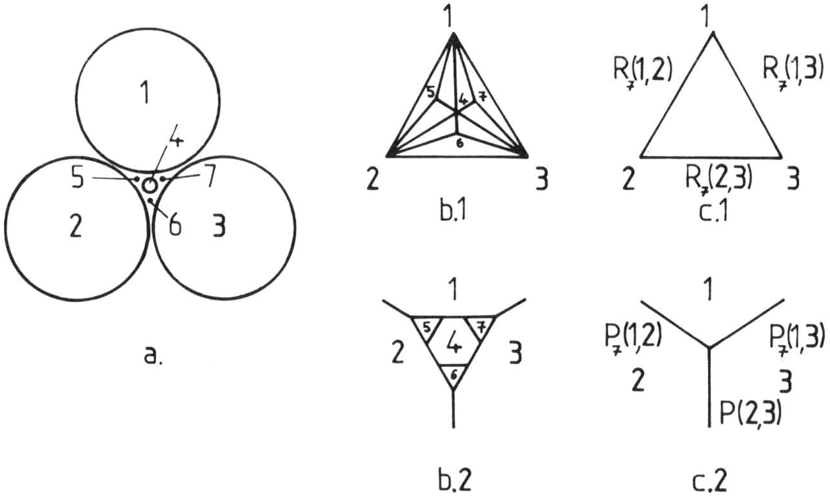

Fig. 4.1 - Leibniz packings. (a) The construction process is illustrated up to n = 2. The corresponding network for conduction and convection are shown in b1 and b2 respectively. These networks may be simplified into the equivalent networks shown in c.

one another ; in the interstices between them, a fourth disk tangent to the three former ones can be added. In the three new interstices which appear, three new disks may be added and so on... In the present case, the disks are assumed not to be exactly tangent. A gap is left between them ; it is assumed to be small with respect to the radius of the disks between which it is located ; it is a constant fraction of the radius of the smallest disk. The actual value of the radius a(i) of the disk i is equal to

$$a(i) = (1-\varepsilon) . a_m(i) \qquad (4.1)$$

where $a_m(i)$ is the largest possible value of the radius of disk i. ε is a dimensionless parameter.

For sake of simplicity, let us consider the transversal properties of these packings in the lubrication limit. For conduction, the conductivity k_p of the disks needs to be assumed much larger than the conductivity k_f of the continuous phase ; as an immediate consequence, each disk i has a constant temperature T(i). In the lubrication limit when ε is small with respect to 1, the temperature difference between two disks is related to the heat flux q(i,i') per unit depth by

$$T(i) - T(i') = [g(i,i').(\frac{1}{a(i)} + \frac{1}{a(i')})]^{1/2} . \frac{q(i,i)}{\pi \ k_f} \tag{4.2}$$

where g(i,i') is the gap between the two disks.

Next, let us consider a Newtonian fluid flowing across such a Leibniz packing. Across an elementary gap between two cylinders i and i, the flow rate per unit length may be expressed as a function of the pressure difference by

$$\bar{q}(i,i') = 4\sqrt{2}. [g^5(i,i').(\frac{1}{a(i)} + \frac{1}{a(i')})]^{1/2} . \frac{\Delta p}{\frac{9\pi}{\sqrt{2}}} \tag{4.3}$$

Thus, the lubrication approximation reduces this situation to the calculation of networks, which are shown in Fig. 4.1b. It can be shown that the rates of heat flow $Q_N(i,i')$ per unit depth between the three initial disks are related to the temperature differences by

$$T(i) - T(i') = R_N(i,i').Q_N(i,i')/\pi k_f \quad (i,i' = 1,2,3) \tag{4.4}$$

where the three resistances $R_N(1,2)$, $R_N(2,3)$ and $R_N(3,1)$ can be calculated as functions of N_n, the number of filling disks. Similarly, for permeability, the packing may be viewed as a star electrical network ; the pressure at the center of the equivalent star is denoted by p_c ; it can be shown that the flow rates per unit depth $\bar{q}(i,i')$ of fluid flowing inside the gap (i,i') are proportional to the pressure difference

$$\bar{q}(i,i') = a^2(1) \ . \ P_N(i,i').(p(i,i') - p_c)/(\frac{9\pi}{\sqrt{2}} \ \mu) \quad (i,i'=1,2,3) \tag{4.5}$$

where the three coefficients $P_N(1,2)$, $P_N(1,3)$ and $P_N(2,3)$ have to be calculated as functions of N_n.

Let us now split our comments into two parts. For conductivity, results are presented in Fig. 4.2. A power law is very quickly reached, which may be expressed as

$$R_N(1,2) = k \sqrt{\varepsilon} \; N_n^{\alpha} \tag{4.6}$$

where k is a constant, and the exponent α is numerically found to be very close to - 0.464.

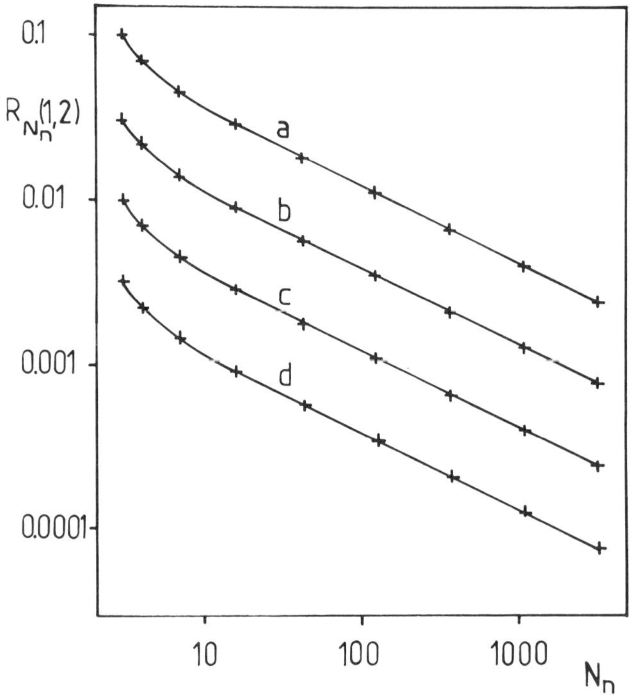

Fig. 4.2 - Equivalent thermal resistances $R_N(1,2)$ for an hexagonal array as a function of the number of disks N_n ; values of ε are : 10^{-2}(a), 10^{-3}(b), 10^{-4}(c), 10^{-5}(d).

The most remarkable feature of this expression is that k is a constant which does not depend upon the initial configuration. The packing may be started from three equal or unequal disks; after a few generations, the resistances $R_N(i,i')$ are very close and given by (4.6). This characteristic enabled us to show that

$$k = 2^{1/2} + \alpha \quad (4.7a)$$

$$\alpha = \frac{\text{Log } 3/5}{\text{Log } 3} \quad (4.7b)$$

values which are very close to the numerical ones.

Permeability data were similarly analysed. Again, a power law is rapidly obtained and may be expressed as

$$P_N(i,i') = \varepsilon^{-5/2} . k(i,i') . N_n^{\beta} \quad (4.8)$$

where the exponent β is numerically found equal to -2.04. ε must be very small, in order to obtain (4.8). The coefficient k(i,i') is numerically found to depend upon the original configuration ; the isotropisation, noticed for conduction, does not exist anymore. An order of magnitude was given for β by a rough argument in I.

This work is being extended in various directions, that we shall mention in our concluding remarks

Longitudinal flow in Sierpinski carpets

If it is relatively easy to analyse the transversal properties of Leibniz packings, longitudinal properties turn out to be simpler in fractals based on Sierpinski carpets. This is the basic reason why we now switch to this structure.

A three-dimensional porous medium may be obtained as illustrated in Fig. 4.3 ; it is composed of unit cells of side a, which are based on the Sierpinski carpets shown in Fig. 2.1, where the removed subsquares are prolongated in solid square bundles [6].

Let us consider a Newtonian fluid which flows, at low Reynolds number, along the solid bundles, i.e. along the z-axis. Then, the Stokes equation (2.6) simplifies to

$$\frac{\partial^2 w}{\partial x^2} + \frac{\partial^2 w}{\partial y^2} = \frac{1}{\mu} . \frac{dp}{dz} \quad (4.8)$$

where dp/dz is a constant which does not depend upon the transversal coordinates x and y ; w denotes the z-component of $\underset{\sim}{v}$.

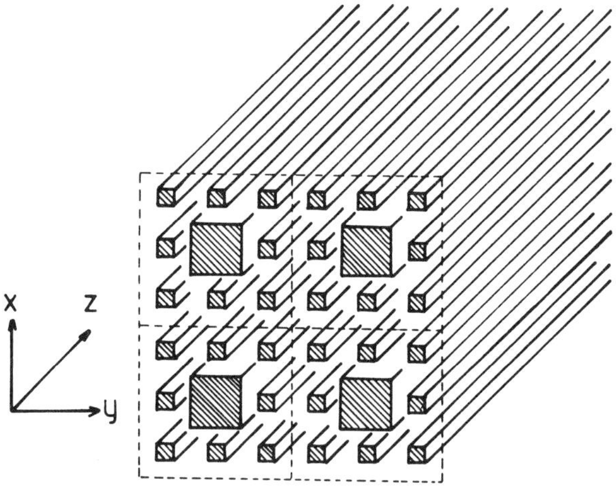

Fig. 4.3 - An example of a porous medium constructed from a Sierpinski carpet. The lattice is shown here at the second construction stage ; several unit cells are displayed for clarity.

The longitudinal component of the permeability tensor may be expressed as

$$\overline{K}_{//,N} = - \overline{w}/\frac{1}{\mu} \cdot \frac{dp}{dz} \tag{4.9}$$

where $\overline{w}$ denotes the seepage velocity.

The major result on Sierpinski carpets is related to the classical Carman-Kozeny law (cf. Happel and Brenner, 1965) [9]. This law is recalled and then it is shown that it can be obtained either by a scaling argument or by a complete numerical integration of equation (4.8).

The Carman-Kozeny law has a special status in the literature about porous media ; it is based on a semi-empirical reasoning and it states that the permeability $\overline{K}$ of a porous medium is given by

$$\overline{K} = \frac{\varepsilon m^2}{k} \tag{4.10}$$

where ε is the porosity, m the hydraulic radius defined as (free volume)/

(wetted area) ; k is the so-called Kozeny constant. Of course, (4.10) is valid for Stokes flow only.

Equation (4.10) has been very successful when compared to experimental data. An excellent agreement is obtained with $k = 4.8$ for random beds of uniform spheres ; (4.10) also holds for beds consisting of a variety of non-spherical particles, though the value of k is slightly different. An other important feature of (4.10) is that it is valid for a large range of porosity ε.

The special status of (4.10) is due to the fact that, in spite of its success when compared with experiments, it is not in very good agreement with theoretical results. Such a comparison has been made for cell models and porous media made up of parallel cylinders. More recently, the permeability of spatially periodic cubic arrays of equal spheres has been calculated (cf. Sangani and Acrivos, 1982 [18] ; Zick and Homsy, 1982 [23]) ; the agreement with (4.10) is fair but these calculations cannot provide a theoretical basis to (4.10).

It is an elementary problem to calculate the permeability $\bar{K}_N$ of the spatially periodic Sierpinski carpets described above, in application of (4.10). In the limit of large generation N, $\bar{K}_N$ is equivalent to

$$\bar{K}_N \quad \alpha\left(\frac{8}{81}\right)^N \tag{4.11}$$

This result may be obtained in a different way which uses the self-similarity of the Sierpinski carpets. Let us first calculate $\bar{K}_{//,N+1}$ when $\bar{K}_{//,N}$ is known. The carpet N+1 can be considered as the union of 8 carpets N but reduced by the size ratio 1/3. It is well known that the flow rate q in a cylinder is proportional to ([9] for Poiseuille flow but this holds for external flows as well)

$$q \;\alpha\; \frac{r^4}{\mu} \cdot \left(-\frac{dp}{dz}\right) \tag{4.12}$$

where r is a characteristic lateral dimension of the cylinder. Hence, for a given overall pressure gradient dp/dz, the flow q_{N+1} in the carpet N+1 is the sum of 8 flows q_N reduced in the ratio $1/3^4$. Hence, relation (4.11) is retrieved by this scaling argument.

In order to confirm this preliminary conclusion, detailed numerical calculations were found necessary. Equation (4.8) was solved by using the so-called Successive Over-Relaxation method.

Let us present briefly the major conclusions which can be drawn from the calculations. First, the flow rates tend to follow a scaling law when the generation number is large enough. Second, this scaling law is independent of the size of the mesh used to discretize this geometry. Third, the ratio between the permeabilities of two generations is equal to

$$\overline{K}_{//,N+1}/\overline{K}_{//,N} = 0.0648, \quad 0.0859, \quad 0.0943, \quad 0.0970 \qquad \text{for} \quad N = 1,\ 2,\ 3,\ 4, \text{ respectively.} \tag{4.13}$$

This ratio has to be compared with the theoretical value 8/81 = 0.0988 (cf. (4.11)).

Hence, the numerical results are in agreement with the Carman-Kozeny law and the scaling argument. The basic reason of this success is that the local velocity field in the elementary carpets become progressively insensitive to the outer boundary conditions ; the scaling based on (4.12) is thus valid.

Some other comments can be made on these results. The Carman-Kozeny law does not make any distinction between the longitudinal and transversal permeabilities ; however, it should be noticed that (4.10) is not valid for the transversal permeability of Leibniz packings as expressed by (4.8) ; this discrepancy is certainly due to the lubrication approximation where most part of the solid surfaces described by (4.10) do not play any role. Obviously, this point requires some further investigations.

The mesh used for the discretization of (4.8) can be viewed as a fractal network, which is obtained by the construction process described in section 3. This may be considered as a first example of a homogeneous fractal, with an increasing number of vertices common to successive generations (cf. Fig. 4.4). When the discretization mesh is thin, it implies that the number of vertices and edges in the basic graph of the network is larger. The independence of the scaling law upon the discretization means that, as for non homogeneous networks, the limiting behavior is only governed by the union of the basic graphs and not by the precise structure of the basic graphs themselves.

In conclusion, the importance of the validity of the Carman-Kozeny law for a particular sort of fractal should be emphasized again. It would be particularly important if it could be extended to other fractals.

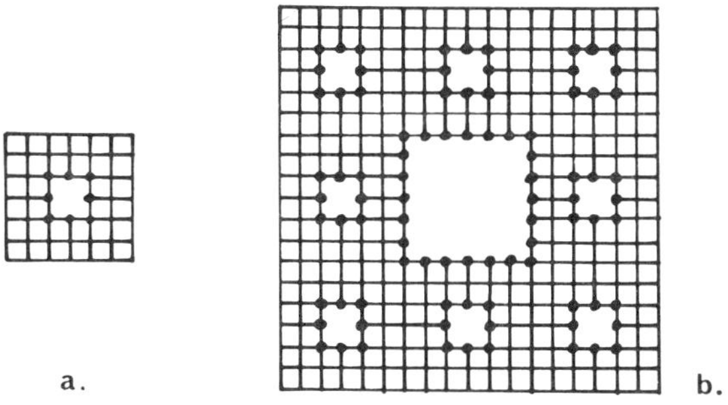

Fig. 4.4 - Construction of the mesh corresponding to a Sierpinski carpet by union of networks. The dotted vertices are maintained to a zero velocity. a : the basic graph. b : union of 8 basic graphs ; this graph should now be reduced by a scaling factor 3 in each direction.

Flow along a Cantor-Taylor brush

Apart from the theoretical interest of studying transport processes along or across a fractal surface, we were motivated (cf. Vignes-Adler et al., 1985) [20] by several specific applications. A first class of applications is related to the determination of the relevant conditions at the boundary of porous media immersed in fluids, which has not been satisfactorily solved yet ; an interesting and new area is the rheology of aggregable suspensions ; the small particles coagulate to form aggregates which were recently found to be fractals (Witten and Sander, 1981) [22]. A second class of applications is related to the transfer processes which may occur across fractal interfaces, such as the one found between two fluids in a porous medium (Jacquin and Adler, 1985) [12].

It was thus highly desirable to define a fractal boundary, which was easy to calculate and where experiments could be performed. Actually, such shapes are not easy to find. The simplest one is, we think, the Cantor-Taylor brush that we have introduced as a modification of the Taylor brush [20]. This brush is composed of identical unit cells which are based on a Cantor set (cf. Fig. 4.5). The usual Cantor set is obtained by dividing a segment of length a in three equal parts and by removing the middle third ; the same operation can be performed on the remaining segments as many times as desired.

Then, a three-dimensional medium is deduced as shown in Fig. 4.5b ; it is composed of unit cells of side a and the removed segments correspond to voids in the solid medium.

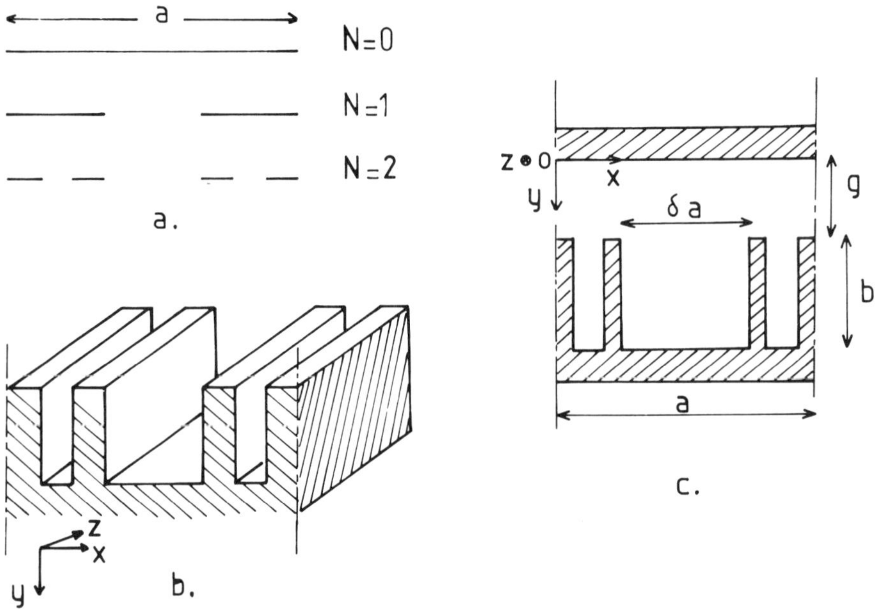

Fig. 4.5 - The Cantor-Taylor brush : (a) construction of the Cantor set ; (b) shows the porous medium at N = 2. In (c) the channel is completed by an upper flat wall ; the geometry is characterized by a, b, g and δ. In (b) and (c), only one lateral period of length a is displayed.

This construction can be generalized by removing a proportion $\delta \neq 1/3$ of the remaining segments at each new generation. The height of the grooves is denoted by b. Moreover, a channel flow may be created by putting a flat plate at a distance g above the teeth. The geometry of the system is characterized by the length scale a and the three dimensionless parameters

$$\delta \ , \ \frac{b}{a} \ , \ \frac{g}{a} \tag{4.14}$$

Let us now consider the two most classical types of flow

(i) Couette flow : $\underset{\sim}{v} = \underset{\sim}{V}_o$ on the flat plate (4.15a)

(ii) Poiseuille flow : the macroscopic pressure gradient $\overline{\nabla} p$ is specified (4.15b)

When we restrict ourselves to longitudinal flows, equation (4.8) is still valid and is solved by the Successive Over Relaxation method.

The major findings of the numerical study can be summarized as follows. In a Couette flow, the average $\overline{\tau}$ of the surface drag on the upper plate was calculated ; in a Poiseuille flow, the longitudinal permeability $\overline{K}_{//}$ is derived from the total flow rate induced by a given pressure drop. It was found that these two quantities tend towards constants when N becomes large

$$\frac{\overline{\tau}}{\frac{\mu V_o}{a}} \rightarrow K_1(\delta, \frac{b}{a}, \frac{g}{a}) \text{ for Couette flow} \tag{4.16a}$$

$$\frac{\overline{K}_{//}}{a^2} \rightarrow K_2(\delta, \frac{b}{a}, \frac{g}{a}) \text{ for Poiseuille flow} \tag{4.16b}$$

This feature was expected on physical grounds. The remarkable fact is how quickly the asymptotic behaviour is obtained, since $\overline{\tau}$ and $\overline{K}_{//}$ are already constant after three generations. Moreover, it is highly plausible that these results are still valid for transversal flows, in the x y-plane. For practical purposes, this conclusion is important since it means that global results are insensitive to the finest details of the geometry.

It should also be emphasized that the asymptotic behaviours (4.16) do not depend upon the discretization mesh, which may be viewed again as an homogeneous fractal.

Finally, it should be reminded that Couette flow is analogous to a heat transfer process (or diffusive one) between the fractal surface of the brush and the upper wall ; $\overline{\tau}$ becomes the average heat transfer between the two surfaces.

5. CONCLUDING REMARKS

Hopefully, fractals were found stimulating by the readers, since we believe that it is a very promising area on both the practical and theoretical sides.

This structure, which completely differs from the ones previously studied, enables us to have a fresh look at classical subjects, such as porous media, aggregates, fluid-fluid interfaces and so on ...

A whole class of new problems is thus opened up. The contributions, which were summed up in this paper, may be extended in four ways, at least. First, the influence of the spatial dimensionality should be investigated ; in this respect, note that, though the real world has three dimensions, it may turn out to be interesting to go beyond this limit. Second, the construction process of fractals may be randomized ; for instance, a disk may be inserted at random in a Leibniz packing ; if a disk is not inserted, no disk will be inserted in the following construction steps ; these random Leibniz packings are being studied in our group. Third, nonlinear phenomena are of very high interest, in connection with inertial effects and non-Newtonian fluids ; such studies, which have already been initiated in capillary networks, may be readily extended to some of the structures which are presented here. Fourth, and it actually represents a very large class, time-dependent phenomena have hardly been touched, with the two examples of Taylor dispersion in networks.

Some challenging questions may also be gathered at the end of this article. It would be very useful to extend what has been done for nonhomogeneous fractals to homogeneous ones, especially in relation with the discretization meshes, which are used in continuous structures ; the independence of the power exponent upon the detailed structure of the basic graph would be an interesting problem to start with. It would also be very useful to develop new basis of orthogonal functions to represent solutions in continuous fractals. Finally, we should look for general relations, valid for whole classes of fractals, between say the fractal exponent of the transport process and the fractal dimension of the medium or any quantity derived from its geometry. Such a proposition is very close in nature to the conjecture of Alexander and Orbach (1982) [7] (which needs however to be carefully restricted to classes of fractals) ; the Carman-Kozeny law may then prove to be a first step in this direction.

NOMENCLATURE

a = characteristic dimension, radius of a disk

$\underset{\approx}{A}_N$ = transfer matrix

D = fractal dimension

$\underset{\approx}{G}, \underset{\approx}{H}$ = matrices (see 3.11)

$\underset{\sim}{j}, J$ = fluxes

k = constant

k_f = conductivity of the fluid

K = compact set

$\overline{K}$ = permeability

L = length

$\underset{\approx}{L}$ = connectivity tensor

M = number of sets K_N in the generation N

N = generation number

N_n = number of sets in K_N

P = pressure

P = probability

r_α = ratio of the similarity S_α

S_α = similarity

t = time

T = temperature

$\underset{\sim}{v}, w$ = velocity

Greek letters

Γ = graph

ε = dimensionless gap, porosity

μ = viscosity

$\overline{\tau}$ = surface drag.

REFERENCES

[1] Adler P.M., Brenner H., Transport process in spatially periodic capillary networks, II. Taylor dispersion with mixing vertices, Physico-Chemical Hydrodynamics, 5, 269-285, 1984.

[2] Adler P.M., Transport processes in fractals, I. Conductivity and permeability of a Leibniz packing in the lubrication limit, Int. J. Multiphase Flow, in press, 1985.

[3] Adler P.M., Transport processes in fractals, II. Stokes flow in fractal capillary networks, Int. J. Multiphase Flow, in press, 1985.a.

[4] Adler P.M., Transport processes in fractals, IV. Non linear flow problems in fractal capillary networks, Int. J. Multiphase Flow, in press, 1985.b.

[5] Adler P.M., Transport processes in fractals, III. Taylor dispersion in two examples of fractal capillary networks, Int. J. Multiphase Flow, in press, 1985.c.

[6] Adler P.M., Transport processes in fractals, VI. Stokes flow through Sierpinski carpets, (submitted for publication, 1985.d.)

[7] Alexander S., Orbach R., Density of states on fractals : "fractons", J. Phys. (Paris), Lett. 43, L. 625-631, 1982.

[8] De Gennes P.G., Scaling laws in polymer physics, Cornell University Press, Ithaca, New York, 1979.

[9] Happel J., Brenner H., Low Reynolds number hydrodynamics, Prentice Hall, 1965.

[10] Hentschel H.G.E., Procaccia I., Relative diffusion in turbulent media : the fractal dimension of clouds, Phys. Rev. A, 29, 1461-1470, 1984.

[11] Hutchinson J.F., Fractals and self-similarity, Indiana Univ. Math. Journal, 30, 713-747, 1981.

[12] Jacquin C.G., Adler P.M., The fractal dimension of a gas-liquid interface in a porous medium (submitted for publication).

[13] Leyvraz F., Stanley H.E., To what class of fractals does the Alexander-Orbach conjecture apply ? Phys. Rev. Lett., 51, 2048-2051, 1983.

[14] Mandelbrot B.B., The fractal geometry of nature, Freeman, San Francisco, 1982.

[15] Mandelbrot B.B., Passoja D.E., Paullay A.J., Fractal character of fracture surfaces of metals, Nature, 308, 721-722, 1984.

[16] Niemeyer L., Pietronero L., Wiesmann H.J., Fractal dimension of dielectric breakdown, Phys. Rev. Lett., 52, 1033-1036, 1984.

[17] Odagaki T., Lax M., A.C. hopping conductivity of a one-dimensional bond percolation model, Phys. Rev. Lett., 45, 847-850, 1980.

[18] Sangani A.S., Acrivos A., Slow flow through a periodic array of spheres, Int. J. Multiphase Flow, 8, 343-360, 1982.

[19] Stauffer D., Scaling theory of percolation clusters, Phys. Rept., 54, 1-74, 1979.

[20] Vignes-Adler M., Adler P.M., Gougat P., Martin F., Transport processes along fractals. I - The Cantor-Taylor brush. Theoretical.(submitted for publication).

[21] Weitz D.A., Oliveria M., Fractal structures formed by kinetic aggregation of aqueous gold colloids, Phys. Rev. Lett., 52, 1433-1436, 1984.

[22] Witten T.A.Jr., Sander L.M., Diffusion-limited aggregation, a kinetic critical phenomenon, Phys. Rev. Lett., 47, 1400-1403, 1981.

[23] Zick A.A., Homsy G.M., Stokes flow through periodic arrays of spheres, J. Fluid Mech., 15, 13-26, 1982.

S HABER & H BRENNER

Taylor–Aris dispersion of N particles with internal constraints — Molecular dispersion

1. Introduction

G.I. Taylor [11,12] and Aris [1] originally addressed the flow and dispersion of pointsize noninteracting solute particles suspended in unidirectional flows occurring within laterally bounded ducts. Brenner [3] demonstrated how Aris' [1] moment scheme could be utilized to obtain the comparable mean flow and dispersion coefficients appropriate to a much broader class of convective-diffusive transport phenomena. This was accomplished by generalizing Horn's theory [5] to include directional- as well as position-dependent tensorial phenomenological coefficients appearing in the constitutive expressions for the convective and diffusive solute fluxes. Additionally, Brenner [3] pointed out the advantages of focusing attention on the stochastic behavior of a single solute corpuscle. This permitted a Lagrangian-like calculation of several global attributes of the probability density function quantifying the stochastic transport process. His procedure incorporated the idea of a multi-dimensional phase space in which such transport processes occur.

Our analysis utilizes tensor notation in place of the original [3] polyadic notation. The problem addressed here considers a single flexible "chain" consisting of N small rigid particles undergoing translational and rotational Brownian movements in an unbounded viscous fluid, the individual particle motions being compatible with (any) prescribed internal constraints. Hydrodynamic interactions between the particles composing the chain are accounted for by use of the Stokesian grand resistance matrix [4]. Thus, rather than dealing with the time-average behavior of rigid bodies, which has been the exclusive focus of all prior Taylor dispersion analyses, attention is directed here towards the time-average behavior of flexible bodies ("chains"). Neither interactions with adjacent chains (if, indeed, any are present) nor with vessel boundaries is considered in our analysis.

As in the case of all Taylor dispersion analyses, our theory is an asymptotic one--valid only after sufficient time has elapsed to permit the chain to sample all accessible internal configurations many times. This assures that the mean values of the configuration-specific phenomenological coefficients (instantaneously characterizing the chain's transport properties) become independent of the initial configuration of the chain at time t=0.

An ℓ-dimensional subspace ($\ell \leqslant 6N$) is introduced, pertaining only to those degrees of freedom which remain after allowing for imposed constraints. Based upon the configuration-specific energy dissipation rate, a positive-definite metric is defined within this space, and used to derive a general Fokker-Planck equation for the temporal evolution of the configurational-positional conditional probability density characterizing the chain's diffusive and convective motions. Linear constitutive laws for the diffusional and convective contributions to the flux of this probability density are formulated using a generalized Stokes-Einstein equation. The moment method, originally introduced by Aris [1] and subsequently generalized by Brenner [3], is exploited to extract from this Fokker-Planck equation the mean velocity vector and dispersivity dyadic of the chain through the fluid. These are expressed jointly in terms of the chain's configuration-specific hydrodynamic resistance coefficients and internal potential energy function. It is this potential which causes the individual particles comprising the chain to behave collectively in the long run as the single entity identifiable as the "chain". This requires, inter-alia, the convergence of all integrals evaluated over the infinite fluid volume. Only those potentials that are attenuated sufficiently rapidly with inter-particle separations lead to such convergence.

Special attention is devoted to assuring that the tensorial formulation of our theory is properly invariant to the explicit choice of coordinate systems. Moreover, it is demonstrated that the mean velocity and mean diffusivity of the chain are invariant to the choice of chain-fixed locator point (i.e., "body"-fixed origin) at which the chain is assumed to be localized. Such invariance is essential if these global properties are to possess physical significance. Finally, the case of an elastic dumbbell (with weak, but nonzero, hydrodynamic interactions between the two spheres of which it is composed) is analyzed in complete detail to illustrate the solution scheme.

2. Problem Statement

A flexible body consisting of N rigid particles of arbitrary shapes joined together by an interparticle potential to form a "chain" is suspended in a quiescent unbounded viscous fluid. The individual particles composing the chain undergo translational and rotational Brownian movements. These motions are required to be consistent with prescribed internal constraints. The mean velocity vector and dispersivity dyadic of the chain in the fluid are sought for the simple circumstance in which no deterministic external forces or torques are exerted on the particles. This corresponds to the case where the chain as a whole undergoes pure molecular diffusion. Inertia forces are neglected, whereas hydrodynamic interactions between particles are taken into account.

3. Configurational Probability Density, P

The instantaneous "configuration" of each of the N particles in the chain is defined by six degrees of freedom; say, the three cartesian coordinates of some body-fixed point within the particle and three Eulerian angles characterizing the particle's orientation relative to a space-fixed reference frame. Let the three-vector $\underset{\sim}{r}_I = \overrightarrow{OO_I}$ denote the displacement vector of the body-fixed point O_I, say, in particle I (I=1,2,...,N) relative to an origin O fixed in space. Additionally, let the "vector" $\underset{\sim}{\phi}_I$ (symbolically) represent the orientation of this particle relative to the space-fixed frame; this triplet of orientational parameters could, for example, represent three Euler angles or some other measure of the rotation group. Each realization of the chain may then be defined by the 6 N degrees of freedom $\underset{\sim}{r}_1, \underset{\sim}{r}_2, \ldots, \underset{\sim}{r}_N, \underset{\sim}{\phi}_1, \underset{\sim}{\phi}_2, \ldots, \underset{\sim}{\phi}_N$.

Assume the existence of holonomic constraints which reduce the number of degrees of freedom to ℓ. Then the $\underset{\sim}{r}_1, \underset{\sim}{r}_2, \ldots, \underset{\sim}{r}_N, \underset{\sim}{\phi}_1, \underset{\sim}{\phi}_2, \ldots, \underset{\sim}{\phi}_N$ are no longer independent entities; rather, ℓ generalized coordinates q^i $(i=1,2,\ldots,\ell)$ suffice to uniquely describe the configuration of the chain. It is possible to relate the set $(\underset{\sim}{r}_I, \underset{\sim}{\phi}_I)$ to the set (q^i) through the following transformation equations:

$$
\begin{aligned}
\underset{\sim}{r}_1 &= \underset{\sim}{r}_1(q^1, q^2, \ldots, q^\ell, t), \\
\underset{\sim}{r}_2 &= \underset{\sim}{r}_2(q^1, q^2, \ldots, q^\ell, t), \\
&\vdots \\
\underset{\sim}{r}_N &= \underset{\sim}{r}_N(q^1, q^2, \ldots, q^\ell, t), \\
\\
\underset{\sim}{\phi}_1 &= \underset{\sim}{\phi}_1(q^1, q^2, \ldots, q^\ell, t), \\
\underset{\sim}{\phi}_2 &= \underset{\sim}{\phi}_2(q^1, q^2, \ldots, q^\ell, t), \\
&\vdots \\
\underset{\sim}{\phi}_N &= \underset{\sim}{\phi}_N(q^1, q^2, \ldots, q^\ell, t).
\end{aligned}
\tag{1}
$$

Note that upper case indices range from 1 to N, whereas lower case indices range only from 1 to ℓ. Since $\underset{\sim}{\phi}_I$ is not a vector quantity the last N "vector" transformation equations only symbolically represent the relations between the orientations of the particles and the generalized coordinates. However, the pseudovector differential $d\underset{\sim}{\phi}_I$, which denotes infinitesimal changes in the orientation of particle I, possesses operational, rather than purely symbolic, significance.

Nonholonomic constraints in the form of nonintegrable differential equations are amenable to a formal solution by the method of Lagrange multipliers. However, such constraints, appearing in the form of inequalities, cannot be systematically analyzed owing to their higher degree of complexity. Henceforth, attention will be confined exclusively to holonomic constraints, where the degrees of freedom can be reduced from 6 N to ℓ through transformation (1).

3.1 Principle of Virtual Work

Since the particles are assumed sufficiently small to permit the neglect of fluid and particle inertia forces, the following equations must be satisfied:

$$
\begin{aligned}
\underset{\sim}{F}_I + \underset{\sim}{F}_I^{Br} &= \underset{\sim}{0}, \\
\underset{\sim}{M}_I + \underset{\sim}{M}_I^{Br} &= \underset{\sim}{0},
\end{aligned}
\qquad (I = 1,2,\ldots,N)
\tag{2}
$$

Here, $\underset{\sim}{F}_I$ denotes all the forces exerted on particle I, excluding the Brownian force $\underset{\sim}{F}_I^{Br}$. Similarly, $\underset{\sim}{M}_I$ denotes all the torques exerted on particle I, excluding the stochastic torque $\underset{\sim}{M}_I^{Br}$. Generally, the force $\underset{\sim}{F}_I$ and torque $\underset{\sim}{M}_I$ can be grouped into three main contributions:

$$\begin{aligned} \underset{\sim}{F}_I &= \underset{\sim}{X}_I + \underset{\sim}{x}_I + \underset{\sim}{F}_I^h, \\ \underset{\sim}{M}_I &= \underset{\sim}{Y}_I + \underset{\sim}{y}_I + \underset{\sim}{M}_I^h \end{aligned} \tag{3}$$

Here, $\underset{\sim}{X}_I$ and $\underset{\sim}{Y}_I$ respectively denote the external force and torque exerted on particle I stemming from the existence of external fields; $\underset{\sim}{x}_I$ and $\underset{\sim}{y}_I$ are the internal forces and torques exerted on particle I, stemming from spring or other attractive or repulsive interparticle forces; $\underset{\sim}{F}_I^h$ and $\underset{\sim}{M}_I^h$ are the respective hydrodynamic Stokes force and torque exerted on particle I due to its motion through the fluid. More will be said of these later.

At a given time t, virtual displacements $\delta\underset{\sim}{r}_I$ and $\delta\underset{\sim}{\phi}_I$ are made to change the configuration of the system, consistent with the constraint forces. By (2), the virtual work of the forces and torques must be zero:

$$\sum_{I=1}^{N} (\underset{\sim}{F}_I + \underset{\sim}{F}_I^{Br})\cdot\delta\underset{\sim}{r}_I + (\underset{\sim}{M}_I + \underset{\sim}{M}_I^{Br})\cdot\delta\underset{\sim}{\phi}_I = 0 \tag{4}$$

The dependent virtual displacements $\delta\underset{\sim}{r}_I$ and $\delta\underset{\sim}{\phi}_I$ are expressed in terms of the independent virtual displacements δq^j by the relations:

$$\begin{aligned} \delta\underset{\sim}{r}_I &= \sum_{j=1}^{\ell} \frac{\partial\underset{\sim}{r}_I}{\partial q^j}\,\delta q^j, \\ \delta\underset{\sim}{\phi}_I &= \sum_{j=1}^{\ell} \frac{\partial\underset{\sim}{\phi}_I}{\partial q^j}\,\delta q^j \end{aligned} \tag{5}$$

No partial derivatives with respect to time appear here since the displacements are assumed to take place at a given time.

If the constraints are time independent (as we shall henceforth assume), the virtual work of the constraint forces is zero for rigid bodies. Thus, only the applied forces and torques must be included in $\underset{\sim}{F}_I$ and $\underset{\sim}{M}_I$, while the unknown forces or torques of constraint can be excluded in (4). In that case, the explicit time dependence of transformation (1) is unnecessary and can be omitted.

Substitute (5) into (4) and recall the independence of the virtual displacements δq^j to obtain:

$$Q_j + Q_j^{Br} = 0 \quad (j = 1,2,\ldots,\ell) \tag{6}$$

where

$$Q_j = \sum_{I=1}^{N} [(\underset{\sim}{X}_I + \underset{\sim}{x}_I + \underset{\sim}{F}_I^h) \cdot \frac{\partial \underset{\sim}{r}_I}{\partial q^j} + (\underset{\sim}{Y}_I + \underset{\sim}{y}_I + \underset{\sim}{M}_I^h) \cdot \frac{\partial \underset{\sim}{\phi}_I}{\partial q^j}] ,$$

$$Q_j^{Br} = \sum_{I=1}^{N} (\underset{\sim}{F}_I^{Br} \cdot \frac{\partial \underset{\sim}{r}_I}{\partial q^j} + \underset{\sim}{M}_I^{Br} \cdot \frac{\partial \underset{\sim}{\phi}_I}{\partial q^j}) \tag{7}$$

It can be easily proven that Q_j and Q_j^{Br} are the covariant components of a vector in ℓ space; they denote the generalized components of the force in the δq^j direction.

3.2 Generalized Forces

Several assumptions are now made to simplify the terms in (7). Assume the known internal forces and torques $\underset{\sim}{x}_I$ and $\underset{\sim}{y}_I$ to be conservative, so that their generalized components derive from a potential V:

$$\sum_{I=1}^{N} (\underset{\sim}{x}_I \cdot \frac{\partial \underset{\sim}{r}_I}{\partial q^j} + \underset{\sim}{y}_I \cdot \frac{\partial \underset{\sim}{\phi}_I}{\partial q^j}) = - \frac{\partial V}{\partial q^j} \tag{8}$$

Here, V is an invariant scalar function, independent of the choice of the generalized coordinates q^j. The relation (8) is also consistent with the requirement of covariance of the generalized force components.

If $\underset{\sim}{u}$ denotes the (assumed) uniform velocity of the undisturbed flow field, the hydrodynamic force and torque exerted on particle I are:

$$\tilde{F}_I^h = - \sum_{S=1}^{N} [{}^t\underset{\approx}{K}_{IS} \cdot (\tilde{U}_S - \tilde{u}) + {}^c\underset{\approx}{K}_{SI}^{\dagger} \cdot \tilde{\Omega}_S],$$

$$\tilde{M}_I^h = - \sum_{S=1}^{N} [{}^c\underset{\approx}{K}_{IS} \cdot (\tilde{U}_S - \tilde{u}) + {}^r\underset{\approx}{K}_{IS} \cdot \tilde{\Omega}_S] \qquad (9)^*$$

Although we shall later assume the fluid to be quiescent ($\tilde{u}=\tilde{0}$), no difficulty exists at this stage in introducing a uniform flow field. Here, $\tilde{U}_S$ denotes the velocity of a point O_S locked in particle S, whereas $\tilde{\Omega}_S$ is the particle's angular velocity. The dyadics ${}^t\underset{\approx}{K}_{IS}$, ${}^c\underset{\approx}{K}_{IS}$ and ${}^r\underset{\approx}{K}_{IS}$ are the translational, coupling and rotational drag coefficients respectively. They depend on the configuration, shape and size of the particles (and viscosity of the fluid). It can be shown that ${}^t\underset{\approx}{K}_{IS}$ is independent of the location of the points O_S and O_I. The coupling dyadic ${}^c\underset{\approx}{K}_{IS}$ depends on the location of point O_I only, whereas ${}^r\underset{\approx}{K}_{IS}$ depends on both O_I and O_S. Moreover, these resistance dyadics satisfy the symmetry conditions:

$${}^t\underset{\approx}{K}_{IS} = {}^t\underset{\approx}{K}_{SI}^{\dagger},$$

$${}^r\underset{\approx}{K}_{IS} = {}^r\underset{\approx}{K}_{SI}^{\dagger} \qquad (10)$$

It should be noted that the indices I and S in (9) do not possess any tensorial significance.

The linear and angular velocities $\tilde{U}_S$ and $\tilde{\Omega}_S$ are related to the generalized coordinates via the equations:

$$\tilde{U}_S = \frac{d\tilde{r}_S}{dt} = \sum_{j=1}^{\ell} \frac{\partial \tilde{r}_S}{\partial q^j} \dot{q}^j ,$$

$$\tilde{\Omega}_S = \frac{d\tilde{\phi}_S}{dt} = \sum_{j=1}^{\ell} \frac{\partial \tilde{\phi}_S}{\partial q^j} \dot{q}^j \qquad (11)$$

---

*The affix † denotes a transposition operation.

where $\dot{q}^j = dq^j/dt$ defines the rate of change of the configuration in ℓ space.

The main difficulty arises from the generalized Brownian force Q_j^{Br}. Kuhn and Kuhn [7,8,9], Kirkwood [6] and Brenner [3] showed the stochastic forces and torques to have a pronounced contribution when a specific location of the particle or its orientation is considered (although their mean must be zero). The stochastic forces and torques cause the system to sample various configurations with different probabilities. A probability distribution function of the configurations can be defined and related to the generalized Brownian force. Equilibrium arguments, similar to those presented by Brenner [3], lead to an entropic-like relation between the potential V^{Br} of the Brownian forces and the probability density function, namely:

$$V^{Br} = kT \ln P \tag{12}$$

where k is Boltzmann's constant, T the absolute temperature of the system, and P the positional-internal configurational probability density.

The definition of the potential,

$$Q_j^{Br} = -\frac{\partial V^{Br}}{\partial q^j} \tag{13}$$

indicates the generalized Brownian force to be conservative. For (12) to be a proper constitutive equation, the function P must be a <u>true</u> scalar, invariant to the choice of generalized coordinates q^j. Since P is a probability <u>density</u> function, a volume element in ℓ space must be furnished; equivalently, a metric in ℓ space must be defined. If g_{ij} is a metric tensor in ℓ space $(i,j = 1,2,\ldots,\ell)$, a volume element invariant to the choice of generalized coordinates is given by [10]:

$$\sqrt{g}\, dq^1 dq^2 \ldots dq^\ell \equiv \sqrt{g}\, d\underset{\sim}{q}$$

where g is the determinant of g_{ij}.

The probability of finding the system in a volume element centered about the point $q^1, q^2, \ldots, q^\ell$ is invariant to the choice of q^i. Hence, if we define $P\sqrt{g}\, dq^1 dq^2 \ldots dq^\ell$ to be this desired probability, P is a true scalar function. A particular choice for the metric tensor is made below.

3.3 Metric Tensor

Substitution of (8), (9), (11) and (13) into (6) and (7) yields the equilibrium equations for the system, namely:

$$\begin{aligned}
&\sum_{m=1}^{\ell}\Bigg(\sum_{I,S=1}^{N}\Bigg[\frac{\partial \underset{\sim}{r}_I}{\partial q^j}\cdot \underset{\approx}{t}_{K_{SI}}\cdot\frac{\partial \underset{\sim}{r}_S}{\partial q^m} + \frac{\partial \underset{\sim}{r}_I}{\partial q^j}\cdot \underset{\approx}{c}_{K_{SI}}^{\dagger}\cdot\frac{\partial \underset{\sim}{\phi}_S}{\partial q^m} + \\
&+ \frac{\partial \underset{\sim}{\phi}_I}{\partial q^j}\cdot \underset{\approx}{c}_{K_{IS}}\cdot \frac{\partial \underset{\sim}{r}_S}{\partial q^m} + \frac{\partial \underset{\sim}{\phi}_I}{\partial q^j}\cdot \underset{\approx}{r}_{K_{IS}}\cdot\frac{\partial \underset{\sim}{\phi}_S}{\partial q^m}\Bigg]\Bigg)\dot{q}^m = \\
&= \sum_{I,S=1}^{N}\left(\frac{\partial \underset{\sim}{r}_I}{\partial q^j}\cdot \underset{\approx}{t}_{K_{IS}} + \frac{\partial \underset{\sim}{\phi}_S}{\partial q^j}\cdot \underset{\approx}{c}_{K_{IS}}\right)\cdot \underset{\sim}{u} - \frac{\partial (V+V^{Br})}{\partial q^j} + \\
&+ \sum_{I,S=1}^{N}\left(\underset{\sim}{X}_I\cdot\frac{\partial \underset{\sim}{r}_I}{\partial q^j} + \underset{\sim}{Y}_I\cdot\frac{\partial \underset{\sim}{\phi}_I}{\partial q^j}\right) \qquad (j = 1,2,\ldots,\ell)
\end{aligned} \tag{14}$$

Equation (14) furnishes ℓ equations among the ℓ unknown components of $\dot{q}^m$. The vector $\dot{q}^m$ is of fundamental importance since it enables us to determine the time evolution of the system.

Rewriting (14) in an abbreviated form gives:

$$\sum_{m=1}^{\ell} g_{jm}\dot{q}^m = b_j \qquad (j = 1,2,\ldots,\ell) \tag{15}$$

where

$$g_{jm} = \sum_{I,S=1}^{N} \left(\frac{\partial \underset{\sim}{r}_I}{\partial q^j} \cdot \underset{\approx}{t_{K_{IS}}} \cdot \frac{\partial \underset{\sim}{r}_S}{\partial q^m} + \frac{\partial \underset{\sim}{r}_I}{\partial q^j} \cdot \underset{\approx}{c_{K_{IS}}^{\dagger}} \cdot \frac{\partial \underset{\sim}{\phi}_S}{\partial q^m} + \right.$$

$$\left. + \frac{\partial \underset{\sim}{\phi}_I}{\partial q^j} \cdot \underset{\approx}{c_{K_{IS}}} \cdot \frac{\partial \underset{\sim}{r}_S}{\partial q^m} + \frac{\partial \underset{\sim}{\phi}_I}{\partial q^j} \cdot \underset{\approx}{r_{K_{IS}}} \cdot \frac{\partial \underset{\sim}{\phi}_S}{\partial q^m} \right) \tag{16}$$

and

$$b_j = \sum_{I,S=1}^{N} \left(\frac{\partial \underset{\sim}{r}_I}{\partial q^j} \cdot \underset{\approx}{t_{K_{IS}}} + \frac{\partial \underset{\sim}{\phi}_S}{\partial q^j} \cdot \underset{\approx}{c_{K_{IS}}} \right) \cdot \underset{\sim}{u} - \frac{\partial (V + V^{Br})}{\partial q^j} +$$

$$+ \sum_{I=1}^{N} \left(\underset{\sim}{X}_I \cdot \frac{\partial \underset{\sim}{r}_I}{\partial q^j} + \underset{\sim}{Y}_I \cdot \frac{\partial \underset{\sim}{\phi}_I}{\partial q^j} \right) \tag{17}$$

It can be easily proven that g_{jm} is a second-rank tensor in ℓ space, covariant in both indices, and that b_j is a covariant vector in ℓ space. Multiplication of (15) by $dq^j dt$ and summation over all j yields:

$$\sum_{j,m=1}^{\ell} g_{jm} dq^m dq^j = dt \sum_{j=1}^{m} g_j dq^j \tag{18}$$

The right-hand side is a true scalar, independent of the choice of the coordinates, since it is obtained by forming the inner product of covariant and contravariant vectors. This invariant of the system is now utilized to define an infinitesimal length element $|d\ell|$ in ℓ space such that its square is given by:

$$d\ell^2 = \sum_{j,m=1}^{\ell} g_{jm} dq^j dq^m \tag{19}$$

It remains to prove that the right-hand side of the above is indeed always positive definite. The rate of energy dissipation Φ in the system is proportional to the following expression:

$$\Phi \sim \sum_{I,J=1}^{N} (d\underset{\sim}{r}_I \cdot {}^t\underset{\approx}{K}_{IJ} \cdot d\underset{\sim}{r}_J + d\underset{\sim}{r}_I \cdot {}^c\underset{\approx}{K}_{JI}^{\dagger} \cdot d\underset{\sim}{\phi}_J + d\underset{\sim}{\phi}_I \cdot {}^c\underset{\approx}{K}_{IJ} \cdot d\underset{\sim}{r}_J +$$

$$+ d\underset{\sim}{\phi}_I \cdot {}^r\underset{\approx}{K}_{IJ} \cdot d\underset{\sim}{\phi}_J)$$

Substitution of the transformation equations (1) into the above expression yields:

$$\Phi \sim \Sigma\, g_{jm} dq^j dq^m$$

where g_{jm} is defined by (16). But the dissipation of energy is always positive definite; hence, (19) can be employed to define the differential length $d\ell$.

Equation (19) is a typical form by which a metric tensor is defined; hence, g_{jm} as defined in (16) furnishes a convenient metric tensor. The contravariant components of the metric tensor are:

$$g^{jm} = \frac{|g|_{jm}}{g} \qquad (j,m = 1,2,\ldots,\ell) \tag{20}$$

where $|g|_{jm}$ is the cofactor and g the determinant of the matrix g_{jm}. Multiplying (15) by g^{nj} and summing over all j yields:

$$\dot{q}^n = g^{nj} b_j = b^n \tag{21}$$

where the b^n are the contravariant components of the vector b_j.

Equation (21) furnishes the desired formula for the rate of change of the generalized coordinates, and serves to facilitate the derivation of the general conservation equation governing the temporal evolution of the probability density function P.

3.4 Generalized Diffusion Equation for P

The flux of the probability density P through a generalized infinitesimal directed area δq^n is given by $P\dot{q}^n$. Assume at time t=0 the configuration of the system to be given by $q^{*1}, q^{*2}, \ldots, q^{*\ell}$; then the conservation equation for P, obtained by utilizing the divergence theorem in ℓ space together with (21), is:

$$\frac{\partial P}{\partial t} + \frac{1}{\sqrt{g}} \frac{\partial}{\partial q^n} (\sqrt{g} b^n P) = \frac{1}{\sqrt{g}} \delta(q^1 - q^{*1}) \delta(q^2 - q^{*2}) \ldots \delta(q^\ell - q^{*\ell}) \delta(t) \tag{22}$$

where δ is the Dirac delta function; Einstein's summation convention has been adopted.

Substitution of (8), (12) and (14) into (21) and (22) yields the general differential equation for the probability density, namely:

$$\frac{\partial P}{\partial t} + \frac{1}{\sqrt{g}} \frac{\partial}{\partial q^n} \{ \sqrt{g}\, g^{nj} [P(X_j + X_j^h - \frac{\partial V}{\partial q^j}) - kT \frac{\partial P}{\partial q^j}] \} = \frac{1}{\sqrt{g}} \delta(\underset{\sim}{q} - \underset{\sim}{q}^*) \delta(t) \tag{23}$$

where

$$X_j = \sum_{I,S=1}^{n} (\underset{\sim}{X}_I \cdot \frac{\partial \underset{\sim}{r}_I}{\partial q^j} + \underset{\sim}{Y}_I \cdot \frac{\partial \underset{\sim}{\phi}_I}{\partial q^j}) \tag{24}$$

are the covariant components of the external forces and torques in ℓ space, and

$$X_j^h = \sum_{I,S=1}^{N} (\frac{\partial \underset{\sim}{r}_I}{\partial q^j} \cdot {}^t\underset{\approx}{K}_{IS} + \frac{\partial \underset{\sim}{\phi}_S}{\partial q^j} \cdot {}^c\underset{\approx}{K}_{IS}) \cdot \underset{\sim}{u} \tag{25}$$

are the covariant components in ℓ space of the hydrodynamic force exerted on the particle as a result of the undisturbed velocity field $\underset{\sim}{u}$.

Equation (23) is a second-order parabolic differential equation in P, possessing a source term at t=0. Normalization of the probability density P provides the global requirement that:

$$\int P \sqrt{g}\, d\underset{\sim}{q} = 1 \tag{26}$$

where the integration is to be carried out over the volume of ℓ space.

A complete solution of (23) is formidable, and will not be attempted. However, the generalized Aris moment method for solving Taylor dispersion problems can be utilized here to obtain simple equations governing the first and second moments of this probability density, at least in the limit of long times, $t \to \infty$, where all internal configurations will have been sampled many times.

4. Mean Chain Velocity and Dispersivity

Replace the general coordinate set $\{q^i\}$ by the particular set $\{Z^1, Z^2, Z^3, z^4, \ldots, z^\ell\}$, where Z^1, Z^2 and Z^3 are the cartesian coordinates of a "locator" point fixed in the chain (as measured from a space-fixed origin in the three-dimensional physical space), and $z^4, z^5, \ldots, z^\ell$ are generalized coordinates used to define the configuration of the chain (relative to the body-fixed chain locator point). In other words, translation of the chain through physical space while keeping its configuration fixed alters $Z^\alpha (\alpha=1,2,3)$ but not z^i $(i = 4, \ldots, \ell)$. The upper case Z's and lower case z's will be referred to as "global" and "local" coordinates, respectively, following the terminology introduced by Brenner [3]. The reasons for explicitly distinguishing the global coordinates Z^α from the local coordinates z^i are two fold: First, we desire to obtain certain mean values of these particular global coordinates (first- and second-order moments); second, (23) can be simplified in such a manner that the desired mean values can be obtained without requiring that (23) be solved explicitly.

The metric tensor g^{ij} is indepdent of Z^α since neither $\dfrac{\partial \underset{\sim}{r}_J}{\partial z^i}$, $\dfrac{\partial \underset{\sim}{\phi}_J}{\partial Z^\alpha}$, $\dfrac{\partial \underset{\sim}{r}_J}{\partial Z^\alpha}$ and $\dfrac{\partial \underset{\sim}{\phi}_J}{\partial z^i}$, nor ${}^t\underset{\approx}{K}_{IJ}$, ${}^c\underset{\approx}{K}_{IJ}$, ${}^r\underset{\approx}{K}_{IJ}$, depend on Z^α. (Translation of the system does not alter these dyadic drag coefficients, which depend rather only on the <u>relative</u> locations of the particles).

The potential V of the internal forces depends only on $z^4, z^5, \ldots, z^\ell$ by definition. If $\underset{\sim}{u}$, $\underset{\sim}{X}_i$ and $\underset{\sim}{Y}_i$ are uniform in the three-dimensional space, then X_j and X_j^h are also independent of Z^α. Hence, the linear differential equation (23) possesses nonconstant phenomenological coefficients that depend only on the <u>local</u> coordinates, but not on the global coordinates.

Thus, (23) is amenable to application of the moment method originally utilized by Aris to solve the Taylor dispersion problem, where the resulting recursive set of differential moment equations thereby replacing (23) may be solved sequentially.

Define the mth- order global moment of P as:

$$M_m^{\alpha_1\alpha_2\cdots\alpha_m} = \int_{\underset{\sim}{Z},\underset{\sim}{z}} Z^{\alpha_1}Z^{\alpha_2}\ldots Z^{\alpha_m}\sqrt{g}\,Pd\underset{\sim}{Z}d\underset{\sim}{z} \qquad (\alpha_1,\alpha_2,\ldots,\alpha_m = 1,2,3) \tag{27}$$

and the mth- order local moment as:

$$\mu_m^{\alpha_1\alpha_2\cdots\alpha_m} = \int_{\underset{\sim}{Z}} Z^{\alpha_1}Z^{\alpha_2}\ldots Z^{\alpha_m}Pd\underset{\sim}{Z} \qquad (\alpha_1,\alpha_2,\ldots,\alpha_m = 1,2.3) \tag{28}$$

Here, $d\underset{\sim}{Z}$ represents the physical-space volume element $dZ^1dZ^2dZ^3$, whereas $d\underset{\sim}{z}$ represents $dz^4dz^5\ldots dz^\ell$. The integration (27) is to be carried out over the entire volume of ℓ space. Subscript m appearing in $M_m^{\alpha_1\alpha_2\cdots\alpha_m}$ and $\mu_m^{\alpha_1\alpha_2\cdots\alpha_m}$ specifies the rank of the tensor only, but bears no tensorial attributes. Since the Z^{α_i} are cartesian coordinates, $M_m^{\alpha_1\alpha_2\cdots\alpha_m}$ and $\mu_m^{\alpha_1\alpha_2\cdots\alpha_m}$ are m-rank cartesian tensors in 3-dimensional space. The global moment $M_m^{\alpha_1\alpha_2\cdots\alpha_m}$ can easily be calculated once $\mu_m^{\alpha_1\alpha_2\cdots\alpha_m}$ is known. Indeed, since g is independent of Z^α,

$$M_m^{\alpha_1\alpha_2\cdots\alpha_m} = \int_{\underset{\sim}{z}} \mu^{\alpha_1\alpha_2\cdots\alpha_m}\sqrt{g}\,d\underset{\sim}{z} \tag{29}$$

Two global moments are of particular interest, these being the first-rank tensor M^{α_1} and the second-rank tensor $M^{\alpha_1\alpha_2}$. This interest arises because the mean velocity vector and dispersivity dyadic of the chain are directly related to these two global moments by the relations:

$$< U^{\alpha_1} > = \lim_{t\to\infty} \frac{d < Z^{\alpha_1} >}{dt} = \lim_{t\to\infty} \frac{dM_1^{\alpha_1}}{dt} \tag{30}$$

and

$$< D_d^{\alpha_1\alpha_2} > = \lim_{t\to\infty} \frac{1}{2}\frac{d}{dt} [<(Z^{\alpha_1} - <Z^{\alpha_1}>)(Z^{\alpha_2} - <Z^{\alpha_2}>)>] =$$

$$= \lim_{t\to\infty} \frac{1}{2} \left(\frac{dM_2^{\alpha_1\alpha_2}}{dt} - M_1^{\alpha_2} \frac{dM_1^{\alpha_1}}{dt} - M_1^{\alpha_1} \frac{dM_1^{\alpha_2}}{dt} \right) \quad (\alpha_1, \alpha_2 = 1,2,3) \tag{31}$$

Here, $< U^{\alpha_1} >$ denotes the mean velocity of the chain locator point, and $< D_d^{\alpha_1\,\alpha_2} >$ the dispersivity appropriate to this point.

4.1 Pure Molecular Diffusion

The (molecular) dispersion dyadic and mean velocity vector of the chain are here derived for circumstances where Brownian forces constitute the only external forces exerted on the particles. Thus, both of the external generalized forces, X_j and X_j^h, stemming from the respective external forces, external moments and uniform velocity $\tilde{u}$ are assumed to be zero. Equation (23) then adopts the simplified form:

$$\frac{\partial P}{\partial t} - \frac{1}{\sqrt{g}} \frac{\partial}{\partial q^i} [kTg^{ij}\sqrt{g}\, e^{-V/kT} \frac{\partial}{\partial q^j} (Pe^{V/kT})] = \frac{1}{\sqrt{g}} \delta(\tilde{q}-\tilde{q}^*)\delta(t) \tag{32}$$

$$(i,j = 1,2, \ldots, \ell)$$

The case of nonzero $\tilde{u}$ will be addressed in a separate paper, where interaction between diffusion and convection occurs. Equation (32) can be rewritten in terms of the cartesian coordinates Z^α and generalized coordinates z^i as:

$$\frac{\partial P}{\partial t} = \frac{\partial}{\partial Z^\alpha}\left(D^{\alpha\beta}\frac{\partial P}{\partial Z^\beta}\right) + \frac{\partial}{\partial Z^\alpha}\left[e^{-V/kT}\tilde{D}^{\alpha i}\frac{\partial}{\partial z^i}\left(Pe^{V/kT}\right)\right] +$$

$$+ \frac{1}{\sqrt{g}}\frac{\partial}{\partial z^i}\left(\sqrt{g}\,\tilde{D}^{i\alpha}\frac{\partial P}{\partial Z^\alpha}\right) + \frac{1}{\sqrt{g}}\frac{\partial}{\partial z^i}\left[\sqrt{g}\,e^{-V/kT}d^{ij}\frac{\partial}{\partial z^j}\left(Pe^{V/kT}\right)\right] +$$

$$+ \frac{1}{\sqrt{g}}\,\delta(\underset{\sim}{Z}-\underset{\sim}{Z}^*)\,\delta(\underset{\sim}{z}-\underset{\sim}{z}^*)\,\delta(t) \tag{33}$$

where the independence of V, g^{ij} and g from Z^α has been accounted for. Here, with the choice of ranges $i,j = 4,5,\ldots,\ell$, and $\alpha,\beta = 1,2,3$, the diffusion components $D^{\alpha\beta}$, $\tilde{D}^{\alpha i}$, $\tilde{D}^{i\alpha}$ and d^{ij} are defined by the partitioned matrix relation:

$$\left[\begin{array}{cc} \begin{bmatrix} D^{11} & D^{12} & D^{13} \\ D^{21} & D^{22} & D^{23} \\ D^{31} & D^{32} & D^{33} \end{bmatrix} & \begin{bmatrix} \tilde{D}^{14} & \ldots & \tilde{D}^{1\ell} \\ \tilde{D}^{24} & \ldots & \tilde{D}^{2\ell} \\ \tilde{D}^{34} & \ldots & \tilde{D}^{3\ell} \end{bmatrix} \\ \begin{bmatrix} \tilde{D}^{41} & \tilde{D}^{42} & \tilde{D}^{43} \\ \vdots & \vdots & \vdots \\ \tilde{D}^{\ell 1} & \tilde{D}^{\ell 2} & \tilde{D}^{\ell 3} \end{bmatrix} & \begin{bmatrix} d^{44} & \ldots & d^{4\ell} \\ \vdots & & \vdots \\ d^{\ell 4} & \ldots & d^{\ell\ell} \end{bmatrix} \end{array}\right] \equiv kT \begin{bmatrix} g^{11} & \ldots & g^{1\ell} \\ \vdots & & \vdots \\ g^{\ell 1} & \ldots & g^{\ell\ell} \end{bmatrix} \tag{34}$$

None of the diffusion coefficients depend on Z^α; hence, (33) is amenable to resolution via the moment method originally utilized by Aris [1] to solve the Taylor dispersion problem.

4.1.1 Zeroth-Order Moment. Integrate (33) over the entire $\underset{\sim}{Z}$ space and assume that $|P(Z^{\alpha})|^{m} \to 0$ as $|Z^{\alpha}| \to \infty$ (for m any positive integer) to obtain:

$$\frac{\partial \mu_0}{\partial t} - L\mu_0 = \frac{1}{\sqrt{g}}\,\delta(z-z^*)\delta(t) \tag{35}$$

where L, defined as:

$$L\mu = \frac{1}{\sqrt{g}}\frac{\partial}{\partial z^i}\left[\sqrt{g}\, e^{-V/kT} d^{ij}\, \frac{\partial (e^{V/kT}\mu)}{\partial z^j}\right] \tag{36}$$

is a second-order linear differential operator. The divergence theorem was extensively used to derive the contributions of the various terms in (33). (Only the two last terms in (33) survive). The local-moment scalar μ_0 satisfies the global relation:

$$\int \sqrt{g}\, \mu_0\, d\underset{\sim}{z} = \begin{cases} 1 & (t > 0)\,, \\ 0 & (t < 0)\,, \end{cases} \tag{37}$$

stemming from (26).

The steady-state solution for μ_0 is simply:

$$\mu_0 e^{V/kT} = C \tag{38}$$

where C is a constant. It can easily be demonstrated that for sufficiently long times the time-dependent solution of μ_0 is of the asymptotic form:

$$\mu_0 = Ce^{-V/kT} + \exp \tag{39}$$

where "exp" symbolically represents terms that decay exponentially rapidly with time. From (37) we have that:

$$C^{-1} = \int e^{-V/kT}\sqrt{g}\, d\underset{\sim}{z} \tag{40}$$

4.1.2 First-Order Moment. The local moment μ_1^{α} is pertinent to calculating the mean velocity of the chain. By definition,

$$\mu_1^{\alpha} = \int Z^{\alpha} P dZ_{\sim}$$

Differentiate μ_1^{α} with respect to time and use (33) to obtain:

$$\frac{\partial \mu_1^{\alpha}}{\partial t} = \int Z^{\alpha} \frac{\partial P}{\partial t} dZ_{\sim} = \frac{1}{\sqrt{g}} \frac{\partial}{\partial z^i} [\sqrt{g}\, e^{-V/kT} d^{ij} \frac{\partial(\mu_1^{\alpha} e^{V/kT})}{\partial z^j}] -$$

$$- \frac{1}{\sqrt{g}} \frac{\partial}{\partial z^i} (\sqrt{g}\, \tilde{D}^{i\alpha} \mu_0) + e^{-V/kT}\, \tilde{D}^{\alpha i} \frac{\partial}{\partial z^i} (\mu_0\, e^{V/kT}) \qquad (41)$$

where the divergence theorem was used to integrate out the contributions arising from various terms of (33); i and j are dummy indices.

The differential equation satisfied by μ_1^{α},

$$\frac{\partial \mu_1^{\alpha}}{\partial t} - L\mu_1^{\alpha} = - \frac{1}{\sqrt{g}} \frac{\partial}{\partial z^i} (\sqrt{g}\, \tilde{D}^{i\alpha} \mu_0) + e^{-V/kT}\, \tilde{D}^{\alpha i} \frac{\partial}{\partial z^i} (\mu_0 e^{V/kT}) \qquad (42)$$

is of the same form as that for μ_0 except for the appearance of the inhomogeneous 'forcing' term, which depends on the zeroth moment μ_0. Thus, a complete solution for μ_0 would appear prerequisite to obtaining a solution of μ_1^{α}. However, as indicated later, a full solution of (42) proves unnecessary in order to obtain the mean velocity of the chain.

4.1.3 Second-Order Moment. The local moment $\mu_2^{\alpha\beta}$ represents the second-order tensor moment of P in Z space. It is relevant to calculating the dispersivity of the chain through the fluid. In accordance with (28), it is defined as:

$$\mu_2^{\alpha\beta} = \int Z^{\alpha} Z^{\beta} P dZ_{\sim}$$

Differentiate $\mu_2^{\alpha\beta}$ with respect to time and use the differential equation (33) to obtain:

$$\frac{\partial \mu_2^{\alpha\beta}}{\partial t} = \int Z^\alpha Z^\beta \frac{\partial P}{\partial t} d\underset{\sim}{Z} = \frac{1}{\sqrt{g}} \frac{\partial}{\partial z^i} [\sqrt{g}\, e^{-V/kT} d^{ij} \frac{\partial}{\partial z^i} (\mu_2^{\alpha\beta} e^{V/kT})] +$$

$$+ 2\mu_0 D^{\alpha\beta} - e^{-V/kT} [\tilde{D}^{\alpha i} \frac{\partial}{\partial z^i} (\mu_1^{\beta} e^{V/kT}) + \tilde{D}^{\beta i} \frac{\partial}{\partial z^i} (\mu_1^{\alpha} e^{V/kT})] -$$

$$- \frac{1}{\sqrt{g}} \frac{\partial}{\partial z^i} [\sqrt{g} (\tilde{D}^{i\beta} \mu_1^{\alpha} + \tilde{D}^{i\alpha} \mu_1^{\beta})] \tag{43}$$

Again, the divergence theorem was utilized to obtain the contributions of the various terms appearing in (33) after integration over $\underset{\sim}{Z}$ space. The differential equation obtained for $\mu_2^{\alpha\beta}$ is thus:

$$\frac{\partial \mu_2^{\alpha\beta}}{\partial t} - L\mu_2^{\alpha\beta} = 2\mu_0 D^{\alpha\beta} - e^{-V/kT} [\tilde{D}^{\alpha i} \frac{\partial}{\partial z^i} (\mu_1^{\beta} e^{V/kT}) +$$

$$+ \tilde{D}^{\beta i} \frac{\partial}{\partial z^i} (\mu_1^{\alpha} e^{V/kT})] - \frac{1}{\sqrt{g}} \frac{\partial}{\partial z^i} [\sqrt{g} (\tilde{D}^{i\beta} \mu_1^{\alpha} + \tilde{D}^{i\alpha} \mu_1^{\beta})] \tag{44}$$

This is of the same form obtained previously for μ_0 and μ_1^α except for the inhomogeneous terms, which herein depend on both μ_0 and μ_1^α. Thus, the solution of (44) for $\mu_2^{\alpha\beta}$ is possible, provided that μ_0 and μ_1^α are already known. A similar procedure was devised by Aris [1], with a recursive set of differential moment equations replacing the general probability density equation ((33) in our case).

It is shown later that the dispersion tensor may, in fact, be obtained without first requiring an explicit solution of $\mu_2^{\alpha\beta}$. Asymptotic solution of the differential equation for μ_1^α as $t \to \infty$ serves to facilitate this dispersivity calculation.

4.2 Boundary Conditions Imposed on the Local Moments

Two different classes of problems are addressed for which boundary conditions are required:

a) The probability density P is defined in some finite domain D, i.e., only certain possible configurations are allowed, whence the flux through the boundary of D must vanish:

$$P\dot{q}^i n_i = 0 \quad \text{on } S \tag{45}$$

where S denotes the boundary of D, and n_i is a unit normal vector on S in ℓ space;

b) There exists a discontinuity in P across some surface S in ℓ space; however, the flux of P through this surface is continuous:

$$(P\dot{q}^i)_1 n_i = (P\dot{q}^i)_2 n_i \quad \text{on } S \tag{46}$$

Here, indices 1 and 2 denote the two sides of surface S. Equation (46) is valid unless there exists some nonzero probability for the system to be concentrated on the surface S, requiring the introduction of a surface-excess flux--and hence destroying the continuity of the normal flux component $P\dot{q}^i n_i$.

Assume the surface S to be defined by the equation:

$$s(q^1, q^2, \ldots, q^\ell) = 0 \tag{47}$$

whence the normal n_i to the surface S is colinear with $\partial s/\partial q^i$:

$$n_i \parallel \frac{\partial s}{\partial q^i} \quad (i = 1,2, \ldots, \ell) \tag{48}$$

If q^1, q^2 and q^3 are the cartesian coordinates Z^1, Z^2 and Z^3 defined previously, and the chain is suspended in an unbounded fluid, the function s is then independent of q^1, q^2 and q^3. Hence, the vector n_i in ℓ space has components along q^4, q^5, ..., q^ℓ only.

The general form of $\dot{q}^i$ is given by (21), and in a more explicit form by the expression:

$$\dot{q}^i = g^{ij}(X_j^h + X_j - \frac{\partial V}{\partial q^j} - kT \frac{\partial \ell n\ P}{\partial q^j})$$

where X_j^h and X_j are defined in (24) and (25). When no external forces exist and the fluid is quiescent we have that:

$$X_j = X_j^h = 0$$

and

$$\dot{q}^i = -g^{ij} (\frac{\partial V}{\partial q^j} + kT \frac{\partial P}{\partial q^j}) \tag{49}$$

where $i,j = 1,2, \ldots, \ell$.

Since $n_1=n_2=n_3=0$, and V is independent of Z^α, (45) can be rewritten in the form:

$$n_i g^{ij} (P \frac{\partial V}{\partial z^j} + kT \frac{\partial P}{\partial z^j}) + n_i g^{i\alpha}(kT \frac{\partial P}{\partial Z^\alpha}) = 0 \tag{50}$$

where $i,j = 4,5, \ldots, \ell$ and $\alpha = 1,2,3$.

Multiply (50) by $Z^{\alpha_1} Z^{\alpha_2} \ldots Z^{\alpha_m}$, integrate over Z space, and utilize the divergence theorem to obtain:

$$n_i d^{ij} \frac{\partial}{\partial z^j} (e^{V/kT} \mu_m^{\alpha_1\alpha_2 \ldots \alpha_m}) =$$

$$= \sum_{k=1}^{m} n_i \tilde{D}^{i\alpha_k} e^{V/kT} \mu_{m-1}^{\alpha_1 \ldots \alpha_{k-1} \alpha_{k+1} \ldots \alpha_m} \tag{51}$$

on S.

Here, D^{ij} and $\tilde{D}^{i\alpha_k}$ are defined in (34), with $i,j = 4,5, \ldots, \ell$ and

$\alpha_1, \alpha_2, \ldots, \alpha_m = 1,2,3$. Dummy indices are summed according to the Einstein convention. Upon successfively setting m = 0, 1 and 2 in (51), the boundary conditions imposed on μ_0, $\mu_1{}^{\alpha}$, $\mu_2{}^{\alpha\beta}$ are obtained respectively as:

$$\left\{\begin{array}{l} n_i d^{ij} \frac{\partial}{\partial z^j} (e^{V/kT} \mu_0) = 0, \\ n_i d^{ij} \frac{\partial}{\partial z^j} (\mu_1{}^{\alpha} e^{V/kT}) = n_i \tilde{D}^{i\alpha} \mu_0 e^{V/kT} , \\ n_i d^{ij} \frac{\partial}{\partial z^j} (\mu_2{}^{\alpha\beta} e^{V/kT}) = n_i (\tilde{D}^{i\alpha} \mu_1^{\beta} + \tilde{D}^{i\beta} \mu_1{}^{\alpha}) e^{V/kT} \end{array}\right. \tag{52}$$

on S.

These boundary conditions must be satisfied together with the differential equations for μ_0, μ_1 and μ_2. Equation (52) shows the relationship between the local moments on the boundaries to be compatible with successive integration of μ_0, μ_1^{α}, $\mu_2^{\alpha\beta}$, etc.

When case (b) is addressed, an equation similar to (51) is obtained, namely,

$$n_i d^{ij} \{ e^{-V_1/kT} [\frac{\partial}{\partial z^i} (e^{V/kT} \mu_m{}^{\alpha_1 \alpha_2 \ldots \alpha_m})]_1 - e^{-V_2/kT} [\frac{\partial}{\partial z^i} (e^{V/kT} \mu_m{}^{\alpha_1 \alpha_2 \ldots \alpha_m})]_2 \}$$

$$= \sum_{k=1}^{M} n_i \tilde{D}^{i\alpha_k} [(\mu_{m-1}{}^{\alpha_1 \ldots \alpha_{k-1} \alpha_{k+1} \ldots \alpha_m})_1 - (\mu_{m-1}{}^{\alpha_1 \ldots \alpha_{k-1} \alpha_{k+1} \ldots \alpha_m})_2] \tag{53}$$

where indices 1 and 2 respectively denote evaluation on each side of the surface S.

Set m = 0, 1 and 2 in the above. The explicit boundary conditions thereby obtained for μ_0, $\mu_1{}^{\alpha}$ and $\mu_2{}^{\alpha\beta}$ are respectively:

for m = 0,

$$n_i d^{ij}\{e^{-V_1/kT}[\frac{\partial}{\partial z^j}(\mu_0 e^{V/kT})]_1 - e^{-V_2/kT}[\frac{\partial}{\partial z^j}(\mu_0 e^{V/kT})]_2\} = 0 \tag{54}$$

for m = 1,

$$n_i d^{ij}\{e^{-V_1/kT}[\frac{\partial}{\partial z^j}(\mu_1{}^{\alpha} e^{V/kT})]_1 - e^{-V_2/kT}[\frac{\partial}{\partial z^j}(\mu_1{}^{\alpha} e^{V/kT})]_2\} =$$

$$= n_i \tilde{D}^{i\alpha}\{[\mu_0]_1 - [\mu_0]_2\} \qquad (\alpha = 1,2,3) \tag{55}$$

for m = 2,

$$n_i d^{ij}\{e^{-V_1 kT}[\frac{\partial}{\partial z^j}(\mu_2{}^{\alpha\beta} e^{V/kT})]_1 - e^{-V_2/kT}[\frac{\partial}{\partial z^j}(\mu_2{}^{\alpha\beta} e^{V/kT})]_2\} =$$

$$= n_i \tilde{D}^{i\alpha}\{[\mu_1{}^{\beta}]_1 - [\mu_1{}^{\beta}]_2\} + n_i \tilde{D}^{i\beta}\{[\mu_1{}^{\alpha}]_1 - [\mu_1{}^{\alpha}]_2\} \quad (\alpha,\beta=1,2,3) \tag{56}$$

These boundary conditions also illustrate the recursive relations existing between the successive moments μ_n and μ_{n-1}.

When the local coordinates form a closed space (e.g., they are three Eulerian angles specifying the orientation of a rigid nonspherical particle), no explicit boundary conditions exist; rather, we demand instead that the solution be continuous and single valued for such "cyclic" coordinates.

4.3 Global Moments and Their Time Derivatives

In section 4 we indicated the importance of the first and second global moments in obtaining the mean velocity and dispersivity of the chain. The differential equations and boundary conditions pertaining to the local moments were addressed in sections 4.1 and 4.2, where special attention was paid to the zeroth-, first- and second-order moments. These solutions are now exploited to obtain the first and second global moments and their time derivatives.

The first-order global moment is defined as (cf. (29)):

$$M_1^{\alpha} = \int \sqrt{g}\, \mu_1^{\alpha} d\underset{\sim}{z}$$

Hence, upon utilizing (41), the mean velocity--expressed in (30) in terms of μ_1^{α} -- is:

$$<U^{\alpha}> = \lim_{t\to\infty} \frac{dM_1^{\alpha}}{dt} = \lim_{t\to\infty} \int \sqrt{g} \frac{\partial \mu_1^{\alpha}}{\partial t} d\underset{\sim}{z} =$$

$$= \lim_{t\to\infty} \left(\int \{\frac{\partial}{\partial z^i} [\sqrt{g}\, e^{-V/kT} d^{ij} \frac{\partial}{\partial z^j} (\mu_1^{\alpha} e^{V/kT})] - \frac{\partial}{\partial z^i} [\sqrt{g} \tilde{D}^{i\alpha} \mu_0]\} d\underset{\sim}{z} + \exp \right) =$$

$$= \int \sqrt{g}\, e^{-V/kT} [d^{ij} \frac{\partial}{\partial z^j} (\mu_1^{\alpha} e^{V/kT}) - e^{V/kT} \tilde{D}^{i\alpha} \mu_0] n_i dS \qquad (57)$$

where "exp" denotes terms decaying exponentially with time arising from the asymptotic solution for μ_0 in (39). (The last equality in (57) was obtained by using the divergence theorem in $\underset{\sim}{z}$ space). But the term in square brackets vanishes on the surface S according to boundary condition (52). Thus, we arrive at the unsurprising conclusion that:

$$< U^{\alpha} > = 0 \qquad (\alpha = 1,2,3) \qquad (58)$$

for the case where no external forces act and when the chain is suspended in a quiescent fluid. This result is invariant to the specific choice of chain locator point as well as of the specific form of the potential energy function V for the internal forces.

The dispersivity of the N-particle chain, defined in (31) and expressed there in terms of the global moments $M_2^{\alpha\beta}$ and M_1^{α} , M_1^{β}, adopts the simplified form:

$$< D_M^{\alpha\beta} > = \lim_{t\to\infty} \frac{1}{2} \frac{dM_2^{\alpha\beta}}{dt} \qquad (59)$$

since the time derivatives of M_1^α and M_1^β vanish. We have here appended the subscript M to the dispersion tensor to stress its purely molecular character.

Substitution of (43) into (59) yields:

$$\frac{dM_2^{\alpha\beta}}{dt} = \int \sqrt{g}\,\frac{\partial \mu_2{}^{\alpha\beta}}{\partial t}\, d\underset{\sim}{z} = 2 \int D^{\alpha\beta}\mu_0 \sqrt{g}\, d\underset{\sim}{z} +$$

$$+ \int \frac{\partial}{\partial z^i} [\sqrt{g}\, e^{-V/kT}\, d^{ij} \frac{\partial}{\partial z^j} (\mu_2{}^{\alpha\beta}\, e^{V/kT})] d\underset{\sim}{z} -$$

$$- \int \sqrt{g}\, e^{-V/kT} [\tilde{D}^{\alpha i} \frac{\partial}{\partial z^i} (\mu_1^\beta\, e^{V/kT}) + \tilde{D}^{\beta i} \frac{\partial}{\partial z^i} (\mu_1{}^\alpha e^{V/kT})] d\underset{\sim}{z} -$$

$$- \int \frac{\partial}{\partial z^i} (\sqrt{g}\, \tilde{D}^{i\alpha}\, \mu_1^\beta + \sqrt{g}\, \tilde{D}^{i\beta} \mu_1{}^\alpha) d\underset{\sim}{z} \qquad (60)$$

Utilization of the divergence theorem and the boundary conditions (52) leads to the following expression for the dispersion tensor:

$$< D_M{}^{\alpha\beta} > = \lim_{t\to\infty} \{\int D^{\alpha\beta}\mu_0 \sqrt{g}\, d\underset{\sim}{z} - \frac{1}{2} \int \sqrt{g}\, e^{-V/kT} [\tilde{D}^{\alpha i} \frac{\partial}{\partial z^i} (\mu_1{}^\beta e^{V/kT}) +$$

$$+ \tilde{D}^{\beta i} \frac{\partial}{\partial z^i} (\mu_1{}^\alpha e^{V/kT})] d\underset{\sim}{z}\} \qquad (61)$$

Since, as $t\to\infty$, μ_0 is already available in (39) in terms of the potential V, the only function that need be determined is $\mu_1{}^\alpha$. The latter satisfies the differential equation:

$$\frac{\partial B^\alpha}{\partial t} - \frac{e^{V/kT}}{\sqrt{g}} \frac{\partial}{\partial z^i} (\sqrt{g}\, e^{-V/kT}\, d^{ij} \frac{\partial B^\alpha}{\partial z^j}) = - \frac{e^{V/kT}}{\sqrt{g}} \frac{\partial}{\partial z^i} (\sqrt{g}\, \tilde{D}^{i\alpha}\mu_0) \qquad (62)$$

where

$$B^{\alpha} \equiv \mu_1{}^{\alpha} e^{V/kT} \tag{63}$$

Only the asymptotic behavior of $\partial B^{\alpha}/\partial z^{i}$ as $t \to \infty$ is needed to evaluate the dispersivity. The generic expressions obtained for the mean velocity vector (Eq. (58)) and dispersivity dyadic (Eq. (62)) constitute the central results of our analysis. These may be evaluated for any prescribed internal potential $V(z^4, z^5, \ldots, z^{\ell})$ and for any collection of rigid bodies composing the chain for which the requisite hydrodynamic resistivity (or mobility) dyadics are available--including hydrodynamic interactions among the particles. By way of example, the case of an elastic dumbbell (with relatively weak hydrodynamic interactions) is addressed in section 5 to illustrate the solution procedure.

4.4 Invariance of the Dispersion Dyadic to Choice of Chain Locator Point

Suppose that a new locator point fixed in the chain is chosen, say $\hat{Z}^{\alpha}$, which differs from our previous locator point Z^{α}. (Recall that both Z^{α} and $\hat{Z}^{\alpha}$ are the cartesian coordinates of a point obtained from different linear combinations of $\underset{\sim}{r}_I$.) The translational transformation:

$$\hat{Z}^{\alpha} = Z^{\alpha} + a^{\alpha}$$

necessarily relates these two points, with a^{α} the fixed distance between them. Thus, the system is defined by a new set of coordinates $\hat{Z}^1, \hat{Z}^2, \hat{Z}^3, \hat{z}^4, \ldots, \hat{z}^{\ell}$, where $\hat{z}^4, \ldots, \hat{z}^{\ell}$ are coordinates related to the new fixed point $\hat{Z}^{\alpha}$. The question we pose is as follows: Does the dispersion tensor change if we track different chain locator points? In other words, what is the transformation law governing the behavior of the dispersion tensor under translation of the body-fixed locator point? (The dispersivity has already been shown to behave as a cartesian tensor under rotation.)

The first- and second-order global moments are defined as:

$$M_1^{\alpha} = \int Z^{\alpha} P \sqrt{g}\, d\underset{\sim}{q}$$

and

$$M_2^{\alpha_1\alpha_2} = \int Z^{\alpha_1} Z^{\alpha_2} P\sqrt{g}d\underset{\sim}{q}$$

Likewise, in the new set of coordinates $\underset{\sim}{\hat{q}}$ we have that:

$$\hat{M}_1^{\alpha} = \int \hat{Z}^{\alpha}\hat{P}\sqrt{\hat{g}}d\underset{\sim}{\hat{q}}$$

and

$$\hat{M}_2^{\alpha_1\alpha_2} = \int \hat{Z}^{\alpha_1} Z^{\alpha_2}\hat{P}\sqrt{\hat{g}}d\underset{\sim}{\hat{q}}$$

But, since $P\sqrt{g}d\underset{\sim}{q}$ remains invariant to the choice of coordinate systems,

$$P\sqrt{g}d\underset{\sim}{q} = \hat{P}\sqrt{\hat{g}}d\underset{\sim}{\hat{q}}$$

Thus, the relations between the global first and second moments, expressed in terms of the two alternative sets of coordinates is:

$$\hat{M}_1^{\alpha} = \int (Z^{\alpha} + a^{\alpha})P\sqrt{g}d\underset{\sim}{q} = M_1^{\alpha} + a^{\alpha}$$

and

$$\hat{M}_2^{\alpha_1\alpha_2} = \int (Z^{\alpha_1} + a^{\alpha_1})(Z^{\alpha_2} + a^{\alpha_2})P\sqrt{g}d\underset{\sim}{q} =$$

$$= M_2^{\alpha_1\alpha_2} + M_1^{\alpha_1}a^{\alpha_2} + M_1^{\alpha_2}a^{\alpha_1} + a^{\alpha_1}a^{\alpha_2}$$

However, from the definition of the dispersion tensor,

$$< D_d^{\alpha_1\alpha_2} > = \lim_{t\to\infty} \frac{1}{2}\frac{d}{dt}(M_2^{\alpha_1\alpha_2} - M_1^{\alpha_1}M_1^{\alpha_2})$$

and

$$< \hat{D}_d^{\alpha_1\alpha_2} > = \lim_{t\to\infty} \frac{1}{2}\frac{d}{dt} (\hat{M}_2^{\alpha_1\alpha_2} - \hat{M}_1^{\alpha_1}\hat{M}_1^{\alpha_2})$$

Upon introducing into these the foregoing relations for $\hat{M}_1^{\alpha}$ and $\hat{M}_2^{\alpha_1\alpha_2}$ we obtain:

$$< \hat{D}_d^{\alpha_1\alpha_2} > = < D_d^{\alpha_1\alpha_2} >$$

Hence, the dispersion tensor is invariant to the particular choice made for the chain locator point.

5. Example: Elastic Dumbbell

Two identical rigid spheres of radii a are connected by an elastic rod or spring that prevents relative rotations of the spheres but allows relative linear displacements of their centers. The force exerted by the rod on each of the spheres is derived from a potential energy function V which depends only on the distance ra between their centers (r being the corresponding nondimensional distance).

Figure 1 illustrates the dumbbell geometry and coordinate systems employed; Z^1, Z^2, Z^3 denote the cartesian coordinates of the center point of the dumbbell. The right-handed trio of body-fixed orthonormal vectors $(\underset{\sim}{e}_1, \underset{\sim}{e}_2, \underset{\sim}{e}_3)$, with $\underset{\sim}{e}_1$ drawn along the line of centers, determine the dumbbell orientation relative to, say, the space-fixed cartesian system Z^1, Z^2, Z^3, whose unit vectors are $(\underset{\sim}{i}, \underset{\sim}{j}, \underset{\sim}{k})$. In accordance with our assumptions, the transformation equations are:

$$\underset{\sim}{r}_1 = \underset{\sim}{R} - \frac{a}{2} r\underset{\sim}{e}_1 \equiv Z^1\underset{\sim}{i} + Z^2\underset{\sim}{j} + Z^3\underset{\sim}{k} - \frac{a}{2} z^7 \underset{\sim}{e}_1 ,$$

$$\underset{\sim}{r}_2 = \underset{\sim}{R} + \frac{a}{2} r\underset{\sim}{e}_1 \equiv Z^1\underset{\sim}{i} + Z^2\underset{\sim}{j} + Z^3\underset{\sim}{k} + \frac{a}{2} z^7 \underset{\sim}{e}_1 ,$$

$$d\underset{\sim}{\phi}_1 = dz^4\underset{\sim}{e}_1 + dz^5\underset{\sim}{e}_2 + dz^6\underset{\sim}{e}_3 ,$$

$$d\underset{\sim}{\phi}_2 = dz^4\underset{\sim}{e}_1 + dz^5\underset{\sim}{e}_2 + dz^6\underset{\sim}{e}_3 ,$$

$$r = z^7 \tag{64}$$

where pseudoscalars dz^4, dz^5, dz^6 denote the components of the infinitesimal rotation pseudovector $d\underset{\sim}{\phi}$. We prefer to use these infinitesimal coordinates rather than, say, the three Euler angles, since they preserve the symmetry of the expressions which follow. At the same time their use simplifies our calculations considerably. According to (64), seven degrees of freedom suffice to locate a point in the phase space. This is consistent with the restrictions imposed on the chain (namely, $d\underset{\sim}{\phi}_1 = d\underset{\sim}{\phi}_2$ as well as rigidity to bending).

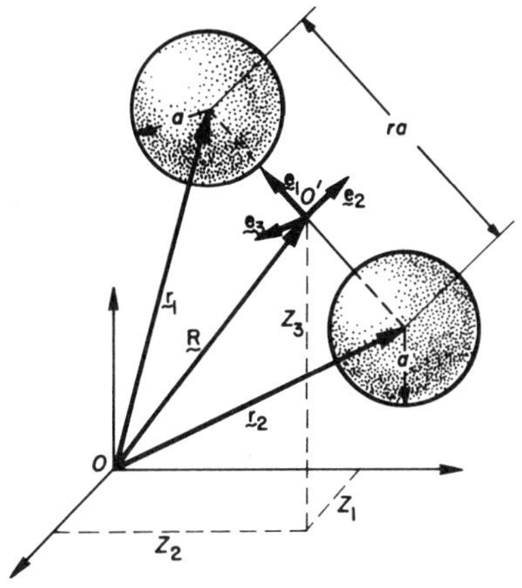

Fig. 1: Coordinate System

Derivatives of $\underset{\sim}{e}_1$, $\underset{\sim}{e}_2$ and $\underset{\sim}{e}_3$ with respect to dz^4, dz^5, dz^6 do not vanish; rather,

$$\frac{d\underset{\sim}{e}_j}{dz_{i+3}} = \varepsilon_{ijk}\underset{\sim}{e}_k \qquad (i,j,k = 1,2,3) \tag{65}$$

where ε_{ijk} is the permutation tensor. The metric tensor may thus be determined by exploiting the following identities:

$$\frac{\partial \underset{\sim}{r}_1}{\partial Z^1} = \frac{\partial \underset{\sim}{r}_2}{\partial Z^1} = \underset{\sim}{i}, \qquad \frac{\partial \underset{\sim}{\phi}_1}{\partial Z^1} = \frac{\partial \underset{\sim}{\phi}_2}{\partial Z^1} = \underset{\sim}{0},$$

$$\frac{\partial \underset{\sim}{r}_1}{\partial Z^2} = \frac{\partial \underset{\sim}{r}_2}{\partial Z^2} = \underset{\sim}{j}, \qquad \frac{\partial \underset{\sim}{\phi}_1}{\partial Z^2} = \frac{\partial \underset{\sim}{\phi}_2}{\partial Z^2} = \underset{\sim}{0},$$

$$\frac{\partial \underset{\sim}{r}_1}{\partial Z^3} = \frac{\partial \underset{\sim}{r}_2}{\partial Z^3} = \underset{\sim}{k}, \qquad \frac{\partial \underset{\sim}{\phi}_1}{\partial Z^3} = \frac{\partial \underset{\sim}{\phi}_2}{\partial Z^3} = \underset{\sim}{0},$$

$$\frac{\partial \underset{\sim}{r}_1}{\partial z^4} = \frac{\partial \underset{\sim}{r}_2}{\partial z^4} = \underset{\sim}{0}, \qquad \frac{\partial \underset{\sim}{\phi}_1}{\partial z^4} = \frac{\partial \underset{\sim}{\phi}_2}{\partial z^4} = \underset{\sim}{e}_1,$$

$$\frac{\partial \underset{\sim}{r}_1}{\partial z^5} = - \frac{\partial \underset{\sim}{r}_2}{\partial z^5} = \frac{1}{2} z^7 a\underset{\sim}{e}_3, \qquad \frac{\partial \underset{\sim}{\phi}_1}{\partial z^5} = \frac{\partial \underset{\sim}{\phi}_2}{\partial z^5} = \underset{\sim}{e}_2,$$

$$\frac{\partial \underset{\sim}{r}_1}{\partial z^6} = - \frac{\partial \underset{\sim}{r}_2}{\partial z^6} = - \frac{1}{2} z^7 a\underset{\sim}{e}_2, \qquad \frac{\partial \underset{\sim}{\phi}_1}{\partial z^6} = \frac{\partial \underset{\sim}{\phi}_2}{\partial z^6} = \underset{\sim}{e}_3,$$

$$\frac{\partial \underset{\sim}{r}_1}{\partial z^7} = - \frac{\partial \underset{\sim}{r}_2}{\partial z^7} = - \frac{1}{2} a\underset{\sim}{e}_1, \qquad \frac{\partial \underset{\sim}{\phi}_1}{\partial z^7} = \frac{\partial \underset{\sim}{\phi}_2}{\partial z^7} = \underset{\sim}{0} \tag{66}$$

By virtue of the transversely isotropic geometric symmetry of the dumbbell about the axis $\underset{\sim}{e}_1$ drawn along its line of centers, the hydrodynamic resistance dyadics possess the following general forms:

$$\left.\begin{aligned} {}^{t}\underset{\approx}{K}_{ij} &= {}^{t}k_{ij}(\underset{\approx}{I} - \underset{\sim}{e}_1\underset{\sim}{e}_1) + {}^{t}\ell_{ij}\underset{\sim}{e}_1\underset{\sim}{e}_1 , \\ {}^{r}\underset{\approx}{K}_{ij} &= {}^{r}k_{ij}(\underset{\approx}{I} - \underset{\sim}{e}_1\underset{\sim}{e}_1) + {}^{r}\ell_{ij}\underset{\sim}{e}_1\underset{\sim}{e}_1 , \\ {}^{c}\underset{\approx}{K}_{ij} &= {}^{c}k_{ij}\underset{\approx}{\underset{\sim}{\varepsilon}}\cdot\underset{\sim}{e}_1 \end{aligned}\right\} \quad (i,j = 1,2) \tag{67}$$

with $\underset{\approx}{I}$ the dyadic idemfactor. The five scalar phenomenlogical coeffticents ${}^{t}k_{ij}$, ${}^{r}k_{ij}$, ${}^{c}k_{ij}$, ${}^{t}\ell_{ij}$ and ${}^{r}\ell_{ij}$ are proportional to the viscosity of the fluid, and depend only upon the radii a of the spheres and the nondimensional distance r between their centers (cf. (76)). Since the spheres are identical, we have further that:

$$\begin{aligned} {}^{t}k_{11} &= {}^{t}k_{22}, & {}^{t}k_{12} &= {}^{t}k_{21}, \\ {}^{t}\ell_{11} &= {}^{t}\ell_{22}, & {}^{t}\ell_{12} &= {}^{t}\ell_{21}, \\ {}^{r}k_{11} &= {}^{r}k_{22}, & {}^{r}k_{12} &= {}^{r}k_{21}, \\ {}^{r}\ell_{11} &= {}^{r}\ell_{22} & {}^{r}\ell_{12} &= {}^{r}\ell_{21}, \\ {}^{c}k_{11} &= -{}^{c}k_{22}, & {}^{c}k_{12} &= -{}^{c}k_{21} \end{aligned} \tag{68}$$

Introduction of (67) and (68) into (16) yields:

$$
\begin{aligned}
g_{11} &= A + B(\underset{\sim}{e}_1 \cdot \underset{\sim}{i})^2, \\
g_{22} &= A + B(\underset{\sim}{e}_1 \cdot \underset{\sim}{j})^2, \\
g_{33} &= A + B(\underset{\sim}{e}_1 \cdot \underset{\sim}{k})^2, \\
g_{44} &= {}^r\ell_{11} + {}^r\ell_{22} + 2\,{}^r\ell_{12}, \\
g_{55} &= \frac{1}{4}\, a^2 r^2 ({}^tk_{11} + {}^tk_{22} - 2\,{}^tk_{12}) + ({}^rk_{11} + {}^rk_{22} + 2\,{}^rk_{12}), \\
g_{66} &= g_{55}, \\
g_{77} &= \frac{1}{4}\, a^2 ({}^t\ell_{11} + {}^t\ell_{22} - 2\,{}^t\ell_{12}), \\
g_{12} &= g_{21} = B(\underset{\sim}{e}_1 \cdot \underset{\sim}{i})(\underset{\sim}{e}_1 \cdot \underset{\sim}{j}), \\
g_{13} &= g_{31} = B(\underset{\sim}{e}_1 \cdot \underset{\sim}{i})(\underset{\sim}{e}_1 \cdot \underset{\sim}{k}), \\
g_{23} &= g_{32} = B(\underset{\sim}{e}_1 \cdot \underset{\sim}{j})(\underset{\sim}{e}_1 \cdot \underset{\sim}{k})
\end{aligned} \tag{69}
$$

where

$$A = {}^tk_{11} + {}^tk_{22} + 2\,{}^tk_{12},$$

$$B = {}^t\ell_{11} + {}^t\ell_{22} + 2\,{}^t\ell_{12} - A$$

All other components of the metric tensor are identically zero.

Armed with these results, the nonzero contravariant components of the metric tensor are readily found to be:

$$
\begin{aligned}
g^{11} &= [A^2 + BA(1 - \underset{\sim}{e}_1\underset{\sim}{e}_1 : \underset{\sim}{i}\underset{\sim}{i})]/g^*, \\
g^{22} &= [A^2 + BA(1 - \underset{\sim}{e}_1\underset{\sim}{e}_1 : \underset{\sim}{j}\underset{\sim}{j})]/g^*, \\
g^{33} &= [A^2 + BA(1 - \underset{\sim}{e}_1\underset{\sim}{e}_1 : \underset{\sim}{k}\underset{\sim}{k})]/g^*, \\
g^{12} &= g^{21} = -AB(\underset{\sim}{e}_1\underset{\sim}{e}_1 : \underset{\sim}{i}\underset{\sim}{j})/g^*, \\
g^{13} &= g^{31} = -AB(\underset{\sim}{e}_1\underset{\sim}{e}_1 : \underset{\sim}{i}\underset{\sim}{k})/g^*, \\
g^{23} &= g^{32} = -AB(\underset{\sim}{e}_1\underset{\sim}{e}_1 : \underset{\sim}{j}\underset{\sim}{k})/g^*, \\
g^{kk} &\equiv \frac{1}{g_{kk}} \quad (k = 4,5,6,7;\ \text{no sum on } k)
\end{aligned} \tag{70}
$$

where

$$g^* = \begin{bmatrix} g_{11} & g_{12} & g_{13} \\ g_{21} & g_{22} & g_{23} \\ g_{31} & g_{32} & g_{33} \end{bmatrix} = 8({}^tk_{11}+{}^tk_{12})^2({}^t\ell_{11}+{}^t\ell_{12}) = A^2(A+B)$$

Upon employing (70), the zeroth-order moment is asymptotically found to be of the form (39), wherein:

$$C^{-1} = 8\pi^2 \int_{r=2}^{\infty} \sqrt{g}\, e^{-V/kT}\, dr \tag{71}$$

Here, g represents $\det g_{\alpha\beta}$, and is a function of $r \equiv z^7$ only. Explicitly,

$$g = g^* g_{44} g_{55} g_{66} g_{77} \tag{72}$$

The molecular dispersivity $< D_d^{\gamma\delta} >$ here possesses the simplified form:

$$< D_M^{\gamma\delta} > = \int D^{\gamma\delta}\, \mu_0 \sqrt{g} d\underset{\sim}{z} \tag{73}$$

since $\tilde{D}^{\gamma i} = 0$ (γ=1,2,3; i=4,5,6,7). Hence, the first local moment μ_1^{γ} is also of no consequence. Substituting (70) into (73) furnishes an explicit expression for the molecular dispersion tensor.

Since $< D_M^{11} > = < D_M^{22} > = < D_M^{33} >$ (there being no preference among $\underset{\sim}{i}$, $\underset{\sim}{j}$ and $\underset{\sim}{k}$), it is sufficient to calculate the trace of $< D_M^{\gamma\delta} >$. After a straightforward calculation we obtain:

$$< D_M^{\alpha\alpha} > = kT \frac{\int_{r=2}^{\infty} \frac{(3A+2B)}{A(A+B)} \sqrt{g}\; e^{-V/kT} dr}{\int_{r=2}^{\infty} \sqrt{g}\, e^{-V/kT} dr} \tag{74}$$

The off-diagonal components of the dispersion tensor vanish identically since:

$$\int \underset{\sim}{e}_1 \underset{\sim}{e}_1 \, dz^4 dz^5 dz^6 = \frac{8\pi^2}{3} \underset{\approx}{I} \tag{75}$$

An approximate value for $< D_M^{\alpha\alpha} >$ can be obtained by utilizing the following asymptotic expressions for the hydrodynamic resistivities appropriate to two distant spheres [2]:

$$\begin{aligned}
t_{\ell_{11}} &= t_{\ell_{22}} = [1 + \tfrac{9}{4} r^{-2} + O(r^{-4})]6\pi\mu a, \\
t_{\ell_{21}} &= t_{\ell_{12}} = -[\tfrac{3}{2} r^{-1} + \tfrac{19}{8} r^{-3} + O(r^{-5})]6\pi\mu a, \\
t_{k_{11}} &= t_{k_{22}} = [1 + \tfrac{9}{16} r^{-2} + O(r^{-4})]6\pi\mu a, \\
t_{k_{12}} &= t_{k_{21}} = -[\tfrac{3}{4} r^{-1} + \tfrac{59}{64} r^{-3} + O(r^{-5})]6\pi\mu a, \\
r_{\ell_{11}} &= r_{\ell_{22}} = [1 - \tfrac{3}{2} r^{-4} + O(r^{-6})]8\pi\mu a^3, \\
r_{k_{11}} &= r_{k_{22}} = [1 + \tfrac{3}{4} r^{-4} + O(r^{-6})]8\pi\mu a^3, \\
r_{\ell_{12}} &= r_{\ell_{21}} = -8\pi\mu a^3 r^{-3} + O(r^{-5}), \\
r_{k_{12}} &= r_{k_{21}} = 4\pi\mu a^3 r^{-3} + O(r^{-5}), \\
c_{k_{11}} &= - c_{k_{22}} = - \tfrac{9}{2} \pi a^2 \mu r^{-3} + O(r^{-5}), \\
c_{k_{12}} &= - c_{k_{21}} = 6\pi a^2 \mu r^{-2} + O(r^{-4})
\end{aligned} \tag{76}$$

Substituting (76) into (74) thereby yields:

$$< D_M^{\alpha\beta} > = \delta^{\alpha\beta} \frac{kT}{12\pi\mu a} \frac{\int_2^\infty [r^2 + r + \frac{337}{48} + O(r^{-1})]e^{-V(r)/kT} dr}{\int_2^\infty [r^2 + \frac{337}{48} + O(r^{-1})]e^{-V(r)/kT} dr} \tag{77}$$

provided that the integral $\int_2^\infty r^2 e^{-V/kT} \, dr$ is convergent.

Equation (77) reveals several important features. As expected, the molecular diffusion tensor is isotropic, as well as being independent of the arbitrary additive constant to within which the potential V is defined. Its components lie very close to $\frac{kT}{12\pi\mu a}$ (the Stokes-Einstein formula for two noninteracting spheres) no matter what potential function V is assumed, so long as $\int_2^\infty r^2 e^{-V/kT}\, dr$ is bounded.

The ratio of the integrals in (77) is bounded below by 1 and above by 1.5. This can be demonstrated by invoking the inequality:

$$\int_2^\infty re^{-V/kT}\, dr \leq \frac{1}{2} \int_2^\infty r^2 e^{-V/kT}\, dr \tag{78}$$

to derive the further inequality:

$$\frac{\int_2^\infty r^2 e^{-V/kT} dr + \int_2^\infty re^{-V/kT} dr + \frac{337}{48}\int_2^\infty e^{-V/kT} dr}{\int_2^\infty r^2 e^{-V/kT} dr + \frac{337}{48}\int_2^\infty e^{-V/kT} dr} \leq$$

$$\leq 1 + 0.5 \left[1 + \frac{\frac{337}{48}\int_2^\infty e^{-V/kT} dr}{\int_2^\infty r^2 e^{-V/kT} dr} \right]^{-1} \tag{79}$$

Additional mean values appropriate to the dumbbell geometry that have not been earlier addressed, and which depend upon the manner in which the coordinates are chosen, can readily be calculated if required. Thus,

$$< \underset{\sim}{e}_i > = \int \underset{\sim}{e}_i P\sqrt{g}\, d\underset{\sim}{q} = \int \mu_0 \underset{\sim}{e}_i \sqrt{g}\, dz^4 dz^5 dz^6 dr = \underset{\sim}{0} ,$$

$$< \underset{\sim}{e}_i \underset{\sim}{e}_j > = \int \underset{\sim}{e}_i \underset{\sim}{e}_j P\sqrt{g} dq = \int \mu_0 \underset{\sim}{e}_i \underset{\sim}{e}_j \sqrt{g}\, dz^4 dz^5 dz^6 dr = \begin{cases} \underset{\sim}{0} \ (i \neq j) , \\ \frac{1}{3} \underset{\approx}{I} \ (i = j), \end{cases}$$

$$< r > \equiv r_{av} = \int rP\sqrt{g}\, dq = \int \mu_0 r\sqrt{g}\, dz^4 dz^5 dz^6 dr = \frac{\int re^{-V/kT}\sqrt{g}\, dr}{\int e^{-V/kT}\sqrt{g}\, dr} ,$$

$$< (r-r_{av})^2 > = \int (r-r_{av})^2 P\sqrt{g}\, d\underset{\sim}{q} = \int (r-r_{av})^2 \mu_0 \sqrt{g}\, dz^4 dz^5 dz^6 dr =$$

$$= \frac{\int (r-r_{av})^2 e^{-V/kT}\sqrt{g}\, dr}{\int e^{-V/kT}\sqrt{g}\, dr} \tag{80}$$

6. Discussion

Equilibrium equations (2) provide the basis of the foregoing theory. Inertia forces depend linearly on the particle masses, and were not included in (2), having been assumed small compared with the viscous and interparticle forces. As a result, the kinetic energy of the system is negligible. Thus, the common approach, in which a quadratic kinetic energy form is used to define a positive-definite metric in phase space, is inadequate. Rather, another invariant of the system, namely the energy dissipation rate quadratic, was exploited. The metric so defined proves to be very convenient for further calculations, and is a direct consequence of (2).

One interesting consequence of our calculation is the disparity existing between the (nondimensional) mean center-to-center spacing $\langle r \rangle$ given by the equilibrium distribution Maxwell-Boltzmann value:

$$\langle r \rangle = \int_2^\infty r^3 e^{-V/kT} dr \Big/ \int_2^\infty r^2 e^{-V/kT} dr \tag{81}$$

(provided that the right-hand numerator is bounded), and the value:

$$\langle r \rangle = \int_2^\infty [r^3 + \frac{337}{48} r + O(1)] e^{-V/kT} dr \Big/ \int_2^\infty [r^2 + \frac{337}{48} + O(r^{-1})] e^{-V/kT} dr \tag{82}$$

furnished by our calculations. Given the nonequilibrium nature of the transport process, such differences are to be expected.

The disparity between the preceding pair of $\langle r \rangle$ values could, of course, be magnified by an appropriately chosen potential, or possibly by the use of more accurate hydrodynamic interaction coefficients than were used for the weak case cited in (76). The difference between these two results can be rationalized in terms of the nonconservative hydrodynamic interaction forces.

The expression (61) obtained for the molecular diffusivity of the chain is valid provided that the length scale of the chain is small compared with its distance from any external boundaries. The computational scheme developed in this paper can, however, be extended to include such wall effects if desired.

6.1 Summary

A general formula is derived for the long-time molecular diffusivity of a single deformable "chain" of hydrodynamically interacting rigid Brownian particles, each of arbitrary size and shape, "joined" together by an internal potential (e.g., springs between adjacent particles) and diffusing through an unbounded quiescent viscous fluid. The formula is expressed in terms of a weighted integral over the configuration-specific hydrodynamic resistivities of the chain particles, including the internal potential. The relative motions of the particles comprising the chain are restricted by any internal constraints included in, or in addition to, the potential, and each particle in the chain is allowed to execute translational and rotational Brownian movements consistent with such restraints.

A new and rigorous approach that avoids the common pre-averaging (equilibrium ensemble) approximation utilizes generalized Taylor dispersion theory to analyze the diffusion equation governing the combined positional-configurational conditional probability density of the N-particle chain. The lower-order physical-space moments of this equation, jointly with the boundary conditions representing the constraints (if any), are calculated in the asymptotic, long-time limit. These asymptotic moments are employed to calculate the mean physical-space velocity vector and dispersivity dyadic of the chain. This velocity is shown to be identically zero for the (pure molecular diffusion) case considered here, where the individual particles comprising the chain are free of external forces and torques imposed upon them from outside of the system. Additionally, the chain diffusion dyadic is shown to be independent of the choice of locator point (i.e., chain-fixed origin) serving to locate the chain in physical space.

Convective or Taylor-like contributions to the dispersivity dyadic, arising from interactions between the configuration-specific Brownian motions and convection, will be addressed in a companion paper (Part II).

The preceding paper in its present form was initially submitted by one of us (S.H.), in 1981, to a leading journal in fluid mechanics. A combination of several factors, including disputes with the referees regarding our tensorial approach in deriving the positive definite metric from the viscous dissipation function rather than from the traditional quadratic kinetic energy function, as well as our broad interpretation of Taylor dispersion theory as opposed to the conventional restricted view of the subject and also a small algebraic error on our part, has delayed its publication until now. The trivial algebraic error, which arose because of our incorrect calculation of the metric-tensor determinant, when corrected by substituting $\sqrt{g} = r^2$ in (80), leads to replacing (82) by (81) and the expression

$$< D_M > / <D_M^\infty > = \int_2^\infty r^2 \,[1 + \frac{1}{2r} + O(r^{-3})]e^{-V/kT}dr / \int_2^\infty r^2 e^{-V/kT}\, dr \quad (83)$$

in place of (77). In (83), the scalar $<D_M>$ is defined by the expression $<D_M^{\alpha\beta}> = \delta^{\alpha\beta}<D_M>$ and $<D_M^\infty> = kT/12\pi\mu a$. Equation (83) was derived by first substituting $\sqrt{g} = r^2$ into (74) to obtain

$$<D_M> = \frac{kT}{3}\int_2^\infty \frac{(3A + 2B)}{A(A+B)}\, e^{-V/kT}\, r^2 dr \,/ \int_2^\infty e^{-V/kT}\, r^2\, dr \quad (84)$$

upon observing that $<D_M> = <D_M^{\alpha\alpha}>/3$. The exact hydrodynamic resistance coefficients A and B required in (84) are available for all separation distances $(2 < r < \infty)$ from the tabulations of Batchelor [Batchelor, G.K., J. Fluid Mech., 74, 1-29 (1976)] and Jeffrey and Onishi [Jeffrey, D.J. and Onishi, Y., J. Fluid Mech., 139, 261-290 (1984)]. In the notation of the former*, (84) becomes

$$<D_M>/<D_M^\infty> = \int_2^\infty [A_{11} + A_{12} + 2(B_{11} + B_{12})]e^{-V/kT} r^2 dr / \int_2^\infty e^{-V/kT} r^2 dr \quad (85)$$

wherein A_{ij} and B_{ij} are nondimensional functions of r. Use in (85) of the asymptotic formulas of Jeffrey and Onishi for the weak interaction case $(r \gg 2)$ then yields (83) in place of the algebraically incorrect (77).

1. Aris, R., Proc. Roy. Soc. (London), A235, 67 (1956).
2. Brenner, H., Adv. Chem. Eng., 6, 287 (1966).
3. Brenner, H., Physico-Chemical Hydrodynamics, 1, 91 (1980); J. Colloid. Interface Sci., 71. 189 (1979).
4. Happel, J. and Brenner, H., "Low Reynolds Number Hydrodynamics", Walters Noordhoff, The Netherlands (1973).
5. Horn, F.J.M., Amer. Inst. Chem. Engrs. J., 17, 613 (1971).
6. Kirkwood, J.G., "Macromolecules", (P.L. Auer, ed.), Gordon and Breach, New York (1967).
7. Kuhn, W. and Kuhn, H., Helv. Chim. Acta, 37, 97 (1944).
8. Kuhn, W. and Kuhn, H., Helv. Chim. Acta, 38, 1533 (1945).
9. Kuhn, W. and Kuhn, H., Helv. Chim. Acta, 39, 71 (1946).
10. Synge, J.L. and Schild, A., "Tensor Calculus", University of Toronto Press, Toronto, Canada (1949).
11. Taylor, G.I., Proc. Roy. Soc. (London), A219, 186 (1953).
12. Taylor, G.I., Proc. Roy. Soc. (London), A225, 473 (1954).

* Equivalently, in Jeffrey and Onishi's notation, $A_{11} = x_{11}^a$, $A_{12} = x_{12}^a$, $B_{11} = y_{11}^a$, $B_{12} = y_{12}^a$.

P O BRUNN

Classification scheme for suspensions with particular emphasis on tube flow

1. Introduction

Solid suspensions are handled in a great variety of mechanical and chemical engineering equipment. Thus, it is no wonder to see that they have been extensively investigated, both experimentally and theoretically. Despite all these efforts, the general behavior of solids in fluids has not been successfully understood nor correlated. Even if the particle concentration is very small, effects like the decrease in viscosity upon addition of the particles to values below the solvent viscosity, can at the present time not be predicted quantitatively. For hydraulic conveying in pipes it is still necessary to treat the five discernable flow regimes (homogeneous flow, heterogeneous flow, intermediate regime, saltation and capsule flow) as separate. No rigorous criteria, based on the parameters of the system, have been found, which would indicate which regime is encountered under prescribed conditions, although various guidelines (often differing drastically from each other) have been proposed on empirical grounds.

The situation is somewhat better for neutrally buoyant suspensions, especially under laminar flow conditions. Yet, even then, totally perplexing results should not be discounted. The recent experimental findings of Goto and Kuno [13] quite clearly belong into that surprise category. Even for unitary neutrally buoyant suspensions in viscometric flows our knowledge is far from complete, experimentally as well as theoretically [10].

In this contribution, we will attempt to summarize, classify and generalize some of the significant facts that have emerged from experimental and theoretical investigations. We shall exclude colloidal forces (for a review of these forces see [22]) and, for the greater part, buoyancy effects as well. No attempt will be made to leave the laminar flow regime of viscometric flows, in which most of the fundamental research has been carried out.

From a purely rheological point of view, the principal question is: what is the equation of state? We shall demonstrate within the framework just outlined that even if an answer to that question could be obtained, it would be utterly useless for solid-fluid flows of practical interest. More specifically, we shall advance the idea that it is far better to study a particular type of flow (e.g. tube flow) in detail, rather than try to obtain answers to the flow of homogeneous suspensions in unbounded simple shear flows. Though shown specifically only for infinitely dilute suspensions, there is no reason to believe that this line of reasoning does not carry over to moderately concentrated suspensions. Some experimental evidence supports that conjecture and demonstrates quite clearly that our understanding of suspensions in that (and higher) concentration range is almost zero. That yield stresses may have to be reckoned within concentrated suspensions has only recently [30] been demonstrated.

2. Classification

One of the factors that makes solid suspensions a difficult material to describe is that it is usually subject to non-homogeneous flow conditions. This being the case, a multitude of Reynolds-numbers can be defined. Alternatively, we can identify several characteristic time scales, each of which is associated with a particular physical process. Following [13] the following identification is made.

Table 1: Characteristic Time Scales

Process	Characteristic Time, t_c
fluid-particle inertia	$t_I = \frac{a^2\rho}{\mu}$
Brownian motion	$t_B = \frac{\mu a^3}{kT}$
sedimentation	$t_S = \frac{\mu}{ga\lvert\Delta\rho\rvert}$
particle forces	$t_F = \frac{\mu a^2}{F}$

Here, μ denotes the shear viscosity of the suspending (Newtonian) fluid, a, a characteristic length scale for the particle, ρ the mass density of the fluid, T the absolute temperature, k the Boltzmann constant, g the standard acceleration of gravity and F a typical inter-or-intra particle force. Table 2 lists some data for rigid particles suspended in water (ρ = 1 g/cm^3, μ = 1 cp) and in oil (ρ = 1 g/cm, μ = 10 p), respectively. All data are evaluated at standard conditions (T = 300°K).

Table 2: Typical Data. The upper row corresponds to water, the lower row to oil, respectively. The density difference $|\Delta\rho|$ in either case is assumed to be 10^{-3} g/cm^3.

in sec:	in cm:	$a = 10^{-5}$	$a = 10^{-3}$	$a = 10^{-1}$
t_I		10^{-8} 10^{-11}	10^{-4} 10^{-7}	10^{0} 10^{-3}
t_B		10^{-4} 10^{-1}	10^{2} 10^{5}	10^{8} 10^{11}
t_S		10^{3} 10^{6}	10^{1} 10^{4}	10^{-1} 10^{2}

While these data would shift somewhat under extreme conditions (e.g. high temperatures) two features can be detected. Firstly, the relation $t_I \ll t_B$ holds for either solvent, and secondly, t_I as well as t_B increase with increasing particle size. Note that the fully suspended state, which we shall consider from now on, is characterized by $t_S \to \infty$.

If t* denotes a characteristic flow time (usually $\dot{\gamma}^{-1}$, where $\dot{\gamma}$ denotes the shear rate) a rheologically important time ratio, or Deborah number De, can be defined:

$$De_c = t_c/t^* \qquad (2.1)$$

Quite clearly,

$$De_I = \frac{a^2\rho}{\mu t^*} \equiv Re \tag{2.2a}$$

can be identified with the particle Reynolds number, while

$$De_B = \frac{\mu a^3}{kTt^*} = Pe \tag{2.2b}$$

corresponds to the diffusional Peclet number. These ratios provide a natural measure of the importance of flow induced change relative to the physical process associated with t_c. This serves to define various rheological regimes, some of which are listed in Table 3.

Table 3: Classification for $De_F = \infty$ and $De_S = \infty$

	$Pe \to 0$	$Pe \cong 1$	$Pe \to \infty$
$Re \to 0$	Newtonian regime	Brownian motion	viscous flow regime
$Re \cong 1$			inertial regime
$Re \to \infty$			generalized Newtonian regime

Note that the sequence Newtonian regime → Brownian motion regime → viscous flow regime → inertial regime → generalized Newtonian regime is warranted by the data of Table 2.

Before studying each regime in detail, it seems important to point out that in tube flow $\dot{\gamma}$ (or $(t^*)^{-1}$) changes from zero to some maximum value with increasing distance from the tube axis. This implies that in tube flow various regimes may coexist. For an order of magnitude argument, we shall associate t^* with $R/<v>$, where R denotes the tube radius and $<v>$ the average flow velocity. Alternatively, we can write:

$$t^* = \frac{\rho R^2}{\mu Re_t} \tag{2.3}$$

with Re_t the tube Reynolds number (based on tube radius). For steady laminar flow in long tube Re_t has to be less than 10^3 and this imposes the restraint:

$$t^* > t^*_m \equiv 10^{-3} \frac{\rho R^2}{\mu} \tag{2.4}$$

on the characteristic flow time. Values of t^*_m for various tube sizes are listed in Table 4, where the upper row corresponds to water and the lower one to oil, respectively, as suspending medium (c.f. Table 2). Note that equation (2.4) implies that small tubes are required if high shear rates are called for. Equation (2.4) implies that for laminar flow in tubes the Deborah number De_c is bounded from above by t_c/t^*_m.

Table 4: The Limiting Flow Time t^*_m for Tube Flow

in sec:	in cm:	$R = 10^{-1}$	$R = 1$	$R = 10$
t^*_m		10^{-3}	10^{-1}	10
		10^{-6}	10^{-4}	10^{-2}

3. Rheological Regimes. Results for Dilute Suspensions.

Having introduced various rheological regimes in the last chapter, we now list the characteristic features of each regime.

3.a. Newtonian Regime

For $Pe \to 0$ and $Re \to 0$ the strength of the flow field is so weak that none of the time scales t_I and t_B, respectively, matter. The suspension shows Newtonian behavior. For rodlike particles of very large aspect ratio s (= a/b, with b as characteristic cross-sectional radius) the relative shear viscosity μ_r is readily calculated using slender body analysis:

$$\mu_r = 1 + \frac{4}{15} \frac{s^2}{\ln s} \phi \tag{3.1}$$

with ϕ the volume fraction of suspended particles.

3.b. Brownian Motion Regime

In this range, Re $\rightarrow$ 0 and Pe $\approx$ 1. This implies that the Brownian motion time scale t_B is of the same order as the flow time t^*. The suspension will therefore be non-Newtonian and it will show memory effects. Figure 1 shows the shear viscosity results for a dilute suspension of prolate spheroids. The shear thinning behavior displayed was to be expected, if we realize that the randomizing effects of Brownian motion are opposed by the ordering effects of the flow field. Note that for dilute suspensions in homogeneous flows only rotational (or orientational) Brownian motion matters. It is due to this fact that a dilute suspension of rigid spheres (s = 1) shows Newtonian behavior even in the Brownian motion regime.

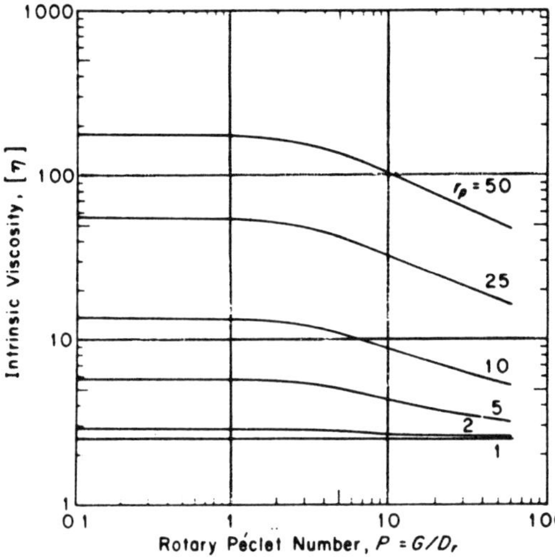

Figure 1: Variation of the Intrinsic Viscosity $(\lim_{\phi \to 0} \frac{(\mu_r - 1)}{\phi})$ with Shear Rate $\dot{\gamma}$ for Prolate Spheroids. The graph is taken from Brenner [3] and covers the Newtonian-Brownian motion regime. P is linearly related to Pe, the constant of proportionality being a complicated function of the aspect ratio s.

3.c. Viscous Flow Regime

For $Re \to 0$, $Pe \to \infty$, i.e. the viscous flow regime, we are at the other end of the spectrum, where neither t_I nor t_B matters. In constrast to the Newtonian regime, however, the strong flow fields needed to bring the suspension into that regime will in general have introduced flow induced anisotropies (alignment of the particles). Thus, while the relation between the shear stress T_{12} and the shear rate $\dot{\gamma}$ will be of the classic Newtonian type (constant shear viscosity), we expect normal stress differences to exist. These can either be directly proportional to the shear stress, or they will be independent of the shear rate. It turns out that dilute suspensions of near spheres and slender, rodlike fibers, respectively, show the latter behavior [15]. Explicitly one finds for the fiber suspension:

$$\mu_r = 1 + 0.315 \frac{s}{\ln s} \phi \qquad (3.2a)$$

and

$$T_{11} - T_{22} = \frac{3}{16} s^2 nkT \qquad (3.2b)$$

with n the number density of rods.

The secondary normal stress difference, T_{22}-T_{33}, turns out to be an order of magnitude smaller than the primary normal stress difference T_{11}-T_{22}.

Note that according to equations (3.1) and (3.2a), respectively, the shear thinning represents a large change (by a factor of s) in the particle contribution to the shear viscosity. This reflects the high degree of particle alignment with the flow at large shear rates together with the fact that the disruption of the basic shear flow is minimized for such an orientation. For spheroids of moderate axis ratios the analogous effect would be considerably smaller (see also Figure 1). As a matter of fact, for near spheres the ratio $\frac{1 + \phi(2.5 + 0.177\varepsilon^2)}{1 + \phi(2.5 + 0.777\varepsilon^2)}$ represents the total shear thinning effect from the Newtonian flow regime to the viscous flow regime. Here the small parameter ε is a measure of departure from sphericity. For these particles it turns out that the viscous flow regime is approached asymptotically, with the magnitude of $[1 + \frac{4}{3} Pe)^2]^{-1}$ as measure of the deviation from that asymptotic limit [15]. Thus, for all practical purposes one can say that a suspension of near spheres is in the viscous flow regime, provided Pe > 10 (and Re $\to$ 0).

3.d. Inertial Regime

With Pe $\to \infty$ any further increase in the strength of the flow field (or increase in particle size) can only affect Re. Thus, in the inertial regime the time scale t_I appears, so that the suspension will (again) be non-Newtonian with memory effects. Only a dilute suspension of spheres has been studied theoretically thus far, and for 0 < Re << 1 the result is:

$$\mu_r = 1 + [2.50 + 1.34\ Re^{3/2}]\phi \tag{3.3}$$

together with a negative first- and a positive second-normal stress difference [21]. As far as I know, there is no simple argument that could be used to understand the shear-thickening behaviour predicted by equation (3.3). Thus, the effect for suspensions of particles other than spheres cannot be assessed at the present time.

3.e. Generalized Newtonian Regime

This regime is characterized by Pe $\to \infty$ and Re $\to \infty$, so that again there is no time scale. The suspension will thus show generalized Newtonian fluid behavior, in which the shear viscosity is constant, and any normal stress differences will either be proportional to the shear stress or they will be independent of the flow rate. No results are available to make quantitative statements.

We should point out that, literally speaking, the requirement Re $\to \infty$ has to be used, although we do expect generalized Newtonian behavior for finite, though possibly large Re (in this connection recall the remarks made at the end of section 3c). For tube flow we have the restriction Re < $10^3\ (a/R)^2$, so that only suspensions with size ratios (a/R) in excess of 0.1 could possibly be in the generalized Newtonian regime. The size ratio may reach somewhat more favorable (i.e. smaller) values for different viscometers, although we expect the generalized Newtonian regime to be more of a limit of the rheological range for steady laminar flow rather than a regime which constantly has to be reckoned with. Figure 2 shows a sketch of the expected behavior, covering all regimes.

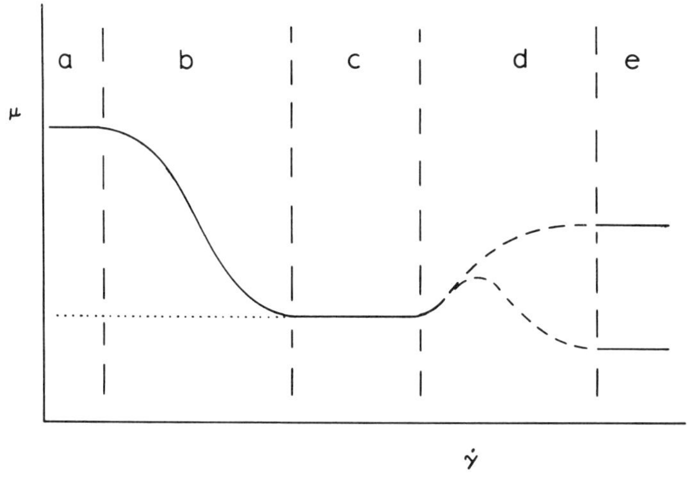

Figure 2: Sketch of the Shear Viscosity as a Function of Shear Rate. The dashed line in the inertial regime e is speculative. The dotted line shows the (singular) behavior of a dilute suspension of rigid spheres.

4. Tube Flow

Strictly speaking, all the results of the last chapter are valid only if (a) the fluid is unbounded and if (b) the flow field is homogeneous, i.e. if it varies linearly with position. Needless to say that none of these two restrictions is met for most flows of practical interest, an example of which is tube flow.

As far as the boundedness of the system is concerned, it is clear that wall effects will play less and less a role, the smaller the ratio a/R is. True, there will always be a layer of thickness δ (of the same order as a) close to the tube wall, which is atypical of the bulk. The concept of a bulk slip velocity ([5,28]) basically is a reflection of that fact. Yet, with a/R decreasing this direct wall effect becomes less and less important in comparison to the bulk.

The nonhomogeneity of the flow field in tube flow, though again linked to a/R, is (or may be) a far more serious matter. As said before, it implies that various rheological regions may coexist close to the tube axis, where the local shear rate is very small one finds the Newtonian regime. Depending upon the actual flow conditions, i.e. upon the tube Reynolds number Re_t, a successive change of different rheological regimes is encountered with increasing distance from the tube axis, which might include all of the regimes introduced in the last chapter. Yet as soon as inertial effects have to be reckoned with (i.e. the inertial regime and the generalized Newtonian regime, respectively) the corresponding rheological results are of no help. Phrased differently, even if the rheological state for the suspension is known over the whole range (i.e. including all of the previously introduced regimes), it is of no use in tube flow (and for most flows of practical interest).

To understand that point we have to realize that sufficiently symmetric particles like spheres, cylinders, and spheroids will move with the fluid in unbounded homogeneous flows. On the other hand, in nonhomogeneous flows (and even in bounded homogeneous flows) the particle will move relative to the fluid, and the slip velocity u_s measures the degree of that relative motion. For example, neglecting wall effects the slip velocity for a sphere in Stokes flow is obtained from Faxen's law. For tube flow only axial slip is encountered, and Faxen's law yields:

$$u_s = -\frac{4}{3}\left(\frac{a}{R}\right)^2 \langle v \rangle \tag{4.1}$$

The negative sign is a consequence of the fact that the sphere lags the fluid. While this expression will undoubtedly change when wall and inertial effects are taken into account, the existence of a slip velocity coupled with the rotational or circulatory part of the flow fields implies the existence of a lift force. This is a direct consequence of inertial effects. For small Reynolds numbers Re (more specifically, for $Re_t < 1$ and $a/R \ll 1$) analyses have been performed for channel flow with the result that the lift forces on an individual sphere work two ways:

close to the channel wall, where the flow field is essentially a simple shear flow, the lift force is directed away from the wall, while the curvature of the flow field, which dominates the axial region, furnishes a lift force, which is directed towards the wall. The sphere will thus migrate towards an eccentric equilibrium position, which according to the calculations of Vasseur and Cox (1976) is at 0.62 of the channel half-width from the axis. Ho and Leal (1974) obtain the value of 0.60 instead of 0.62. As these latter authors have shown, the theoretical results correlate quite well with some of the data of Tachibana [27]. This is remarkable, since in the experiments a square section tube was used, the particles were rather large ($a/B = 0.159$, where B is the half-width of the square section tube) and the "tube" Reynolds number Re_t (based on B) was 16, i.e. not even close to the theoretical $Re_t < 1$ restriction.

For flow in a circular tube no theoretical results are available. The experimentally observed two way migration, called tubular pinch effect leads to an equilibrium position r^* of $0.6R$ for sufficiently small spheres, independent of the initial position of release. As can be seen from Figure 3, r^* is pretty insensitive to Re (or Re_t).

Adopting for simplicity the formalism of the Magnus effect, i.e. assuming that per unit height of the particle the Kutta Joukowski formula is applicable, we obtain for the radial (or lift) force the expression:

$$F_r = -\rho V u_s \dot{\gamma} \tag{4.2}$$

with

$$\dot{\gamma} = - \langle v \rangle \frac{r}{R^2} \tag{4.3}$$

the local shear rate. Here V denotes the volume of the particle and u_s the slip velocity introduced earlier. As already noted by Segre and Silberberg [24], equation (4.2) in conjunction with eq. (4.1) furnishes agreement in order of magnitude with the observed centripedal removal of a sphere from the wall. Note that the experiments of these authors covered the range $7.87 < Re_t < 17.11$, for an a/R variation between 0.069 to 0.138. This implies that the (particle) Reynolds number Re in their experiments varied between 3.7 x 10^{-2} to 0.33. Shizgal, Goldsmith and Mason [26] list $Re^* = 10^{-4} (\frac{R}{a})$ as lower limit, above which inertial migration has to be reckoned with. Although this implies that the particle/tube size matters greatly, it is still safe to say that in the inertial and the generalized Newtonian regime, respectively, non-uniform concentration profiles are to be expected in tube flow. Rheological equations based on a uniform particle distribution are therefore useless. Experiments quite clearly demonstrate that point [25].

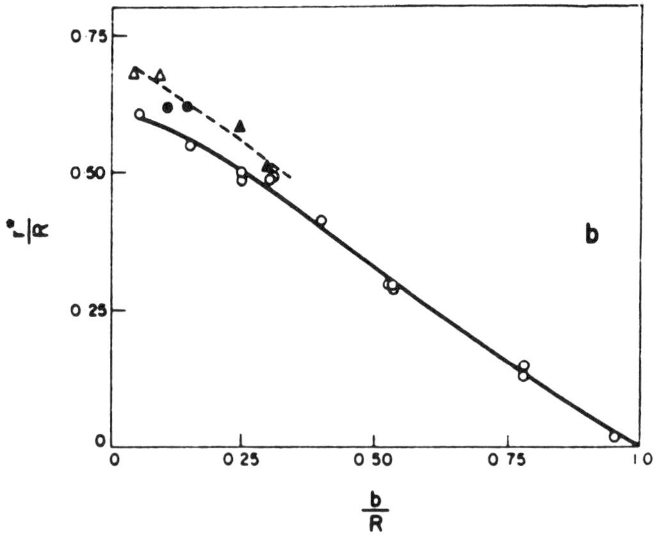

Figure 3: The Equilibrium Position r* in Tube Flow as a Function of Sphere Size a, Taken from Karnis et al. [19]. The graph combines data for different systems, involving a variation of the tube Reynolds number Re_t by a factor of 500, from 0.55 (open circles) to 244 (closed triangles).

5. Concentration Effects

So far, all theoretical results reported were based on the behavior of an individual particle. They are thus relevant only for infinitely dilute suspensions. To extend the results to higher concentrations requires that particle interaction effects have to be accounted for. Taking pair interaction effects between two identical spheres into account Batchelor [2] arrived at the result:

$$\mu_r = 1 + 2.5\phi + 6.2\phi^2 \tag{5.1}$$

for the relative shear viscosity of a dilute suspension of spheres in the Newtonian regime.

Detailed study of the pair-interaction in simple shear reveals that some of the streamlines of a sphere relative to a reference sphere are closed, corresponding to non-separating sphere doublets. Such doublets have been observed [12]. Besides these permanent doublets there are also temporary ones, in which two spheres approach each other, and after apparent contact rotate like a rigid dumbbell, before separating and final recession. To get an idea about the average number of such temporary doublets we estimate the collision frequency f by using Smoluchowski's formula, derived for shear induced coagulation, $f = (8/n)\phi\dot{\gamma}$. At statistical equilibrium, the number of doublets n_B per unit volume thus is $n_b = n\tau f/2$, with n the number density of single spheres and τ the mean life time of a doublet. The latter one can be estimated from the "collision dynamics". Assuming for simplicity a rectilinear approach furnishes $\tau = 5\pi/6\dot{\gamma}^{-1}$ and thus [12].

$$\phi_D = \frac{20}{3}\phi^2 \tag{5.2}$$

with ϕ_D the concentration (volume fraction) of doublets. While this result should be taken more qualitatively, rather than quantitatively, it does indicate a certain trend: multiplets have to be reckoned with. According to equation (5.2), almost 15 percent of the spheres present would, on average, be in the (temporary) doublet stage at a concentration as low as 2 percent ($\phi = 0.02$). According to Goldsmith and Mason [12], one should not expect to find single spheres beyond a sphere concentration of 12 percent and above 20 percent one is dealing with a system which at any given instant contains only triplets and higher-order multiplets. It has been demonstrated that such structures greatly influence the behavior of the suspension from the one predicted by our classification in chapter two.

For tube flow Karnis, Goldsmith and Mason [20] found that the parabolic flow changed to partial plug flow at a sphere concentration above 15 percent. Figure 4, based on results for Re ≈ 10^{-6}, Pe ≈ 10 , which we would classify as viscous flow regime, quite clearly demonstrates that.

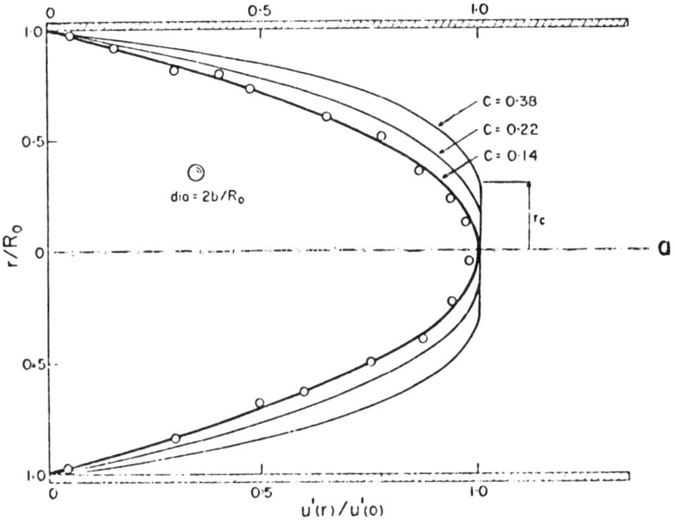

Figure 4: Graph Taken from Karnis et al. [20] Showing the Development of Partial Plug Flow with Increasing Sphere Concentration for a/R = 0.028. (Re ≈ 10^{-6}, Pe ≈ 10).

Note that these authors also found an increase of the plug flow layer with increasing ϕ, and a complete independence of the dimensionless velocity profile on the tube Reynolds number Re_t, provided Re was less than its critical value Re*.

Perhaps even more surprising are the results of Gadala-Maria and Acrivos [10]. Utilizing a R-17 Weissenberg Rheogoniometer, the shear viscosity (at a given $\dot{\gamma}$) for suspensions of spheres $\phi > 0.3$ was found to drift for many hours until an asymptotic value was reached (Figure 5).

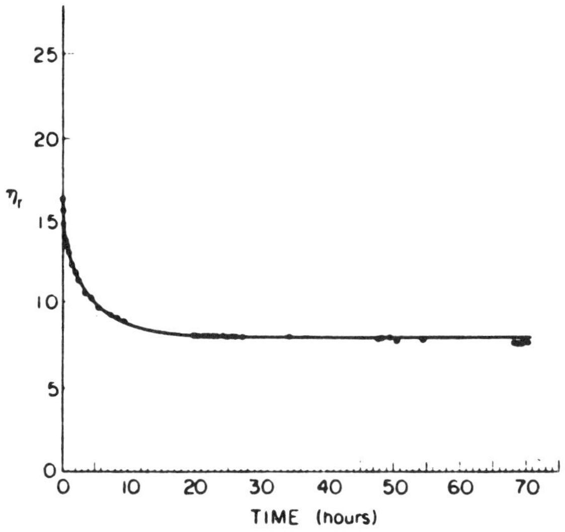

Figure 5: Graph Taken from Gadala et al. [10], Showing the Transient Behavior of μ_r for a Suspension of Spheres in Couette Flow. (ϕ = 0.45, Re = 10^{-4}, Pe $\approx 10^6$).

These asymptotic values displayed shear thinning behavior (Figure 6). Note that these experiments were carried out in the range $2.2 \times 10^{-7} < \text{Re} < 2.2 \times 10^{-4}$ and $10^4 < \text{Pe} < 10^7$, respectively.

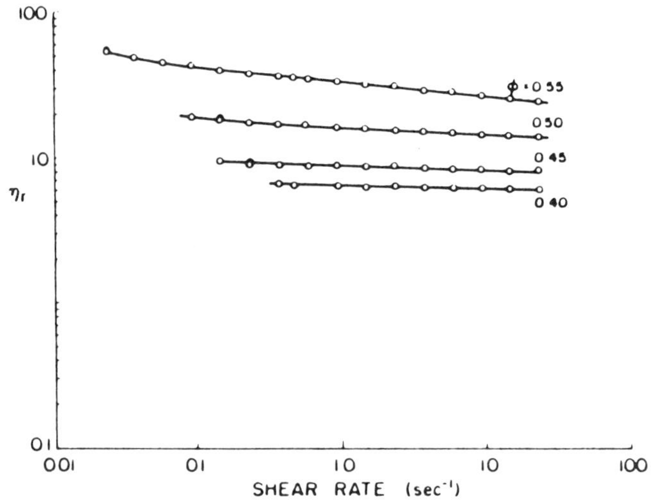

Figure 6: Shear Rate Dependence in the Viscous Regime ($2.2 \times 10^{-7} < Re < 2.2 \times 10^{-4}$; $10^4 < Pe < 10^7$) of the (Steady State) Shear Viscosity for Concentrated Suspensions (Gadala et al., [10]).

To understand, why, in a range previously classified as purely viscous, time dependent non-Newtonian behavior results, we cite three possible reasons (we are still assuming $De_s = \infty$).

a) The length scale of a structure, rather than that of an individual sphere matters. The resulting increase in the inertial time scale t_I could bring us into the inertial regime.

b) The gap width between spheres of a given structure matters. This would lead to a decrease of the Brownian motion time scale, and behavior characteristic of the Brownian regime could result.

c) Since particles in a structure are close to each other, interparticle forces (Van der Waals, Coulombic) can no longer be neglected. As demonstrated in chapter two, the existence of such forces would require a corresponding time scale. Time dependent behavior, hitherto unaccounted for, would have to be reckoned with.

As soon as structures are incorporated, a novel feature emerges: stability. It is interesting that in the first study, in which a discontinuity in μ was shown to be caused by such a stability problem (Figure 7), the explanation was sought in terms of an imbalance between Van der Walls attraction, double layer repulsion and hydrodynamic forces, respectively [17,18].

Note that the viscosity of concentrated suspensions has been a subject of much study. The discrepancy of the results reported (e.g. [8]) might be due, a) to the fact that a steady final state had not been reached (see Figure 4), b) to the fact that in different viscometers different structures are induced which in turn would lead to difference viscosities, and, c) to the fact that different materials have been used. This latter fact would be closely linked to the existence of interparticle forces. Experimentally, it should be easy (using different materials in the same viscometer) to test this latter possibility and to either confirm or reject it.

At higher Reynolds numbers concentrated suspensions develop a particle free zone close to the wall [20]. As a result of the formation of the particle-free layer and two-phase flow of the suspension, there is a drop in the pressure gradient at a given volume flow rate, which is advantageous in hydraulic conveying. The stability of such stratified fluids needs to be investigated.

For fiber suspensions, where increased concentration enhances the tendency towards mutual parallelism of the particles [7], one thus has a particle free layer close to the wall, surrounding a core of fibers, all essentially parallel to the flow direction. In this case, some qualitative understanding is possible if we assume that in plane normal to the flow the

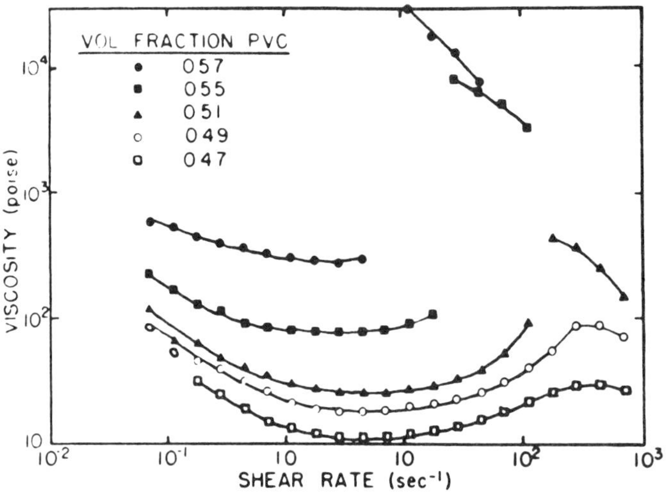

Figure 7: Graph Taken from Hoffman [17] Showing Discontinuous Viscosity Behavior for Concentrated Suspension of Spheres. According to our classification, the results cover the Brownian motion and viscous flow regime ($10^{-9} < Re < 10^{-5}$; $2 < Pe < 10^5$).

particles (or at least their cross-sections) are dilute. It thus suffices to concentrate on an individual fiber. Close to the wall the flow field can be represented by simple shear (shear rate $\dot{\gamma}$) and the wall can be represented by the equation $x_2 = 0$. For rodlike particles parallel to the x_1-axis of very large aspect ratio $s = a/b$, the flow field will be essentially undirectional (for $b/R << 1$), and thus satisfy to dominant order:

$$0 = \nabla^2 v, \quad v = v_1(x_2, x_3) \tag{5.3}$$

Here, the subscripts 1, 2 and 3 refer to the flow direction, the gradient direction, and the indifferent direction, respectively. If the particle translates steadily with velocity v_o in the x_1-direction, the boundary conditions are:

$$v = 0 \quad \text{at } x_2 = 0 \tag{5.4a}$$

$$v = v_o \quad \text{at particle surface} \tag{5.4b}$$

We shall determine v_o from the requirement that no viscous forces act on the particle. Note that if the symmetry axis of the particle is at $x_2 = d$ then the slip velocity u_s is given by:

$$u_s = v_o - \dot{\gamma}d \tag{5.5}$$

To solve that problem, we introduce bipolar cylinder coordinates (ψ, η, z). These are related to the cartesian coordinates via:

$$x_2 = \frac{c\sinh\eta}{\Delta}, \qquad x_3 = \frac{c\sin\psi}{\Delta} \qquad \Delta = \cosh \quad - \cos\psi \tag{5.6}$$

The curves given by the parameter $\eta = \eta_o$ = constant are a family of non-intersecting circles, with center at $(x_2 = c\coth\eta_o, x_3 = 0)$ and radius $|c/\sinh\eta_o|$. Thus, the wall $x_2 = 0$ is given by $\eta = 0$. If $\eta_o > 0$ describes the cross-sectional surface of the rod (radius b) we have the identification (see Figure 8a).

$$c = \sqrt{d^2 - b^2}$$

$$\eta_o = \ln(d/b + [(d/b)^2 - 1]^{1/2}) \tag{5.7a}$$

To secure a geometric interpretation of the bipolar coordinates ψ and η, denote by R_1 the distance from the focal point $F_1 = (c,0)$ and by R_2 the distance from the focal point $F_2 = (-c,0)$, i.e.

$$R_{1/2}^2 \equiv (x_2 \pm c)^2 + x_3^2 = \frac{2c^2}{\Delta} e^{\pm\eta}$$

Then, quite clearly:

$$\eta = \ln (R_2/R_1)$$
$$\psi = \psi_2 - \psi_1 \tag{5.7b}$$

where ψ_i is the angle (measured counterclockwise) R_i makes with the x_3-axis (see Figure 8b).

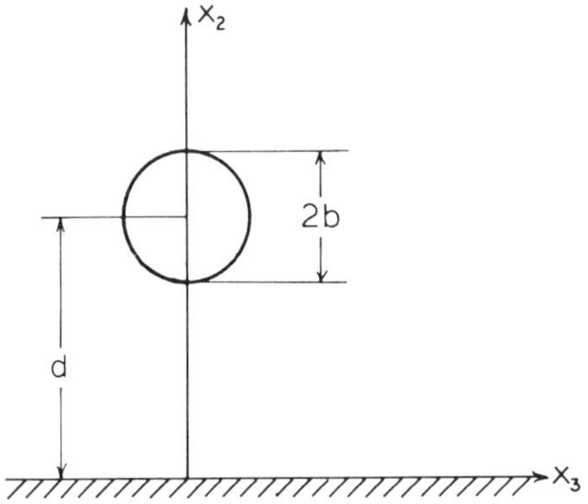

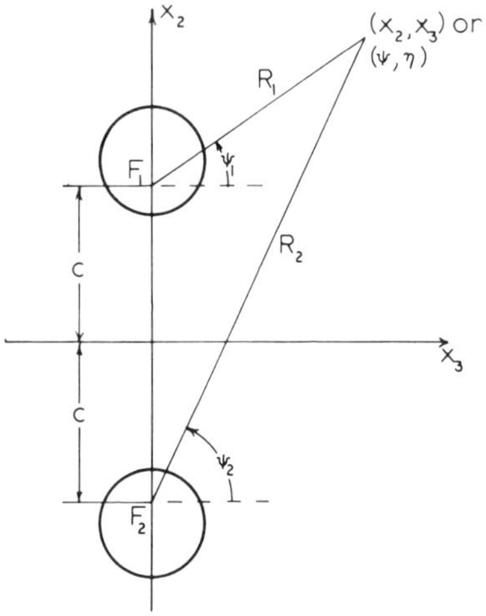

Figure 8: (a) Cross-Sectional View of a Thin Fiber Close to a Solid Wall. The flow is in the x_1-direction. (b) Geometrical Interpretation of the Bipolar Cylinder Coordinates ψ, η.

Note that η and ψ are related by the cosine law: $(2c)^2 = R_1^2+R_2^2-2R_1R_2\cos\psi$. As far as v is concerned we make the Ansatz (suggested by a separation of variables):

$$v = \dot{\gamma}\,\frac{c\sinh\eta}{\Delta} + c_o\eta + \sum_{j=1}^{\infty} c_j\sinh(j\eta)\cos(j\psi) \qquad (5.8)$$

It is readily checked that this function satisfies the differential equation (5.3) and the boundary condition (5.4a). The coefficient c_o is zero on account of our zero viscous force assumption, and the no-slip condition (5.4a) at the particle surface $\eta = \eta_o$ furnishes:

$$v_o = c\dot{\gamma} \qquad (5.9a)$$

$$c_j = -2c\dot{\gamma}[\coth(j\eta_o) - 1], \quad j = 1,2,... \qquad (5.9b)$$

Note that this implies:

$$u_s = -\dot{\gamma}d\,\{1 - [1 - (b/d)^2]^{-1/2}\} \qquad (5.10)$$

i.e. the fiber lags the fluid. According to equation (4.2) this implies that the fiber experiences a lift force away from the wall. The lift-coefficient f_L is:

$$f_L \equiv \frac{F_L}{4ba\frac{1}{2}\rho(\dot{\gamma}d)^2} = \pi\,\frac{b}{d}\,[1 - [1 - (b/d)^2]^{1/2} \qquad (5.11)$$

and this is plotted in Figure 9. While this equation seems to imply that all particles will concentrate at the tube axis, this is actually not the case. If the non-homogeneity of the flow field is taken into account, it is easy to show that the lift force associated with this nonhomogeneity is directed towards the wall. Yet, for concentrated suspensions we do not know the magnitude of the non-homogeneity. But, we do know that other particles surround the one we studied. Repeating for such a case the calculation just outlined, it follows that the cylinders repel each other

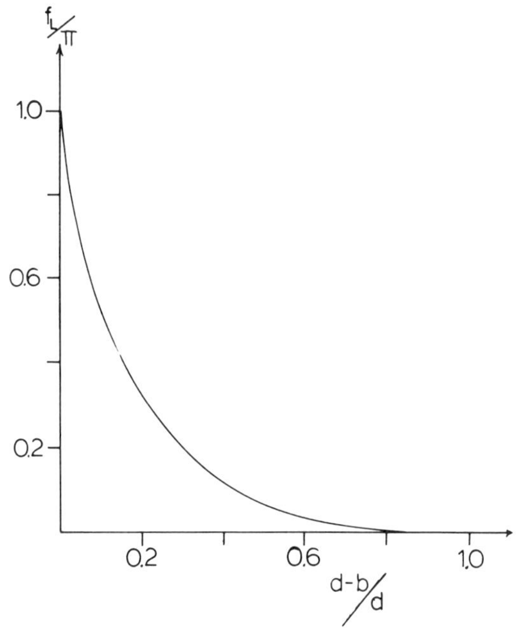

Figure 9: The Lift Coefficient According to Equation (5.11) as a Function of the Distance d to the Wall.

in the x_2-direction such that the lift force, which has only a 2-component, on a cylinder is given by:

$$F_L = \rho V d \cos\alpha \{1 - (1 - (b/d)^2)^{1/2}\} \dot{\gamma}^2 \qquad (5.12)$$

where d is the half distance of the interacting cylinders and α the angle of the cylinder in question relative to the x_2-axis (see Figure 10). Thus, for a concentrated fiber suspension the following picture emerges in the case of negligible viscous effects: close to the tube axis the fibers repel each other and the distribution of fibers is dictated by fiber-fiber interactions. Closer to the wall, however, the more one sided fiber-fiber repulsion is balanced by the counteracting forces of the wall. A particle

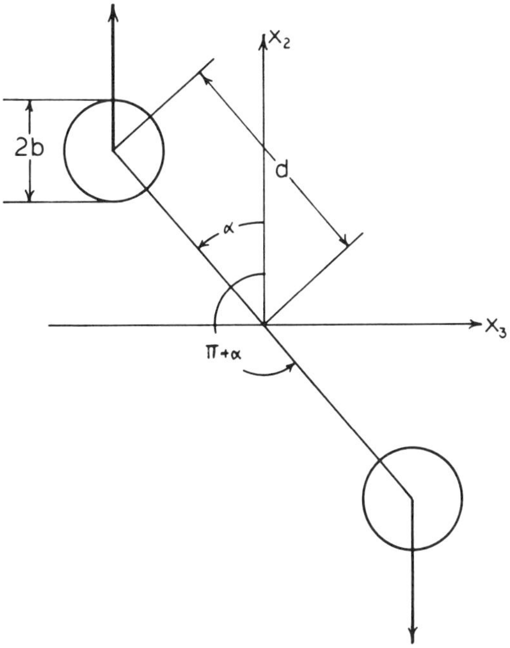

Figure 10: Cross-Sectional Geometry for Two Interacting Fibers. The thick arrows indicate the direction of the force, resulting from hydrodynamic interaction.

free layer close to the wall is the consequence. This does, at least qualitatively, agree with the observed behavior. The fact that experimental findings show a quadratic dependence of the wall-lift force on the flow velocity [23] puts additional credance on the method used. However, far more experimental and theoretical studies are needed before one can hope to somehow understand suspensions in tube flow.

6. Non-Neutrally Buoyant Suspensions

Neutrally buoyant suspensions are characterized by $\Delta\rho = 0$. In general, however, it will be almost impossible to exactly match the densities. In that case, the additional time scale t_s, with all its rheological consequences to be considered too.

As far as flow in a horizontal pipe is concerned, density differences will lead to a separation effect, with the heavier (lighter) particles concentrating near the bottom (top) of the pipe. As long as inertial effects are negligible, it is not hard to see that the steady state density distribution in the cross-sectional area for a dilute spherical suspension is uncoupled from the flow field [4], i.e. it is governed by the barometric formula. For the same situation in a vertical pipe, however, coupling effects appear such that the density may be nonuniform in the cross-sectional area, even in a regime previously described as viscous.

There is one additional complication associated with a nonvanishing density difference. All the results reported in chapter three were based on the premise that the bulk stress can be obtained from a volume average of the local stress fields. As such, the bulk stress will always be related to a volume averaged rate of strain dyadic. It is well known from the theory of mixtures that the classic conservation equations for bulk quantities involve the mass-averaged velocity field. For example, Newton's law of viscosity is always understood to be the mass average velocity. If one utilizes the volume averaged expression for the bulk stress and replaces the volume averaged velocity field in that expression by means of its relation to a mass averaged velocity field, a rheological behavior is predicted which depends explicitly on the density ratio of the two phases.

One way out of this dilema is to realize that a suspension comprises a statistical system and that it should be treated as such. Thus, bulk quantities should be represented by ensemble averages. An additional benefit of these averages is that they commute with space and time differential operators. Applied to the equations of motion for each phase this approach immediately furnishes the unconditioned bulk conservation equations for each phase (multiphase fluids). Unfortunately, this system of equations is not closed since singly conditioned flow fields in the vicinity of a reference particle have to be known [6]. Closure of the conditioned equations, which govern these fields requires doubly conditioned fields. Repeating this process one obtains an infinite hierarchy of systems of conditioned fields and inevitably the problem of truncation of this hierarchy arises. Note also that this approach does not furnish a rheological equation of state for the suspension. Rather, the evaluation of the bulk stress requires that the previous mentioned conditioned field equations be solved before its relation to other bulk quantities (velocity gradient, etc.) can be established.

Conceptually, this approach is free from any objections, although the inevitable closure problem clearly will introduce errors into the analysis. For a dilute suspension of spheres in the low Reynolds number regime Buyevich and Shchelchkova [6] deduce equations characteristic of a Newtonian fluid, with $\rho = \phi_{\rho}^{P} + (1 - \phi)\rho^{f}$ the mean density and $\mu_r = (1 - 2.5)^{-1}$ the relative viscosity. To obtain that result the authors had to assume a constant suspension concentration. For vertical tubes this requires Pe $\rightarrow \infty$, while for horizontal tubes the limiting case Pe/De$_s \rightarrow 0$ is needed. It would be nice to see the modification required if these restraints are dropped, and to incorporate inertia effects. For a full understanding of the problem, such results are clearly called for.

Besides these theoretical difficulties there are experimental ones, too. It is not hard to see that measuring viscosities of settling suspensions by using conventional apparatus involves quite a bit of difficulties. To overcome such difficulties, Ferrini et al. [14], modified a narrow gap Couette viscometer with rotating inner cylinder into a bop-cup metering system, allowing for recirculation of the slurry. While the helical flow encountered in such a system is viscometric (see Figure 11), it is viscometric relative to the shear axes $\hat{\underline{\delta}}_i$, i = 1,2,3. These are related to the unit vectors $\underline{\delta}_r$, $\underline{\delta}_\phi$ and $\hat{\underline{\delta}}_z$ of a cylindrical coordinate system unit vectors by:

$$\hat{\underline{\delta}}_1 = \frac{1}{\dot{\gamma}} [r \frac{d\omega}{dr} \underline{\delta} + \frac{dv}{dr} \underline{\delta}_z] \tag{6.1a}$$

$$\hat{\underline{\delta}}_2 = \hat{\underline{\delta}}_r \tag{6.1b}$$

$$\hat{\underline{\delta}}_3 = \hat{\underline{\delta}}_1 \times \hat{\underline{\delta}}_2 = \frac{1}{\dot{\gamma}} [-r \frac{d\omega}{dr} \underline{\delta}_z + \frac{dv}{dz} \underline{\delta}_\phi] \tag{6.1c}$$

with

$$|\dot{\gamma}| = \{[r(\frac{d\omega}{dr})]^2 + (\frac{dv}{dr})]^{1/2}\} \quad (6.2)$$

the magnitude of the shear rate.

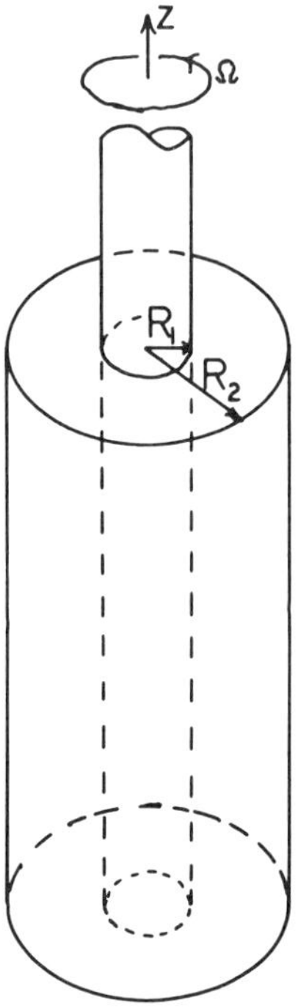

Figure 11: Representation of Helical Flow

The velocity $\underline{v}$ is of the form:

$$\underline{v} = r\omega(r)\,\underline{\delta}_\phi + v(r)\underline{\delta}_z \quad (6.3)$$

and this implies that the shear rate $\dot{\gamma}$ depends on both velocity gradients. With $\eta = \eta(\dot{\gamma})$ the viscosity function we thus have for the cylindrical coordinate components of the stress tensor $\underline{\underline{T}}$,

$$T_{r\phi} = \eta(\dot{\gamma}) r \frac{d\omega}{dr} = \frac{M}{2\pi r^2} \quad (6.4a)$$

$$T_{rz} = \eta(\dot{\gamma}) \frac{dv}{dr} = -\frac{1}{2} Ar + \frac{B}{2} \quad (6.4b)$$

The second equality signs in each of these equations are a consequence of the equations of motion. M is the torque per unit height exerted on a cylindrical surface of fluid, the constant A is the driving force per unit height and unit cross section which is exerted in the axial direction,

$$A = -\frac{dP}{dz} - \rho g \quad (6.5)$$

(the gravitational force per unit mass is $g = -g\underline{\delta}_z$), and the constant B is related to the radius $\tilde{r}$, at which $dv/dr = 0$, i.e.

$$B = \frac{1}{2} A\tilde{r}^2 = \frac{1}{2} A \frac{\int_{R_1}^{R_2} dr \frac{r}{\eta}}{\int_{R_1}^{R_2} \frac{dr}{r\eta}} \quad (6.6)$$

where $R_1(R_2)$ denotes the radius of the inner (outer) cylinder. Note that equations (6.4) imply:

$$|\dot{\gamma}\eta| = \{(\frac{M}{2\pi r^2})^2 + [-\frac{1}{2} Ar + \frac{B}{r}]^2\}^{1/2} \quad (6.7)$$

While some simplifications are possible for very small gap width (e.g. $T_{r\phi} \approx M/2\pi R^2$ = constant) the fact that the rotational and axial flow fields cannot be decoupled in general, poses great problems. In this connection one should note that small gap widths do not imply that the shear rate $\dot{\gamma}$ will vary over only a narrow range.

The quantities that can readily be measured for that flow are a) the applied torque, b) the applied pressure difference Δp, and thus A,

c) the angular velocity Ω of the inner cylinder:

$$\Omega = \omega(R_1) = -\frac{M}{2\pi} \int_{R_1}^{R_2} \frac{dr}{r^3 \eta} \tag{6.8}$$

and d) the volumetric flow rate:

$$Q = 2\pi \int_{R_1}^{R_2} dr \, rv(r) = \pi \int_{R_1}^{R_2} dr \frac{[\frac{1}{2} Ar^3 - Br]}{\eta} \tag{6.9}$$

In general, there is not much hope to simplify these relations. The exception being when the settling speed, and thus Q, A and B, are small relative to the rotational speeds. If ε denotes this ratio by order of magnitude, i.e. $\varepsilon = 0(Q/[R_1^2\Omega(R_2 - R_1)])$ then it is not hard to see that we have for $|\varepsilon| << 1$,

$$\begin{aligned} \dot{\gamma} &= \gamma_0 \, [1 + 0(\varepsilon^2)] \\ \eta &= \eta_0 \, [1 + 0(\varepsilon^2)] \end{aligned} \tag{6.10}$$

where the subscripts zero denote quantities appropriate for circular Couette flow. In all other cases, even in the extreme limit that sedimentation greatly dominates the rotation, $|R_1^2\Omega(R_2 - R_1)/Q| << 1$, the situation is extremely complicated. Needless to say that none of the methods appropriate for pure cylindrical Couette flow and to Poiseuille flow, respectively, are applicable. Ferrini et al. [14] realized that the "axial flow obviously modifies the flow field". How they were able to list shear rates and to measure viscosities of their device without taking such "modifications" into account, is beyond this author's grasp. Independent studies, both theoretically and experimentally, are clearly in order.

7. Other Influences and Future Research

Almost all results of this article have been restricted by the fact that a) there are only two time scales (t_I and t_B), and b) that these time scales are of a different magnitude. As shown in the last chapter, when another time scale has to be added, a far more complex behavior will in general result. Especially complicated is the case in which two or more time scales are of the same order of magnitude. Maybe one should refrain in such cases looking for a constitutive equation which would be valid for a wide range of shear rates. In this connection a statement Batchelor [1] made in a related, though somewhat different context comes to mind, "... it is an almost hopeless task, indeed one that is not worthwhile to attempt, to find a single constitutive equation between mean stress and mean rate of strain that applies to all flow fields". The results of this paper seem to prove Batchelor's point.

Even if all time scales could properly be accounted for, the results would strictly be valid only for homogeneous particles, identical in every respect. If particles of different shapes are used, exact theoretical results seem not to be forthcoming in the near future. For particles of the same shape, but different size, a dependence upon the size ratio might have to be included in the transport properties. Alternatively, and especially so for particles of widely different size, one could think of a rheological behavior directly influenced by time scales appropriate for the various size fractions themselves. The complicated response, depicted in Figure 12, recently reported for a suspension of spheres of two different sizes (size ratio varying between 1.31 and 9.71, but constant solid volume fraction ϕ of 0.2) seem to point in that direction [13]. As stated by these authors (and others), that behavior is still open for further study. Hopefully, this article will stimulate some research in that (and related) areas.

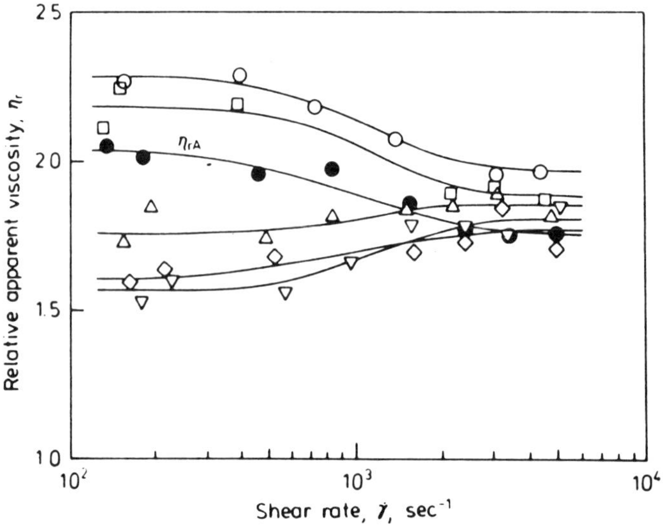

Figure 12: (a) $\dot{\gamma}$ = 250 sec^{-1}

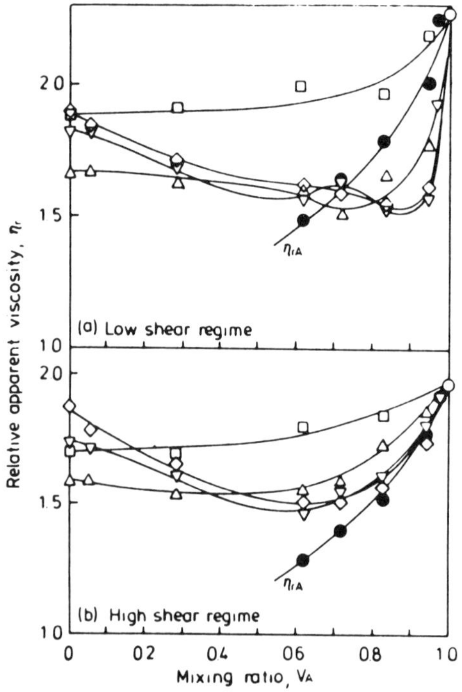

(b) $\dot{\gamma}$ = 4000 sec^{-1}

The Relative Viscosity for a Binary Suspension as a Function of the Mixing Ratio V_A. The graphs are taken from Goto et al. [13], where all data are found. The solid circles correspond to a unitary solid suspension of the larger spheres (Φ = 0.194).

Nomenclature

a	=	characteristic length scales for particle
a/R	=	size ratio
A, B	=	arbitrary constants
b	=	characteristic cross-sectional radius
c	=	defined by Equation 5.7(a)
d	=	distance of the symmetry axis of the particle
De, De_c	=	Deborah number
De_I	=	Deborah number associated with fluid-particle inertia, defined in Equation (2.2a)
De_B	=	Deborah number associated with Brownian motion, defined in Equation (2.2b)
F	=	inter or intra particle force
F_r	=	radial force defined in Equation (4.2)
f	=	collision frequency
f_L	=	lift force coefficient, defined in Equation (5.11)
F_L	=	lift force
g	=	acceleration due to gravity
k	=	the Boltzmann constant
n	=	number density of rods
n_b	=	number of doublets per unit volume
Pe	=	Diffusional Peclet number
Q	=	volume flow rate
Re	=	Particle Reynolds number
r^*	=	equilibrium position of the particle in tube flow
s	=	aspect ratio of the particle (= a/b)
t_I	=	characteristic time scale associated with fluid-particle motion, defined in Table 1
t_B	=	characteristic time scale for Brownian motion, defined in Table 1
t_S	=	characteristic time scale for sedimentation, defined in Table 1
t_F	=	characteristic time associated with particle forces, defined in Table 1
t^*	=	characteristic flow time, also defined in Equation (2.3)
T	=	absolute temperature
t_m^*	=	defined by Equation (2.4)
t_C	=	characteristic time

T_{ij} = stress tensor
$T_{11}-T_{22}$ = primary normal stress difference
$T_{22}-T_{33}$ = secondary normal stress difference
u_s = slip velocity
$\underset{\sim}{v}$ = velocity vector
V = volume of the particle
v_o = translational velocity of the particle
(ψ,η,z) = bipolar cylindrical coordinates
μ = shear viscosity of the suspending fluid
ρ = mass density of the fluid
$\dot{\gamma}$ = shear rate
$\Delta\rho$ = density difference
μ_r = relative shear viscosity
ϕ = volume fraction of suspended particles
ε = parameter measuring the departure from sphericity
ϕ_D = volume fraction of doublets
τ = mean life time of a doublet
$\underset{\sim}{\delta}$ = unit vectors defined in Equations (6.1a)-(6.1c)
$\eta\ (\dot{\gamma})$ = viscosity function
Ω = angular velocity of the inner cylinder defined in Equation (6.8)

References

1. G.K. Batchelor, Transport Properties of Two Phase Materials with Random Structure. Ann. Rev. Fluid Mech. 6, 227-255 (1974).
2. G.K. Batchelor, The Effect of Brownian Motion on the Bulk Stress in a Suspension of Spherical Particles. J. Fluid Mech. 83, 97-117 (1977).
3. H. Brenner. Rheology of a Dilute Suspension of Axisymmetric Brownian Particles. Int. J. Multiphase Flow 1, 195-341 (1974).
4. P.O. Brunn, The Effect of Brownian Motion for a Suspension of Spheres. Rheol. Acta 15, 104-119 (1976).
5. P.O. Brunn, The Hydrodynamic Wall Effect for a Disperse System. Int. J. Multiphase Flow 7, 221-234 (1981).
6. Y.A. Buyevich and I.N. Shchelchkova, Flow of Dense Suspensions. Prog. Aerospace Sci. 18, 121-150 (1978).
7. J.M. Burgers, On the Motion of Small Particles of Elongated Form Suspended in a Viscous Liquid, Chapter 3, 113-184 in "Second Report on Viscosity and Plasticity", Amsterdam Acad. Sci., Amsterdam (1938).
8. J.S. Chong, E.B. Christiansen and A.D. Baer. Rheology of Concentrated Suspensions. J. Appl. Polym. Sci. 15, 2007-2021 (1971).
9. A.C. Dierckes and W.R. Schowalter, Helical Flow of a Non-Newtonian Polyisobutylene Solution, I & EC Fund. 5, 263-271 (1966).
10. F. Gadala-Maria and A. Acrivos, Shear Induced Structure in a Concentrated Suspension of Solid Spheres. J. Rheol. 24, 799-814 (1980).
11. J.D. Goddard, Memory Materials without Characteristic Time and Their Relation to the Rheology of Certain Particle Suspensions. Adv. Colloid Interface Sci., 17, 241-262 (1982).
12. H.L. Goldsmith and S.G. Mason, The Microrheology of Dispersions in Rheology, 4 (F. Eirich, ed.). Academic H Vol., Press, 85-250, New York (1967).
13. H. Goto and M. Kuno, Flow of Suspensions Containing Particles of Two Different Sizes through a Capillary Tube II. Effect of the Particle Size Ratio. J. Rheol. 28, 197-205 (1984).
14. F. Ferrini, D. Ercolani, B. de Cinto, L. Nicodemo, L. Nicolais and S. Ranando, Shear Viscosity in Settling Suspensions. Rheol. Acta 18, 289-296 (1979).
15. E.J. Hinch and L.G. Leal, The Effect of Brownian Motion on the Rheological Properties of a Suspension of non-Spherical Particles. J. Fluid Mech. 52, 683-712 (1972).
16. B.P. Ho and L.G. Leal, Intertial Migration of Rigid Spheres in Two-Dimensional Unidirectional Flows. J. Fluid Mech. 65, 365-400 (1974).
17. R.L. Hoffmann, Discontinuous and Dilatant Viscosity Behavior in Concentrated Suspensions I. Observations of a Flow Instability. Trans. Soc. Rheol. 16, 155-173 (1972).
18. R.L. Hoffmann, Discontinuous and Dilatant Viscosity in Concentrated Suspensions II. Theory and Experimental Tests. J. Colloid Interface Sci. 46, 491-506 (1974).
19. A. Karnis, H.L. Goldsmith and S.G. Mason. The Flow of Suspensions through Tubes V. Inertial Effects. Can. J. Chem. Eng. 44, 181-193 (1966a).
20. A. Karnis, H.L. Goldsmith and S.G. Mason, The Kinetics of Flowing Dispersions I. Concentrated Suspensions of Rigid Particles. J. Colloid Interface Sci. 22, 531-553 (1966b).

21. C.J. Lin, J.H. Peery and W.R. Schowalter, Simple Shear Flow Round a Rigid Spheres: Inertial Effects and Suspensions Rheology. J. Fluid Mech. 44, 1-17 (1970).
22. W.B. Russell, Review of the Role of Colloidal Forces in the Rheology of Suspensions. J. Rheol. 24, 287-317 (1980).
23. F. Schultz-Grunow. Entmishung makromolekularer Losungen in Scherstromungen. Rheol. Acta 1, 289-296 (1958).
24. G. Segre and A. Siberberg, Radial Particle Displacements in Poiseuille Flow of Suspensions. Nature, 189, 209-210 (1961).
25. G. Segre and A. Siberberg, Non-Newtonian Behavior of Dilute Suspensions of Macroscopic Spheres in a Capillary Viscometer. J. Colloid Sci. 18, 312-317 (1963).
26. S. Shizgal, H.L. Goldsmith and S.G. Mason, The Flow of Suspensions through Tubes IV: Oscillatory Flow of Rigid Spheres. Can. J. Chem. Engng. 43, 97-101 (1965).
27. M. Tachibana, On the Behavior of a Sphere in Laminar Tube Flows. Rheol. Acta 12, 58-69 (1973).
28. A. Tozeren and R. Skalak, Stress in a Suspension near Rigid Boundaries. J. Fluid Mech. 82, 289-307 (1977).
29. P. Vasseur and R.G. Cox, The Lateral Migration of a Spherical Particle in Two Dimensional Shear Flow. J. Fluid Mech. 78, 385-413 (1976).
30. C.R. Wildemuth and M.C. Williams, Viscosity of Suspensions Modeled with a Shear Dependent Maximum Packing Fraction. Rheol. Acta 23, 627-635 (1984).

P J CARREAU & M GRMELA

Modeling of the rheological behaviour of polymeric fluids

1. INTRODUCTION

It is well known that most polymeric liquids do not obey Newton's law of viscosity. They exhibit shear-thinning and viscoelastic effects. An excellent description of particularly interesting phenomena that are encountered with non-Newtonian liquids can be found in the books of Bird, Armstrong and Hassager [11] and of Schowalter [55].

An adequate description of the rheological behaviour (stress-strain rate relationship) is required in order to solve flow problems that arise in the fabrication, processing and other manipulations. The need for relevant rheological models or constitutive equations becomes more and more obvious with the increasing demand for computer simulation and control of most of the polymer processes. For a given application, the choice of a rheological model may not be obvious: a computer simulation cannot describe a given flow process better than is the rheological model on which the algorithm is based on; however, the use of a complex and fully predictive model will lead inevitably to unacceptably long computer times and other computation problems. Therefore, at least for simulation work, the choice of a rheological equation will necessarily be a compromise between completeness and computation facility. Rheological equations find interesting uses also in the characterization of polymer systems. First of all, a rheological model may be needed to organize, interpret and understand results collected from various experiments conducted for a given class of polymeric liquids. A rheological model, if chosen appropriately, should make it possible to extract from the results the pertinent material characteristics and to predict the rheological behaviour under other flow conditions. Finally, if molecular considerations are built in the model, model parameters evaluated from rheological measurements should relate directly to the molecular structure of the polymer. This is a useful information for the fabrication of products with specified mechanical properties and for the synthesis of more performing polymers.

Many constitutive equations or rheological models have been proposed in the literature in the last two decades to describe the rheological behaviour of polymer solutions, of melts, of suspensions, of foodstuffs, etc. Two fundamental approaches have been followed: i) first, constitutive equations have been developed from principles of continuum mechanics and thermodynamics and by using insights from experimental investigation: the second approach makes uses of kinetic theories. The second approach combines simple descriptions of the macromolecules and non equilibrium statistical mechanics to obtain relationships between measurable quantities such as viscosity, normal stress coefficient, etc. and parameters related to the description of the macromolecules. The second approach is more challenging and possibly it could lead to more useful results, at least for the characterization of polymeric liquids.

In this chapter, we review some of the most important theories based on molecular considerations: dumbbell-type models developed for dilute polymer solutions, reptation and network theories proposed for polymer melts and concentrated solutions. The avantages and the limitations of each group of theories are discussed. Both the first (phenomenological) and the second (molecular) approaches to constitutive relations are then used in the last section to formulate a simple recipe for constructing rheological models. The objective is to give a potential user a tool with the help of which he or she can construct a rheological model that suits best his or her needs. The reader will see, from the particular examples chosen, that such models are highly flexible and can describe most of the rheological properties encountered with polymeric liquids.

1.1 Rheological Functions. As we are mostly concerned here with rheological behaviour of polymers in relation to processing, we introduce in this section only the rheological or material functions commonly used to describe the non-linear behaviour. The steady and transient simple shear flow is defined by the following velocity profile:

$$V_1(x_2,t) = \dot{\gamma}(t)x_2 \qquad (1.1)$$

$$V_2 = V_3 = 0$$

where $\dot{\gamma}(t) = (\partial V_1/\partial x_2)$ = shear rate.

For steady shear flow, $\dot{\gamma}$ is constant and the material functions are

$$\eta(\dot{\gamma}) = -\tau_{12}/\dot{\gamma} \tag{1.2}$$

$$\Psi_1(\dot{\gamma}) = -(\tau_{11} - \tau_{22})/\dot{\gamma}^2 \tag{1.3}$$

$$\Psi_2(\dot{\gamma}) = -(\tau_{22} - \tau_{33})/\dot{\gamma}^2 \tag{1.4}$$

For stress relaxation after cessation of steady simple shear

$$\dot{\gamma}(t) = \dot{\gamma}_o\ [1 - h(t)] \tag{1.5}$$

where $h(t)$ is the unit step function: $h(t) = 0$ for $t < 0$ and $h(t) = 1$ for $t > 0$. The constant $\dot{\gamma}_o$ is the initial constant shear rate. The shear stress and normal stress relaxation functions are introduced by

$$\eta^-(t;\dot{\gamma}_o) = -\tau_{12}/\dot{\gamma}_o \tag{1.6}$$

$$\Psi_1^-(t;\dot{\gamma}_o) = -(\tau_{11} - \tau_{22})/\dot{\gamma}_o^2 \tag{1.7}$$

For stress growth after onset of steady simple shear,

$$\dot{\gamma}(t) = \dot{\gamma}_\infty\ h(t) \tag{1.8}$$

and

$$\eta^+(t;\dot{\gamma}_\infty) = -\tau_{12}/\dot{\gamma}_\infty \tag{1.9}$$

$$\Psi_1^+(t;\dot{\gamma}_\infty) = -(\tau_{11} - \tau_{22})/\dot{\gamma}_\infty^2\ , \tag{1.10}$$

where $\dot{\gamma}_\infty$ is the constant applied shear rate.

In the case of uniaxial elongation at constant volume, the flow is non-viscometric and the velocity profile is given by

$$V_1(x_1,t) = \dot{\varepsilon}x_1$$
$$V_2(x_2,t) = -\frac{\dot{\varepsilon}}{2}x_2,\ V_3(x_3,t) = -\frac{\dot{\varepsilon}}{2}x_3 \tag{1.11}$$

where $\dot{\varepsilon}$ is the elongational rate (constant for steady state). The elongation viscosity is defined by

$$\eta_E = - \frac{\tau_{11} - \tau_{22}}{\dot{\varepsilon}} \qquad (1.12)$$

2. DILUTE POLYMER SOLUTIONS

Beginning in the 1930's considerable efforts have been devoted to the development of molecular or kinetic theories for dilute polymer solutions. An excellent and comprehensive review of these theories and their relevance to rheology have been presented by Williams [63]. Until recently the focus has been on obtaining relationships between linear viscoelastic behaviour (small deformation flows) and molecular or structural parameters such as molecular weight, chain flexibility, branching, strechability, etc... These theories are, nevertheless, of limited interest to the polymer engineer as they are unable of describing important non-linear viscoelastic phenomena such as a monotone decreasing shear-rate-dependent viscosity. The so-called shear-thinning behaviour is observed for most polymer solutions at shear rates encountered in the manufacturing or transformation processes.

The recent work of Bird et al. [13] is partly successful in extending kinetic theories to describe some of the important features of non-linear behaviour. As our work on rheological equations (see section 4) will appear to be a natural extension of the work of Bird et al. [13], we summarize here their important results. Excellent reviews of these theories are presented by Bird [8,9].

2.1 Dumbbell Models. In the simplest model, the polymer chain is viewed as a dumbbell made of two beads jointed by an elastic connector. The stress tensor for the polymer solution is given by [12]:

$$\underline{\underline{\tau}} = \underbrace{- \eta_s \dot{\underline{\underline{\gamma}}}}_{\text{Solvent contribution}} \underbrace{- n \langle \underline{F}^{(c)} \underline{R} \rangle}_{\text{Connector-force contribution}} \underbrace{+ n k_B T \underline{\underline{\delta}}}_{\text{Brownian-motion contribution}} \qquad (2.1)$$

where η_s is the solvent viscosity, $\dot{\underline{\underline{\gamma}}}$ is the rate of deformation tensor; n is the number density of dumbbells; $\underline{F}^{(c)}$ is the force acting on the connector; $\underline{R}$ is the end-to-end vector of the dumbbell; k_B is Boltzmann's constant; T is the temperature and $\underline{\underline{\delta}}$ is the unit tensor. The brackets mean average with respect to a configurational distribution function Ψ, which can be in principle obtained as a solution of the diffusion equation [12]:

$$\frac{\partial \Psi}{\partial t} = - \Big(\underbrace{\frac{\partial}{\partial \underline{R}} \cdot [\underline{\underline{\kappa}} \cdot \underline{R}]\Psi}_{\text{hydrodynamic forces}} - \underbrace{\frac{2k_BT}{\zeta} \frac{\partial}{\partial \underline{R}} \Psi}_{\text{Brownian forces}} - \underbrace{\frac{2}{\zeta} \underline{F}^{(c)} \Psi}_{\text{Connector forces}} \Big) \tag{2.2}$$

Here $\underline{\underline{\kappa}}$ is the transpose of the velocity gradient tensor $(\nabla \underline{v})^+$ and ζ is the friction coefficient of a bead. This equation is a continuity equation corresponding to the dynamical equation of two beads of the dumbbell. Three types of forces are considered in the dynamics of the beads:

Brownian forces

$$\underline{F}_1^{(B)} = - k_BT \frac{\partial}{\partial \underline{r}_1} \ln \Psi (\underline{R},t) \tag{2.3}$$

Drag or friction forces:

$$\underline{F}_1^{(f)} = - \zeta (\dot{\underline{r}}_1 - \underline{u}_1) \tag{2.4}$$

where $\dot{\underline{r}}_1$ is the time-derivative of the position vector of bead 1, and $\underline{u}_1$ its velocity.

Connector forces:

$$\underline{F}^{(c)} = \underline{F}_2^{(c)} - \underline{F}_1^{(c)} = H \underline{R} \tag{2.5}$$

where H is the modulus of the connector, possibly a function of $\underline{R}$.

Explicit solutions of equations (2.1) and (2.2) can be obtained for a limited number of cases.

a) Hookean Dumbbell

Giesekus [27] assumed that the modulus is a constant ($H=H_o$) to obtain the so-called upper convected Maxwell model:

$$\underline{\underline{\tau}} = -\eta_s \dot{\underline{\underline{\gamma}}} + \underline{\underline{\tau}}_p \tag{2.6}$$

with the polymer contribution given by:

$$\underline{\underline{\tau}}_p + \lambda_H \frac{\delta}{\delta t} \underline{\underline{\tau}}_p = -nk_BT\,\lambda_H \dot{\underline{\underline{\gamma}}} \tag{2.7}$$

where $\delta/\delta t$ is the upper convected derivative:

$$\frac{\delta}{\delta t}\underline{\underline{\tau}} = \frac{\partial}{\partial t}\underline{\underline{\tau}} + \underline{v}\cdot\nabla\underline{\underline{\tau}} - \underline{\underline{\kappa}}\cdot\underline{\underline{\tau}} - \underline{\underline{\tau}}\cdot\underline{\underline{\kappa}}^+ \tag{2.8}$$

and $\lambda_H = \zeta/4H_o$.

This model predicts a constant steady-shear viscosity and a constant primary normal stress coefficient. The secondary normal stress coefficient is equal to zero and the steady elongational viscosity goes to infinity at finite elongational rate.

b) FENE-P Dumbbell

Bird et al. [13] used the original idea due to Warner [62] that the dumbbell connector is finitetly extensible non-linear elastic, with the following modulus:

$$H = H_o/[1 - (R/R_o)^2] \tag{2.9}$$

where R_o is the maximum extensibility. However, in order to obtain a specific rheological model, Bird et al. introduced the Peterlin [50] approximation that consists of pre-averaging the term $1-(R/R_o)^2$ in equation (2.9) to write:

$$H = H_o/[1 - \langle (R/R_o)^2 \rangle] \tag{2.10}$$

Then the solution to equations (2.1) and (2.2) yields the following rheological equation (for the polymer contribution):

$$z\,\underline{\underline{\tau}}_p + \lambda_H \frac{\delta}{\delta t}\underline{\underline{\tau}}_p - (\underline{\underline{\tau}}_p - nk_BT\underline{\underline{\delta}})\,\lambda_H \frac{D}{Dt}\ln z = -nk_BT\lambda_H\dot{\underline{\underline{\gamma}}} \tag{2.11}$$

with $z = 1 + (3/b)(1 - \mathrm{tr}\,\underline{\underline{\tau}}_p/3nk_BT)$ (2.12) where $b=H_oR_o^2/k_BT$ and D/Dt is the substantial derivative.

Equation (2.11) is known as the Tanner equation as Tanner [56] previously obtained this result assuming that the configurational distribution Ψ could be represented by a Dirac delta function. The Maxwell model is obtained as a special case by taking the limit in which R_o or b tends to ∞.

Although the FENE-P dumbbell is a very crude description of polymer molecules, the incorporation of a finite extensible connector results into qualitative predictions of non-linear effects observed with polymer solutions. For steady-shear flow, the following results are obtained [13]:

$$\Psi_1 = 2(\eta - \eta_s)^2/nk_BT \tag{2.13}$$

$$\Psi_2 = 0 \tag{2.14}$$

$$\text{For} \quad \dot{\gamma} \to 0, \ \eta - \eta_s = nk_BT\lambda_H b/(b+3) \tag{2.15}$$

$$\text{For} \quad \dot{\gamma} \to \infty, \ \eta - \eta_s = nk_BT\lambda_H[(2/b)(\lambda_H\dot{\gamma})^2]^{-1/3} \sim \dot{\gamma}^{-2/3} \tag{2.16}$$

Thus shear-thinning behaviour is predicted at high shear rate, but slopes of -2/3 for η and -4/3 for Ψ_1 are too restrictive. Figures 2.1 and 2.2 compare the predictions of the FENE-P model with the experimental data of Tsai and Darby [57] for dilute aqueous solutions of polyacrylamide (Dow Separan AP-30). In the figures, the parameter λ_E is defined by:

$$\lambda_E = \frac{\eta_o - \eta_s}{c} \frac{M_w}{RT} = \lambda_H b/(b+3) \tag{2.17}$$

where η_o is the zero-shear viscosity, M_w the molecular weight and R the gas constant. The equality on the right-hand side holds only in the limit as the polymer concentration, c, tends to zero. This is not exactly the case for the data shown in the figures, where λ_E was obtained from the zero-shear viscosity data: λ_E increases with concentration indicating appreciable intermolecular interaction. Clearly, as shown in Figures (2.1) and (2.2), the model is not flexible enough. Nevertheless, the model suggests a time constant, λ_E, with which shear viscosity and primary normal stress data for various polymer concentrations can be correlated.

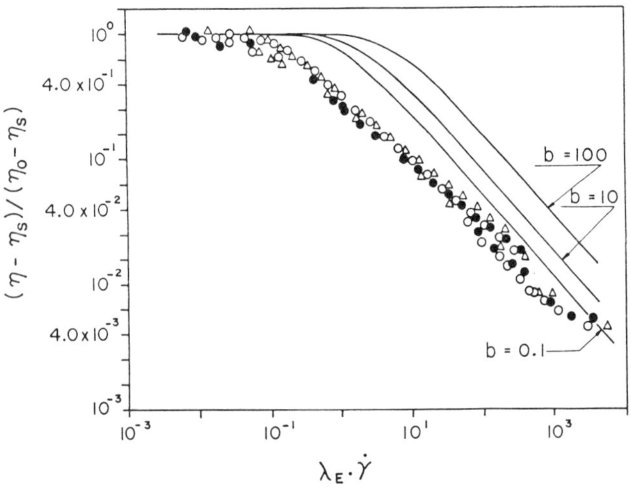

Figure 2.1 Comparison of the FENE-P dumbbell model predictions with steady-shear viscosity data of polyacrylamide solutions (data of ref. [18,57]).

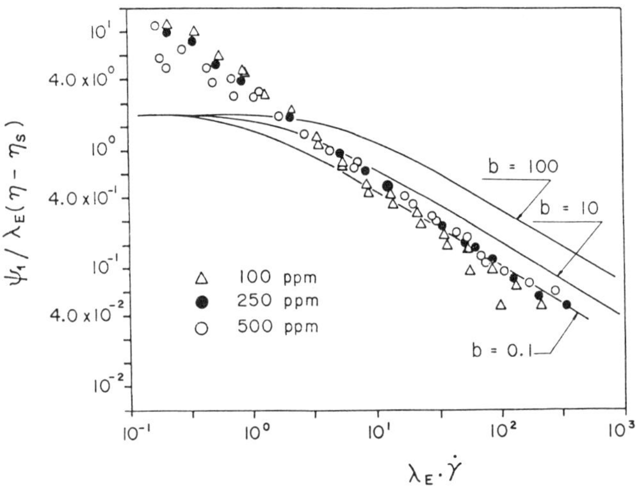

Figure 2.2 Comparison of the FENE-P model predictions with steady-shear primary normal stress data of polyacrylamide solutions (data of ref. [18,57]).

Another interesting feature of the FENE-P dumbbell model is the predictions for elongational viscosity.

For $\dot{\varepsilon} \to 0$,

$$\eta_E - 3\eta_s = 3\, nk_B T \lambda_H b/(b+3) \tag{2.18}$$

and for $\dot{\varepsilon} \to \infty$,

$$\eta_E - 3\eta_s = 2(b+3)(\eta_o - \eta_s) \tag{2.19}$$

As the elongational rate increases, the elongational viscosity is monotanously increasing to reach a plateau given by equation (2.19) at high elongational rate. Although there is not experimental data yet to confirm this result, it appears to be more realistic than the unbounded value predicted by the Maxwell model.

2.2 Flexible-Chain Model. In flexible-chain models, such as originally proposed by Rouse [52] for the draining case and by Zimm [66] for the non draining case (strong hydrodynamics interaction), the macromolecules are viewed as linear chains of beads joined together with some kind of connectors. For freely jointed FENE-P chains, the stress tensor is given by [13]:

$$\underbrace{\underline{\underline{\tau}} = -\eta_s\dot{\underline{\underline{\gamma}}}}_{\text{solvent contribution}} - nH_o \sum_{j=1}^{N-1} \underbrace{\frac{\langle \underline{Q}_j\,\underline{Q}_j \rangle}{1 - \langle Q_j^2/Q_o^2 \rangle}}_{\text{connector-force contribution}} + \underbrace{(N-1)\,nk_BT\underline{\underline{\delta}}}_{\text{Brownian motion contribution}} \tag{2.20}$$

where $\underline{Q}_j$ is the end-to-end vector, Q_o is the maximum extensibility, $\langle\ \rangle$ represents the average with respect to the configurational distribution function $\Psi(t, \underline{Q}_1, \underline{Q}_2 \ldots)$ given by the equation of diffusion:

$$\frac{\partial \Psi}{\partial t} = -\sum_{j=1}^{N-1} \frac{\partial}{\partial \underline{Q}_j} \cdot \{[\underline{\underline{\kappa}} \cdot \underline{Q}_j]\,\Psi - \frac{1}{\zeta}\sum_{k=1}^{N-1} A_{jk}[k_BT \frac{\partial}{\partial \underline{Q}_k}\Psi + \underline{F}_k^{(c)}\Psi]\} \tag{2.21}$$

where the A_{jk} are the elements of the Rouse matrix: $A_{jk} = +2$ for $j=k$, $A_{jk} = -1$ for $j = k \pm 1$, $A_{jk} = 0$ otherwise. The solution of equations (2.20) and (2.21) yields the following rheological equation:

$$\underline{\underline{\tau}} = - \eta_s \underline{\underline{\dot{\gamma}}} + \sum_{j=1}^{N-1} \underline{\underline{\tau}}_j$$

$$z_j \underline{\underline{\tau}}_j + \lambda_j \frac{\delta}{\delta t} \underline{\underline{\tau}}_j - (\underline{\underline{\tau}}_j - nk_B T \underline{\underline{\delta}}) \lambda_j \frac{D \ln}{Dt} z_j = -nk_B T \lambda_j \underline{\underline{\dot{\gamma}}} \tag{2.22}$$

where $z_j = 1 + \frac{3}{b} (1 - \text{tr } \underline{\underline{\tau}}_j / 3nk_B T)$

$b = H_o Q_o^2 / k_B T$

$\lambda_j = \zeta C_j / 2H_o$

$C_j = 1/[4 \sin^2 (j\pi/2N)]$

Since it contains a series of relaxation time, λ_j, the FENE-P chain model is more flexible than the FENE-P dumbbell model to describe non-linear viscoelastic effects. The limiting expressions for η and Ψ_1 under steady-shear flow are:

For $\dot{\gamma} \to 0$

$$\eta - \eta_s = \eta_o - \eta_s = nk_B T \lambda_E \tag{2.23}$$

where $\lambda_E = [\frac{\zeta b}{2H_o (b+3)}] \sum_{j=1}^{N-1} C_j$

$$\Psi_1 = \Psi_{1o} = \frac{2(\eta_o - \eta_s)^2}{nk_B T / A_o} \tag{2.24}$$

where $A_o = \sum_{j=1}^{N-1} C_j^2 / (\sum_{j=1}^{N-1} C_j)^2$

For $\dot{\gamma} \to \infty$

$$\eta - \eta_s = \frac{nk_B T \lambda_H}{[(1/b)(\lambda_H \dot{\gamma})^2]^{1/3}} \sum_{j=1}^{N-1} C_j^{1/3} \tag{2.25}$$

$$\sim \dot{\gamma}^{-2/3}$$

$$\Psi_1 = \frac{2(\eta - \eta_s)^2}{nk_B T / A_\infty} \sim \dot{\gamma}^{-4/3} \tag{2.26}$$

where $A_\infty = \sum_{j=1}^{N-1} C_j^{2/3} / (\sum_{j=1}^{N-1} C_j^{1/3})^2$

In the case of the FENE-P dumbbell (N=2), $A_o = A_\infty = 1$, so it is obvious that the chain model is more adequate to describe the primary normal stress data. Nevertheless, the power-law regions remain just as for the dumbbell model with slope of -2/3 and -4/3 for $\eta - \eta_s$ and Ψ_1 respectively. The predictions for the elongational viscosity are very similar to those of the dumbbell model. Bird et al. [13] have included equilibrium-averaged hydrodynamic interaction. The Rouse eigenvalues (C_j in equation 2.21) are replaced by the Zimm eigenvalues. This does not change the flexibility of the model in regard to fitting non-linear data.

3. POLYMER MELTS AND CONCENTRATED SOLUTIONS

Two groups of molecular theories have been developed to describe the rheological properties of polymer melts or concentated solutions: the network and the reptation theories. The network theories, which have been inspired by the successful theories on rubber elasticity, are rather simple. The major drawback of these theories is their lack of molecular weight dependent parameters. However, the network theories have served as the framework to develop highly successful constitutive equations. More recently, Doi and Edwards [23] have used the concept of reptation, as elaborated by de Gennes [21], to derive a complete constitutive relation. The idea of a macromolecular chain reptation in an imaginary tube, that represents the constraints of the surroundings, is closer to the molecular description used in the kinetics theories of dilute solutions. Considerable research is being now conducted to evaluate the merits of the reptation theories.

In this section, we discuss a few theories of both groups and present some rheological tests used to assess rheological models derived from network theories. Some of the limitations of the network and reptation theories are stressed, but at this stage, it is not possible to decide which type of theories will eventually prove to be the most useful to polymer rheologists.

3.1 Network Theories. The network theories origin in the early work of Green and Tobolsky [29], but it was Lodge [45,46] and Yamamoto [64] who fully developed the concept to obtain complete constitutive relations. These theories visualize the polymer in the melt or solution as a network of entangled polymer chains, as illustrated in Figure 3.1-a. The entanglements or junctions could be of different nature: mechanical, physical or

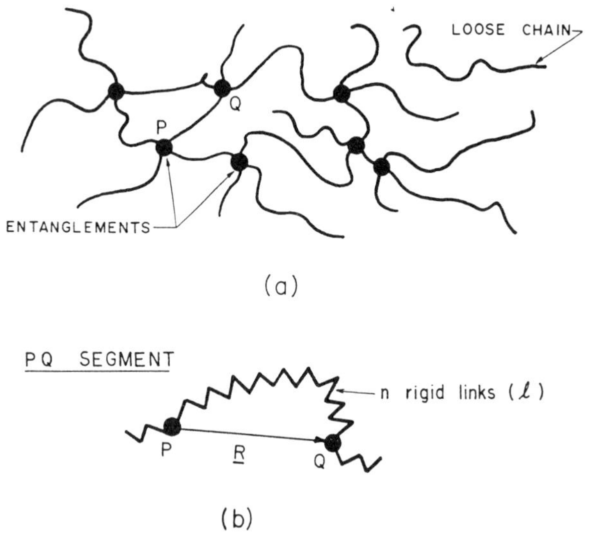

Figure 3.1 Polymer representation in network theories; a) network of entangled chains; b) detail of a n-segment.

weak chemical bounds. For polymeric liquids, the entanglements have a temporary life which is assumed to be much shorter than a characteristic time associated with the macroscopic flow. The contribution to the extra stress tensor is then assumed to arise from the deformation of the segments formed by adjacent entanglements. Such a segment made of n links and of end-to-end distance vector $\underline{R}$ is shown in Figure 3.1-b. The Helmoltz free energy per unit volume of a network of Gaussian segments made of n freely-rotating jointed rigid links is given by [45]:

$$A(t) = \text{constant} + kT \sum_n b_n \int F_n(\underline{R},t) R^2 d^3x \tag{3.1}$$

where $$b_n = \frac{3}{2nl^2} \tag{3.2}$$

The constant in equation (3.1) represents the contributions of the solvent and of the loose segments; F_n is the probability of the n-segments to have end-to-end distance is the range (R, R+dR). Lodge [45] introduced another index to account for various complexities (or different nature) of the entanglements. This, however, does not lead to more flexible results and will not be further discussed here. Using the assumption of affine deformation (non-slip hypothesis), equation (3.1) gives the following expression for the contribution of the segments to the stress tensor:

$$\underline{\underline{\tau}} = -\sum_n H_n \langle \underline{R}\,\underline{R} \rangle_n \tag{3.3}$$

where H_n are constant moduli given by:

$$H_n = 3k_B T/nl^2 \tag{3.4}$$

and $\langle\ \rangle$ refers to average with respect to the probability function F_n. In comparison with the kinetic theories for dilute solutions, the segments are taken as Hookean springs and there is no drag force acting on the segments. The loose chain, as the solvent, do not contribute to the extra stress tensor.

The probability or distribution function is obtained from a gain-loss balance of the n-segments. This balance yields the following time evolution equation:

$$\frac{\partial F_n(\underline{R},t)}{\partial t} = -\left(\frac{\partial}{\partial \underline{R}} \cdot [\underline{\underline{\kappa}} \cdot \underline{R}]F_n\right) + L_n(\underline{R},t) - F_n/\lambda_n(t) \tag{3.5}$$

net change in distribution due to fluid motion — rate of creation of n-segments — rate of loss of n-segments

This is a first order differential equation that can be integrated and combined with equation (3.3) to give the following rheological equation:

$$\underline{\underline{\tau}} = -\int_{-\infty}^{t} m(t,t')\, \underline{\underline{C}}^{-1}(t,t')\, dt' \tag{3.6}$$

where $\underline{\underline{C}}^{-1}$ is the Finger deformation tensor and m(t,t') is a memory function or functional given by:

$$m(t,t') = \sum_n H_n \bar{L}_n (t') \exp \{- \int_{t'}^{t} \frac{dt''}{\lambda_n(t'')} \} \tag{3.7}$$

The $\bar{L}_n(t')$ are defined by:

$$\bar{L}_n(t') = \frac{4\pi}{3} \int_0^\infty R^4 \, L_n(R,t)dR \tag{3.8}$$

For constant λ_n and $\bar{L}_n$, the rheological equation reduces to the rubberlike-liquid equation of Lodge [44]:

$$\underline{\underline{\tau}} = - \int_{-\infty}^{t} \sum_n \frac{\eta_n}{\lambda_n^2} \exp \{ - \frac{(t-t')}{\lambda_n}\} \underline{\underline{C}}^{-1} (t,t')dt' \tag{3.9}$$

The η_n are parameters with units of viscosity and equal to $H_n\bar{L}_n \lambda_n^2$. Equation (3.9) is identical to the generalized upper convected Maxwell model. It is interesting to note that the network theory, designed for concentrated solutions or melts, yields in its simplest form the same results as the Hookean dumbbell model for dilute solutions. Obviously, the theory presented in section 2.1 can be easily generalized by summing over a series of non-interacting dumbbells of different moduli. As in the case of the Hookean dumbbell model, the rubberlike-liquid equation of Lodge predicts, under steady-shear flow, a constant viscosity and a constant primary normal stress coefficient; the secondary normal stress coefficient is equal to zero. The elongational viscosity is a monotonously increasing function of the elongational rate and goes to infinity at a finite rate.

Lodge has examined [45] the effects on the results of using a non-Gaussian distribution for the segments. This leads to a non-zero secondary normal stress coefficient, but the shear-dependence of the viscosity and of the normal stress coefficients is not acceptable. In the work of Yamamoto [64,65], the rates of creation and of loss of segments are allowed to depend on the segment length and orientation. His theory does not yield an explicit constitutive equation and it is difficult to assess the merits of the choices retained by Yamamoto. Several attempts to modify empirically equation (3.6) have been quite successful. In most alterations of the Lodge network theory, the rates of creation and the rates of loss of entanglements are taken as functions of the invariants of the deformation or of the rate of deformation tensor. The most successful models are probably those of Wagner [59 to 61] who considered the invariants of the deformation tensor and those of Bogue [14], Meister [48], Carreau [16], Macdonald [47] and DeKee and Carreau [22] who introduced dependences on the second invariant of the rate of deformation tensor. Other choices made by Kaye [40] and by Acierno et al. [1 to 3], who took the rates to depend on the stress invariants, lead to constitutive equations that must be solved by iterative procedures. The so-called Marrucci equation (Acierno et al. [1 to 3] appears to contain, at least qualitatively, all the desired feature of a rheological model.

For more information, the reader is refered to the chapter of this book written by DeKee, who discusses of the merits of various models derived from the network theories. Our next section is devoted to rheological tests based on transient experiments. These tests can be used to discriminate between classes of models which incorporate invariants of the deformation tensor and classes which make use of the rate of deformation invariants.

We conclude this section by mentionning the interesting idea proposed recently by Jongschaap et al. [38]. They considered the contribution to the extra-stress tensor of the free (or loose) chains as well as that of the fixed segments. The time evolution of the fixed segments for a given configuration is given by:

$$\frac{\partial F_1}{\partial t} = - \nabla \cdot (F_1 \dot{\underline{R}}_1) + g F_2 - hF_1 \qquad (3.10)$$

and for the free segments:

$$\frac{\partial F_2}{\partial t} = - \nabla \cdot (F_2 \dot{\underline{R}}_2) - g F_2 + hF_1 \qquad (3.11)$$

In these equations the creation and loss functions g and h may depend on the concentration of segments and on invariants of the stress or rate of deformation tensor. The rates of creation of fixed segments are proportional to the concentration of free segments (F_2) and are equal to the rates of loss of free segments. Summing over all configurations, the net rates of change of segments concentrations N_1 and N_2 are:

$$\frac{dN_1}{dt} = - \frac{dN_2}{dt} = g-h \qquad (3.11a)$$

Using the affine deformation hypothesis and assuming that the free segments behave like elastic dumbbells, Jongschaap et al. [38] have shown that their theory reduces to the Marrucci model as a special case. They also compared their theory to data obtained for a S.I.S. block-copolymer solution in tetradecane. The shear-viscosity data showed a thickening effect at a critical shear rate so that two different rate parameters had to be used to fit the data.

The Jongschaap et al.'s idea is worth further investigation. However, some of the physics behind equations (3.10) to (3.12) have to be clarified. For high molecular weight polymer, one may expect that the number of entanglements per unit macromolecule be considerably larger than one. So, the rates of loss of fixed segments are not equal to the rates of creation of free segments as postulated in equations (3.10) and (3.11). Moreover, free segments do not have the same configuration as fixed segments from which they originate. Refering to Figure 3.1, the loss of one entanglement between a n and a m-segment will result into a (m+n)- segment with an end-to-end vector being the vectorial sum of the initial end-to-end vectors. As far as we are aware, no one has attempted a statistical approach to obtain a balance being the rates of creation and the rates of loss of entanglements. This is a direction for future research which is worth consideration.

3.2 Rheological Tests for Rheological Models from Network Theories. As we mentionned above, some of the rheological models are quite successful in describing the rheological properties of various classes of polymeric materials. All those models, however, contain empirical functions or parameters proposed from experience and often evaluated from a tedious procedure. In this section, we discuss some of the rheological tests proposed in the recent literature to discriminate between two classes of integral constitutive equations derived from network theories. These tests are based on relationship between two and more material functions and require no prior evaluation of model parameters. The following is taken from Attané et al. [6].

The first class could be appropriately refered to as the Kaye-Bernstein-Kearsley-Zapas equation [11]:

$$\underline{\underline{\tau}} = - \int_{-\infty}^{t} \{m_1(t-t',I_c,II_c)[\underline{\underline{C}}^{-1}(t')-\underline{\underline{\delta}}]+m_2(t-t',I_c, II_c)[\underline{\underline{C}}(t')-\underline{\underline{\delta}}]\}dt' \tag{3.12}$$

where $\underline{\underline{C}}^{-1}$ and $\underline{\underline{C}}$ are respectively the Finger and the Cauchy-Green deformation tensor, $\underline{\underline{\delta}}$ is the unit tensor, m_1 and m_2 are functions of the first and second invariants of the deformation tensor, $\underline{\underline{C}}^{-1}$. Many rheological models can be obtained as special cases of this equation. For example the Wagner equation [59] is obtained by taking

$$m_1 = m(t-t') \,.\, h(I_c,II_c) \tag{3.13}$$

$$m_2 = 0$$

The second class can be refered to as the Carreau equation [16]. It can be expressed as:

$$\underline{\underline{\tau}} = - \int_{-\infty}^{t} M(t-t',II_{\dot\gamma})\{(1+\frac{\varepsilon}{2})[\underline{\underline{C}}^{-1}(t')-\underline{\underline{\delta}}] + \frac{\varepsilon}{2}[\underline{\underline{C}}(t')-\underline{\underline{\delta}}]\}dt' \tag{3.14}$$

where M is a functional of the second invariant of the rate-of-strain tensor ($II_{\dot\gamma} = \dot\gamma : \dot\gamma$) and is given by:

$$M(t-t',II_{\dot\gamma}) = \sum_{p=1}^{N} \frac{\eta_p f_p(II_{\dot\gamma}(t'))}{\lambda_p^2} \exp - \int_{t'}^{t} \frac{dt''}{\lambda_p\, g_p(II_{\dot\gamma}(t''))} \tag{3.15}$$

and λ_p and η_p are material parameters describing the linear viscoelasticity and f_p and g_p are functions which take into account the effects of the rate of deformation on the rates of loss and rates of creation of entanglements. For different choices of f_p and g_p, various rheological models can be obtained: Bogue and coworkers [14 , 25], Carreau A and B [16], M.B.C. [47], DeKee and Carreau [22] etc. The Bird-Carreau [10] model is readily obtained by taking g_p=1 and the Lodge elastic model by taking f_p=g_p=1 and ε=0. We note also that there two classes of rheological models are compatible with Gaussian network theories only when the second term of the integral vanishes, i.e. for m_2 and $\varepsilon=0$.

For stress relaxation after steady simple shear flow, the following relations are obtained [6]:

K-BKZ

$$\frac{1}{\dot{\gamma}^2} \int_0^\infty u \, \Psi_1^- (u,t) du = \int_t^\infty \eta^- (\dot{\gamma},t) dt \qquad (3.16)$$

or $$-\frac{1}{2} \frac{\partial \Psi_1^-}{\partial t} (\dot{\gamma},t) = \eta^- (\dot{\gamma},t) + \frac{\dot{\gamma}}{2} \frac{\partial \eta^-}{\partial \dot{\gamma}} (\dot{\gamma},t) \qquad (3.17)$$

At the limit $t \to 0$, $\eta^- (\dot{\gamma},0) = \eta(\dot{\gamma})$ and relation (3.17) becomes:

$$-\frac{1}{2} \frac{\partial \Psi_1^-}{\partial t} (\dot{\gamma},0) = \eta(\dot{\gamma}) + \frac{\dot{\gamma}}{2} \frac{\partial \eta}{\partial \dot{\gamma}} (\dot{\gamma}) \qquad (3.18)$$

Carreau

$$\Psi_1^- (\dot{\gamma},t) \leqslant 2 \int_t^\infty \eta^- (\dot{\gamma},t) dt \qquad (3.19)$$

or $$-\frac{1}{2} \frac{\partial \Psi_1^-}{\partial t} (\dot{\gamma},t) \leqslant \eta^- (\dot{\gamma},t) \qquad (3.20)$$

where the equality holds for the Bird-Carreau model [10] and at the limit of $\dot{\gamma} \to 0$ for the Carreau equation. With the equality sign, this relation is known as the Yamamoto relation.

With the help of reliable data, relations (3.16) to (3.20) can be used as rheological tests to discriminate between these two classes of constitutive equations. Accurate transient and steady-shear data of solutions of nearly monodisperse polystyrenes in dibutylphtalate have been obtained on a modified Weissenberg rheogoniometer [5]. Only one set of data, for the higher molecular weight ($M_w = 1.6 \times 10^6$), is presented here. The other polystyrene solutions show similar behaviour.

Figure 3.2 compares the relation (3.19) with the experimental data of six solutions of different concentrations. It is obvious that the equality holds only at low shear rate, where the viscosity is approximately equal to the zero-shear viscosity. Hence the Bird-Carreau model is not flexible

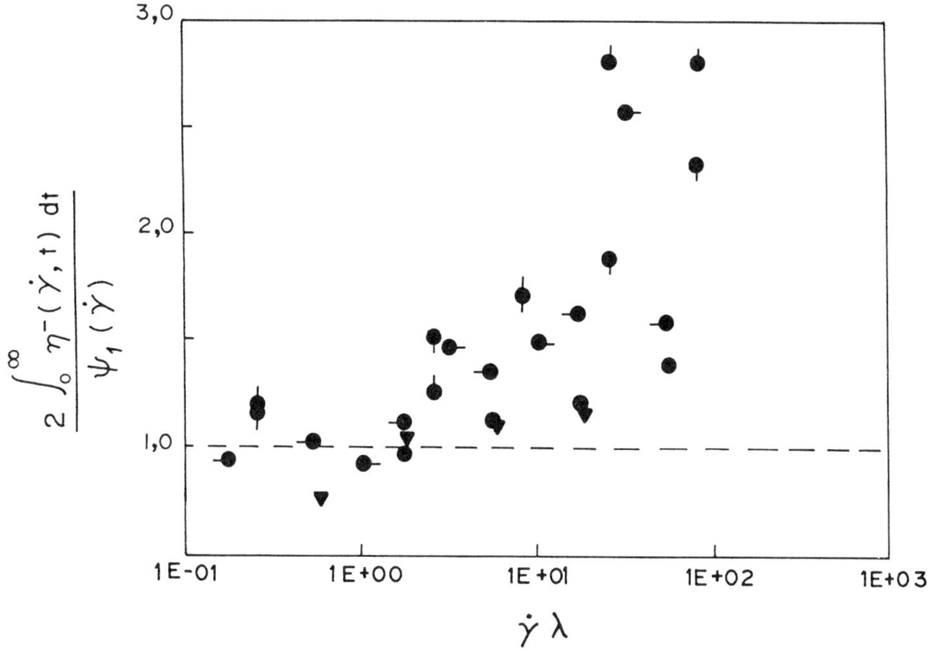

Figure 3.2 Experimental evaluation of relation (3.19). The symbols are defined in Table 3.1 -------- Predictions of the Bird-Carreau equation.

Table 3.1 Characteristics of the Polystyrene Solutions ($M_w = 1.6 \times 10^6$)

Symbol	Concentration weight %	η_o Pa.s	λ^* s
▲	5	4.8	0.025
●	7	20	0.082
-●	10	110	0.25
●|	15	1450	1.5
●-	20	13500	7.0
|●	25	42600	15.0

* The characteristic elastic time is taken as $\lambda = \Psi_{1o}/2\eta_o$ where Ψ_{1o} is the zero-shear normal stress coefficient and η_o is the zero-shear viscosity.

enough to predict the shear-rate dependence at high shear rate. Similar failure is observed for the K-BKZ equation. This is shown in Figure 3.3 where the same experimental data are plotted according to equation (3.16). In principle, these data can be accurately described by the Carreau equation through the appropriate choices of the functions $g_p(\dot{\gamma})$.

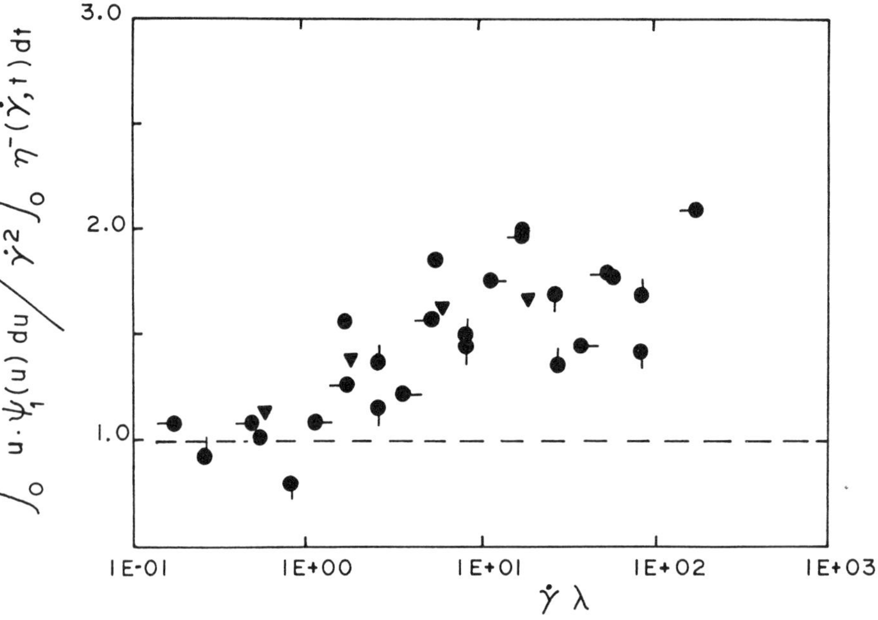

Figure 3.3 Experimental evaluation of relation (3.16). The symbols are defined in Table 3.1 ----- Predictions of the K-BKZ equation.

A different pattern is shown in Figure 3.4 when the data are plotted as suggested by equation (3.20). The limits at t=0 are correctly predicted by the Bird-Carreau model whereas large deviations between the shear relaxation function and the derivative of the normal stress relaxation function are observed at finite times for large shear rates.

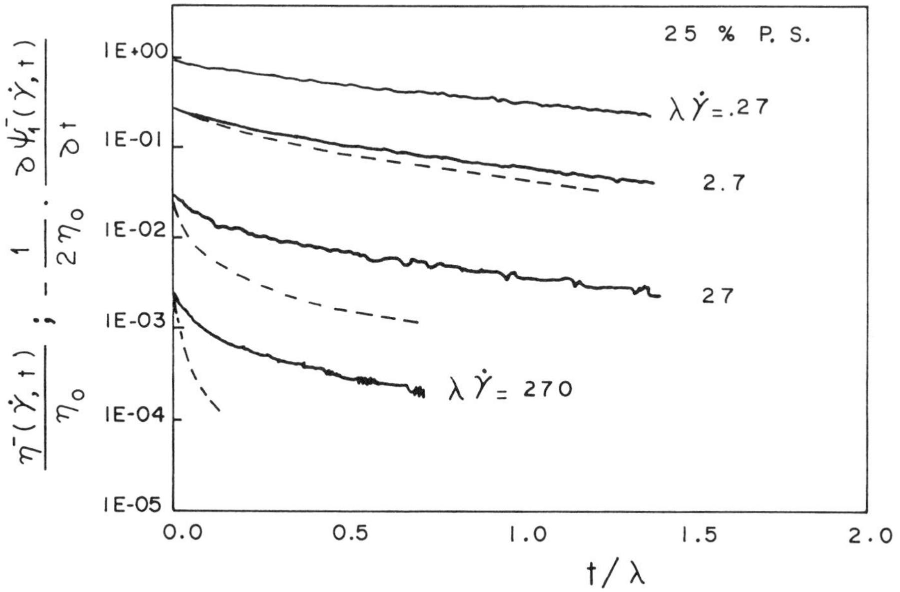

Figure 3.4 Experimental evaluation of relation (3.20) for the 25% polystyrene solution, ———— $\eta^{-}(\dot{\gamma},t)/\eta_o$ --------- $\frac{\partial\Psi_1^{-}(\dot{\gamma},t)/2\eta_o}{\partial t}$

On the contrary, the K-BKZ and Carreau equations can describe the differences observed at finite times, but incorrectly predict different limits at t=0 for large shear rates. Clearly none of these constitutive equations is capable of describing both the initial and final rates of relaxation at large shear rate. This suggests that a totally new approach has to be considered for the insertion of a strain or rate-of-strain dependence in the memory function. One possibly successful route is the inclusion of the invariants of the stress tensor, as proposed by Acierno et al. [1 to 3].

Van Es and Christensen [58] have proposed a test for the evaluation of the Bird-Carreau equation based on stress growth data.

The Van Es-Christensen test can be written in the following form:

$$\Gamma(\dot{\gamma},t) = \Psi_1^+(\dot{\gamma},t) - t\eta^+(\dot{\gamma},t) + \int_o^t \eta^+(\dot{\gamma},t)dt \qquad (3.21)$$

where the expressions of $\Gamma(\dot{\gamma},t)$ are the following:

Carreau

$$\sum_{p=1}^{N} \eta_p\, g_p\, (\dot{\gamma})\, [\lambda_p\, g_p\, (\dot{\gamma})\, \{1 - e^{-t/\lambda_p g_p(\dot{\gamma})}\} - te^{-t/\lambda_p g_p(\dot{\gamma})}] \qquad (3.22)$$

K-BKZ

$$\frac{1}{\dot{\gamma}} \int_0^{\dot{\gamma}} [t\eta^+(\dot{\gamma},t) - \int_0^t \eta^+(\dot{\gamma},t)dt]d\dot{\gamma} \qquad (3.23)$$

The expression for the Bird-Carreau model is obtained by setting g_p=1 in the expression for the Carreau equation.

Figure 3.5 shows the experimental values of $\Gamma(\dot{\gamma},t)$ obtained from the right-hand side of equation (3.21) with the η^+ and Ψ_1^+ data of a 25% polystyrene solution. At very low shear rate $\Gamma(\dot{\gamma},t)$ is a monotonously increasing function of time. At larger shear rate, $\Gamma(\dot{\gamma},t)$ reaches rapidly a plateau the magnitude of which decreases markly with increasing shear-rate. A slight maximum is also observed. Except for the maximum, the shear-rate dependence of Γ can be adequately described by the Carreau equation. It is obvious that the Bird-Carreau model (obtained by setting all g_p equal to 1 in equation 3.22) will fail considerably with no shear-rate dependence in the function Γ. The K-BKZ equation is more flexible than the Carreau equation. The analysis of equation (3.23) shows that $\Gamma(\dot{\gamma},t)$ can describe a maximum closely related to the maximum predicted for the shear growth function $\eta^+(\dot{\gamma},t)$.

The times at which the maxima of $\eta^+(\dot{\gamma},t)$ and $\Psi_1^+(\dot{\gamma},t)$ (stress overshoots) are observed can be used as more critical tests. For the Carreau equation, the following relation is obtained:

$$(t\dot{\gamma})_{\eta^+_{max}} = \frac{1}{2}\, (t\dot{\gamma})_{\Psi^+_{1max}} = f(\dot{\gamma}) \qquad (3.24)$$

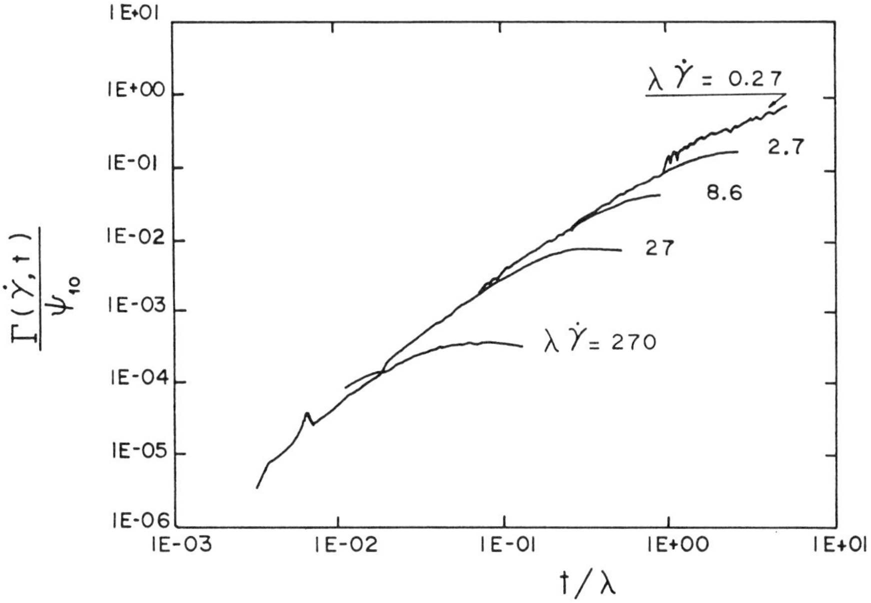

Figure 3.5 Stress growth function for a 25% solution of polystyrene

where $f(\dot{\gamma})$ depends on the specific choices of the functions $f_p(\dot{\gamma})$ and $g_p(\dot{\gamma})$. A priori, the K-BKZ equation appears to be the most flexible. However, for the specific memory functions chosen by Wagner [59] with $m_1 = m(t-t') \cdot e^{-n(t-t')\dot{\gamma}}$ and $m_2 = 0$, we obtain:

$$(t\dot{\gamma})_{\eta^+_{max}} = \frac{1}{2}\ (t\dot{\gamma})_{\Psi^+_{1max}} = \frac{1}{n} \qquad (3.25)$$

where n is a material parameter.

All the literature data [7] show that the time of Ψ_1^+ max is twice that of η^+ max, as predicted by the three constitutive equations. Wagner have shown that the maximum for low density polyethylene melts are observed at constant deformation. In contrast, for solutions $(\dot{\gamma}t)_{\eta^+_{max}}$ or $(\dot{\gamma}t)_{\Psi^+_{1max}}$ is an increasing function of the shear rate.

None of the two types of constitutive equations is capable of describing the whole spectrum of rheological behaviour observed in transient experiments. The initial rate of relaxation of polystyrene solutions after steady shear flow is independent of the initially applied shear-rate. This suggests that stress invariants have to be introduced in the memory functions.

3.3 Reptation Theories . The reptation theories are at present the most popular molecular theories used for the modeling of the rheological behaviour of polymer melts or concentrated solutions. The initial concept proposed by de Gennes [21] was developed by Doi and Edwards [23, 24] to obtain a complete constitutive relation. They based their development on the idea of a macromolecule reptating inside an imaginary tube with a given time life. The tube represents the constraints of the surrounding polymer chains. The mathematical formulation, however, is not clear and we will rather summarize the findings of Curtiss and Bird [19, 20] who developed their theory from a general phase-space kinetic formalism. The macromolecules are modeled as Kramers freely jointed bead-rod chains. The stress equation is given by:

$$\underline{\underline{\tau}} = -Nnk_BT \left[\int_0^1 < \underline{u}\,\underline{u} - \frac{1}{3}\underline{\underline{\delta}} > d\sigma + \varepsilon\lambda\,\underline{\underline{\kappa}} : \int_0^1 < \underline{u}\,\underline{u}\,\underline{u}\,\underline{u} > \sigma(1-\sigma)d\sigma \right. \qquad (3.26)$$

where N is the number of beads describing the polymer chains, n is the number of chains per unit volume, $\underline{u}$ is the local orientation vector; $\underline{\underline{\delta}}$ is the unit tensor, ε is a parameter related to the anisotropy of the chain motion and λ is a characteristic time defined by:

$$\lambda = N^{3+\beta}\,\zeta\,l^2/2\,k_BT \qquad (3.27)$$

The parameter β is a contraint exponent which accounts for possible entanglements. The first term on the right-hand side equation (3.26) describes the Brownian motion contribution whereas the second term represents the hydrodymanics contribution. The < > means average with respect to the orientation distribution function given by the following diffusion equation:

$$\frac{\partial f}{\partial t} = \frac{1}{\lambda} \frac{\partial^2 f}{\partial \sigma^2} - \left(\frac{\partial}{\partial \underline{u}} \cdot G_t \ (\underline{u}) f \right) \tag{3.28}$$

where the operator G_t is:

$$G_t(\underline{u}) = \underline{\underline{\kappa}} \cdot \underline{u} - \underline{\underline{\kappa}} : \underline{u}\,\underline{u}\,\underline{u} \tag{3.29}$$

The complete constitutive equation obtained by Curtiss and Bird can be found in references, [19 ,20 , 8 or 9]. We summarize here some of the interesting features of their equation. Under steady-shear flow the zero-shear viscosity and normal stress coefficients are given by:

$$\eta_o = \frac{N\rho RT}{M_w} \lambda \left(\frac{1}{60} + \frac{\varepsilon}{90} \right) \tag{3.30}$$

$$\Psi_{1o} = \frac{N\rho RT \ \lambda^2}{300 \ M_w} \tag{3.31}$$

$$\Psi_{2o} = -(2/7) \ (1-\varepsilon) \ \Psi_{1o} \tag{3.32}$$

If one assumes that N is proportional to M_w, then $\eta_o \sim \lambda \sim M_w^{3+\beta}$, $\Psi_{1o} \sim M_w^{6+2\beta}$ and for $\beta = 0.4$, the theory predicts the well-established relation for linear polymer melts of high M_w: $\eta_o = K_1 M_w^{3.4}$. It is interesting to note that secondary normal differences (eq. 3.32) are predicted only in the case of anisotropic motion, i.e. for $\varepsilon < 1$.

The Curtiss-Bird theory has been compared [53] with steady and transient shear flow data obtained for concentrated polystyrene solutions. The data are well described by the theory for ε values ranging between 0.3 and 0.5.

The Curtiss-Bird constitutive equation appears to be more flexible than the Doi-Edwards equation which can be approximately recovered by setting $\varepsilon = 0$ and $\beta = 0$ in the Curtiss-Bird equation. The most serious limitation of the reptation theories is the high-shear-rate predictions. For example, at high-shear-rate, the Doi-Edwards theory predicts a viscosity which is proportional to $\dot{\gamma}^{-1.5}$ whereas for the Curtiss-Bird equation with $\varepsilon > 0$, $\eta \sim \dot{\gamma}^{-1.0}$. This is unrealistic and modifications to the theories have to be proposed to correct that undesired feature. As the mathematical formulation is already quite complex, this is not an obvious task.

4. MASTER RHEOLOGICAL MODEL

In this last section, we shall recognize four steps in the process of constructing a rheological model. Advantages of this are the following:

(i) A certain selfconsistency of the models and their agreement with results of some observations is automatically guaranteed if the rules introduced in the four steps are followed.

(ii) The first three steps require to make some choices. Any considerations, in particular those based on an insight, experience gained by regarding results of measurements, molecular theories, and the intended use of the model, can be used to make the choices.

A detailed knowledge of the molecular theories is not required. Our intention is to formulate the steps in such a way that any potential user of rheological models is able to construct, by following the steps and by using an insight and an experience, a model that suits best his or her needs.

This section is based on results that were reported in Grmela [30], [31], [32] and Grmela et al. [33-35].

4.1 Construction of Rheological Models

First step - Choice of State Variables. From the point of view of modeling, the main difference between polymeric and classical fluids is in the separability of the time evolution of hydrodynamic fields (i.e. the fields of mass, momentum and energy) and the time evolution of the internal (molecular) structure. Under the conditions that correspond to most situations of interest in fluid mechanics, changes on the molecular level in classical fluids take place in the time scale that is much smaller than the time scale on which hydrodynamic fields change. It can be therefore assumed that the fluid is locally at equilibrium (the so called local equilibrium assumption). The hydrodynamic fields evolve in time independently of the time evolution of molecules. In polymeric fluids, on the other hand, the internal (molecular) structure evolves in a time scale that is comparable with the time scale on which hydrodynamic fields change. Both the hydrodynamic fields and the internal structure have to be therefore considered together in models of polymeric fluids. The first question that arises is how the internal structure is characterized. We shall now list some possible candidates for the additional state variables that characterize the internal structure. Our focus in on practical usefulness and not on completeness and generality. Before presenting the candidates for the additional state variables, we note that we do not require them to be directly measurable. An indirect (i.e. mediated by the model) information about them is obtained by comparing results of standard rheological measurements with results predicted by a model that uses them.

It has been suggested (see section 2) to model a polymer molecule as a chain of beads connected by either elastic springs or rods . The additional state variable that corresponds to this point of view is the one chain phase space distribution function. We refer to Bird et al. [12] for a review of results that have been obtained by pursuing this choice. A simpler view of polymeric fluids is obtained by modeling polymeric molecules as dumbbells (see section 2). The corresponding convenient additional state variable is a dumbbell configuration space distribution function $\Psi(\underline{r},\underline{R},t)$, where $\underline{r}$ is the position vector of, say, center of mass of the dumbbell and $\underline{R}$ is the vector connecting the two beads of the dumbbell, t is the time. Still simpler and convenient additional state variable is a symmetric positive definite tensor $\underline{\underline{c}}(\underline{r},t)$ that is usually called a configuration tensor (see Giesekus [28]). The tensor $\underline{\underline{c}}$ has the physical meaning of an internal strain. In terms of the distribution function $\Psi(\underline{r},\underline{R},t)$, the configuration tensor $\underline{\underline{c}}$ may be introduced as

$$\underline{\underline{c}}(\underline{r},t)= <\underline{R}\ \underline{R}> = \int \underline{R}\ \underline{R}\ \Psi(\underline{r},\underline{R},t)\ d\underline{R} \tag{4.1}$$

In the illustrations of the master model, we shall use $\underline{\underline{c}}(t)$ as the additional state variable. It means that we shall assume that the fluids under consideration are in states in which the internal structure can be considered to be independent of the position vector $\underline{r}$.

By choosing more microscopic additional state variables (i.e. those that contain detailed information about macromolecules) we are in position to formulate the model in truly molecular terms, and finally, to obtain a relation between molecular and rheological properties. A disadvantage of such a choice is the complexity of the governing equations. The equations cannot be solved without introducing ad hoc simplifying assumptions. Experience seems to show that it is convenient to build the bridge between molecular and rheological properties in several stages. The stage that will be in the center of our interest is a bridge between mesoscopic point of view in which the additional state variable is the configuration tensor $\underline{\underline{c}}$ and rheological properties. It should be emphasized however that the steps in the construction of rheological models that follow apply to any choice of the additional state variable.

Second step - Choice of a Generating Functional. Having chosen the additional state variable, we need to find equations governing its time evolution and the way the additional state variables enter the time evolution equations for hydrodynamic fields. To write the governing equations means to analyze systematicaly all causes of changes of the additional state variable (see e.g. the analysis of forces on beads of a dumbbell in section 2). This analysis depends, of course, on the nature of the chosen additional state variable. There are however general rules that have to be respected in order that the time evolution equations are intrinsically compatible. This and the following steps present these rules. Our aim is not a complete generality and completeness. Rather, we want to present the rules as an organizing frame that facilitates construction of rheological models. The reader who is interested in more theoretical aspects of the rules is refered to Grmela [30 ,31 ,32], Grmela et al. [33].

It has been observed in Grmela [30 ,31], that every time evolution equation that is compatible with equilibrium thermodynamics is associated with a functional. We shall call it a generating functional and denote it by G. We use the term functional since G is a real valued function of state variables. Since the state variables are, in general, functions themselves, G is a function of functions and thus, by using the usual terminology, a functional. The generating functional G is a linear combination of a functional M, that has the meaning of the total mass, E having the meaning of the total energy, and another functional S. The physical meaning of the functional S will be introduced later. Now, we shall discuss the functionals M, E, S one after the other. We have to introduce a terminology. By $\rho(\underline{r},t)$, $\underline{v}(\underline{r},t)$, $e(\underline{r},t)$ we denote the hydrodynamic fields, ρ is the mass density, $\underline{v}$ the velocity and e the specific internal energy. The additional state variable will be denoted formally by $\Psi(\underline{r},x,t)$, where x is an unspecified vector. As we have already said, in illustrations we shall use $\Psi(\underline{r},x,t) \equiv \underline{\underline{c}}(t)$, which means that x $\equiv$ tensor indices.

First, we turn our attention to the functional M that has the physical meaning of the total mass. In most cases the additional state variable Ψ is chosen in such a way that it does not enter the functional M. Usually, we have

$$M = \rho(\underline{r},t)\ d\underline{r} \tag{4.2}$$

Next, we consider the total energy

$$E = \tilde{E}\ (\rho,\ \underline{v},\ e) + \int \rho(\underline{r},t) e_{int}\ (\Psi;\ \underline{r},t)\ d\underline{r} \tag{4.3}$$

The energy associated with coupling the additional state variable Ψ with the hydrodynamic fields has been neglected.

If we choose $\Psi \equiv \underline{\underline{c}}(t)$, then the energy corresponding to elastic dumbbells is

$$e_{int}(\underline{\underline{c}}) = 1/2\ H_o tr\ \underline{\underline{c}} \tag{4.4}$$

(see e.g. Bird et al. [13]), where H_o is a constant modulus. We shall use later

$$e_{int}(\underline{\underline{c}}) = U(tr\ \underline{\underline{c}}) \tag{4.5}$$

and $$1/2\ H(tr\ \underline{\underline{c}}) = \frac{dU}{d(tr\ \underline{\underline{c}})}, \tag{4.6}$$

where U is an arbitrary function of tr $\underline{\underline{c}}$. The equation (4.6) introduces the modulus in this general case.

Finally, we turn our attention to the functional S. Its physical meaning is determined by the following properties. Let

$$G = -S(\rho,\underline{v},e,\Psi) + \frac{1}{T_{th}} E(\rho,\underline{v},e,\Psi) - \frac{\mu_{th}}{T_{th}} M(\rho,\underline{v},e,\Psi) + \frac{P_{th}}{T_{th}} V_{th} \tag{4.7}$$

where T_{th}, μ_{th}, P_{th}, V_{th} denote respectively the thermodynamic temperature, chemical potential pressure and volume. Solutions of

$$\frac{\delta G}{\delta \rho} = 0, \quad \frac{\delta G}{\delta \underline{v}} = 0$$
$$\frac{\delta G}{\delta e} = 0, \quad \frac{\delta G}{\delta \Psi} = 0 \tag{4.8}$$

are equilibrium states. We shall denote them $(\rho_{eq}, \underline{v}_{eq}, e_{eq}, \Psi_{eq})$. The symbols $\delta/\delta f, \ldots$ denote the functional derivative with respective to a function f; if f is not a function but an element of a finite dimensional space, $\delta/\delta f$ reduces to the usual derivative. The functionals M, E, S evaluated at $(\rho_{eq}, \underline{v}_{eq}, e_{eq}, \Psi_{eq})$ become respectively the thermodynamic mass, the thermodynamic energy and the thermodynamic entropy. The thermodynamic equation of state associated with the functional G is

$$G(\rho_{eq}, \underline{v}_{eq}, e_{eq}, \Psi_{eq}; T_{th}, \mu_{th}, P_{th}) = 0 \tag{4.9}$$

The reader who wants to find out more about the generating functional is refered to Grmela [30 ,31]. In most rheological models

$$S = \tilde{S}\ (\rho, \underline{v}, e,) + \int \rho(\underline{r},t)\ s_{int}(\Psi; \underline{r},t) d\underline{r} \tag{4.10}$$

It means that the hydrodynamic fields are again similar as in equation (4.3), decoupled from the additional state variable Ψ. In the case $\Psi \equiv \Psi(\underline{r}, \underline{R}, t)$ we may suggest (see Boltzmann [15])

$$s_{int}(\Psi,\underline{r},t) = -\int \Psi(\underline{r},\underline{R},t) \log \Psi(\underline{r},\underline{R},t) d\underline{R} \tag{4.11}$$

In the case $\Psi \equiv \underline{\underline{c}}$, we suggest

$$s_{int}(\underline{\underline{c}},t) = 1/2 \log(\det \underline{\underline{c}}) \tag{4.12}$$

We note (Sarti and Marrucci [54]) that the expressions (4.11) and (4.12) are compatible if $\underline{\underline{c}}$ and $\Psi(\underline{R},t)$ are related by equation (4.1) and

$$\Psi(\underline{R},t) = (2\pi)^{-3/2}(\det \underline{\underline{c}})^{-1/2} \exp(\underline{R}\,\underline{\underline{c}}^{-1}\,\underline{R}) \tag{4.13}$$

We also notethat if the functional S is chosen as in (4.10), (4.11) or (4.12) then the polymer molecules are, from the point of view of their contribution to the thermodynamic equation of state, considered as an ideal gas. This is a good approximation in the case of dilute polymer solutions but certainly not in the case of polymer melts. Different, more realistic choices of the functionals E and S are being considered (see Grmela [32]). In this chapter we shall be however content with the choices (4.3), (4.5), (4.10) and (4.12).

Third step - Choice of Governing Equations. We look for an equation

$$\frac{\partial\Psi(\underline{r},x,t)}{\partial t} = \hat{\Psi}\ (\rho,\ \underline{v},\ e,\ \Psi;\ \underline{r},\ x,\ t) \tag{4.14}$$

where $\hat{\Psi}$ denotes formally the right hand side. It is useful to write

$$\hat{\Psi} = \hat{\Psi}^- + \hat{\Psi}^+, \tag{4.15}$$

where $\hat{\Psi}^-$ is an odd function of $\underline{v}$ (i.e. if $\underline{v} \to -\underline{v}$ then $\hat{\Psi}^- \to -\hat{\Psi}^-$) and $\hat{\Psi}^+$ is an even function of $\underline{v}$ (i.e. if $\underline{v} \to -\underline{v}$ then $\hat{\Psi}^+ \to \hat{\Psi}^+$), and consider $\hat{\Psi}^-$ and $\hat{\Psi}^+$ separately. The term $\hat{\Psi}^-$ is a convection term. It denotes the time reversible changes of $\hat{\Psi}$. The term $\delta\Psi/\delta t - \hat{\Psi}^-$ is usually denoted by $\delta\Psi/\delta t$ and called a generalized time derivative. In the case $\Psi \equiv \underline{\underline{c}}$, $\delta\Psi/\delta t$ may be chosen to be for example the upper convected derivative (2.8) or its generalizations (see e.g. Olbricht et al. [49]). The term $\hat{\Psi}^+$ is a diffusion (dissipation) term. It denotes the time irreversible changes of Ψ. The second law of thermodynamics tells us that (see more in Grmela [31])

$$\iint \frac{\delta G}{\delta\Psi(\underline{r},x,t)}\ \hat{\Psi}^+(\underline{r},x,t)\ d\underline{r}\ dx \lesssim 0 \tag{4.16}$$

The diffusion term $\hat{\Psi}^+$ has to be thus chosen in such a way that the inequality (4.16) is satisfied. If Ψ is chosen to be the configuration tensor $\underline{\underline{c}}$ then the usual choice of $\hat{\Psi}^+$ (see Giesekus [28]) is

$$\hat{\Psi}^{+}_{ij} = - \Lambda\, c_{ik} \frac{\partial G}{\partial c_{kj}} , \tag{4.17}$$

where Λ denotes the mobility. If $\Lambda > 0$ and $\underline{\underline{c}}$ is positive definite then the inequality (4.16) is clearly satisfied. The mobility Λ can depend on tr $\underline{\underline{c}}$ (see Hinch [36] and de Gennes [21]) and it can be also non isotropic, i.e. Λ can be a tensor (see Giesekus [28]). A different form of $\hat{\Psi}^{+}$ was used by Leonov [43].

Fourth sept - Formula for the Stress Tensor. Finally, we turn our attention to the appearence of the additional state variable Ψ in the stress tensor (we limit our interest to isothermal processes and ignore the heat flux). It has been found in Grmela [30] that the requirement of the compatibility of the hydrodynamic equations and the equation (4.14) with equilibrium thermodynamics implies

$$\tau_{ij} = -\rho T \int \frac{\delta \hat{\Psi}^{-}}{\delta \kappa_{ji}} \frac{\delta G}{\delta \Psi(\underline{r},x,t)} \, dx, \tag{4.18}$$

where $\underline{\underline{\tau}}$ is the extra stress tensor and $\kappa_{ji} = \partial v_j / \partial r_i$. It means that once the generating functional G and the generalized time derivative are chosen then the extra stress tensor is determined uniquely and universally by equation (4.18). In the case $\Psi \equiv \underline{\underline{c}}$, the formula (4.18) becomes

$$\tau_{ij} = - \rho T \frac{\partial \hat{\Psi}^{-}_{kl}}{\partial \kappa_{ij}} \frac{\partial G}{\partial c_{kl}} \tag{4.19}$$

The summation convention has been used in equation (4.19). The temperature T has been used in this section as having the physical dimension of energy. If we want to use T in degrees of Kelvin, we have to replace T by $k_B T$ where k_B is the Boltzmann constant.

Summary. A specific rheological model is obtained by choosing the additional state variable Ψ, the functionals e_{int}, s_{int} (see equations (4.3) and (4.10)) and $\hat{\Psi}^{-}$, $\hat{\Psi}^{+}$ (see equations (4.14) and (4.15)). The choice of $\hat{\Psi}^{+}$ is restricted by the inequality (4.16), the choice of Ψ, e_{int}, s_{int}, $\hat{\Psi}^{-}$ is unrestricted. The advantages of the master model are the following: i) All rheological models corresponding to all possible choices of Ψ,

e_{int}, s_{int}, $\hat{\Psi}^-$ and $\hat{\Psi}^+$ (the inequality (4.16) is assumed to be satisfied) are guaranteed to be compatible with equilibrium thermodynamics. It means that in the case of no flow (i.e. $\underline{\underline{\kappa}} \equiv 0$) the results of the models agree with the experimental observations (i.e. a fluid subjected to no external forces reaches an equilibrium state; at this state, the fluid properties are described well by equilibrium thermodynamics). The equilibrium thermodynamics implied by the rheological model is determined by the thermodynamic entropy S_{th}, the thermodynamic energy E_{th}, and the thermodynamic mass M_{th}, where S_{th}, E_{th}, M_{th} are the functionals, S, E, M introduced in the second step and evaluated at (ρ, $\underline{v}$, e, Ψ) that correspond to the equilibrium state (see more in Grmela [30 , 31]).

ii) The master model provides a convenient setting for a unification of various existing rheological models (see section 4.2).

iii) A choice of Ψ, e_{int}, s_{int}, $\hat{\Psi}^-$, $\hat{\Psi}^+$ represents a mathematical formulation of an intuitive insight into the structure and dynamics of polymeric fluids under consideration. Everyone who has such insight can suggest Ψ, e_{int}, s_{int}, $\hat{\Psi}^-$, $\hat{\Psi}^+$ and thus construct the rheological model corresponding to the insight.

4.2 Examples. Finally, we shall illustrate the master model. The first choice of Ψ, e_{int}, s_{int}, $\hat{\Psi}^-$, $\hat{\Psi}^+$ that we shall consider is the following: the internal state variable Ψ is chosen to be a configuration tensor $\underline{\underline{c}}(t)$ that is assumed to be symmetric, positive definite and independent of the position vector $\underline{r}$ (see Giesekus [28]). The term $\partial\underline{\underline{c}}/\partial t - \hat{\Psi}^-$ is chosen to be the upper convected derivative (2.8), $\hat{\Psi}^+$ is chosen as in equation (4.17), where Λ is left to be an unspecified function of tr $\underline{\underline{\tau}}$. The function e_{int} is chosen as in equation (4.5) and (4.6), the modulus H is left to be an unspecified function of tr $\underline{\underline{c}}$. The function s_{int} is chosen as in equation (4.12). The resulting rheological model is then given by the following set of equations:

$$\frac{dc_{ij}}{dt} = c_{kj}\,\kappa_{ik} + c_{ik}\,\kappa_{jk} + \frac{1}{2n}\,\Lambda(\mathrm{tr}\,\underline{\underline{\tau}}^{(P)})\,\tau_{ij}^{(P)} \tag{4.20}$$

$$\tau_{ij}^{(P)} = nk_BT\,\delta_{ij} - n\,H(\mathrm{tr}\,\underline{\underline{c}})c_{ij} \tag{4.21}$$

$$\tau_{ij} = \tau_{ij}^{(S)} + \tau_{ij}^{(P)}, \tag{4.22}$$

where the supperscripts P and S stand for polymer and solvent respectively. As in the case of kinetic theories of dilute polymer solutions (see section 2), the solvent contribution to the stress tensor has been added; n is the number of macromolecules per unit volume (the mass density ρ in section 4.1). Equations (4.20) and (4.21) are two tensorial equations for two unknowns tensor $\underline{\underline{c}}$ and $\underline{\underline{\tau}}^{(P)}$.

We consider steady shear flows (equation (1.1) with $\dot{\gamma}(t) = \dot{\gamma}$ = constant) and steady uniaxial elongational flows (equation (1.13) with $\dot{\varepsilon}(t) = \dot{\varepsilon}$ = constant). It means that the tensor $\underline{\underline{\kappa}}$ is known. Our objective is to calculate η, Ψ_1, Ψ_2 (equations (1.2) - (1.4) and η_E (equation(1.14)). We shall try to postpone the choice of $\Lambda(\mathrm{tr}\ \underline{\underline{\tau}}^{(P)})$ and $H(\mathrm{tr}\ \underline{\underline{c}})$ as late as possible. Before listing the results, we make a few comments about the rheological model defined by equations (4.20) - (4.22):

First, we note that if equation (4.21) can be solved to obtain $\underline{\underline{c}}$ as an explicit function of $\underline{\underline{\tau}}^{(P)}$, then the solution can be inserted into equation (4.20) and we obtain in this way one tensorial equation for one unknown tensor $\underline{\underline{\tau}}^{(P)}$ (the so-called rheological equation of state). There are however physically interesting cases for which equation (4.21) cannot be solved explicitely (e.g. if the modulus H exhibits maxima and minima). We keep therefore the more general form of the rheological equation of state that consists of the three equations, the first one determining the time evolution of the additional (configurational) state variable, the second being a relation between the contribution of the polymer to the extra stress tensor and the additional state variable, and the third being the sum of the polymer and the solvent contributions. The physical insight that is included in the rheological model (4.20) - (4.22) is the following. The choice of $\hat{\Psi}^-$ is based on the assumption that the configuration tensor $\underline{\underline{c}}$ deforms in the same way as the whole fluid (affine deformation). The choice of s_{int} (see equation (4.12)) corresponds to the assumption of an isotropic Brownian motion. A configuration dependent but isotropic mobility Λ is considered in the choice of $\hat{\Psi}^+$. The energy e_{int} associated with the configuration tensor $\underline{\underline{c}}$ is assumed to be arbitrary. Not included in the model (4.20) - (4.22) are: a slip (see for examples Phan-Thien and Tanner [51] and Johnson and Segalman [39]), an internal viscosity (Kuhn and Kuhn [41] and Cerf [17]) an anisotropic mobility (Giesekus [28]) and an anisotropic Brownian motion (Curtiss and Bird [19, 20]). Consequences of some of these generalizations will be briefly analyzed in the last part of this section. If Λ = constant and H = constant, then the equations (4.20) - (4.22) reduce to the upper convected Maxwell model. If Λ = constant and $H = H_o(1-\text{tr}\underline{\underline{c}}/R_o^2)$ then we obtain the FENE-P model (see section 2.1).

Now we proceed to solve equations (4.20) - (4.22) for steady shear and uniaxial elongation flows. First, we look for invariants of the rheological model (4.20) - (4.22). We say that a given property is an invariant of the rheological model if it is independent of the choice of $\Lambda(\text{tr}\,\underline{\underline{\tau}}^{(P)})$ and $H(\text{tr}\underline{\underline{c}})$. The invariants thus clearly indicate limitations of the model and can be used as rheological tests (see section 3.2). If we compare the invariants with observations and find a disagreement, we know that the disagreement cannot be fixed by a choice of $\Lambda(\text{tr}\,\underline{\underline{\tau}}^{(P)})$ and $H(\text{tr}\,\underline{\underline{c}})$. The disagreement would indicate that the physical processes that are not included in the model play an important role. We have found (see Grmela et al. [35]) the following invariants of the rheological model (4.20) - (4.22):

$$\Psi_2 = 0 \tag{4.23}$$

$$\Psi_1 = 2(\eta - \eta_s)^2/nk_BT \tag{4.24}$$

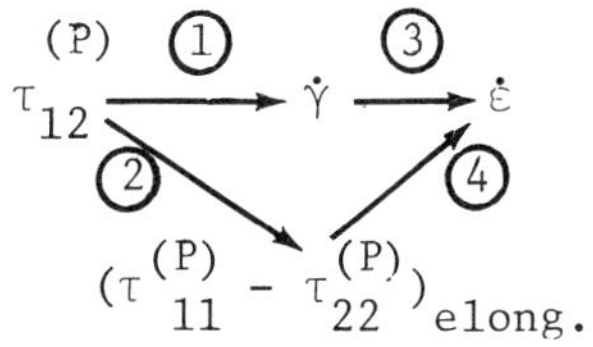

(4.25)

The equations (4.23) and (4.24) are clear, the relation (4.25) shows how the elongational viscosity $\eta_E(\dot{\varepsilon})$ can be obtained from $\eta(\dot{\gamma})$. The passage ① is the function $\eta(\dot{\gamma})$; the passage ② is:

$$(\tau_{11}^{(p)} - \tau_{22}^{(p)})_{\text{elong.}} = -\tau_{12}^{(P)\,2}/2\,nk_BT + \tau_{12}^{(P)}\{\tfrac{9}{4}\tau_{12}^{(P)\,2}/(nk_BT)^2+3\}^{1/2} \tag{4.26}$$

the passage ③ is:

$$\dot{\varepsilon} = \dot{\gamma}\, \tau_{12}^{(P)} / (\tau_{11}^{(P)} - \tau_{22}^{(P)})_{elong.} \tag{4.27}$$

and the passage ④ determines the elongational viscosity $\eta_E(\dot{\varepsilon})$. It can be shown easily that relation (4.25) implies the Trouton relation:

$$\lim_{\dot{\varepsilon} \to 0} \eta_E(\dot{\varepsilon}) = 3 \lim_{\dot{\gamma} \to 0} \eta(\dot{\gamma}) \tag{4.28}$$

and in addition the relation

$$m' = 2n'/(1-n') \tag{4.29}$$

where m' and n' are respectively the power-law indices of the elongational viscosity, $\eta_E(\dot{\varepsilon}) \sim \dot{\varepsilon}^{m'-1}$ for $\dot{\varepsilon} \to \infty$ and of the shear viscosity, $\eta(\dot{\gamma}) \sim \dot{\gamma}^{n'-1}$ for $\dot{\gamma} \to \infty$.

In Figure 4.1, we compare relation (4.24) with five sets of data of various polymer solutions obtained by different investigators. The 1.0 and

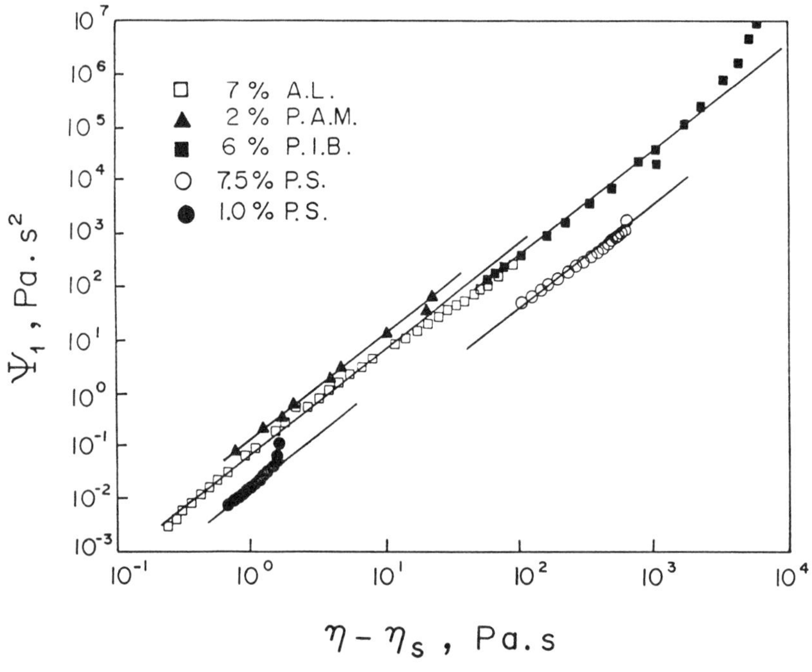

Figure 4.1 Experimental evaluation of relation (4.24).

7.5 P.S. are respectively 1.0% and 7.5% solutions of narrow molecular weight polystyrene (M_w = 860,000) in Aroclor 1248. The data are from Ashare [4a]. The7.0% A.L. is a 7% solution of aluminum laurate in decalin and m-cresol. The data are from Huppler et al.[36a]. The 2.0% P.A.M. is a 2% solution of polyacrylamide (A.P. 30 of Dow Chemical) in a 50%/50% mixture of water and glycerine. The 6% P.I.B. is a 6% solution polyisobutylene ($M_w \sim 1.5 \times 10^7$) in Primol 355. These two set of data are from our laboratory. The range of rheological properties covered by these solutions is quite large, with variations of Ψ_1 from 10^{-3} to 10^{+7}. Although most of these solutions are ill-characterized, the molecular weight and the distribution of the molecular weight of the polymers used being unknown, and are not dilute solutions, it is surprising to observe a very good agreement in all cases, as shown by the straight lines of slope 2, except possibly for the low shear-rate data (higher values of $\eta - \eta_s$ and of Ψ_1) for which it is well known that the Ψ_1 data are not reliable. It is clear from these results, that anisotropy or slip effects do not play an important role in the rheological behaviour of polymer solutions. The situation appears to be totally different in the case of polymer melts for which relation (4.24) is no longer valid. This is being investigated and will be reported elsewhere.

<u>4.2-1 Specific choices for the modulus and the mobility</u>. Now, we shall solve equations (4.20), (4.21) for some specific choices of the modulus H and the mobility Λ. As it follows from the relations (4.23) - (4.25), it suffices to calculate only shear viscosity $\eta(\dot{\gamma})$. First, we focus our attention on the asymptotic behaviour $\dot{\gamma} \to \infty$ and $\dot{\gamma} \to 0$. The following result can be easily obtained from equations (4.20) and (4.21) (see Grmela et al. [35]) of

$$H(\mathrm{tr}\underline{\underline{c}}) \sim (\mathrm{tr}\underline{\underline{c}})^p \text{ as } (\mathrm{tr}\underline{\underline{c}}) \to \infty, \quad \lim_{(\mathrm{tr}\underline{\underline{c}})\to 0} H(\mathrm{tr}\underline{\underline{c}}) = H_o \tag{4.30}$$

and

$$\Lambda(\mathrm{tr}\underline{\underline{\tau}}^{(P)}) \sim |\mathrm{tr}\underline{\underline{\tau}}^{(P)}|^q \text{ as } |\mathrm{tr}\underline{\underline{\tau}}^{(P)}| \to \infty, \quad \lim_{|\mathrm{tr}\underline{\underline{\tau}}^{(P)}|\to 0} \Lambda(\mathrm{tr}\underline{\underline{\tau}}^{(P)}) = \Lambda_o \tag{4.31}$$

then

$$(\eta - \eta_s) \sim \dot{\gamma}^{n'-1} \text{as } \dot{\gamma} \to \infty \tag{4.32}$$

and

$$\lim_{\dot{\gamma} \to 0} (\eta - \eta_s) = \frac{nk_BT}{\Lambda_o H_o} \tag{4.33}$$

where

$$n' = \frac{p + 1}{2pq + 2q + 3p + 1} \tag{4.34}$$

It means that we can match any power law exponent n' by choosing appropriately the asymptotic behaviour of the modulus and the mobility. We have already mentioned that the upper convected Maxwell model corresponds to H = const., Λ = const. (i.e. $p = 0$, $q = 0$) and the FENE-P model to $H = H_o(1 - \mathrm{tr}\underline{\underline{c}}/R_o^2)$, Λ = const. (i.e. $p \to \infty$, $q = 0$). By using the formula (4.34) we obtain the well known power law exponent $n'=1$ for the upper convected Maxwell model and $n'=1/3$ for the FENE-P model.

Now we shall calculate completely the shear viscosity $\eta(\dot{\gamma})$. The results corresponding to the choices H = constant, Λ = constant and $H = H_o/(1-\mathrm{tr}\underline{\underline{c}}/R_o^2)$, Λ = constant have been reported in section 2. Here, we consider another choice:

$$H = \frac{H_o}{(1 - \mathrm{tr}\underline{\underline{c}}/R_o^2)} - \frac{E}{2} \frac{1}{(\mathrm{tr}\underline{\underline{c}})^{3/2}} \tag{4.35}$$

$$\Lambda = \frac{1}{\zeta_o(1 + \beta(\mathrm{tr}\underline{\underline{c}}/R_o^2)^{1/2})}, \tag{4.36}$$

where H_o, E, ζ_o, β are constant parameters. From the physical point of view, the first term on the right hand side of equation (4.35) is the FENE-P modulus, the second term is the modulus corresponding to the Coulombic force. The parameter E is an effective electrical charge. The Coulombic force has been introduced into the dumbbell model of Dunlap and Leal [26]. The mobility (4.36) has been introduced by Tanner [56]. The Tanner choice of Λ corresponds to the assumption that the friction coefficient equals a constant plus a linear function of the length (that is proportional to $(\mathrm{tr}\underline{\underline{c}})^{1/2}$) of the macromolecule. We have introduced the choice (4.35) and (4.36) in order to explain measurements of the shear viscosity of polyelectrolyte solutions (see Ait Kadi [4]). In Figure 4.2, we compare the model predictions with steady-shear viscosity data obtained by Ait Kadi [4] for various solutions of polyacrylamide (Pusher-700 of Dow Chemicals) in a mixture 50%/50% per weight of water and glycerine. The solutions contain also 20 g/l of NaCl. The data are reported for four polymer concentrations as

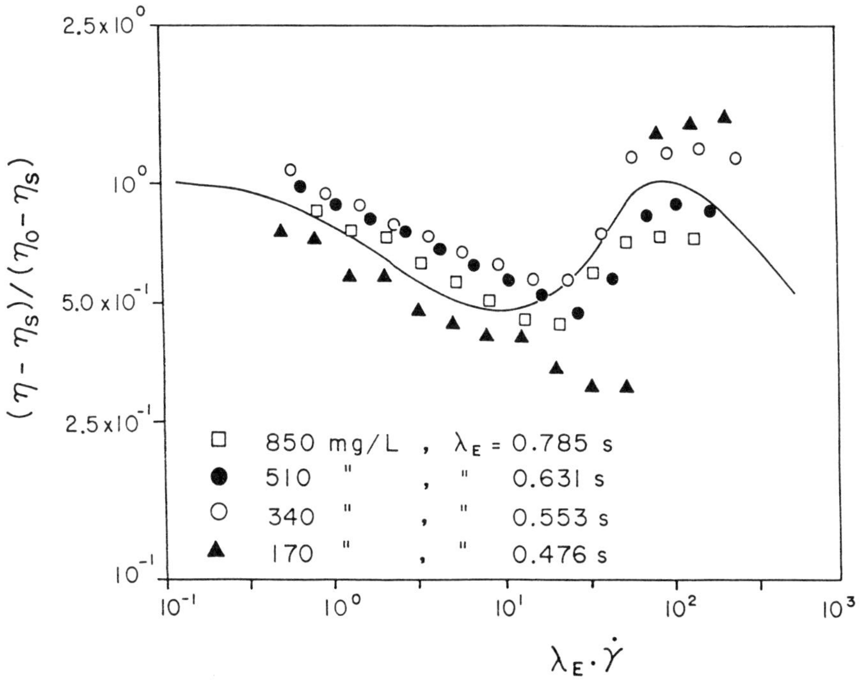

Figure 4.2 Comparison of the configuration model predictions with steady-shear viscosity data of polyacrylamide solutions. Taken from Ait Kadi [4]. The parameters are $b=5\times10^4$, $\beta=5$ and $e=ER_o^3/k_BT = 0.05$.

a reduced viscosity as a function of a dimensioneless shear rate $\lambda_E\dot{\gamma}$, where λ_E is defined in equation (2.17). These partially hydrolysed polyacrylamide solutions exhibit a shear-thickening behaviour above a critical shear rate.

It is interesting to note that the model gives a good description of the observed phenomenon, which is accounted for by the conformation-dependence parameter β. The values of λ_E were estimated from intrinsic viscosity measurements, correcting partially for polymer-polymer interaction. Clearly, the differences between the viscosity data for the different polymer concentrations indicate more important interactions than predicted by the Huggins equation [37].

4.2.2 Some Generalizations. How the relations (4.23) - (4.25) change if the terms $\hat{\Psi}^-$ and $\hat{\Psi}^+$ are generalized? A partial answer to this question is the following. Let $\hat{\Psi}^-$ be generalized to include a slip (see for example Phan-Thien and Tanner [51] and Johnson and Segalman [39]), i.e.

$$\Psi^-_{ij} = 1/2(g+1)c_{kj}\kappa_{ik} + 1/2(g+1)c_{ik}\kappa_{jk} + 1/2(g-1)c_{ik}\kappa_{kj} + 1/2(g-1)c_{kj}\kappa_{kj}, \tag{4.37}$$

and $\hat{\Psi}^+$ is generalized to include the tensorial mobility, (see Giesekus [28]) i.e.

$$\hat{\Psi}^+_{ij} = -(\Lambda_{ik}\, c_{kl}\, \frac{\partial G}{\partial c_{lj}})_{sym}, \tag{4.38}$$

where $(\quad)_{sym}$ denotes the symmetric part. We note that if the slip coefficient g=1, then $\partial \underline{\underline{c}}/\partial t - \hat{\Psi}^-$ is the upper convective derivative used before. Similarly, if $\Lambda_{ik} = \Lambda\delta_{ik}$, we get the term $\hat{\Psi}^+$ used in section 4.2-1. It can be shown (see Grmela et al. [35]) that if $\hat{\Psi}^-$ and $\hat{\Psi}^+$ are given by equations (4.37) and (4.38) then equation (4.23) generalizes into

$$(g+1)(\Lambda_{22}\tau_{22}+\Lambda_{12}\tau_{12}) = (g-1)(\Lambda_{11}\tau_{11}+\Lambda_{12}\tau_{12}) \tag{4.39}$$

and equation (4.24) into

$$(\Lambda_{11}\tau_{11}+\Lambda_{12}\tau_{12})\left(\frac{2g^2}{g+1}\rho k_B T - \tau_{22} - \frac{g-1}{g+1}\tau_{11}\right) = -(\Lambda_{11}+\Lambda_{22})\tau_{12}^2 - \Lambda_{12}\tau_{12}(\tau_{11}+\tau_{22}) \tag{4.40}$$

More complete results will be published elsewhere.

5. CONCLUDING REMARKS

We have illustrated in this chapter various approaches to the rheological modeling of polymer solutions and melts. This review is clearly incomplete and some recent ideas, possibly quite promising, have been omitted for reason of space and difficulty of treating completly the subject. Our emphasis has been on presenting concepts and theories which are based on a molecular description of the polymer molecules, but which will lead to the reasonable predictions or descriptions of the flow properties in engineering applications, the so-called non-linear rheological properties. It is obvious that none of the theories presented here give a correct description of the relaxation spectrum of the macromolecules as one can determine from linear dynamic experiments under a large range of frequency. The kinetic theories such as FENE-P chain and reptation models incorporate relaxation spectra, but these are too simple to represent correctly real situations; the network theories have also been criticized for not incorporating a priori information or details of the relaxation spectrum.

We nevertheless believe that a detailed and corrected relaxation spectrum is not necessary for the description of non-linear rheological properties such as shear-thinning viscosity, normal stress differences and elongational viscosity under steady-state or transient conditions. One or hopefully only a few relaxation times are needed to characterize non-linear effects. Those are macroscopic properties which can be characterized by integral-average types of relaxation times, possibly a short relaxation time for rapidly changing flow situations and a long relaxation time for molecular or diffusional processes. Evidences of that can be found in the work of DeKee and Carreau [22] and of Soong and Shen [55a].

The most successful and popular kinetic theories such the FENE-P chain and reptation theories cannot be easily generalized to incorporate more realistic descriptions of the polymer chains. The solution of the coupled stress and diffusion equations becomes an impossible task. The network concepts still represent interesting alternatives to the modeling of the rheological behaviour of concentrated polymer solutions or melts. The recent work of Jongschaap [38] and of Soong and Shen [55a] who proposed a more detailed kinetics for the rates of creation and of loss of entanglements is a clear indication of potential success.

Another and possibly highly successfull and more general route is to adopt a mesoscopic view as we have done in section 4. We have organized the process of constructing a rheological model into four steps. Everyone who has an insight into the structure of polymeric liquids, based on experience, can construct by following the steps proposed a model which will fit best the needs required. As an illustration, we have introduced a family of rheological models that explain the universality of the relation between the shear viscosity and the first normal stress differences found in experiments with polymer solutions. In another example, we have proposed a model that describes shear-thickening effects observed with polyelectrolyte solutions.

ACKNOWLEDGMENTS

We wish to acknowledge the most appreciated help of Mr. A. Ait Kadi who carried all the calculations and the experimental evaluations presented in sections 2 and 4. We also wish to acknowledge the financial support received from the National Science and Engineering Research Council of Canada.

NOTATION

A	Helmoltz free energy per unit volume
b	chain flexibility parameter in FENE-P model, $H_o R_o^2/k_B T$
b_n	parameters in network theories
c	polymer concentration
$\underline{\underline{c}}$	configuration state tensor
C_j	Rouse eigenvalues in equation (2.21)
$\underline{\underline{C}}$	Cauchy-Green strain tensor
$\underline{\underline{C}}^{-1}$	Finger strain tensor
e	internal specific energy or parameter in configurational model
e_{int}	part of the specific energy that depends on the additional state variable
f	distribution function in the Curtiss-Bird theory
f_p	functional dependence of the rates of creation of segments in the Carreau theory
F	distribution function in network theories
$\underline{F}$	force acting on beads in molecular theories
g	rate of creation of free segments in the Jongschaap theory or slip coefficient in configurational rheological models.
g_p	function dependence of the rate of loss of segments in the Carreau theory
G	generating functional
h	rate of loss of free segments in the Jongschaap theory
$h(t)$	Heaviside function

H modulus
k_B Boltzmann's constant
l length of a rigid link in network theories
L_n rates of creation of segments in network theories
m' power-law index for the elongational viscosity
m, m_1, m_2 memory functions in network theories
M total mass
$M(t-t, II)$ functional defined by equation (3.15)
M_w molecular weight
n number density of dumbbells, parameter in the Wagner model or index of segments in network theories
n' power-law index for the shear viscosity
N number of chain elements
P index of segments in the Carreau theory
P_{th} equilibrium pressure
$\underline{Q}_j$ end-to-end vector in FENE-P chain model
$\underline{r}$ position vector
$\underline{R}$ end-to-end vector of a dumbbell
R_o maximum extensibility of a dumbbell
tr trace of a tensor
T temperature
T_{th} equilibrium temperature
$\underline{u}$ chain orientation vector in the Curtiss-Bird theory
U total energy
$\underline{v}$ velocity vector

Greek letters

β conformation parameter in configurational model
$\dot{\gamma}$ shear rate
Γ stress growth function defined (by equation (3.21))
$\underline{\underline{\delta}}$ unit tensor
ε parameter in Carreau or Curtiss-Bird theories
$\dot{\varepsilon}$ elongational rate
ζ bead friction coefficient
η shear viscosity
η_E elongational viscosity
$\underline{\underline{\kappa}}$ $\nabla\underline{v}^+$
λ time constant
λ_E time constant defined by equation (2.17)
μ_{th} equilibrium chemical potential
ρ mass density
$\underline{\underline{\tau}}$ stress tensor
Ψ distribution function or additional state variable
Ψ_1 primary normal stress coefficient (equation 1.3)
Ψ_2 secondary normal stress coefficient (equation 1.4)
$\hat{\Psi}$ right hand side of the governing equation of the additional state variable
$\hat{\Psi}^{\pm}$ even or odd part of $\hat{\Psi}$

Operators and indices

D/Dt substantial or material derivative

δ/δ_t	functional derivation
$\mathfrak{d}/\mathfrak{d}_t$	upper convected derivative defined in equation (2.8)
I_c	first invariant of the Finger strain tensor
II_c	second invariant of the Finger strain tensor
$II_{\dot{\gamma}}$	second invariant of the rate of strain tensor
n	index of segments in network theories
o	equilibrium value
P	polymer contribution
s	solvent contribution
+	stress growth function
-	stress relaxation function

REFERENCES

1. Acierno, D., F.P. LaMantia, G. Marrucci, and G. Titomanlio, J. NNFM, 1, 125 (1976).
2. Acierno, D., F.P. LaMantia, G. Marrucci, G. Rizzo and G. Titomanlio, J. NNFM, 1, 147 (1976).
3. Acierno, D., F.P. LaMantia, G. Marrucci, J. NNFM, 2, 271 (1977).
4. Ait Kadi, A., "Comportement rhéologique des polymères utilisés en récupération du pétrole", Ph.D. Thesis, Ecole Polytechnique, Montréal (1985)
4a. Ashare, E., Ph.D., Thesis, University of Wisconsin, Madison (1967).
5. Attané, P., P. LeRoy and G. Turrel, J. NNFM, 6, 269 (1980).
6. Attané, P., J.M. Pierrard, and P.J. Carreau, in Advances in Rheology, Vol. 1, p. 337, edited by B. Mena, A. Garcia-Rejon and C. Rangel-Nafaile (1984).
7. Attané, P., G. Turrel, J.M. Pierrard and P.J. Carreau, "Rheological Tests for Integral Constitutive Equations", submitted to J. Rheol. (1985).
8. Bird, R.B., J. Rheol., 26, 277 (1982).
9. Bird, R.B., Chem. Eng. Commun., 16, 175 (1982).
10. Bird, R.B. and P.J. Carreau, Chem. Eng. Sci., 23, (1968).
11. Bird, R.B., R.C. Armstrong, and O. Hassager, "Dynamics of Polymeric Liquids", Volume I, Wiley, N.Y. (1977).
12. Bird, R.B., O. Hassager, R.C. Armstrong, and C.F. Curtiss, "Dynamics of Polymeric Liquids", Volume II, Wiley, N.Y. (1977).
13. Bird, R.B., P.J. Dotson and N.L. Johnson, J. NNFM, 7, 213 (1980).
14. Bogue, D.C. and J.O. Doughty, Ind. Eng. Chem. Fundam., 5, 243 (1966).
15. Boltzmann, L., "Wissenschaftlichen Aghandlungen von Ludwig Boltzmann, Vol. 2, Chelsea, N.Y. (1968).
16. Carreau, P.J., Trans. Soc. Rheol., 16, 99 (1972).
17. Cerf, R., J. Polym. Sci., 23, 125 (1957).
18. Chang, H.F. and R. Darby, J. Rheol., 27, 77 (1983).
19. Curtiss, C.F. and R.B. Bird, J. Chem. Phys. 74, 2016 (1981).
20. Curtiss, C.F. and R.B. Bird, J. Chem. Phys. 74, 2026 (1981)
21. de Gennes, P.G., J. Chem. Phys., 60, 5030 (1974).
22. DeKee, D. and P.J. Carreau, J. NNFM, 6, 127 (1979).
23. Doi, M. and S.F. Edwards, J. Chem. Soc. Faraday, Trans. II, 74, 1789, 1802, 1818 (1978).
24. Doi, M. and S.F. Edwards, J. Chem. Soc. Faraday, Trans II, 75, 38, (1979).
25. Doughty, J.O. and D.C. Bogue, Ind. Eng. Chem. Fund., 6, 388 (1967).
26. Dunlap, R.N. and L.G. Leal, Rheol. Acta, 23, 238 (1984).
27. Giesekus, H., Rheol. Acta, 5, 29 (1966).

28. Giesekus, H., J. NNFM, 11, 69 (1982).
29. Green, M.S. and A.V. Tobolsky, J. Chem. Phys., 14, 80 (1946).
30. Grmela, M., Phys. Letters 111A, 36, 41, (1985).
31. Grmela, M., "Diffusion-Convection Equations", submitted to Physica D. (1985).
32. Grmela, M., "Non-equilibrium Extensions of the Simha-Somcynsky Equilibrium Theory of Polymeric Fluids", to appear in J. Rheol (1986).
33. Grmela, M. and P.J. Carreau, in Advances in Rheology, Vol. 1, p. 525, edited by B. Mena, A. Garcia-Rejon and C. Rangel-Nafaile (1984).
34. Grmela, M. and P.J. Carreau, in Recent Developments in Structured Continua, p. 111, edited by D. DeKee and P.N. Kaloni, University of Windsor (May 1985).
35. Grmela, M. and P.J. Carreau, "Consequences of a Family of Rheological Models in Steady Shear and Elongational Flows", submitted to J. NNFM (1985).
36. Hinch, E.J. Colloques Internationaux du C.N.R.S., No. 233, 241, (1974).
36a. Huppler, J.D., Ph.D. Thesis, University of Wisconsin, Madison (1965).
37. Huggins, M.L., J. Am. Chem. Soc., 64, 2716 (1942).
38. Jongschaap, R.J.J., H. Kamphuis, and D.K. Doeksen, Rheol. Acta, 22, 539 (1983).
39. Johnson Jr., M.W. and D. Segalman, J. NNFM, 2, 225 (1981).
40. Kaye, A., Br. J. Appl. Phys., 17, 803 (1966).
41. Kuhn, W. and H. Kuhn, Helv. Chim. Acta, 28, 1533 (1945).
42. Larson, R.G., J. NNFM, 13, 279 (1983).
43. Leonov, A.I., Rheol. Acta, 15, 85 (1976).
44. Lodge, A.S., "Elastic Liquids", Academic Press, N.Y. (1964).
45. Lodge, A.S., Rheol. Acta, 7, 379 (1968).
46. Lodge, A.S., R.C. Armstrong, M.H. Wagner, and H.H. Winter, "Constitutive Equations from Gaussian Molecular Network Theories in Polymer Rheology", IUPAC Division Working Party Report (1979).
47. Macdonald, I.F., Rheol. Acta, 14, 801, 899, 906 (1975).
48. Meister, B.J., Trans. Soc. Rheol, 15, 63 (1971).
49. Olbricht, W.L., J.M. Rallison and L.G. Leal, J. NNFM, 10, 291 (1982).
50. Peterlin, A., J. Polym. Sci., Polym. Lett., 4B, 287 (1966).
51. Phan-Thien, N., and R.I. Tanner, J. NNFM, 2, 353 (1977).
52. Rouse, P.E., J. Chem. Phys., 21, 1272 (1953).
53. Saab, H.H., R.B. Bird and C.F. Curtiss, University of Wisconsin Rheology Research Center, Report No. 79, (1982).
54. Sarti, G.C. and G. Marrucci, Chem. Eng. Sci., 28, 1053 (1973).
55. Schowalter, W.R., "Mechanics of Non-Newtonian Fluids", Pergamon P.(1978)
55a. Soong, O.S. and M. Shen, Polym. Eng. Sci., 20, 1177, (1980).
56. Tanner, R.I., Trans. Soc. Rheol., 19, 557 (1975).
57. Tsai, C.F., and R. Darby, J. Rheol., 22, 219 (1978).
58. van Es, H.E. and R.M. Christensen, Trans. Soc. Rheol., 17, 325 (1973).
59. Wagner, M.H., Rheol. Acta, 15, 136 (1976).
60. Wagner, M.H., J. NNFM, 4, 39 (1978).
61. Wagner, M.H., Rheol. Acta, 18, 33 (1979).
62. Warner Jr. H.R., Ind. Eng. Chem. Fund., 11, 379 (1972).
63. Williams, M.C., AIChE J., 21, 1, (1975).
64. Yamamoto, M., J. Phys. Soc. Jpn., 11, 413 (1956).
65. Yamamoto, M.J. Phys. Soc. Jpn., 12, 1148 (1957) and 13, 1200 (1958).
66. Zimm, B.H., J. Chem. Phys. 24, 256 (1956).

D DE KEE

Equations of state from network theories in polymer rheology

1. Introduction

Several constitutive equations have been proposed over the years, in order to describe the flow behaviour of polymer solutions and melts. Periodically, review papers such as for example those by Spriggs et al. [44], Bogue and Doughty [7] and Carreau and De Kee [8] have appeared in the literature, describing the state of the art. More recently, the volumes by Bird et al. [5,6] which are now being rewritten, also provided a considerable amount of information in our area of interest.

This contribution reviews some of the efforts, dealing with equations of state inspired by network theories, which have been reported in the last decade. These models cannot be considered as being derived from a pure molecular theory because they are based on assumptions about the response of the molecules to macroscopic disturbances as opposed to deriving these responses from a molecular model. Equations derived from molecular reptation theories such as those by Doi and Edwards [18-21] and the more general approach by Curtis and Bird [11-13] are not discussed in this paper. Relations based on a molecular network which exhibits rubberlike behaviour and relations where linear viscoelastic behaviour is associated with an equilibrium structure under zero shear and where deviations from linearity are described by structural kinetics as well as the incorporation of a yield stress are treated here.

An overview of several of these recent equations is timely in view of some of the new tests which have been developed in the last few years, allowing for a better discrimination among the proposed rheological models and in view of the more accurate data which can be expected from newly developed test equipment.

2. General

In network theories, polymer molecules are assumed to form a network of temporary junctions. When the sample is in motion, the molecules slide past each other, loosing and forming junctions. Figure 1 shows a typical polymeric network.

Lodge [27,28] treated the macromolecular system as an incompressible, isotropic fluid for which the Helmholtz free energy per unit volume consists of a contribution of the segments (associated with the stress) and contributions from the solvent, from unattached polymer molecules and from the loose ends. Also, the times associated with changes in flow and with the creation and loss of segments are considered to be far superior to the times associated with the Brownian motion. That is to say, the methods of equilibrium statistical mechanics can be applied to calculate the stress.

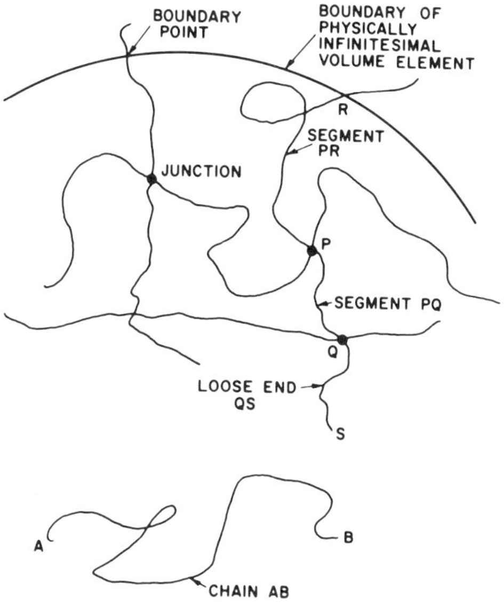

Figure 1: Polymer Network

For a network composed of Gaussian strands, where a Gaussian strand is such that if one end if at point 0 and the other end is within a volume element dV about a second point P, where OP = r, the configurations available are of equal potential energy and of number density $K\ \exp(-br^2)dV$, with K and b constant, the Helmholtz free energy per unit volume is given in terms of a convected segment distribution function by:

$$A(t) = \text{const.} + kT\ \hat{g}_{ij}(t) + \Sigma\ b_n \iiint_{-\infty}^{\infty} F(\hat{x},\hat{n},\hat{t})\hat{x}^i\hat{x}^j d^3\hat{x} \tag{2-1}$$

where $F(\hat{x},n,t)d^3\hat{x}$ represents a per unit volume number of segments whose end-to-end vectors are in the range $(\hat{x},\hat{x}+d\hat{x})$. The $\hat{x}^i$ are the convected coordinates and the $\hat{g}_{ij}$ are the covariant components of the body metric tensor. The constants b_n are defined by:

$$b_n = \frac{3}{2n\ \ell^2} \tag{2-2}$$

where n is the number of freely-jointed rigid links, each of length ℓ, which form a segment. In order to generate an expression for the segment distribution, one can characterize the earlier so called $(\hat{x},n)$-segments by an additional complexity parameter k. One can further assume that the now $(\hat{x},n,k)$ segments have the same probability τ_{kn}^{-1} (II) of leaving the network. On physical grounds, this probability can be related to the rate of deformation. Similarly, one assumes that the (n,k)-segments are created at the same rate per unit volume L_{kn} (II) (also a function of the rate of deformation) and that they have, at the instant of creation, the same distribution of $\hat{x}$-values as a set of free n-chains [47]. Following Carreau [9] one obtains a first order differential equation by performing a $(\hat{x},n,k)$-segment balance over a unit volume element $d^3\hat{x}$ over a time interval dt, resulting in the following expression:

$$\frac{d}{dt} F(\hat{x},n,k,t) + \frac{F(\hat{x},n,k,t)}{\tau_{kn}\ (II)} =$$

$$L_{kn}(II)\left(\frac{b_n}{\pi}\right)^{3/2} \exp[-b_n\ \hat{x}^r\hat{x}^s\hat{g}_{rs}(t)] \tag{2-3}$$

Solving for F and after simplification for homogeneous flow histories, one obtains the following relation for the Helmholtz free energy per unit volume:

$$A(t) = \text{const.} + \frac{1}{2}\ kT\ \hat{g}_{ij}(t) \int_{-\infty}^{t} N^*(t-t',II)\hat{g}^{ij}(t')dt' \tag{2-4}$$

where

$$N^{*}(t-t',II) = \sum_{k,n} L_{kn}[II(t')]\exp\{-\int_{t'}^{t} \frac{dt''}{\tau_{kn}[II(t'')]}\} \qquad (2\text{-}5)$$

As we know, the body components of the extra stress tensor are related to the Helmholtz free energy, assuming that the network behaves reversibly for small isothermal deformations, as follows:

$$dA = -\frac{1}{2}\hat{\tau}^{ij}\, d\,\hat{g}_{ij} \qquad (2\text{-}6)$$

From the symmetry of $\hat{g}_{ij}$ and from the incompressibility condition it further follows that:

$$\hat{\tau}^{ij} + p\hat{g}^{ij} = -kT \int_{-\infty}^{t} N^{*}(t-t',II)\hat{g}^{ij}(t')dt' \qquad (2\text{-}7)$$

where p is a constant and N^{*} is equivalent to a memory function. The number of segments per unit volume is given by:

$$N(t,II) = \int_{-\infty}^{t} N^{*}[t-t',II(t')]dt' \qquad (2\text{-}8)$$

In order to obtain the form of the WJFLMB model [45], which is a modification of Lodge's [29] elastic liquid model, by accounting for a dependence on the second invariant of the rate-of-deformation tensor, one introduces a combination of covariant and contravariant strain tensors and one replaces $\hat{g}^{ij}(t')$ of equation (7) by $\hat{g}^{ij}(t') - \hat{g}^{ij}(t)$.

In fixed coordinates we then obtain the following expression for the extra stress tensor:

$$\tau^{ij} = -pg^{ij} - \int_{\infty}^{t} m[t-t',II(t')]\{[1 + \frac{\varepsilon}{2}]\overline{\Gamma}^{ij}(t')$$

$$- \frac{\varepsilon}{2} g^{ir}(x)g^{js}(x)\Gamma_{rs}(t')\}dt' \qquad (2\text{-}9)$$

where the strain tensors $\overline{\Gamma}^{ij}$ and Γ_{rs} are defined by:

$$\overline{\Gamma}^{ij}(t') = -g^{ij}(x) + (\partial x^i/\partial x'^m)(\partial x^j/\partial x'^n)g^{mn}(x') \quad (2\text{-}10)$$

$$\Gamma_{ij}(t') = g_{ij}(x) - (\partial x'^m/\partial x^i)(\partial x'^n/\partial x^j)g_{mn}(x') \quad (2\text{-}11)$$

The g^{ij} and g_{ij} are the contravariant and covariant components of the fixed metric tensor, ε is a material constant and the x and x′ are the positions in space occupied by a material element at times t and t′, respectively.

The memory function $m = kTN^*$ can be written as:

$$m[t-t',II(t')] = \sum_{P=1}^{M} \frac{n_p f_p[II(t')]}{\lambda_p^2} \exp\{-\int_{t'}^{t} \frac{dt''}{\lambda_p g_p[II(t'')]}\} \quad (2\text{-}12)$$

where $n_p(= L_{kn}\,\tau_{kn}^2)$ and $\lambda_p(= \tau_{kn})$ are constants with units of viscosity and time, respectively. The dependence on the second invariant of the rate-of-deformation tensor is introduced through the functions f_p and g_p. The function f_p is related to the rate of creation of segments and the function g_p is associated with the probability of loss of segments. In the limit:

$$f_p = g_p = 1 \quad \text{as } II \rightarrow 0 \quad (2\text{-}13)$$

Several equations of state can thus be formulated through appropriate choices for the functions f_p and g_p. As always, the idea is to generate a constitutive equation capable of predicting simultaneously, a variety of steady-state material functions and functions accounting for the transient behaviour, in terms of a small number of physically meaningful parameters.

The Carreau model B [9] is still one of the most successful equations to date. The remaining sections of this contribution review several equations which were introduced during the last decade.

3. Models with Structural Parameters

In 1976, Marrucci's group [1 - 2] introduced a constitutive equation to describe the flow behaviour of concentrated polymer solutions and melts. Their model was a physically based empirical modification of the generalized Maxwell model and is given by the following set of equations:

$$\tau^{ij} = \sum_{P=1}^{\infty} \tau_p^{ij} \tag{3-1}$$

$$\frac{\tau_p^{ij}}{G_p} + \lambda_p \frac{\delta}{\delta t}\left(\frac{\tau_p^{ij}}{G_p}\right) = 2\lambda_p \dot{\gamma}^{ij} \tag{3-2}$$

$$G_p = G_{op}\, x_p; \qquad \lambda_p = \lambda_{op}\, x^{1.4} \tag{3-3}$$

$$\frac{dx_p}{dt} = \frac{1-x_p}{\lambda_p} - \frac{a\, x_p}{\lambda_p}\sqrt{\frac{\frac{1}{2} I_{\tau_p}}{G_p}} \tag{3-4}$$

where I_{τ_p} is the first invariant of the extra stress tensor and $\delta/\delta t$ is the convected derivative defined by:

$$\frac{\delta\bar{\bar{A}}}{\delta t} = \frac{\partial\bar{\bar{A}}}{\partial t} + \bar{v}\cdot\bar{\nabla}\bar{\bar{A}} - \bar{\nabla}\bar{v}\cdot\bar{\bar{A}} - \bar{\bar{A}}\cdot(\bar{\nabla}\bar{v})^{+} \tag{3-5}$$

G_{op} and λ_{op} are equilibrium values, describing the material behaviour in the linear viscoelastic range. The x_p describe the degree of structural non-equilibrium. The elastic modulus G_p is proportional to the junction concentration and the time dependent structural parameter x_p is a function of both the junction creation due to Brownian motion, which in turn is proportional to the junction concentration difference between the equilibrium and the actual states, and the rate of loss of junctions due to the stresses in the system.

In 1981, De Cleyn and Mewis [14] also proposed an equation based on the concept of structural kinetics. Their model represents a modification of Marrucci's ideas in that equation (3-4) is replaced by:

$$\frac{dx_p}{dt} = \frac{A}{\lambda_p^{0.3}} \left(\frac{1}{1 + a\sqrt{\frac{\frac{1}{2} I_{\tau_p}}{G_p}}} - x_p \right) \tag{3-6}$$

adding one additional parameter A.

Two years later, Mewis and Denn [36] published an equation of state based on the transient network concept, assuming that the rate of breakdown is proportional to the number of chains present and that the rate of formation is a Brownian process, proportional to the equilibrium distribution function of end-to-end vectors. This leads to a kinetic equation of the form:

$$\frac{dx_p}{dt} = a_p(1 - x_p) - b_p \, x_p \tag{3-7}$$

where $x_p = \frac{N_p}{N_{op}}$ represents the fraction relative to equilibrium of P-segments and a_p and b_p are parameters associated with the rates of formation and loss respectively. As such, a link is provided between the network models and the structural models.

The model can be written as:

$$\frac{1}{a_p + b_p} \frac{\hat{D} \, \tau_p^{ij}}{\hat{D}t} + \tau_p^{ij} = \frac{N_p \, k \, T}{a_p + b_p} \, 2(1 - \xi)\dot{\gamma}^{ij} \tag{3-8}$$

with

$$\tau^{ij} = \sum_{P=1}^{\infty} \tau_p^{ij} \tag{3-1}$$

$\frac{\hat{D}}{\hat{D}t}$ is a non-affine differential operator defined by Phan-Thien and Tanner [38]:

$$\frac{\hat{D}}{\hat{D}t}\bar{\bar{\tau}} = \frac{D}{Dt}\bar{\bar{\tau}} - \bar{\bar{L}}\,\bar{\bar{\tau}} - \bar{\bar{\tau}}\,\bar{\bar{L}}^{+} \qquad (3\text{-}9)$$

where the effective velocity gradient L is given by:

$$\bar{\bar{L}} = \bar{\nabla}\bar{v} - \xi\left[\frac{\bar{\nabla}\bar{v} + (\bar{\nabla}\bar{v})^{+}}{2}\right] \qquad (3\text{-}10)$$

and where $\frac{D}{Dt}$ is the substantial derivative $(= \frac{\partial}{\partial t} + \bar{v}\cdot\bar{\nabla})$. For $\xi = 0$ (affine deformation) this operator reduces to the convected derivative of equation (3-5). For $\xi = 1$, $\frac{\hat{D}}{\hat{D}t}$ corresponds to the Jaumann co-rotational derivative.

Soong and Shen [42] in the meantime introduced a simple equation to calculate the shear-rate-dependent viscosities of entangled polymers and particle suspensions. The structural state being determined by two competing processes: - structural breakdown which is caused by the imposed shear and which is given by:

$$\frac{dn_{\ell}}{dt} = k_{\ell}\,\dot{\gamma}^{m}\,n \qquad (3\text{-}11)$$

where k_{ℓ} is the loss rate constant, n is the prevailing number of intact structural points and m is a parameter which can be related to the elasticity of the medium, and - structural reformation, which is promoted by Brownian diffusion (independent of the flow field) and which is given by:

$$\frac{dn_{c}}{dt} = \frac{k_{c}}{\lambda^{m}}(n_{o} - n) \qquad (3\text{-}12)$$

where k_c is the creation rate constant, λ is a characteristic diffusion time and n_o represents the equilibrium number of structural points.

At steady state, the loss and creation rates are equal and the viscosity is computed as follows:

$$\frac{\eta(\dot{\gamma})}{\eta_{o}} = \frac{n(\dot{\gamma})}{n_{o}} = P(\dot{\gamma}) = \frac{1}{1 + b\dot{\gamma}^{m}} \qquad (3\text{-}13)$$

with $b = k_{\ell} \lambda^m/k_c$. P is the probability for a given entanglement to exist at shear rate $\dot{\gamma}$. Equation (3-11) does not account for the contribution of monomeric friction.

In 1981, Liu, Soong and Williams [25] discussed transient flow predictions, where the time dependent fluid structure is given by:

$$P(t,\dot{\gamma}) = \frac{n(t,\dot{\gamma})}{n_0} = P + (1-P)\exp[-k_{\ell}\dot{\gamma}^m t/(1-P)] \qquad (3\text{-}14)$$

A Maxwell model, for which the constants η_p and λ_p depend on the fluid structure, is further chosen to predict polymer flow characteristics.

Evaluation of the Models

The Marrucci model predictions are good in steady state. The secondary normal stress coefficient is zero, and the parameter a is determined from steady shear data. The model qualitatively predicts most nonlinear effects. Deviations for stress growth are appreciable at high shear rates. The difference between this model and Carreau's [9] model is that the relaxation times as well as the rates of junction creation and loss are assumed by Carreau to depend on the instantaneous value of the rate of strain while they depend on the past history of motion in the Marrucci approach. That is to say; the relaxation times are associated with the structural variables x_p. Therefore, the memory function for this model represents a functional relation over the flow history. A reduction of relaxation times is achieved only after an equilibrium modification. The dependence of the degree of non-equilibrium x_p on the first invariant of the stress tensor could possibly be modified to yield better results. Also, for these models, the rheological behaviour is described by coupled differential equations, resulting in a time consuming fit of experimental data and parameter determination. The values of λ_{op} and G_{op} have to be determined from the spectrum $H(\lambda)$.

In a 1981 paper, Jongschaap [23] showed that it was possible to derive both the constitutive equation (3-2) and the kinetic equation (3-4) of the Marrucci model from a balance law of the segment - distribution function in the transient network model. This makes it possible to identify which assumptions about this balance law are implicitly made in the Marrucci theory. Jongschaap's approach can also be applied to a special type of non-affine deformation. This involves an effective velocity gradient of the network and leads to a theory of the type formulated by Phan Thien and Tanner [38].

The ideas put forward by Mewis, improved on the flexibility of the Marrucci type model via the introduction of a second nonlinear parameter. Both models predict a total breakdown of the microstructure as $\dot{\gamma} \to \infty$. One could possibly consider a limiting structural state at high shear rate.

The model proposed by De Cleyn and Mewis does not differ from the Marrucci model under equilibrium conditions. These models predict the functions η, η' and η'' quite well. Comparisons are shown [14] with data for polyisobutylene and polyacrylamide solutions obtained using a modified (more rigid) Weissenberg rheogoniometer. The samples were also tested under parallel superposition flow for which the 1, 2-component of the shear rate tensor is given by:

$$\dot{\gamma}(t) = \dot{\gamma} + \omega\gamma_0 \, e^{i\omega t} \tag{3-15}$$

where γ_0 is the amplitude of the oscillatory deformation. The dynamic viscosity (η') predictions under parallel superposition are better than those under orthogonal superposition. Relaxation after cessation of flow $\eta^-(t,\dot{\gamma}_0)$ is rather well described and is shown to be somewhat insensitive to the structural kinetics. That is, changing the value of the parameter A in equation (3-6) does not affect the result to a great extent. Transient superposition experiments are much more sensitive to the additional kinetic parameter A. The same model parameters describe shear and extensional flow. Both the Marrucci and De Cleyn-Mewis models are less successful when it comes to predict stress growth functions. Marrucci's model tends to systematically underestimate the maxima in the $\eta^+(t,\dot{\gamma}_\infty)$ versus time curves.

Mewis and Denn [36] point out that the problem of parameter estimation increases considerably when non-affine deformation is considered . A simple kinetic formulation requires that two parameters be determined in addition to the linear viscoelastic spectrum, and unique choices do not exist. They formulated a kinetic equation of the form:

$$\frac{dx}{dt} = \frac{k_c}{\lambda^m}(1 - x) - k_\ell \dot{\gamma}^m x \tag{3-16}$$

to represent Soong's ideas in a Marrucci form and concluded that the dependence of x on $\dot{\gamma}$ precludes proper reduction to linear viscoelasticity. This however, is not easily justifiable.

The model by Soong et al. contains six parameters, several of which are determined from steady state shear stress data. The model is mathematically simple, quite versatile and can be applied to various complex flows. Liu et al. [25] show quite reasonable quantitative predictions for both the stress growth and the stress relaxation of a concentrated solution of monodisperse polystyrene. The prediction of these transient material functions show a discontinuity at t=0 as a consequence of the segmental contributions which lead to η_∞ in steady flow. De Kee [15] obtained a similar result earlier, using a different approach as pointed out in the next section. The existence of these offsets at t=0 is however still very difficult to ascertain experimentally. Liu et al. further report on the versatility of their model by showing model predictions related to i) interrupted flow, demonstrating that apparent disappearance of the stress is not a good indicator that a true equilibrium entanglement structure has been reestablished in the fluid, ii) a step increase in shear rate, which leads to the suggestion that such a gradual increase can lead to decreased stress overshoots, which could for example minimize melt fractures, iii) a step decrease in shear rate, iv) pre-steady state stress relaxation, etc. Their model differs from the Marrucci equation primarily in the kinetic equation and in the number of relaxation times involved. This greatly simplifies computation and allows for an easy adoption to solve practical engineering problems involving complicated flows.

4. Carreau Type Models

The Carreau model B [9] mentioned in section 2 is obtained by empirically defining the functions f_p and g_p, which introduce the second invariant of the rate-of-deformation tensor in equation (2-12), so as to obtain simple results for the non-Newtonian viscosity η and for the primary normal stress coefficient ψ_1. These functions are defined by:

$$f_{p-1}[II(t')] = \frac{1+[\frac{1}{2}(2^{\alpha}t_1)^2 II(t')]^s/P^{2\alpha}}{[1+(c^2/2)\lambda^2 II(t')]^{2R}} \qquad (4\text{-}1)$$

$$g_{p-1}[II(t'')] = \frac{[1 + (c^2/2)\lambda^2 \; II(t'')]^R}{1 + [\frac{1}{2}(2^{\alpha}t_1)^2 \; II(t'')]^s/P^{2\alpha}} \tag{4-2}$$

where R, s, t_1 and c are parameters related to nonlinear behaviour. A seven constant model is obtained by taking c=1.

In 1975, MacDonald [30-32] defined the functions f_p and g_p by:

$$f_p = \frac{1 + |(\frac{1}{2}\lambda_{1p}^2 \; II)^{1/2}|}{1 + |(\frac{1}{2}\lambda_{2p}^2 \; II)^{1/2}|} \tag{4-3}$$

$$g_p = \frac{[1 + |(\frac{1}{2}\lambda_{2p}^2 \; II)^{1/2}]^{0.5}}{[1 + |(\frac{1}{2}\lambda_{1p}^2 \; II)^{1/2}]^{1.5}} \tag{4-4}$$

where

$$\lambda_{1p} = \frac{2^{\alpha 1} \lambda_1}{(P+1)^{\alpha_1}} \tag{4-5}$$

$$\lambda_{2p} = \frac{2^{\alpha_2} \lambda_2}{(P+1)^{\alpha_2}} \tag{4-6}$$

$$\eta_p = \eta_o \frac{\lambda_{1p}}{\sum_{P=1}^{\infty} \lambda_{1p}} \tag{4-7}$$

These equations lead to a six parameter rheological model, capable of quite satisfactory predictions for high amplitude data. The 2-1 component of stress for large amplitude sinusoidal flow is calculated to be:

$$\tau_{21}(t) = \frac{\eta_0 \dot{\gamma}^o}{(2^{\alpha_2} \lambda_2)^2 [z(\alpha_1) - 1]\omega} \times$$

$$\int_o^\infty \sum_{P=2}^\infty \frac{P^{3\alpha_2}[P^{\alpha_1}+2^{\alpha_1}\lambda_1\dot{\gamma}^o|\cos \omega(t-\tau)|]}{P^{2\alpha_1}[P^{\alpha_2}+2^{\alpha_2}\lambda_2\dot{\gamma}^o|\cos \omega(t-\tau)|]}$$

$$[\sin \omega t - \sin \omega(t-\tau)] \times [\exp - t \int_{-\tau}^{t}$$

$$\frac{P^{1.5\alpha_2}[P^{\alpha_1}+2^{\alpha_1}\lambda_1\dot{\gamma}^o|\cos \omega t''|]^{1.5}\, dt''}{2^{\alpha_2}\lambda_2 P^{1.5\alpha_1}[P^{\alpha_2}+2^{\alpha_2}\lambda_2\, \dot{\gamma}^o|\cos \omega t''|]^{0.5}}]d\tau \tag{4-8}$$

In 1976, Pearson and Middleman [37], in an attempt to improve on the stress growth model predictions proposed the following forms for the functions f_p and g_p:

$$f_p = [1 + 0.24\lambda\sqrt{\left| \frac{II(t')-II(t)}{2} \right|}\,]^{-1/2} \tag{4-9}$$

$$g_p = [1 + c\lambda\sqrt{\frac{II(t'')}{2}}\,]^{-1} \tag{4-10}$$

where

$$c = \frac{0.4}{1 + (0.012\lambda\sqrt{II/2})^{0.775}} \tag{4-11}$$

This leads to the following equations for some of the material functions of interest:

$$\eta = \frac{\eta_o}{1 + (a\lambda\dot{\gamma})^{\beta}} \tag{4-12}$$

$$\frac{\eta^+(t,\dot{\gamma}_\infty)}{\eta(\dot{\gamma}_\infty)} = f_p(1 + c\lambda\dot{\gamma}_\infty)\left(\frac{t}{\lambda_e}\right)^2 e^{-t/\lambda_e} + \left[1-e^{-t/\lambda_e}\left(1 + \frac{t}{\lambda_e}\right)\right] \tag{4-13}$$

with

$$\lambda_e = \frac{\lambda}{1+c\lambda\dot{\gamma}_\infty} \tag{4-14}$$

In 1977, De Kee [15-17] defined the functions f_p and g_p as follows:

$$f_p = \exp\left[-\sqrt{\tfrac{1}{2}\, II}\;\; t_p(-2c+3)\right] \tag{4-15}$$

$$g_p = \exp\left[-\sqrt{\tfrac{1}{2}\, II}\; t_p(c-1)\right] \tag{4-16}$$

The constants t_p have the units of time whereas c is a dimensionless parameter. These definitions for f_p and g_p result in simple exponential functions for the products, $f_p g_p$, $f_p g_p^2$ and $f_p g_p^3$, through which the different material functions are calculated.

A reduction of the constants η_p in a manner suggested by molecular theory (see equation (4-7)) yields the following expressions for η and ψ_1:

$$\eta = \sum_{P=1}^{k} \eta_p \exp(-t_p\dot{\gamma}) + \eta_\infty \tag{4-17}$$

with

$$\eta_\infty = \eta_o \sum_{P=k+1}^{M} (\lambda_p/\Sigma\lambda_p) \tag{4-18}$$

$$\psi_1 = 2\sum_{P=1}^{k} \eta_p\lambda_p \exp(-ct_p\dot{\gamma}) + \psi_{1\infty} \tag{4-19}$$

with

$$\psi_{1\infty} = 2 \sum_{P=k+1}^{M} \eta_p \lambda_p \tag{4-20}$$

Here, $t_p=0$ and $\lambda_p \to 0$ for $P>k$. k can be interpreted as the number of representative macromolecular segments that are being affected by $\dot{\gamma}$. k takes the value 1, 2 or 3 depending on the data.

The relaxation functions are given by:

$$\eta^-(t,\dot{\gamma}_o) = \sum_{P=1}^{k} \eta_p \exp(-t_p\dot{\gamma}_o)\exp(-t/\lambda_p) + \eta_\infty[1-h(t)] \tag{4-21}$$

$$\psi_1^-(t,\dot{\gamma}_o) = 2 \sum_{P=1}^{k} \eta_p\lambda_p \exp(-ct_p\dot{\gamma}_o)\exp(-t/\lambda_p) + \psi_{1\infty}[1-h(t)] \tag{4-22}$$

The stress growth functions are:

$$\eta^+(t,\dot{\gamma}_\infty) = \eta(\dot{\gamma}_\infty) + \sum_{P=1}^{k} [\eta_p\{\frac{t}{\lambda_p}[1-\exp(-t_p\dot{\gamma}_\infty(2-c))] - \exp(-t_p\dot{\gamma}_\infty)\} \times$$

$$\exp\{-t/\lambda_p \exp(-t_p\dot{\gamma}_\infty(c-1))\}] + \eta_\infty[h(t)-1] \tag{4-23}$$

$$\psi_1^+(t,\dot{\gamma}_\infty) = \psi_1(\dot{\gamma}_\infty) + \sum_{P=1}^{k} [\eta_p\{\frac{t^2}{\lambda_p} [1-\exp(-t_p\dot{\gamma}_\infty(2-c))]$$

$$- 2t \exp(-t_p\dot{\gamma}_\infty) - 2\lambda_p \exp(-ct_p\dot{\gamma}_\infty)\}$$

$$\exp\{-t/\lambda_p \exp(-t_p\dot{\gamma}_\infty(c-1))\}] + \psi_{1\infty}[h(t)-1] \tag{4-24}$$

and the steady elongational viscosity is given by:

$$\bar{\eta}(\bar{\gamma}) = 3 \sum_{P=1}^{k} \frac{\eta_p \exp(-\sqrt{3}\,\bar{\gamma}\,t_p)}{\{1-2\lambda_p\bar{\gamma}\exp(-\sqrt{3}\,\bar{\gamma}t_p(c-1))\}\{1+\lambda_p\bar{\gamma}\exp(-\sqrt{3}\,\bar{\gamma}t_p(c-1))\}}$$

$$+ 3\,\eta_\infty \tag{4-25}$$

Evaluation of the Models

The Carreau model B fits simultaneously and rather remarkably well the steady shear, complex viscosity, stress growth and stress relaxation functions. The model parameters are determined by fitting the complex viscosity, shear viscosity and primary normal stress difference data. Because of the empiricism of the functions f_p and g_p, it is not possible to directly relate the nonlinear parameters to the molecular structure of the fluids. The use of the Carreau model B is laborious, especially for complex flows. Initially [9], experimental data on three fluids, representative of eight viscoelastic fluids, were used to test the model in various flow situations. In particular, for stress growth, the agreement with the data was remarkable. Since its publication, the Carreau model has been used successfully by many researchers and has been referred to in just about every issue of most rheological journals.

MacDonald, through a judicious choice of the functions f_p and g_p obtained slightly better predictions for stress growth, stress relaxation and large amplitude oscillatory shear flows. He also showed [33] that the claim that rate dependent memory functions are inadmissible is not justified.

Pearson and Middleman presented a single relaxation time fluid model, obtained by empirically modifying the Meister model [34]. The empiricisms take the form of two functions of deformation rate, chosen in order to quantitatively predict the time and the magnitude of the stress overshoot in $\eta^+(t, \dot{\gamma}_\infty)$. They showed that the model compares reasonably well with data on polystyrene, aluminum soap, polyisobutylene and polyacrylamide. Their model contains four parameters: a, β, η_0 and λ, which are determined from oscillatory (λ) and steady shear data. Obviously, this model describes the stress growth function well. The predictions are however inferior to those of the Carreau model B when it comes to compare steady-state (η and ψ_1), normal stress growth ($\psi_1^+(t,\dot{\gamma}_\infty)$ and stress relaxation ($\eta^-(t,\dot{\gamma}_0)$) functions. The stress relaxation predictions show a discontinuity at the origin. This discontinuity increases with increasing shear rate. While Pearson and Middleman report this situation as objectionable, one can interpret it as a shift towards Newtonian like behaviour at high shear rate. The other transient functions should preferably show a similar trend, as is the case for the exponential model (4-21 - 4-24).

Due to the exponential nature of equations (4-17) and (4-19), the model parameters are best estimated from a semilogarithmic representation of the viscosity and the primary normal stress coefficient versus the shear rate. The usefulness of the simplified (series truncated) equations has been established and the model has been successfully evaluated with typical viscoelastic data on polystyrene, polyacrylamide, polyisobutylene and carboxymethylcellulose [15-17]. This exponential model fits the functions η and ψ_1 very well, using at most three terms of the series expansion. A reduction in the number of model parameters can be achieved by assuming that $t_p = 10\ t_{p+1}$.

For a value of the parameter c>1.5, both the rates of creation and the probabilities of loss of segments are increasing functions of the rate of strain. For 1<c<1.5 the rates of creation are decreasing functions, whereas the probabilities of loss are increasing functions. One expects the first case to be more realistic. Both cases are however consistent with the observation that the primary normal stress coefficient is a more rapidly decreasing function than the non-Newtonian viscosity.

The number of terms used in the series expansion (1, 2 or 3) has to be checked against a shear stress-shear rate plot, to assure a physically acceptable parameter determination. The components of the complex viscosity are given by:

$$\eta' = \sum_{P=1}^{k} \frac{\eta_p}{1+(\omega\lambda_p)^2} + \sum_{P=k+1}^{M} \frac{\eta_p}{1+(\omega\lambda_p)^2} \tag{4-26}$$

$$\eta'' = \sum_{P=1}^{k} \frac{\eta_p\ \omega\lambda_p}{1+(\omega\lambda_p)^2} + \sum_{P=k+1}^{M} \frac{\eta_p\omega\lambda_p}{1+(\omega\lambda_p)^2} \tag{4-27}$$

For $k \leqslant 3$ and with $\lambda_p=0$ for P>k, the predicted values decrease too rapidly with increasing frequency. This model is however capable of describing the dynamic behaviour over a large frequency span, provided one chooses an appropriate form for the constants λ_p. For example, setting:

$$\lambda_p = \frac{2^{\alpha}\lambda}{(P+1)^{\alpha}} \tag{4-28}$$

results in the Carreau expressions for η' and η'', given by:

$$\eta' = \frac{\eta_o}{z(\alpha)-1} \sum_{P=2}^{\infty} \frac{P^{\alpha}}{P^{2\alpha}+(2^{\alpha}\lambda\omega)^2} \tag{4-29}$$

$$\eta'' = \frac{2^{\alpha}\eta_o\lambda\omega}{z(\alpha)-1} \sum_{P=2}^{\infty} \frac{1}{P^{2\alpha}+(2^{\alpha}\lambda\omega)^2} \tag{4-30}$$

Although this exponential model yields good results for a variety of material functions, the complexity of equation (4-24) can cause problems. That is to say that for a given set of model parameters, it is feasible that the plot of the shear rate versus the time at which the maximum in the $\psi_1^+(t,\dot{\gamma}_\infty)$ function occurs may not be monotonically declining. The experimental data on stress growth may therefore not always be represented correctly. Promising suggestions to correct this problem include:

i) new defining functions f_p and g_p of the form:

$$f_p = [1 + (\lambda_p\dot{\gamma})^2]^{\frac{2m_2 - 3m_1}{2}} \tag{4-31}$$

$$g_p = [1 + (\lambda_p\dot{\gamma})^2]^{m_1 - m_2} \tag{4-32}$$

resulting in a series truncated model composed of Carreau model A [9] like terms for η and ψ_1 or ii) a model generalization allowing for a large number of series terms to be used, without significantly altering the number of model parameters. This could be achieved by defining λ_p and η_p, as suggested by equations (4-6) and (4-7) respectively and by defining time constants t_p and t_p' by relations of the form:

$$t_p = \frac{2^n\, t_1}{(P+1)^n} \tag{4-33}$$

The products $f_p g_p^{\,2}$ and $f_p g_p^{\,3}$ would then be given by $e^{-\dot{\gamma} t_p}$ and $e^{-\dot{\gamma} t_p'}$ respectively. The viscosity can then be computed in terms of the Riemann zeta function as:

$$\eta = \frac{\eta_o}{z(\alpha)-1} \sum_{P=2}^{M} \frac{1}{P^{\alpha}} e^{-(2nt_1\dot{\gamma})/P^n} \tag{4-34}$$

For $\dot{\gamma}\to\infty$, one can calculate an asymptotic expression, in terms of the gamma function, of the form:

$$\eta = \frac{\eta_o}{[z(\alpha)-1]n} \Gamma \left(\frac{\alpha-1}{n}\right) |2^n\ t_1\dot{\gamma}|^{(1-\alpha)/n} \tag{4-35}$$

with a slope in the power law region given by $(1-\alpha)/n$. A similar type of relation can be obtained for $\psi_1(\dot{\gamma})$. Here, the slope in the power law region is given by $2 + (1-2\alpha)/n'$. Taking $t_1 = t_1'$, results in a six constant rheological equation with three non-linear parameters (t_1, n and n′), from which equations (4-29) and (4-30) can be retrieved.

5. Models Accounting for a Yield Stress

Surprisingly little has been done in this area. In 1981, White and Tanaka [48] reported on a comparison of a plastic-viscoelastic constitutive equation with rheological measurements on a polystyrene melt reinforced with small particles. They proposed the following equations for the steady state rheological behaviour of a filled system. The viscosity is given by:

$$\eta = \frac{\tau_o}{\dot{\gamma}\sqrt{1 + \frac{4}{3}(\lambda_{eff}\dot{\gamma})^2}} + f(\phi)G^o\lambda_{eff} \tag{5-1}$$

and the primary normal stress difference is given by:

$$N_1 = \frac{2\ \tau_o\ \lambda_{eff}\dot{\gamma}}{\sqrt{1 + \frac{4}{3}(\lambda_{eff}\dot{\gamma})^2}} + 2f(\phi)(\lambda_{eff}\dot{\gamma})^2 \tag{5-2}$$

where

$$\lambda_{eff} = \frac{\lambda_o}{1 + a\,\lambda_o\dot{\gamma}} \tag{5-3}$$

For uniaxial elongational flow $\bar{\eta}$ is given by:

$$\bar{\eta} = \frac{\sqrt{3}\,\tau_o}{\bar{\dot{\gamma}}} + \frac{3f(\phi)G^o\,\lambda_{eff}}{(1+\lambda_{eff}\bar{\dot{\gamma}})(1-2\lambda_{eff}\bar{\dot{\gamma}})} \tag{5-4}$$

with

$$\lambda_{eff} = \frac{\lambda_o}{(1 + \sqrt{3}\,a\,\lambda_o\bar{\dot{\gamma}})} \tag{5-5}$$

The superscript o refers to unfilled systems and the function $f(\phi)$ is taken to be equal to the dependence of viscosity or modulus on volume fraction for a system of noninteracting spherical particles of volume fraction ϕ.

Liu, Soong and De Kee [26] expanded on the ideas described in section 3, in order to be able to consider multiphase systems, possessing a yield stress. The magnitude of the yield stress in a material depends on the state of the structure of the sample. The yield stress τ_o should therefore be treated as a variable. Liu et al. however assumed, for simplicity, that the yield stress was a fixed contribution to the overall stress; that is to say:

$$\tau(t) = \tau_o + \tau_{st}(t) + \tau_m(t) \tag{5-6}$$

where τ_{st} represents the stress contributed by the material structure;

$$\tau_{st}(t) = \eta_o\,P(t,\dot{\gamma})\dot{\gamma} \tag{5-7}$$

and where the residual matrix viscosity contributes the following time dependent stress:

$$\tau_m(t) = \eta_o \beta \dot{\gamma} \tag{5-8}$$

where β is a small number representing the relative importance of the residual viscous dissipation.

Summarizing, one obtains the following expression for the shear viscosity under steady state conditions:

$$\eta(\dot{\gamma}) = \frac{\tau_o}{\dot{\gamma}} + \frac{\eta_o(1 - \beta)}{1 + b\,\dot{\gamma}^m} + \eta_o \beta \tag{5-9}$$

In 1984, Ekong and Jayaraman [22] presented a kinetic network model representing the behavior of block copolymer systems with spherical microdomains. The model involves two parameters which may be related to a yield stress. Their rate terms incorporate a segment distribution function F, which obeys the evolution equation of Yamamoto:

$$\frac{\partial F}{\partial t} + \overline{\nabla}\cdot(\dot{\overline{R}}F) = f(\overline{R},N) - \beta(\overline{R},N)F \tag{5-10}$$

where the terms on the right side denote respectively the rate of creation and the coefficient of destruction of segments with N subunits. $\overline{R}$ denotes the nondimensional position $\overline{r}/N\ell$, where $N\ell$ is the extended length of the segment. $\dot{\overline{R}}$ denotes the velocity of such segments:

$$\dot{\overline{R}} = (\overline{\overline{L}} - \xi\,\dot{\overline{\overline{\gamma}}})\cdot\overline{R} \tag{5-11}$$

where ξ is a slip coefficient.

$$f(\overline{R},N) = c\,\frac{e^{2a}}{1+2a}\left(\frac{3N}{2\pi}\right)^{3/2} \exp\left(\frac{a^2}{NR^2} - \frac{3NR^2}{2}\right) \tag{5-12}$$

where c is a constant rate coefficient and R is the magnitude of vector $\overline{R}$. Increasing the parameter "a" means that the end-to-end distance of the most probable segments is increased. The rate coefficient of destruction β is given by:

$$\beta(\bar{R}, N) = \beta_0(1 + \frac{3\ NR^2}{2} + \frac{\varepsilon a^2}{NR^2}) \quad (5\text{-}13)$$

and the rate of destruction is βF. For $\varepsilon << 1$, the initial segment distribution can be approximated by:

$$F(\bar{R},N,t=0) = G(\bar{R},N)/\beta_0 \quad (5\text{-}14)$$

where ε describes the dependence of junction destruction on deformation.

Evaluation of the Models

White and Tanaka investigated the steady state shear and elongational flow behavior of three polystyrene melt compounds reinforced with 30 vol. % carbon black, calcium carbonate and titanium dioxide. Their equation for viscosity compares rather well with the data. The deviations between model predictions and experimental data were more severe in the case of the primary normal stress difference versus shear stress and for the elongational viscosity versus elongational rate; especially at higher shear stress and at higher elongational rates. Typical values for G^o, λ_o and a were reported as 6 x 10^3Pa, 4 s and 0.7, respectively. Values obtained for τ_o were close to 10^4 Pa and $f(\phi)$ for ϕ = 0.3 was 3.6.

The model proposed by Liu, Soong and De Kee, which is an extension of previous ideas [42], incorporates a number of important concepts such as yield stress, pseudoplasticity, thixotropy and viscoelasticity. Simulations for several sets of model parameters show a high degree of flexibility in the qualitative representations of viscosity, stress growth and hysteresis behaviour, both for purely viscous systems as well as for viscoelastic materials. Also, upon repeated cycling in the hysteresis test, the stress rise in the second loop is not nearly as high as for the first loop, which is indicative of a substantial structural decay of the primary material structure during the first cycle.

The difference between the second and third loops is much smaller, indicating an asymptotic approach to stable structure fluctuations. These model predictions all agree with reported properties of suspensions supporting the applicability of the model to such systems. Dilatant and rheopectic behaviour could be introduced by making equation (3-12) shear rate dependent.

At steady state, the model by Ekong and Jayaraman, results in an equation for the primary normal stress difference, which reduces to Lodge's rubberlike liquid model, if $a = \varepsilon = 0$. For $a = 0$ and $\varepsilon \neq 0$, Wagner's equation is recovered. The value of the parameter "a", which describes the range of repulsion between segments attached to spherical domains, correlates with the concentration of filler in the material. Ekong and Jayaraman present curves for steady-state and transient stress in uniaxial elongational flows. Their model predicts an apparent yield stress at low elongational rates.

6. Concluding Remarks

There are no fixed criteria through which one can select the best rheological model. There is also not a single model capable of characterizing all polymeric materials in all flow situations.

All models published in the past decade or so are capable of describing steady state material functions such as for example the non-Newtonian viscosity $\eta(\dot{\gamma})$. Several authors have reported predictive abilities for steady and elongational flows. This may contribute to the understanding of the isotropic nature of the material but it is obvious from this short write-up that an accurate quantitative prediction of material functions such as the shear stress growth $\eta^{+}(t,\dot{\gamma}_{\infty})$ and primary normal stress growth $\psi_1^{+}(t,\dot{\gamma}_{\infty})$ are probably more severe tests for most constitutive equations. Stastna and De Kee [46] proposed new tests relating shear stress to normal stress differences, both in steady state and in the transient regimes. Other experimental tests are described by Attane et al. [3], Kearsley and Zapas [24] and by Soong [43]. Although further studies in this direction could reveal the relative importance of the assumptions used in a given theory, these efforts may very well be premature considering on the one hand that the vast majority of the reported data are data on very poorly characterized systems and considering on the other hand that several measurements are probably in error due to phenomena such as radial inflow, because the measuring instrument may not be stiff enough, or due to effects of cone angle and possible other geometric factors, which may contribute to the production of erroneous results. Menezes and Graessly [35] succeeded in achieving responses on the order of 30 ms using a stiffened

Weissenberg rheogoniometer, keeping the ratio of the mechanical response time to the material response time less than 0.1.

As future research possibilities, one could consider relating the extra stress tensor to a combination of memory and relaxation functions which could be influenced by invariants of both deformation and stress tensors, so as to encompass as many useful modifications as possible, such as for example; i) the possibility of predicting negative primary normal stress differences reported by Chaffey and Porter [10], or ii) the incorporation of information on say the molecular weight distribution into the network model. At the same time, the number of model parameters should remain reasonable and should ideally be related to the molecular structure. De Kee and Carreau [17] have reported modest success in this direction, relating the time constants t_p from equation (4-15) to the zero shear rate viscosity η_o and to the molecular weight M_w.

Phillips [39-41] focussed on the selection of a strain measure in connection with a study on the prediction of time-dependent nonlinear stresses. Using a Bird-Carreau type equation, he showed that a variety of known constitutive equations such as for example the BKZ model [4] could be recovered.

In general, computational difficulties peculiar to each model arise as a result of the particular choices of proposed defining functions.

In this model building appropriate forms should be suggested based on the best information available from molecular theories, continuum mechanics and thermodynamics, combined with reliable data on well characterized systems covering a wide variety of material functions.

Models based on continuum mechanics are not designed to explain effects of molecular structure. Their model parameters are usually determined from steady state experiments and it is difficult to relate the nonlinear parameters to the molecular structure. Models based on molecular theories on the other hand, are presently not as successful as the theories based on continuum mechanics when it comes to predicting time dependent nonlinear flow properties.

The need for suitable and easy to use rheological equations providing important parameters for material characterization and for process design will be present for the foreseeable future. In this respect, an already substantial degree of success has been achieved using models derived from molecular network considerations.

Acknowledgements

The author would like to thank Professors P.J. Carreau and P.N. Kaloni for their constructive comments.

Nomenclature

a	=	model parameter (equations (3-4) and (4-12)) and (5-3)
A	=	Helmholtz free energy per unit volume of solution/model parameter (equation (3-6))
b	=	model parameter in equation (3-11)
b_n	=	$3/(2n\ell^2)$ in Gaussian theories
b_p	=	model parameters (equation (3-7))
c	=	material constant in equation (4-10)
$f_p(II)$	=	functional dependence of the rates of creation of segments on the second invariant of the rate-of-strain tensor
$F(\hat{x},n,t)d^3\hat{x}$	=	concentration of $(\hat{x},n)$-segments
$\hat{D}/\hat{D}t$	=	non-affine differential operator (equation (3-8))
g^{ij},g_{ij}	=	components of metric tensor, fixed coordinate system
$\hat{g}^{ij},\hat{g}_{ij}$	=	components of metric tensor, convected coordinate system
$g_p(II)$	=	functional dependence of the probabilities of loss of segments
$H(\lambda)$	=	relaxation spectrum
k	=	Boltzmann constant/index of complexity of junctions in network theories
k_ℓ	=	loss rate constant
k_c	=	creation rate constant
ℓ	=	length of a link of a segment
$L_{kn}(t)$	=	rate of creation per unit volume of (n,k)-segments
m	=	memory function of rheological models
m_1,m_2	=	model parameters in equations (4-31),(4-32)
n	=	number of freely-jointed rigid links in a segment; number of intact structural points, and parameter in equation (4-33)
n_o	=	equilibrium number of structural points in equation (3-10)
$N^*(t-t')dt'$	=	concentration at time t of segments created during interval $(t', t'+dt')$
N_1	=	primary normal stress difference = $-(\tau_{11}-\tau_{22})$
N_2	=	secondary normal stress difference = $-(\tau_{22}-\tau_{33})$
p	=	pressure
$P(t,\dot{\gamma})$	=	time dependent fluid structure in equation (3-12)

R	=	material constant in equation (4-1)
s	=	material constant in equation (4-1)
t	=	current time
t', t''	=	past times
T	=	absolute temperature (K)
x, x'	=	position occupied at t,t' in fixed coordinate system
$\hat{x}^i$	=	convected coordinate
x_p	=	structural parameter
$z(\alpha)$	=	Riemann zeta function
$\alpha, \alpha_1, \alpha_2$	=	model constants associated with power-law behaviour
β	=	material parameter in equation (4-12)
$\dot{\gamma}, \dot{\gamma}_o, \dot{\gamma}_\infty$	=	shear rate
$\bar{\gamma}$	=	elongational rate
$\bar{\Gamma}^{ij}, \Gamma_{ij}$	=	strain tensors defined by equations (2-10) and (2-11), respectively
$\delta/\delta t$	=	convectived derivative
η	=	non-Newtonian viscosity
$\bar{\eta}$	=	elongational viscosity = $-\tau_{11}/\bar{\gamma}$
η_p	=	constants of dimensions of viscosity
η_0	=	zero shear rate viscosity
η', η''	=	real and imaginary parts of complex viscosity η^*
$\eta^-(t, \dot{\gamma}_o)$	=	shear stress relaxtion function = $-\tau_{21}(t)/\dot{\gamma}_o$
$\eta^+(t, \dot{\gamma}_\infty)$	=	shear stress growth function = $-\tau_{21}(t)/\dot{\gamma}_\infty$
λ	=	characteristic diffusion time in equation (3-10)
$\lambda, \lambda_1, \lambda_2$	=	time constants
λ_p	=	time constants
ψ_1	=	primary normal stress coefficient in steady simple shear flow = $-(\tau_{11}-\tau_{22})\dot{\gamma}^2$
$\tau^{ij}, \hat{\tau}^{ij}$	=	components of the stress tensor in fixed and convected coordinates
τ_o	=	yield stress
τ_{21}	=	shear stress
$-(\tau_{11}-\tau_{22})$	=	primary normal stress difference
$\tau_{kn}(II)$	=	probability of loss of (n,k)-segments
I	=	first invariant
II(t)	=	second invariant of the rate-of-strain tensor = $\dot{\gamma}^{mn}(t)\dot{\gamma}_{mn}(t)$

References

1. Acierno, D., La Mantia, F.P., Marrucci, G. and Titomanlio, G., J. Non-Newtonian Fluid Mech., 1, 125 (1976).
2. Acierno, D., La Mantia, F.P., Marrucci, G., Rizzo, G. and Titomanlio, G., J. Non-Newtonian Fluid Mech., 1, 147 (1976).
3. Attane, P., Pierrard, J.M. and Carreau, P., Proc. IX Intl. Congress on Rheol., Acapulco, I, 337 (1984).
4. Bernstein, B., Kearsley, E.A. and Zapas, L.J., Trans. Soc. Rheol., 8, 391 (1963).
5. Bird, R.B., Armstrong, R.C. and Hassager, O., Dynamics of Polymeric Liquids, Volume I, Fluid Mechanics, Wiley, New York (1977).
6. Bird, R.B., Hassager, O., Armstrong, R.C. and Curtiss, C.F., Dynamics of Polymeric Liquids, Volume II, Kinetic Theory, Wiley, New York (1977).
7. Bogue, D.C. and Doughty, J.O., I.E.C. Fund., 5, 243 (1966) and 6, 388 (1967).
8. Carreau, P.J. and De Kee, D., Can. J. Chem. Eng., 53, 3 (1979).
9. Carreau, P.J., Trans. Soc. Rheol., 16, 1, 99 (1972).
10. Chaffey, C.E. and Porter, R.S., J. Rheol., 29 (3) 281 (1985).
11. Curtis, C.F. and Bird, R.B., J. Chem. Phys., 74, 2016 (1981).
12. Curtis, C.F. and Bird, R.B., J. Chem. Phys., 74, 2026 (1981).
13. Curtis, C.F. and Bird, R.B., Physica, 118A, 191 (1983).
14. De Cleyn, G. and Mewis, J., J. Non-Newtonian Fluid Mech., 9, 91 (1981).
15. De Kee, D., Ph.D. Thesis, University of Montreal (1977).
16. De Kee, D. and Carreau, P.J., J. Non-Newtonian Fluid Mech., 6, 127 (1979).
17. De Kee, D. and Carreau, P.J., J. Rheol., 24, (3), 319 (1980).
18. Doi, M. and Edwards, S.F., J. Chem. Soc. Faraday Trans. II, 74, 1789 (1978).
19. Doi, M. and Edwards, S.F., J. Chem. Soc. Faraday Trans. II, 74, 1802 (1978).
20. Doi, M. and Edwards, S.F., J. Chem. Soc. Faraday Trans. II, 74, 1818 (1978).
21. Doi, M. and Edwards, S.F., J. Chem. Soc. Faraday Trans. II, 75, 32 L979).
22. Ekong, A. and Jayaraman, K., J. Rheol., 28, 45 (1984).
23. Jongschaap, R.J.J., J. Non-Newtonian Fluid Mech., 8, 138 (1981).
24. Kearsley, E.A. and Zapas, L.J., Trans. Soc. Rheol., 20 (4), 623 (1976).
25. Liu, T.Y., Soong, D. and Williams, M., Polym. Eng. Sci., 21, 11, 675 (1981).
26. Liu, T.Y., Soong, D.S. and De Kee, D., Chem. Eng. Commun., 22, 273 (1983).
27. Lodge, A.S., Rheologica Acta, 7, 4, 379 (1968).
28. Lodge, A.A., Armstrong, R.C., Wagner, M.H. and Winter, H.H., Pure & Appl. Chem., 54, 7, 1349 (1982).
29. Lodge, A.S., Elastic Liquids, Academic Press, New York (1964).
30. MacDonald, I.F., Rheol. Acta, 14, 801 (1975).
31. MacDonald, I.F., Rheol. Acta, 14, 809 (1975).
32. MacDonald, I.F., Rheol. Acta, 14, 906 (1975).
33. MacDonald, I.F., Rheol. Acta, 15, 223 (1976).
34. Meister, B.J., Trans. Soc. Rheol., 15, 63 (1971).

35. Menezes, E.V. and Graessley, W.W., Rheol. Acta, 19, 38 (1980).
36. Mewis, J. and Denn, M., J. Non-Newtonian Fluid Mech., 12, 69 (1983).
37. Pearson, G. and Middleman, S., Trans. Soc. Rheol., 20 (4), 559 (1976).
38. Phan Thien, N. and Tanner, R.I., J. Non-Newtonian Fluid Mech., 2, 353 (1977).
39. Phillips, M.C., J. Non-Newtonian Fluid Mech., 2, 109 (1977).
40. Phillips, M.C., J. Non-Newtonian Fluid Mech., 2, 123 (1977).
41. Phillips, M.C., J. Non-Newtonian Fluid Mech., 2, 139 (1977).
42. Soong, D. and Shen, M., Polym. Eng. Sci., 20, 17, 1177 (1980).
43. Soong, D., Rubber Chemistry and Technology, 54, 3, 641 (1981).
44. Spriggs, T.W., Huppler, J.D. and Bird, R.B., Trans. Soc. Rheol., 10, 1, 191 (1966).
45. Spriggs, T.W., Huppler, J.D. and Bird, R.B., Trans. Soc. Rheol., 10, 1, 191 (1966).
46. Stastna, J. and De Kee, D., Rheol. Acta, 23, 250 (1984).
47. Wall, F.T., J. Chem. Phys., 10, 485 (1942).
48. White, J.L. and Tanaka, H., J. Non-Newtonian Fluid Mech., 8, 1 (1981).

J D GODDARD

Microstructural origins of continuum stress fields — A brief history and some unresolved issues

0. ABSTRACT

The following‡ is a survey of various methods for the derivation of an effective continuum stress field from the statistical micromechanics of particulate and heterogeneous media. The Cauchy stress emerges as the sum of a configurational term, in the form of an internal force dipole, plus a kinetic part consisting of a momentum-flux dipole.

Detailed attention is paid to systems of point masses interacting according to a general force law. The stress tensor derived by the classical method of Cauchy is compared with that given by the modern statistical mechanics of Kirkwood and coworkers. With appropriate generalizations, the two agree and both involve multipolar effects, which become important in media with large property gradients.

We also discuss the compatibility of the derived stress with energy principles, with continuum kinematics, and the principle of material frame indifference.

1. INTRODUCTION

"One way of introducing the notion of stress into an abstract conceptual scheme of Rational Mechanics is to accept it as a fundamental notion derived from experience...that of mutual action between two bodies in contact, or between two parts of the same body separated by an imagined surface...

In such theories as Cauchy's the apparent contact actions are traced to distance actions between 'molecules' ...Thus a second way of introducing the notion of stress is to base it upon on an hypothesis concerning intermolecular forces.

A third way is found in an application of the theory of energy..."

A. E. H. Love 26 , Note B, pp. 616ff

------

‡ This work is dedicated to my esteemed colleague and friend, Professor C. S. Yih, on his 67th birthday.

One could hardly imagine a more eloquent or lucid survey of the conceptual issues and techniques of the day than offered by the above treatise. There, one will find the following definition of the stress tensor, for a solid body consisting of interacting point masses contained in volume V †:

$$\underset{\sim}{T} = \underset{\sim}{T}_C \equiv \frac{1}{V} \Sigma \underset{\sim}{f}\underset{\sim}{\ell}, \quad (\text{or} \quad T_{\alpha\beta} = \frac{1}{V} \Sigma f_\alpha \ell_\beta) \tag{1.1}$$

where $\underset{\sim}{f}$ and $\underset{\sim}{\ell}$ denote, respectively, the pairwise force of interaction and distance of separation, while Σ denotes a sum over the distinct pairs of particles in V.

The tensor moment of force defined by (1.1) as a dyadic (or tensor) product of $\underset{\sim}{f}$ and $\underset{\sim}{\ell}$, is nowadays easily identified as the cohesive force dipole (or dipolar internal force)†† per unit volume, thanks largely to the pioneering work of Burgers [8] and Batchelor [2] on suspension rheology. As such, (1.1) generally represents only one part of the stress tensor, which we denote by "configurational" [33] or "cohesive", to distinguish it from the "kinetic" part:

$$\underset{\sim}{T}_K = - \frac{1}{V} \sum_i \underset{\sim}{p}_i' \underset{\sim}{v}_i' \quad , \tag{1.2}$$

long familiar in the kinetic theory of dilute gases as the (negative) pressure tensor or molecular-momentum flux. Here, m_i, $\underset{\sim}{v}_i'$ and $\underset{\sim}{p}_i'$ denote mass, linear velocity and linear momentum of particle i, with the latter quantities measured relative to a suitable mass-average velocity.

In a sense (1.1) and (1.2) typify two extremes in the classical states of matter [10], the condensed solid state ---

---

†We employ Greek suffixes to denote tensor components, reserving Roman $i,j,\ldots n$ for discrete particle labels. Also, tildes beneath symbols indicate vectors or second-rank tensors.
††which has been called the "tensor virial" [17] (see below).

where intermolecular forces are dominant, and the rarified gaseous state where momentum transport by molecular motion prevails. The latter also characterizes a massless photon "gas", in which (1.2) represents the wave-mechanical radiation stress. Also it is a matter of some historical interest [26,29] that (1.1) serves to define the Maxwell stress in a system of electrostatic dipoles, each consisting of charges ±Q separated by distance $\underset{\sim}{\ell}$, possessing thus a dipole moment $\underset{\sim}{\ell}Q/2$, and situated in an electric field of magnitude $\underset{\sim}{f}/Q$ [29]. (This formula also carries over to free space, without actual point charges, and represents stress in MacCullagh's hypothetical aether.)

In intermediate states of matter such as liquids or other dense fluids both the stress contributions (1.1) and (1.2) can be comparable and, generally, one must take

$$\underset{\sim}{T} = \underset{\sim}{T}_C + \underset{\sim}{T}_K \qquad (1.3)$$

The purpose of this article is to survey the body of work, leading from Cauchy [9] to the present, which serves to establish (1.1)-(1.3), as a general form, relating what today is called the *Cauchy stress* in the literature on rational continuum mechanics to various microstructural or molecular theories. The continuum notion of stress, referred to in the opening lines above, hardly needs elaboration at this point in history [23,37].

The main subject of our survey is the configurational stress $\underset{\sim}{T}_C$, which over the years has been the subject of the most controversy. Thus, we recall how early doubts over the famous Cauchy relations among the elastic constants of periodic arrays of attracting mass points were subsequently dispelled by the more general lattice models of Born and coworkers [6,26]. (The latter models have further elaborated upon in recent works [27].)

In the modern literature on solid-state physics, the validity of (1.1)-(1.3) has been argued on the grounds of the

Hellman-Feynman theorem [12,30,31,38], which provides a quantum-mechanical recipe for the derivation of the effective forces $\underset{\sim}{f}$ in (1.1) from the appropriate Hamiltonian. Here as in classical mechanics the concept of force itself occupies an insecure position without some such appeal to energy principles.

The present article shall not deal with epistomological questions of the above nature but rather assumes in the Newtonian spirit [36] that all forces ultimately can be specified in a manner appropriate to the system under consideration. Not only does this allows one to discuss conservative and Brownian-dynamical systems [3,20], with forces derived from suitable potentials, but it also admits kinetic theories of nonconservative systems, such as granular media with frictional forces or other heterogeneous continua involving dissipative effects [2,16,19,23].

For systems of interacting point masses or other discrete particles, we require only that the mutual forces be pairwise additive and subject to Newton's principle of action-reaction. Thus if $\underset{\sim}{f}_i$ denotes the force exerted on particle i by all other particles in our system, then we require that

$$\underset{\sim}{f}_i = \sum_j \underset{\sim}{f}_{ij} \tag{1.4}$$

where

$$\underset{\sim}{f}_{ij} = -\underset{\sim}{f}_{ji} \tag{1.5}$$

is the force exerted on particle i by particle j, for $i,j = 1,2,\ldots$ It is worth noting that (1.1) then follows from the more general moment

$$\underset{\sim}{T}_C = -\frac{1}{V} \sum_i \underset{\sim}{f}_i \underset{\sim}{r}_i \tag{1.6}$$

where the vector $\underset{\sim}{r}_i$ represents the spatial position of particle i or its mass centroid, with respect to an arbitrary origin.

In the case of heterogeneous continua, our definitions need only a slight alteration in form. In particular, the force dipole $\underset{\sim}{M}_0$ associated with a region V_0 containing a heterogeneity or "inclusion", in an otherwise well-defined continuous medium or "matrix" endowed with Cauchy stress $\underset{\sim}{T}$, is defined by

$$\underset{\sim}{M}_0^T = \int_{S_0} \underset{\sim}{r}d\underset{\sim}{f} = \int_{S_0} \underset{\sim}{r}\underset{\sim}{T}\cdot\underset{\sim}{n}dS \tag{1.7}$$

where S_0, with unit outer normal $\underset{\sim}{n}$, is the bounding surface of V_0. Here $\underset{\sim}{r}$ denotes spatial position relative to a suitably defined center of mass for V_0 and, as below, the superscript T indicates the transpose (or operator-adjoint) of second-rank tensors.

In a medium of volume V filled with such inclusions, the analogous form to (1.1) is

$$\underset{\sim}{T}_C = \frac{1}{V} \Sigma \underset{\sim}{M}_0 \tag{1.8}$$

where Σ denotes a sum over all the associated regions V_0. Interactive force fields require further terms of the form (1.1).

Equation (1.7) is valid for pointwise singular inclusions as well as for a disperse phase of discrete particles imbedded in the matrix and also having a well-defined stress field $\underset{\sim}{T}'$, say. In the latter instance, and for the case of quasi-static or inertialess media, (1.7) can be written by means of the divergence theorem as

$$\underset{\sim}{M}_0 = \int_{V_0} \underset{\sim}{T}'dV + \int_{S_0} \underset{\sim}{r}(\underset{\sim}{T}-\underset{\sim}{T}')\cdot\underset{\sim}{n}dS \tag{1.9}$$

where V_0 now denotes the actual volume of a given particle, and where (1.9) includes any singular surfaces over which surface tensions and the associated stress discontinuity $(\underset{\sim}{T}-\underset{\sim}{T}')\cdot\underset{\sim}{n}$ do not vanish. Equation (1.9) serves as the main justification for the use of volume-average stresses in heterogeneous media [2]. As further discussed in [2], an accounting for inertial effects requires that we substract from (1.7) a kinetic contribution of the form

$$\underset{\sim}{\Pi}_0 = \int_{V_0} (\rho\underset{\sim}{v}\underset{\sim}{v})'dV \tag{1.10}$$

where $(\rho\underset{\sim}{v}\underset{\sim}{v})'$ denotes momentum flux relative to a suitably defined average. Equation (1.10) defines a kinetic "pressure tensor" and in strict analogy to (1.2) $\underset{\sim}{T}_K$ now is given by a sum of the form (1.8) with $\underset{\sim}{M}_0$ replaced by $-\underset{\sim}{\Pi}_0$.

The relations (1.7), (1.8) and (1.10) prove indispensible to the interpretation of numerous theories for the rheology of heterogeneous continua, such as particle suspensions and composite materials, where they lend themselves to a variety of disperse-phase morphologies, for example, filamentary particles represented by line singularities [2,16,34]. Indeed, we can regard (1.7), (1.8) and (1.10) as general statements from which (1.1)-(1.3) follows as singular limits, corresponding to point particles in free space.

In a related domain of application, it appears that all the proposed expressions for stress which emerge from various macromolecular kinetic theories are but variants on the above formulae [5,14,15,25]. In this context macromolecular chains, like filamentary reinforcing agents, serve as the propagators or "correlators" of force over distances $\underset{\sim}{\ell}$ which are large compared to ordinary atomic dimensions. This accounts for the relatively large stress levels or "load transfers" which are characteristic of such systems.

The main goal of the present article is to juxtapose two rather distinct approaches to the derivation of the effective continuum stress field in terms of the micromechanics of a discrete particulate medium. The more modern and somewhat more formal method, which can be attributed to Kirkwood and coworkers [22], is based on the momentum balance. The second and more direct method can be traced back to Cauchy's [9] calculation of the cohesive stress in a system of material points. This type of calculation, referred to in our epigrammatic citation and discussed in some detail by Love [26], deals only with the configurational stress $\tilde{T}_C$. However, the reasoning is based on the same type of arguments employed in the kinetic theory of gases to derive the molecular momentum transport term $\tilde{T}_K$. With this in mind, it will be seen that both the above methods lead essentially to the same result for the complete stress tensor $\tilde{T}$. As will also become evident, both methods involve a certain indeterminancy in $\tilde{T}$, which becomes physically significant in strongly non-homogeneous fluids, for example, near vapor-liquid phase boundaries [11,32,33,39].

As signaled in the opening quotation from Love, yet another derivation of stress can be based on energy methods, which enjoy a venerable history in the rheological literature. Alongside numerous elasticity calculations [6], of a type which continue to be popular [1], one can also cite various dissipation arguments of the kind originated by Einstein for the viscosity of particle suspensions [34]. Apart from their relevance to certain variational techniques, for deriving bounds on the linear viscoelastic properties of heterogeneous media, we do not regard energy methods as being distinct generally from the methods discussed above. (Indeed, one might hope that methods like those of Green and Rivlin [18,23] for continua could also be employed to derive all microscopic balances from a suitable microscopic energy balance. However, see the concluding comments.) Hence, beyond a few remarks in the Conclusion regarding compatibility of the results with energy methods, we shall not discuss the latter.

To illustrate the methods of interest, we consider the special case of a medium composed of interacting material points, subject to the force laws (1.4)-(1.5). Out of this model we show how existing theories allow one to extract the (Noll) simple continuum [37], with Cauchy stress defined in terms of dipolar moments like (1.1)-(1.2). Consideration of more complex microstructures involving microscopic couples or of higher-order moments of the form $\underset{\sim}{f}\underset{\sim}{\ell}\underset{\sim}{\ell}$, $\underset{\sim}{f}\underset{\sim}{\ell}\underset{\sim}{\ell}\underset{\sim}{\ell}$, etc., would introduce at the outset new microscopic length scales and lead to more complex continuum models (multipolar or Cosserat-Mindlin materials) [10,23,36,37]. As discussed in the Conclusions, higher-order moments of the above type can still arise for strongly non-homogeneous states, even in the elementary system considered here.

The considerations of the preceding paragraph have implications for the symmetry of the stress tensor $\underset{\sim}{T}$, since higher-order terms enter into lower-order equations in the typical hierarchy of continuum moment balances [10,23,36], reflecting a similar coupling at the microscopic level. The symmetry of $\underset{\sim}{T}$, as assured by vanishing of the microscopic internal couple:

$$\Sigma\ \underset{\sim}{f}\times\underset{\sim}{\ell} = \underset{\sim}{0}$$

as in the classical central-force model, will therefore have to rest on a further analysis.

2. THE KIRKWOOD METHOD

We now present a derivation of the stress tensor for a classical mechanical system of N interacting particles consisting of simple mass points. Our derivation is based on the formal method pioneered by Kirkwood and coworkers [22] and subsequently employed by several others [33,35]. The previous works generally assume conservative forces derivable from suitable potential energy functions, whereas, in line with the introductory remarks we allow here for non-conservative forces.

We denote, respectively, the mass, position and linear momentum of the ith particle by m_i , $\underset{\sim}{r}_i = \underset{\sim}{r}_i(t)$, and $\underset{\sim}{p}_i = \underset{\sim}{p}_i(t)$ or, collectively, by the phase-space vector

$$\underset{\sim}{z}_i = (\underset{\sim}{r}_i,\underset{\sim}{p}_i)\ ,\ \text{with}\ \ \underset{\sim}{w}_i \equiv \dot{\underset{\sim}{z}}_i\ \ \text{for}\ i = 1,2,\ldots,N \qquad (2.1)$$

where, in the standard notation of mechanics,

$$\underset{\sim}{p}_i = m_i \underset{\sim}{v}_i \quad , \quad \underset{\sim}{v}_i = \dot{\underset{\sim}{r}}_i \tag{2.2}$$

We then represent the set of particle coordinates by

$$\underset{\sim}{r}^N = \{\underset{\sim}{r}_i\} \equiv \{\underset{\sim}{r}_1, \underset{\sim}{r}_2, \ldots, \underset{\sim}{r}_N\} \tag{2.3}$$

with similar notation for $\underset{\sim}{p}^N$, $\underset{\sim}{z}^N$ and $\underset{\sim}{w}^N$.

Newton's Law for particle i , taken together with the above definition, gives

$$\underset{\sim}{w}_i = (\underset{\sim}{v}_i, \underset{\sim}{f}_i) \tag{2.4}$$

where $\underset{\sim}{f}_i$ is the force exerted on particle i by all other particles and external agents, including external force fields and container boundaries.

Given any autonomous dynamical scalar, vector or tensor function $\underline{A} = \underline{A}(\underset{\sim}{z}^N)$, that is, one which depends uniquely on the dynamical variables $\underset{\sim}{z}^N$, we have

$$\dot{\underline{A}} = \underset{\sim}{w}^N \cdot \underset{\sim}{\partial}_N \underline{A} \equiv \sum_i \underset{\sim}{w}_i \cdot \underset{\sim}{\partial}_i \underline{A} \ , \tag{2.5}$$

where

$$\underset{\sim}{\partial}_N \equiv \partial/\partial \underset{\sim}{z}^N \equiv \{\underset{\sim}{\partial}_i\} \equiv \{\partial/\partial \underset{\sim}{z}_i\}$$

(For conservative dynamical systems we recall that $\underset{\sim}{w}^N \cdot \underset{\sim}{\partial}_N \underline{A}$ reduces to the Poisson bracket [17,35].) In the case where $\underline{A}$ is distributed over the particles, such that

$$\underline{A} = \sum_i \underline{A}_i \qquad \text{with} \qquad \underline{A}_i = \underline{A}_i(\underset{\sim}{z}_i) \tag{2.6}$$

our system of point particles serves to map $\underline{A}$ onto physical space through an "$\underline{A}$ - density" $\delta_A(\underset{\sim}{r}, t)$, given by

$$\delta_A(\underset{\sim}{r}, t) = \sum_i \underline{A}_i \delta(\underset{\sim}{r} - \underset{\sim}{r}_i) \tag{2.7}$$

where $\delta(\underset{\sim}{r}-\underset{\sim}{r}_i)$ denotes the Dirac delta. More generally, we could replace $\delta(\underset{\sim}{r}-\underset{\sim}{r}_i)$ by densities $\delta_i(\underset{\sim}{r},t)$ representing continuous distributions of matter and having appropriately defined "velocities" $\underset{\sim}{v}_i$, such that

$$\partial_t\delta_i + \underset{\sim}{v}_i\cdot\underset{\sim}{\nabla}\delta_i = 0, \text{ where } \partial_t = \frac{\partial}{\partial t} \text{ and } \nabla = \frac{\partial}{\partial \underset{\sim}{r}} \qquad (2.8)$$

In the scheme of Kirkwood and coworkers, Eq. (2.7) serves as the fundamental connection between the discrete particulate system and its continuum counterpart, wherein δ_A represents a macroscopic density [17,35]. As such, it serves as the point of departure for the definition of the fluxes which appear in various macroscopic conservation laws, in terms of the particulate dynamics and statistical mechanics†. By forming the time rate of change of (2.7) followed by suitable statistical averaging one is able to identify the relevant spatial flux $\underset{\sim}{j}_A$, say, associated with the quantity $\underline{A}$.

Thus the time-rate of change of δ_A is found from (2.7) as

$$\partial_t\delta_A = \sum_i(\underset{\sim}{w}_i\cdot\underset{\sim}{\partial}_i\underline{A}_i)\delta(\underset{\sim}{r}-\underset{\sim}{r}_i) - \nabla\cdot\left[\sum_i\underline{A}_i\underset{\sim}{v}_i\delta(\underset{\sim}{r}_i-\underset{\sim}{r})\right] \qquad (2.9)$$

where we have employed [33]

$$\frac{\partial}{\partial\underset{\sim}{r}_i}\delta(\underset{\sim}{r}-\underset{\sim}{r}_i) = \frac{\partial}{\partial\underset{\sim}{r}}\delta(\underset{\sim}{r}-\underset{\sim}{r}_i)$$

to cast the second term on the r.h.s. term in the form of a

---

†The formalism of the Kirkwood School suffers from the mild disadvantage of employing generalized functions. Indeed, in the seminal paper [22], use is made of a Taylor series expansion for $\delta(\underset{\sim}{r})$ (with, however, the results carefully corroborated by an independent derivation in the Appendix.) The latter is generalized in the subsequent work of Schofield and Henderson [33], which we follow here. It is plausible that generalized functions could be dispensed with altogether by an appropriate adaptation of the hypervirial theorem (a generalization of the famous Clausius theorem [7,13,21]) to define stress. The present versions of the theorem rely, however, on statistical stationarity in time and a description of container-wall stress which appears somewhat to beg the question. See Gray and Gubbins [17], Appendix E, for an admirably concise summary.

divergence. This is the first step toward identifying a macroscopic flux.

Following a slightly more specialized analysis of Schofield and Henderson [33], we next observe that the first term can also be written formally as a divergence:

$$- \nabla \cdot \left[\sum_i \underset{\sim}{w}_i \cdot \underset{\sim}{\partial}_i \underline{A}_i \oint_{\underset{\sim}{r}_0}^{\underset{\sim}{r}_i} \delta(\underset{\sim}{r}-\underset{\sim}{x}) d\underset{\sim}{x} \right] \qquad (2.10)$$

provided that

$$\sum_i \dot{\underline{A}}_i = \sum_i \underset{\sim}{w}_i \cdot \underset{\sim}{\partial}_i \underline{A}_i = \underline{0} \qquad (2.11)$$

The integral sign in (2.10) indicates integration along an abitrary contour with $\underset{\sim}{r}_0$ as an arbitrary initial point.

The condition (2.11) is similar in form to the condition of stationarity in the mean employed in various forms of the hypervirial theorem [17]. Ultimately, the present treatment also requires only that (2.11) be true for general $\underline{A}$ in some appropriate mean, $\langle \Sigma \dot{\underline{A}}_i \rangle = 0$. However, for the momentum flux of interest here, (2.11) is in fact guaranteed strictly by (1.4)-(1.5) and without the further conditions of [33].

Substitution of (2.10) into (2.9) leads to a relation having the form of a conservation law:

$$\partial_t \delta_A + \nabla \cdot \underset{\sim}{j}_A = 0 \qquad (2.12)$$

with spatial flux defined by

$$\underset{\sim}{j}_A(r,t) = \sum_i \left[\underset{\sim}{w}_i \cdot \underset{\sim}{\partial}_i \underline{A}_i \oint_{\underset{\sim}{r}_0}^{\underset{\sim}{r}_i} \delta(\underset{\sim}{r}-\underset{\sim}{x}) d\underset{\sim}{x} + \underline{A}_i \underset{\sim}{v}_i \delta(\underset{\sim}{r}-\underset{\sim}{r}_i) \right]$$

...(2.13)

(which has tensorial rank one degree higher than that of $\underline{A}$.)

As emphasized by preceding workers [33,39], there is an arbitrariness in j_A arising from the initial point r_0 and the undefined contour of integration, as well as from the possibility of an additive solenoidal (divergence-free) term in (2.13) [22,33,35]. However, it is easy to show that an integral

$$\underset{\sim}{i}(\underset{\sim}{r}) \equiv \oint f(\underset{\sim}{r}-\underset{\sim}{x})d\underset{\sim}{x} \quad , \qquad (2.14)$$

involving integration around a closed contour of a function f with suitably defined gradient, is solenoidal so that the arbitrary contour in (2.13) engenders at worst an additive solenoidal term. Thus the above-mentioned sources of arbitrariness are not all distinct.

In the case of primary interest we have

$$\underline{A}_i = \underset{\sim}{p}_i \, , \quad \underline{A} = \underset{\sim}{p} \equiv \sum_i \underset{\sim}{p}_i , \quad \text{and} \quad \underset{\sim}{w}_i \cdot \underset{\sim}{\partial}_i \underline{A}_i = \dot{\underset{\sim}{p}}_i = \underset{\sim}{f}_i \qquad (2.15)$$

where we recall that $\underset{\sim}{f}_i$ is the force on particle i . Since the presence of external force fields poses no special difficulty and is adequately treated in other works [33,35], we simplify the present discussion by considering only the interparticle forces. We further assume the latter satisfy (1.4) and (1.5) with

$$\underset{\sim}{f}_{ij} = \underset{\sim}{f}_{ij}(\underset{\sim}{z}^N) \qquad (2.16)$$

All such forces are assumed to be translation invariant (i.e., unchanged by $\underset{\sim}{r}^N \to \underset{\sim}{r}^N + \underset{\sim}{r}_0^N$, where $\underset{\sim}{r}_0^N$ is an arbitrary constant.)

The condition (1.5) obviously guarantees (2.11) and allows us to write the flux (2.13) in the form

$$\underset{\approx}{j}_p = \sum_{i>j} \underset{\sim}{f}_{ij} \oint_{\underset{\sim}{r}_j}^{\underset{\sim}{r}_i} \delta(\underset{\sim}{r}-\underset{\sim}{x})d\underset{\sim}{x} + \sum_i \underset{\sim}{p}_i \underset{\sim}{v}_i \delta(\underset{\sim}{r}-\underset{\sim}{r}_i) \qquad (2.17)$$

in which the arbitrary point r_0 no longer appears, so that the only arbitrariness is associated with choice of integration contour. As with (2.13), this is tantamount to an arbitrary additive solenoidal term

$$\oint \delta(\underset{\sim}{r}-\underset{\sim}{x})d\underset{\sim}{x}$$

involving an arbitrary closed circuit.

The macroscopic or continuum stress field $\underset{\sim}{T}(\underset{\sim}{r},t)$ follows from (2.17) as

$$\underset{\sim}{T} = -\langle \underset{\sim}{j}'_p \rangle \equiv \rho \underset{\sim}{v}\underset{\sim}{v} - \langle \underset{\sim}{j}_p \rangle = \underset{\sim}{T}_K + \underset{\sim}{T}_C \text{ , say} \tag{2.18}$$

with

$$\rho = \langle \sum_i m_i \delta(\underset{\sim}{r}-\underset{\sim}{r}_i) \rangle \tag{2.19}$$

and

$$\underset{\sim}{v} = \frac{1}{\rho} \langle \sum_i \underset{\sim}{p}_i \delta(\underset{\sim}{r}-\underset{\sim}{r}_i) \rangle \tag{2.20}$$

where

$$\underset{\sim}{T}_K = -\langle \sum_i \underset{\sim}{p}'_i \underset{\sim}{v}'_i \delta(\underset{\sim}{r}-\underset{\sim}{r}_i) \rangle, \text{ with } \underset{\sim}{v}'_i = \underset{\sim}{v}_i - \underset{\sim}{v}, \quad \underset{\sim}{p}' = m_i \underset{\sim}{v}'_i \tag{2.21}$$

and

$$\underset{\sim}{T}_C = \langle \sum_{i>j} \sum \underset{\sim}{f}_{ij} \oint_{\underset{\sim}{r}_i}^{\underset{\sim}{r}_j} \delta(\underset{\sim}{r}-\underset{\sim}{x})d\underset{\sim}{x} \rangle \tag{2.22}$$

yield the kinetic and configurational stress, respectively. The brackets $\langle\ \rangle$ denote statistical phase-space averages of the form

$$\langle A \rangle = \int_{Z^N} A(\underset{\sim}{z}^N)\psi(t,\underset{\sim}{z}^N)dZ^N \tag{2.23}$$

with respect to a suitable distribution $\psi(t,\underset{\sim}{z}^N)$, which may also depend on $\underset{\sim}{r}$ in the case of highly non-homogeneous states. Then, with

$$dZ^N = dV^N dP^N \quad , \quad dV^N = dV(\underset{\sim}{r}_1)\ldots dV(\underset{\sim}{r}_N) \quad , \quad \text{and}$$

$$dP^N = dP(\underset{\sim}{p}_1)\ldots dP(\underset{\sim}{p}_N) \tag{2.24}$$

denoting the respective volume elements in phase, position and momentum space, we have the various marginal position-space number distributions (denoted by $n^{(m)}$ in [21], p. 83):

$$\rho^{(1)}(t,\mathbf{r}^N) = \frac{1}{(N-1)!}\int_{V^{N-1}} \rho^{(N)}(t,\mathbf{r}_1,\mathbf{r}^{N-1})dV^{N-1} \qquad (2.25)$$

$$\rho^{(2)}(t,\mathbf{r}_1,\mathbf{r}_2) = \frac{1}{(N-2)!}\int_{V^{N-2}} \rho^{(N)}(t,\mathbf{r}_1,\mathbf{r}_2,\mathbf{r}^{N-2})dV^{N-2} \qquad \ldots(2.26)$$

etc., with

$$\rho^{(N)}(t,\mathbf{r}^N) = N!\int_{P^N} \psi(t,\mathbf{z}^N)dP^N \qquad (2.27)$$

representing the N-particle spatial distribution.

Although the above treatment allows for general force laws, in which interparticle forces may depend on particle velocities as well as positions, we focus attention here on the special case of velocity-independent forces. Then, the configurational stress $\mathbf{T}_C$ is given by

$$\mathbf{T}_C = \frac{1}{2N!}\sum_{i>j}\sum \int_{V^N}\oint_{\mathbf{r}_i}^{\mathbf{r}_j} \delta(\mathbf{r}-\mathbf{x})\mathbf{f}_{ij}(\mathbf{r}^N)\rho^{(N)}(\mathbf{r}^N)d\mathbf{x}dV^N$$

where for brevity we henceforth suppress notation for dependence on time t.

Since we are considering identical particles, all terms in the sum (2.28) are essentially the same and (2.28) can be replaced by

$$\mathbf{T}_C = \frac{1}{2(N-2)!}\int_{V^{N-2}}\int_V\int_V\oint_{\mathbf{r}_1}^{\mathbf{r}_2} \delta(\mathbf{r}-\mathbf{x})\mathbf{f}_{12}(\mathbf{r}_1,\mathbf{r}_2,\mathbf{r}^{N-2})$$

$$\otimes\ \rho^{(N)}(\mathbf{r}_1,\mathbf{r}_2,\mathbf{r}^{N-2})d\mathbf{x}dV(\mathbf{r}_1)dV(\mathbf{r}_2)dV^{N-2} \qquad \ldots(2.29)$$

As an exception to the Gibbs notation employed elsewhere, we employ the standard symbol $\otimes$ for dyadic products which have factors on different lines of text. Then, making use of the new variables of integration:

$$\bar{\underset{\sim}{r}} = \frac{\underset{\sim}{r}_1+\underset{\sim}{r}_2}{2} \quad , \underset{\sim}{r}_{12} = \underset{\sim}{r}_2-\underset{\sim}{r}_1 \quad , \underset{\sim}{y} = \underset{\sim}{x}-\bar{\underset{\sim}{r}} \tag{2.30}$$

and the fundamental property of the Dirac δ , (2.29) becomes

$$\underset{\sim}{T}_C = \frac{1}{(N-2)!} \int_{V^{N-2}} \int_V \oint_{\frac{1}{2}\underset{\sim}{r}_{12}}^{\frac{1}{2}\underset{\sim}{r}_{12}} \underset{\sim}{f}_{12}(\underset{\sim}{r}-\underset{\sim}{y}-\tfrac{1}{2}\underset{\sim}{r}_{12},\underset{\sim}{r}-\underset{\sim}{y}+\tfrac{1}{2}\underset{\sim}{r}_{12},\underset{\sim}{r}^{N-2})$$

$$\otimes\ \rho^{(N)}(\underset{\sim}{r}-\underset{\sim}{y}-\tfrac{1}{2}\underset{\sim}{r}_{12},\underset{\sim}{r}-\underset{\sim}{y}+\tfrac{1}{2}\underset{\sim}{r}_{12},r^{N-2})d\underset{\sim}{y}dV(\underset{\sim}{r}_{12})dV^{N-2} \qquad \ldots(2.31)$$

If, finally, we choose the straight line path of integration in (2.31):

$$\underset{\sim}{y} = (\alpha-\tfrac{1}{2})\underset{\sim}{r}_{12} \ , \text{ with } 0\le\alpha\le 1 \ , \text{ and } \ d\underset{\sim}{y} = \underset{\sim}{r}_{12}d\alpha \tag{2.32}$$

then we get the Irving-Kirkwood form [22,32,33]:

$$\underset{\sim}{T}_C = \frac{1}{2(N-2)!} \int_{V^{N-2}} \int_V \int_0^1 \underset{\sim}{f}_{12}(\underset{\sim}{r}-\alpha\underset{\sim}{r}_{12},\underset{\sim}{r}-\alpha\underset{\sim}{r}_{12}+\underset{\sim}{r}_{12},\underset{\sim}{r}^{N-2})$$

$$\times\ \underset{\sim}{r}_{12}\rho^{(N)}(\underset{\sim}{r}-\alpha\underset{\sim}{r}_{12},\underset{\sim}{r}-\alpha\underset{\sim}{r}_{12}+\underset{\sim}{r}_{12},\underset{\sim}{r}^{N-2})d\alpha dV(\underset{\sim}{r}_{12})dV^{N-2} \tag{2.33}$$

We note that with the standard approximation wherein $\underset{\sim}{f}_{12}(\underset{\sim}{r}_1,\underset{\sim}{r}_2,\underset{\sim}{r}^{N-2})$ depends only on its first two arguments, i.e., only on the positions of the members of interacting pair "12", all the formulae (2.28)-(2.33) can be simplified and expressed in terms of $\rho^{(2)}$, by integration over $\underset{\sim}{r}^{N-2}$ and application of (2.26). We also recall that (2.33) is arbitrary up to an additive term of the form

$$\frac{1}{(N-2)!}\int_{V^{N-2}}\int_{V}\oint \underset{\sim}{f}_{12}(\underset{\sim}{x}-\underset{\sim}{r}_{12},\underset{\sim}{x},\underset{\sim}{r}^{N-2})\rho^{(N)}(\underset{\sim}{x}-\underset{\sim}{r}_{12},\underset{\sim}{x},\underset{\sim}{r}^{N-2})$$

$$\otimes\, d\underset{\sim}{x}dV(\underset{\sim}{r}_{12})dV^{N-2} \qquad (2.34)$$

Because, however, of the postulated translation invariance of the force $\underset{\sim}{f}_{12}$ we can replace the function $\underset{\sim}{f}_{12}(\underset{\sim}{r}_1,\underset{\sim}{r}_2,\underset{\sim}{r}^{N-2})$ by one having argument $(\underset{\sim}{r}_{12},\underset{\sim}{r}^{N-2}-\underset{\sim}{r}_1)$ and, hence, the function $\underset{\sim}{f}_{12}$ in (2.34) by one with argument

$$(\underset{\sim}{r}_{12},\underset{\sim}{r}^{N-2}-\underset{\sim}{x}) \text{ , where } \underset{\sim}{r}^{N-2}-\underset{\sim}{x} \equiv \{\underset{\sim}{r}_3-\underset{\sim}{x},\ldots,\underset{\sim}{r}_N-\underset{\sim}{x}\} \qquad (2.35)$$

As observed by Irving and Kirkwood [22] in slightly different terms, if the fluid is homogeneous such that $\rho^{(N)}$ is also translation invariant then it is invariant to the same transformation of argument, in (2.34). Then, by changing the variable of integration $\underset{\sim}{r}^{N-2}$ to $\underset{\sim}{r}^{N-2}-\underset{\sim}{x}$, one sees that (2.34) vanishes identically as does the arbitrariness in $\underset{\sim}{T}_C$. Otherwise, one sees by the same change of integration variables that (2.34) reduces to an integral of the form

$$\int_{V^{N-2}}\int_{V} \underset{\sim}{f}(\underset{\sim}{r}_{12},\underset{\sim}{r}^{N-2})\left[\oint \rho^{(N)}(\underset{\sim}{x}-\underset{\sim}{r}_{12},\underset{\sim}{x},\underset{\sim}{r}^{N-2}+\underset{\sim}{x})d\underset{\sim}{x}\right]dV(\underset{\sim}{r}_{12})dV^{N-2}$$

which, in effect, corresponds to an arbitrary additive term in the sum (1.1) of the form $\underset{\sim}{f}\underset{\sim}{\ell}_0$. As discussed in the recent literature, this type of arbitrariness leads to certain indeterminancies in the so-called mechanical theory of surface tension [11,24,32,39]. As also indicated in the Conclusions, the reasoning of the preceding paragraph can be employed to simplify (2.33), reducing it basically to (1.1). We now turn to a review of the classical approach to (2.28) and (2.33).

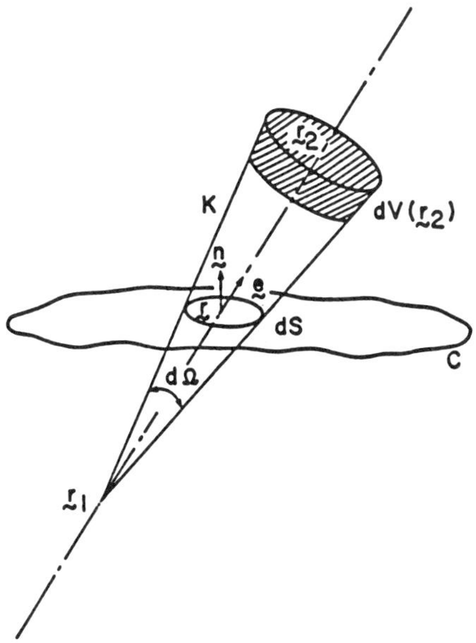

FIGURE 1. GEOMETRY OF A PAIRWISE INTERACTION ACROSS A SURFACE S.

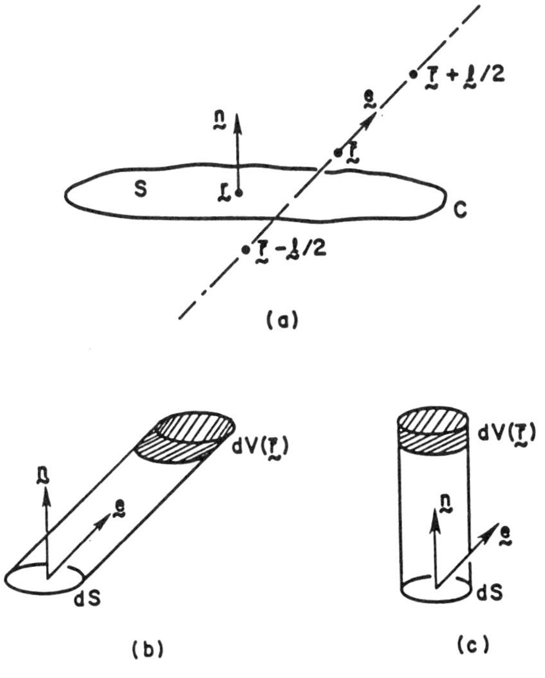

FIGURE 2. ALTERNATIVE DESCRIPTION OF AN INTERACTING PAIR.

3. THE CAUCHY METHOD

By considering all the possible pairs of particles which can interact across a given surface, say, S bounded by the closed curve C as shown in Figure 1, we calculate their contribution to the contact force on an elemental area dS of S situated at position $\underset{\sim}{r}$ on S . With the first particle situated at position $\underset{\sim}{r}_1$ on one side of S , we construct a cone K having apex $\underset{\sim}{r}_1$ and generators passing through the boundary of dS , which subtend a solid angle

$$d\Omega = d\Omega(\underset{\sim}{e}) = \underset{\sim}{e}\cdot\underset{\sim}{n}dS/r^{*2} \tag{3.1}$$

where $\underset{\sim}{n}$ is the unit normal to dS on the side opposite $\underset{\sim}{r}_1$, while

$$r^* = |\underset{\sim}{r}^*| \quad , \quad \text{and} \quad \underset{\sim}{e} = \underset{\sim}{r}^*/r^* \quad , \tag{3.2}$$

where $\underset{\sim}{r}^* = \underset{\sim}{r}-\underset{\sim}{r}_1$ (3.3)

is the vector connecting $\underset{\sim}{r}_1$ to $\underset{\sim}{r}$.

The particle at $\underset{\sim}{r}_1$ can interact directly across dS with any particle at position $\underset{\sim}{r}_2$ lying in the base of the cone K , such that $(\underset{\sim}{r}_2-\underset{\sim}{r})\cdot\underset{\sim}{n}$ is non-negative. The associated volume element is

$$dV(\underset{\sim}{r}_2) = r_{12}{}^2 dr_{12} d\Omega(\underset{\sim}{e}) = (r_{12}/r^*)^2 dr_{12}\underset{\sim}{e}\cdot\underset{\sim}{n}dS \tag{3.4}$$

where of course

$$r_{12} = |\underset{\sim}{r}_{12}| \quad \text{with} \quad \underset{\sim}{r}_{12} = \underset{\sim}{r}_2-\underset{\sim}{r}_1 = \underset{\sim}{e}r_{12} \tag{3.5}$$

The probability of such an interacting pair is given by

$$\rho^{(N)}(\underset{\sim}{r}_1,\underset{\sim}{r}_2,\underset{\sim}{r}^{N-2})dV(\underset{\sim}{r}_1)dV(\underset{\sim}{r}_2)dV^{N-2}$$

$$= \frac{1}{(N-2)!}\Big[\rho^{(N)}(\underset{\sim}{r}_1,\underset{\sim}{r}_1+\underset{\sim}{e}r_{12},\underset{\sim}{r}^{N-2})\underset{\sim}{e}(r_{12}/r^*)^2 dr_{12}dV(\underset{\sim}{r}_1)$$

$$\times\, dV^{N-2}\Big]\cdot\underset{\sim}{n}dS \qquad \ldots(3.6)$$

where $\underset{\sim}{r}^*$ is given by (3.3). Multiplication of (3.6) by the pairwise force

$$\underset{\sim}{f}_{12}(\underset{\sim}{r}_1,\underset{\sim}{r}_2,\underset{\sim}{r}^{N-2}) = \underset{\sim}{f}_{12}(\underset{\sim}{r}_1,\underset{\sim}{r}_1+\underset{\sim}{e}r_{12},\underset{\sim}{r}^{N-2}) \quad ,$$

followed by integration of r_{12} over (r^*, ∞) and of $dV(\underset{\sim}{r}_1)dV^{N-2}$ over V^{N-1} yields the contribution of all such pairs to the contact force $d\underset{\sim}{f}_n$ acting on dS (now multipled by a factor 2, since we have relaxed the above restriction $(\underset{\sim}{r}_2-\underset{\sim}{r})\cdot\underset{\sim}{n} \geq 0$ and thus have counted pairs twice). By subsitution of the variable $\underset{\sim}{r}^*$ in (3.3) for $\underset{\sim}{r}_1$ we then find that the resulting stress on dS is given by

$$\underset{\sim}{t}_n \equiv d\underset{\sim}{f}_n/dS = \underset{\sim}{T}_C\cdot\underset{\sim}{n}$$

where

$$\underset{\sim}{T}_C = \frac{1}{2(N-2)!}\int_{V^{N-2}}\int_V\int_{r_{12}=r^*}^{\infty} \underset{\sim}{f}_{12}^{(N)}\,(\underset{\sim}{r}-\underset{\sim}{r}^*,\underset{\sim}{r}-\underset{\sim}{r}^*+\underset{\sim}{e}r_{12},\underset{\sim}{r}^{N-2})\underset{\sim}{e}$$

$$\times\ (r_{12}/r^*)^2 dr_{12}dV(\underset{\sim}{r}^*)dV^{N-2} \tag{3.7}$$

in which $\underset{\sim}{e}$ is defined by (3.2) in terms of $\underset{\sim}{r}^*$ and in which we have written, for brevity,

$$\underset{\sim}{f}_{12}^{(N)}(\underset{\sim}{r}^N) \equiv \rho^{(N)}(\underset{\sim}{r}^N)\ \underset{\sim}{f}_{12}(\underset{\sim}{r}^N) \tag{3.8}$$

Noting, however, that

$$\underset{\sim}{r}_{12} = \underset{\sim}{e}r_{12} \quad , \quad dV(\underset{\sim}{r}^*) = r^{*2}dr^*d\Omega(\underset{\sim}{e}) \quad ,$$

and

$$dV(\underset{\sim}{r}_{12}) = r_{12}{}^2 dr_{12}d\Omega(\underset{\sim}{e}) \quad , \tag{3.9}$$

we can convert the integral (3.7) from its present form:

$$\int_V \int_{r_{12}=r^*}^{\infty} \underset{\sim}{F}\ dr_{12}dV(\underset{\sim}{r}^*)$$

involving r_{12} and $\underset{\sim}{r}^*$ as integration variables, to a form involving r^* and $\underset{\sim}{r}_{12}$:

$$\int_V \int_{r^*=0}^{r_{12}} \underset{\sim}{F}(r^*/r_{12})^2 dr^* dV(\underset{\sim}{r}_{12})$$

in which all terms in $\underset{\sim}{r}^*$ are to be replaced by $r^*\underset{\sim}{e}$, the unit vector $\underset{\sim}{e}$ being defined now in terms of $\underset{\sim}{r}_{12}$ by (3.9). If we further let

$$r^* = \alpha r_{12} \qquad (0 \leq \alpha \leq 1)$$

with α as a variable of integration in place of r^*, then (3.7) becomes

$$\underset{\sim}{T}_C = \frac{1}{2(N-2)!} \int_{V^{N-2}} \int_V \int_0^1 \underset{\sim}{f}_{12}^{(N)}(\underset{\sim}{r}-\alpha\underset{\sim}{r}_{12}, \underset{\sim}{r}-\alpha\underset{\sim}{r}_{12}+\underset{\sim}{r}_{12}, \underset{\sim}{r}^{N-2})$$

$$\otimes \underset{\sim}{r}_{12} d\alpha dV(\underset{\sim}{r}_{12}) dV^{N-2} \qquad (3.10)$$

which of course is identical with (2.33). We now consider a form which contains the arbitrariness of (2.28).

3.1 <u>An Alternative Form</u>. For a slightly different derivation of the pair contribution to stress, we let

$$\frac{1}{(N-2)!} \hat{\rho}^{(N)}(\bar{\underset{\sim}{r}}, \underset{\sim}{\ell}, \underset{\sim}{r}^{N-2}) dV(\bar{\underset{\sim}{r}}) dV(\underset{\sim}{\ell}) dV^{N-2} \qquad (3.11)$$

denote the probability of finding an arbitrarily selected pair having midpoint $\bar{\underset{\sim}{r}}$ and separation distance $\underset{\sim}{\ell}$, with all N-2 remaining particles in positions $\underset{\sim}{r}^{N-2}$. Also, we let $\underset{\sim}{f}(\bar{\underset{\sim}{r}}, \underset{\sim}{\ell}, \underset{\sim}{r}^N)$ denote the force exerted by one member of the pair, at $\bar{\underset{\sim}{r}}+\underset{\sim}{\ell}/2$, on the other, at $\bar{\underset{\sim}{r}}-\underset{\sim}{\ell}/2$. By means of the associated transformation of variables with unit Jacobian:

$$(\bar{\underset{\sim}{r}}, \underset{\sim}{\ell}) \leftrightarrow (\underset{\sim}{r}_1, \underset{\sim}{r}_2) \quad \text{with} \quad \underset{\sim}{\ell} = \underset{\sim}{r}_{12} \qquad (3.12)$$

where $\bar{\underset{\sim}{r}}$ and $\underset{\sim}{r}_{12}$ are defined by (2.30), we see that $\hat{\rho}^{(N)}$ of

(3.11) is related to the distribution function (2.27) by

$$\hat{\rho}^{(N)}(\underset{\sim}{r},\underset{\sim}{\ell},\underset{\sim}{r}^{N-2}) = \rho^{(N)}(\underset{\sim}{r}-\underset{\sim}{\ell}/2,\underset{\sim}{r}+\underset{\sim}{\ell}/2,\underset{\sim}{r}^{N-2}) \qquad (3.13)$$

We also have similar relation between the above force $\hat{\underset{\sim}{f}}$ and that of (2.28).

The distribution $\hat{\rho}$ is essentially the same as that giving position and orientation of the "bead-spring" or "dumbell" model which is familiar in the literature on macromolecules [5]. By arguments which are also familiar in that same literature, we can determine the contribution of our arbitrarily selected particle pair to the stress on an element of area S , as shown in Figure 2a. However, there are different ways in which we can choose to select the volume element $dV(\bar{\underset{\sim}{r}})dV(\underset{\sim}{\ell})$ containing the pair in question and, thence, to perform the integration over a suitably restricted range of $\bar{\underset{\sim}{r}}$ and $\underset{\sim}{\ell}$.

For example, and as illustrated in Figure 2b, we may select a prism containing the axis $\underset{\sim}{e} = \underset{\sim}{\ell}/\ell$ and center $\bar{\underset{\sim}{r}}$ of the pair, having an element dS of S as base and having

$$dV(\bar{\underset{\sim}{r}}) = \underset{\sim}{e}\cdot\underset{\sim}{n}dSd\bar{r} \qquad (3.14)$$

This corresponds to the type of direct interaction across dS considered in the preceding section, and an appropriate integration with respect to $\bar{r}$ and $\underset{\sim}{\ell}$ leads again to the (3.10).

Instead of the above, we may choose a cylinder normal to S containing $\underset{\sim}{r}$ and having base dS , as shown in Figure 2c, with

$$dV(\bar{\underset{\sim}{r}}) = \underset{\sim}{n}\cdot d\bar{\underset{\sim}{r}}dS \qquad (3.15)$$

In this case, a pair which acts across dS must have

$$\pm[(\bar{\underset{\sim}{r}}\pm\underset{\sim}{\ell}/2)-\underset{\sim}{r}]\cdot\underset{\sim}{n} > 0 \qquad (3.16)$$

where either the upper or the lower pair of signs must be chosen, corresponding to the condition that the pair straddle dS . Thus, the expected contribution to the force acting on dS from the given pair is found to be

$$d\underset{\sim}{f}_n = \frac{1}{2(N-2)!}\left[\int_{V^{N-2}}\int_{V}\oint_{\underset{\sim}{r}-\underset{\sim}{\ell}/2}^{\underset{\sim}{r}+\underset{\sim}{\ell}/2} \hat{\underset{\sim}{f}}(\bar{\underset{\sim}{r}},\underset{\sim}{\ell},\underset{\sim}{r}^{N-2})\hat{\rho}^{(N)}(\bar{\underset{\sim}{r}},\underset{\sim}{\ell},\underset{\sim}{r}^{N-2}) \otimes d\bar{\underset{\sim}{r}}dV(\underset{\sim}{\ell})dV^{N-2}\right]\cdot\underset{\sim}{n}d\underset{\sim}{S} \qquad (3.17)$$

where we have included a factor 1/2 in order properly to weigh the cases $\pm\underset{\sim}{\ell}\cdot\underset{\sim}{n}>0$.

The appearance of the integral in (3.17) involving integration along an arbitrary path with endpoints $\underset{\sim}{r}\pm\underset{\sim}{\ell}/2$ is the result of an abitrariness, up to an additive vector perpendicular to $\underset{\sim}{n}$, in the location $\underset{\sim}{r}$. This corresponds to a lateral displacement, parallel to S , of the pair center. (Of course, such displacements are confined roughly to lie within the area S , whose linear dimensions are much larger than ℓ , such that we count only those particle pairs having centers in immediate or "molecular" proximity to S .)

Upon substituting the functions $\hat{\underset{\sim}{f}}$ and $\hat{\rho}^{(N)}$, with arguments transformed as in (3.13) above, we see that (3.17) gives the same expression for the stress vector $\underset{\sim}{t}_n$ as (2.28).

4. CONCLUSIONS

Having reached the end of our detailed analysis, we observe that the elementary relations (1.1)-(1.3) postulated at the outset can be reinterpreted now as

$$\underset{\sim}{T} = \nu\ [\ \overline{\underset{\sim}{f}\underset{\sim}{\ell}} - \overline{\underset{\sim}{p}'\underset{\sim}{v}'}] \qquad (4.1)$$

where $\nu=N(N-1)/2V$ denotes the number of distinct particle pairs per unit volume and the overbars denote numerical averages of the form

$$\bar{A} = \frac{1}{\nu V}\Sigma A \qquad (4.2)$$

where, as before, Σ denotes a sum over all (νV) pairs or a sum over all particles, as appropriate.

We may now compare (4.1) with the Kirkwood form (2.33). Based on the arguments immediately following (2.33), we see that the term $\underset{\sim}{f}_{12}\underset{\sim}{r}_{12}\rho^{(N)}$ appearing in the integrand can be replaced by

$$\underset{\sim}{f}_{12}(\underset{\sim}{0},\underset{\sim}{r}_{12},\underset{\sim}{r}^{N-2})\underset{\sim}{r}_{12}\rho^{(N)}(\underset{\sim}{r}-\alpha\underset{\sim}{r}_{12},\underset{\sim}{r}-\alpha\underset{\sim}{r}_{12}+\underset{\sim}{r}_{12},\underset{\sim}{r}^{N-2}+\underset{\sim}{r}-\alpha\underset{\sim}{r}_{12})$$

owing to the translation in variance of $\underset{\sim}{f}_{12}$ and thus, subsequently, by

$$\underset{\sim}{f}_{12}(\underset{\sim}{0},\underset{\sim}{r}_{12},\underset{\sim}{r}^{N-2})\underset{\sim}{r}_{12}\rho^{(N)}(\underset{\sim}{0},\underset{\sim}{r}_{12},\underset{\sim}{r}^{N-2})$$

for homogeneous media. Furthermore, in the latter case the reasoning of Section 2 establishes the uniqueness of (2.33). Therefore, for a statistically homogeneous system, and with the usual assumption that number averages can be equated to (ensemble) averages $< >$ based on (2.23)-(2.27), we see that (4.1) is equivalent to the result put forth in the literature on statistical mechanics and hydrodynamics.

In the case of strongly non-homogeneous systems, the next-to-last of the preceding expressions applies, and the term in $\rho^{(N)}$ can be written formally in terms of a differential operator [10,22] as

$$\exp\{-\alpha\underset{\sim}{r}_{12}\cdot\nabla\}\rho^{(N)}(\underset{\sim}{r},\underset{\sim}{r}+\underset{\sim}{r}_{12},\underset{\sim}{r}^{N-2}+\underset{\sim}{r}) \ , \text{ where } \nabla = \frac{\partial}{\partial\underset{\sim}{r}}$$

The Taylor series expansion of this operator in α justifies a related expansion of $\delta(\underset{\sim}{r})$ [22] and, simultaneously, generates a set of moments $\underset{\sim}{f}\underset{\sim}{\ell}\underset{\sim}{\ell}$, $\underset{\sim}{f}\underset{\sim}{\ell}\underset{\sim}{\ell}\underset{\sim}{\ell}$, etc., all of which were mentioned above in the Introduction. As indicated there, one can interpret such terms as signaling the demise of the simple continuum and the emergence of a multipolar medium, engendered by spatial gradients ∇ which are large on the microscale ℓ . Along with these effects there also emerges an arbitrary additive stress field, which is divergence-free and hence self-equilibrated, of the type discussed above in Section 2. Although the physical significance is not entirely clear, this stress appears to be associated with a kind of "loop tension" arising from the inhomogeneity, much like that associated with mathematical dislocations [26]. Such effects evidently reflect the state of affairs in the molecular theory of capillarity [11,39]. Furthermore, one sees that the Cauchy stress is represented by the zeroth-order terms in α, both in the above expansions and the integrand of (2.33).

Although we have restricted attention to systems of structureless point masses, there should be little doubt that the basic forms (1.1)-(1.3) would also serve to define the Cauchy stress, as a force (plus momentum-flux) dipole, in other situations. This expectation is borne out by existing treatments of multicomponent mixtures of interacting particles [4,11], even though new effects such as partial stress and ("chemical") body forces arise. In systems with still more complex microstructure, as envisioned in the general analysis of Dahler and Scriven [10] and in the numerous works they survey, one would of course be obliged to include internal force dipoles, intrinsic to particles with (deformable) microstructure. Examples from suspension rheology are already evident [2,34].

Possible exceptions to the simple forms (1.1)-(1.3) could occur in the case of systems with interactions limited by signal speed, for example, as might occur in certain hydrodynamic models of cosmological structures. Even in these cases we suspect that (1.1)-(1.3) would still provide a model of an effective continuum stress, with the kinetic term now including the spatial momentum flux associated with propagation of the relevant force carriers (as with the radiation stress mentioned in the opening paragraphs). Such considerations would no doubt take us beyond the classical scope of the present article.

A comment should be made on the compatibility with energy principles of forms like (1.1)-(1.3) and their statistical counterparts, since such principles ultimately must undergird the concept of continuum stress. In particular, the instantaneous volumetric rate of internal ("stress") working,

$$\dot{W} = \underset{\sim}{T}:\underset{\sim}{L}, \quad \text{with} \quad \underset{\sim}{L} = (\nabla \underset{\sim}{v})^T \tag{4.3}$$

where $\nabla\underset{\sim}{v}$ is an effective-continuum velocity gradient, serves to define the present stress $\underset{\sim}{T}$ following any deformation history, given an arbitrary instanteously imposed $\underset{\sim}{L}$. Then, considering only the configurational stress term in (1.1) we see that the associated rate of working is

$$\dot{W}_C = \frac{1}{V} \Sigma \, \underset{\sim}{f}\cdot(\underset{\sim}{L}\cdot\underset{\sim}{\ell}) \tag{4.4}$$

which is precisely what one would calculate assuming that particle pairs move "affinely", with the instantaneously imposed velocity gradient.

Except for very special cases, and as assumed in various treatments of linear elasticity [1,6,26], one does not anticipate such affine or homogeneous microstructural motion. Instead, we expect to have an additional relative velocities between particles $\Delta\underset{\sim}{v}'$, say, so that an additional term $\Sigma\underset{\sim}{f}\cdot\Delta\underset{\sim}{v}'$ must be added to the sum in (4.4) in order to obtain the true work effect. Since $\underset{\sim}{f}$ generally is statistically correlated with $\Delta\underset{\sim}{v}'$, such a term will involve non-zero configurational energy effects, for example, interparticle potential energy.

In the key statistical mechanics literature [22,35], an energy balance is simultaneously formulated, in such a way as to include work terms of the above type in a nominal heat-flux vector. If this were generally valid it would appear to imply a principle of virtual work, whereby the present stress $\underset{\sim}{T}(t)$, following an arbitrary history of motion, is determined by the work done in every virtual instantaneous deformation, as represented by $\underset{\sim}{L}dt$. This, incidentally, produces the same results as obtained by assuming homogeneous motions in the linear theory of elasticity for regular lattices [6,26]. Without some such principle, it seems we should have to regard the effective continuum velocity gradient $\underset{\sim}{L}$ as being generally different from the gradient of the mass-average velocity (2.20). This corresponds to the type of "polarization" envisaged by Dahler and Scriven [10] and to the notions of intrinsic microstructural kinematics in general theories of structured continua [23,36,37]. However, the latter course does not appear to be appropriate to the simple continuum approximation, and a further analysis would be desirable. At any rate, the question takes on a certain practical imporatnce in certain current applications, where energy methods are being employed for systems with highly disordered microstructure [1].

As a closing remark related to the preceding consideration, we note the question of compatibility with energy principles appears related to the well-known principle of material frame indifference. The latter would be necessary for application, at the microstructural level, of the technique of Green and Rivlin [18,23] mentioned in the Introduction, and here we encounter a conceptual problem. In particular, while true that the dyadic forms in $\underset{\sim}{f},\underset{\sim}{\ell},p,\underset{\sim}{v}$ appearing in (1.1)-(1.2) transform compatibly with the stress tensor $\underset{\sim}{T}$ under instantaneous changes of frame, the microscopic dynamics and, hence, the statistical distributions and averages < > will not generally exhibit the required indifference to a time-dependent history of such frame changes. (We note that the Euclid invariance postulated in theories of structural elastic continua is of a weaker variety, than that required here. See [36], p. 29.) Thus to rescue the principle, it appears that one would have to accord it the status of the Second Law of thermodynamics, in which certain symmetries of the microstructural dynamics are not manifest in the overlying continuum.

ACKNOWLEDGEMENT

The author gratefully acknowledges the outstanding work of Karen Woo in preparing the typescript and he also expresses thanks to those who organized the conference in which the paper is presented.

NOMENCLATURE

Roman

A	autonomous dynamical function
$\underset{\sim}{e}$	unit vector in direction $\underset{\sim}{\ell}$
$\underset{\sim}{f}$	interparticle force
$\underset{\sim}{j}$	flux
$\underset{\sim}{\ell}$	interparticle separation
$\underset{\sim}{M}$	force dipole
$\underset{\sim}{n}$	unit normal to a surface
N	number of particles
$\underset{\sim}{p}$	linear momentum
$\underset{\sim}{r}$	(relative) position of particle(s)
S	surface
$\underset{\sim}{T}$	Cauchy stress
t	time
$\underset{\sim}{v}$	velocity
V	volume
$\underset{\sim}{w}$	phase-space velocity
$\dot{W}$	work rate
$\underset{\sim}{x}$	spatial position
$\underset{\sim}{z}$	phase-space position

Greek

α	dummy variable (2.33)
δ	density or Dirac delta
ρ	spatial number density (2.27)
$\underset{\sim}{\Pi}$	momentum-flux dipole
ψ	phase-space density
Ω	solid angle

Indices

$\alpha, \beta, \ldots$	vector and tensor indices
C	configurational (stress)
$i, j, \ldots$	(subscripts) particle labels
K	kinetic (stress)
$\sim$	vector or tensor (Gibbs dyadic notation employed)

REFERENCES

1. Alexander, S., "Is the Elastic Energy of Amorphous Materials Rotationally Invariant?" J. Physique, 45, 1939 (1984).

2. Batchelor, G. K., "The Stress System in a Suspension of Force-free Particles", J. Fluid Mech., 41, 545 (1970).

3. Batchelor, G. K., "The Effect of Brownian Motion on the Bulk Stress in a Suspension", J. Fluid Mech., 83, 97 (1977).

4. Bearman, R. J., and Kirkwood, J., "Equations of Transport in Multicomponent Systems", J. Chem. Phys., 28, 136 (1958).

5. Bird, R. B., Hassager, O., Armstrong, R. C. and Curtiss, C. F., "Dynamics of Polymeric Liquids, Vol. II Kinetic Theory", John Wiley, 1977, see pp. 484ff.

6. Born, Max, and Huang, Kun, "Dynamical Theory of Crystal Lattices", Clarendon Press, Oxford, 1954. pp. 129 ff.

7. Brush, S. G., "Kinetic Theory", Pergamon Press, 1965, Vol. 1, p. 172.

8. Burgers, J. M., in "Second Report on Viscosity and Plasticity", Royal Netherland Acad., Amsterdam, 1938.

9. Cauchy, A. L., "De la Pression ou Tension Dans un Systeme de Points Materiels", Exercices de Mathematiques, t. 3, De Bure Freres, Paris, 1828, pp. 211ff.

10. Dahler, J. and Scriven, L. E., "Theory of Structured Continua", Proc. Roy. Soc., Lond. A275, 504 (1963).

11. Davis, H. T. and Scriven, L. E., "Stress and Structure in Fluid Interfaces", Adv. Chem. Physics, 49, 357-454 (1982). See esp. pp. 365-373.

12. Feynmann, R. P., "Forces on Molecules", Phys. Rev., 56, 340, (1939).

13. Fowler, R. H., "Statistical Mechanics", Cambridge University Press, 1929, pp. 211 ff.

14. Giesekus, H., "Die rheologische Zustandsgleichung" Rheol. Acta., 1, 2 (1958).

15. Giesekus, H., "Elasto-Viskose Flussigkeiten fur die in Stationaren Schichtstromungen Samtliche Normalspannungs komponenten Vershieden gross sind", Rheol. Acta., 2, 50-62 (1962).

16. Goddard, J. D., Huang, Y.-H., and Huang, L.-C., "Rational Predictions of Composite Properties Based on Asymptotic Micromechanics", Proc. Ninth U. S. Congress Appl. Mech., 197, (1982).

17. Gray, C. G. and Gubbins, K., "Theory of Molecular Fluids. Vol. 1: Fundamentals", esp. Appendix E, "Virial and Hypervirial Theorems", pp. 602-615, Clarendon Press, Oxford, 1984.

18. Green, A. E., and Rivlin, R. S., "On Cauchy's Equations of Motion", ZAMP, 15, 290 (1964).

19. Haff, P. K., "Grain Flow as a Fluid Mechanical Phenomena", J. Fluid Mech., 134, 401 (1983).

20. Herczynski, R. and Pienkowska, I., "Toward a Statistical Theory of Suspension", Ann. Rev. Fluid Mech., 12, 237 (1980).

21. Hirschfelder, J. O., Curtiss, C. E. and Bird, R. B., "Molecular Theory of Gases and Liquids", J. Wiley, 1954, pp. 41-43.

22. Irving, J. H., and Kirkwood, J. G., "The Statistical Mechanical Theory of Transport Properties. IV. The Equations of Hydrodynamics", J. Chem. Phys., 18, 817 (1950).

23. Jaunzemis, W., "Continuum Mechanics", Macmillan, 1967, pp.223ff.

24. Kirkwood, J. G., and Buff, F. P., "The Statistical Mechanical Theory of Surface Tension", J. Chem. Phys., 17, 338 (1949).

25. Kramers, H. A., "Het Gedrag von Macromoleculen in een Stroomende Vloeistof", Physica, 11, 1-19 (1944).

26. Love, A. E. H., "A Treatise on the Mathematical Theory of Elasticity", Fourth ed., Dover, 1944. See esp. pp. 8-9 and 616 ff.

27. Ludwig, W. E. W., "Theory of Elastic Constants in Lattices with Additional Degrees of Freedom", in Continuum Models of Discrete Systems (J. W. Provan, ed.) U. of Waterloo Press, 1977.

28. Lun, C. K. K., Savage, S. B., Jeffrey, D. J. and Chepurniy, N., "Kinetic Theories for Granular Flow...", J. Fluid Mech., 140, 223 (1984).

29. Maxwell, J. C., Electricity and Magnetism", Vol. 1, 3rd ed., Oxford, 1982, p. 167.

30. Musher, J. I., "Comments on Some Theorems of Quantum Chemistry", Am. J. Physics, 34, 267 (1966).

31. Nielsen, O. H. and Martin, R. M., "First Principles Calculation of Stress", Phys. Rev. Lett., 50, 697 (1983).

32. Rowlinson, J. S. and Widom, B., "Molecular Theory of Capillarity", Clarendon Press, Oxford, 1982. See esp. pp. 85-89 and 122-124.

33. Schofield, P. and Henderson, J. R., "Statistical Mechanics of Inhomogeneous Fluids", Proc. Roy. Soc. Lond., A379, 231-246 (1982).

34. Schowalter, W. R., "Mechanics of non-Newtonian Fluids", Pergamon, 1978. pp. 264ff.

35. Steele, W. A., "Time Correlation Functions", Chap. 8 in "Transport Phenomena in Fluids" (H. J. M. Hanley, ed.) M. Dekker (1969).

36. Truesdell, C. "Six Lectures on Modern National Philosophy", Springer, 1966, p. 23ff and 95.

37. Truesdell, C., and Noll, W., "The Non-Linear Field Theories of Mechanics", Encylopedia of Physics, III/3, Springer-Verlag, 1965.

38. Wallace, D. C., Schiferl, S. K., and Straub, G. K., "Stresses and Elastic Constants of Metals with Classical Ion Motion", Phys. Rev. A., 30, 616 (1984).

39. Walton, J. P. R. B., Tildesley, D. J., Rowlinson, J. S. and Henderson, J. R., "The Pressure Tensor at the Planar Surface of a Liquid", Mol. Phys., 48, 1357-1368 (1983).

H L GOLDSMITH, S P THA, D N BELL & S SPAIN

Interactions between human blood cells in shear flow

1. INTRODUCTION

There exists a substantial body of theoretical and experimental work on the shear-induced interactions of neutrally buoyant spheres and spheroids suspended in viscous fluids subjected to Couette or Poiseuille flow [37]. In particular, the fluid mechanical problem of predicting the trajectories of two colliding spheres has been solved [1,3,5,45], including the case when interaction forces, $F_{int}(h)$, other than hydrodynamic operate where sphere surfaces approach to within a distance $h < 100$ nm [20,65,71]. The theory has been applied to rigid latex spheres of colloidal size ($\sim 10^{-6}$m) interacting in Poiseuille flow [59,60,66,67], as has the behaviour of doublets of such spheres when cross-linked by polymer [61,62]. This paper describes the application of the above cited investigations to suspensions of human blood cells.

From a fluid dynamic viewpoint, mammalian blood may be considered to be a concentrated suspension (40 to 45% by volume) of deformable red blood cells ~ 8 μm diameter in plasma (a Newtonian aqueous solution of salts and proteins) subjected to pulsatile flow in vessels from 25 mm down to 5 μm diameter. The mechanics of the motion is complex and the flow regimes in large arteries and veins [46] differ markedly from those in small vessels [33] and in the microcirculation [34]. Because of the high particulate volume concentration, there are continuous collisions not only between the red cells but also betweeen the less numerous and smaller platelets (~ 3 μm diameter, ~ 0.3% volume concentration). The blood cells also collide with the cells of the endothelium lining the walls of the vessels. At the high shear rates normally prevailing in the circulation cell-cell collisions do not result in the formation of aggregates, and cell-wall collisions do not result in adhesion to intact endothelium. In certain situations, however, such interactions play an important role in normal as well as in abnormal processes such as haemostasis and thrombosis which involve aggregation of platelets and their adhesion to damaged vessel wall. Other examples are immunologic reactions involving the agglutination of red cells by antibody cross-linked between adjacent cell surfaces, cancer metastasis in which circulating tumour cells adhere to endothelial cells in the capillaries of a microcirculatory bed and from there invade and grow into the surrounding tissue [70], and the aggregation of red cells at low shear rates (e.g. in circulatory shock) into straight and branched chain rouleaux in which the cells are cross-linked by fibrinogen and form a network in the core of the vessel.

The following deals with recent work in our laboratory concerned with three aspects of cellular interactions in human blood subjected to flow in tubes: (i) the measurement of the hydrodynamic force required to break up doublets of red cells of antigenic type A or B cross-linked by the corresponding antibody; (ii) the two-body collision capture efficiency and the kinetics of aggregation of platelets activated with adenosine diphosphate (ADP); and (iii) the aggregation of red cells in blood of normal haematocrit and the effect on the distribution of white cells.

2. THEORETICAL BACKGROUND: TWO-BODY INTERACTIONS BETWEEN RIGID SPHERES

2.1. Trajectories.

We consider two equal-sized neutrally buoyant, non-conducting, charged rigid spheres of radius b suspended in an incompressible Newtonian fluid of viscosity η containing electrolyte. The suspension is subjected to laminar viscous flow in a circular tube of radius R_o (Fig. 1) in which the fluid velocity in the axial, x_3-direction at a radial distance R is given by:

$$u_3(R) = \frac{2Q}{\pi R_o^4}(R_o^2 - R^2) , \qquad (1)$$

where Q is the volume flow rate.

The equations governing the trajectories of the spheres in a linear shear field have been solved [65]. Assuming that the interaction forces $F_{int}(h)$ act along the line joining the centres of the spheres, the relative velocity of the centres separated by a distance r is given by:

$$\frac{dr}{dt} = A(r^*)Gb\sin^2\theta_1\sin2\phi_1 + \frac{C(r^*)F_{int}(h)}{3\pi\eta b} . \qquad (2)$$

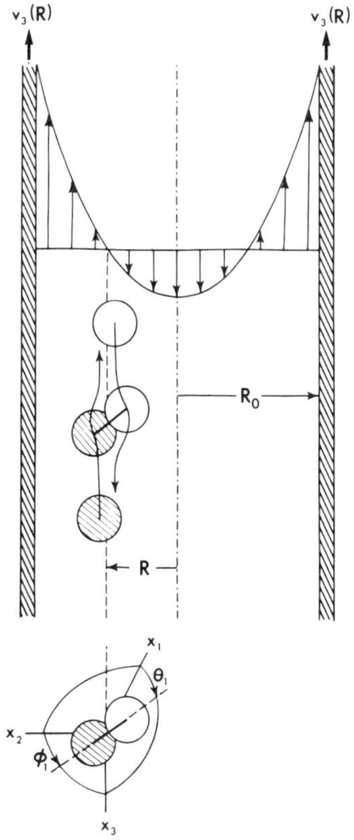

FIGURE 1. Schematic diagram of a two-body collision in Poiseuille flow between rigid spheres forming a transient doublet. Shown is the median plane of a tube of radius R_o being moved upward with the velocity, $v_3(R)$, of the downward flowing doublet whose centre is at a radial distance R from the tube axis. Cartesian (x_1, x_2, x_3) and polar coordinates (θ_1, ϕ_1) referred to x_1 are constructed at the mid-point of the doublet axis. (After [40])

The angular velocity of the doublet is given by:

$$\frac{d\theta_1}{dt} = \tfrac{1}{4}GB(r^*)\sin 2\theta_1 \sin 2\phi_1 \ , \tag{3}$$

$$\frac{d\phi_1}{dt} = \tfrac{1}{2}G\left(1 + B(r^*)\cos 2\phi_1\right), \tag{4}$$

where θ_1 and ϕ_1 are the respective polar and azimuthal angles with x_1 as the polar axis; G is the shear rate, $A(r^*)$ and $C(r^*)$ are functions of $r^* = r/b$ [65], and $B(r^*) = \{r_e^2(r^*)-1\}/\{r_e^2(r^*)+1\}$, $r_e(r^*)$ being the equivalent ellipsoidal axis ratio [37]; $B(r^*) = 0.5941$ for a dumbbell of touching spheres [3]. Equations (2) - (4) have been shown to apply in Poiseuille flow provided the ratio of doublet to tube radius, $2b/R_o << 1$ [59,60].

In the absence of interaction forces, $F_{int}(h) = 0$, the trajectories of approach and recession of the spheres are symmetrical about $\phi_1 = 0$, as experimentally found for neutral spheres [36,47]. In the case of charged spheres surrounded by a diffuse ionic electrical double layer, the paths of approach and recession are no longer symmetrical, $F_{int}(h) \neq 0$, while sphere surfaces are within 50 nm of each other and subject to double layer repulsion and van der Waals attraction [21,69]:

$$F_{int}(h) = F_{attr}(h) + F_{rep}(h) \; , \tag{5}$$

where the van der Waals attractive force is given by:

$$F_{attr}(h) = -\frac{Ab}{12h^2} f(p), \tag{6}$$

and the double layer repulsive force is given by:

$$F_{rep}(h) = 2\pi K b \varepsilon_o \Psi_o^2 \frac{e^{-\kappa h}}{1 \pm e^{-\kappa h}} \; . \tag{7}$$

Here, A is the Hamaker constant, p is the retardation parameter = $2\pi h/\lambda$, λ being the London wavelength; Ψ_o is the surface potential at $h = \infty$, K the dielectric constant, κ the reciprocal Debye length and ε_o the permittivity of free space.

In dilute suspensions of polystyrene latex spheres it was shown that, from the asymmetry of the trajectories, net repulsive or attractive interaction forces as small as 10^{-13}N could be detected, and applying Eqs. (6) and (7) values of the Hamaker constant (3×10^{-21}J) and the retardation parameter (200 nm) were obtained [60].

2.2. Application to biological systems. Equation (6) was derived by Hamaker [41] assuming pairwise additivity of individual interatomic interactions, applicable strictly to rarefied gases and not to a condensed medium. In biological systems, there is the additional problem of dealing with the hydrocarbon lipid layer of the membrane situated between two aqueous media. Ninham and Parsegian [48,51] overcame these problems by using the Lifshitz theory [44] for calculating the van der Waals attractive force, which takes into account many-body forces acting through a continuum. They also considered the effects of divalent ions in the cellular milieu on electrostatic repulsion, and estimated the effect of a glycoprotein layer extending from the membrane into the suspending medium [48,49]. Using the above theory, Brooks et al. [12] compared experimentally measured Hamaker coefficients with those predicted by the Lifshitz theory for monoglyceride-alkane thin films in polar liquids. The work of these authors indicates that A for the red cell membrane lies between 10^{-22}J and 10^{-23}J.

Nevertheless, application of colloid stability theory, so successful in model particle systems, appears to have been much less successful in predicting the observed interactions between living cells. Thus, calculations using a model of a lipid bilayer coated with charged mucoprotein have shown that there is a secondary energy minimum with the interaction potential $\sim 10^2 kT/\mu m^2$, more than enough to hold cells together [51]. Even in the absence of fibrinogen, therefore, red cells would be expected to be strongly aggregated at low or zero shear rates, contrary to experiment. When the Smoluchowski equation for the electrophoretic mobility of a charged colloidal particle is applied to the red cell, the surface charge is underestimated by a factor of 2 to 3 [54]. Levine et al. have proposed a model to account for the lower mobility of red cells which takes into account the extracellular mass coating the membrane bilayer consisting of polyelectrolyte molecules anchored to the membrane, the glycocalyx [43].

Experiments from this laboratory showed that the trajectories of colliding, swollen sphered red blood cells rigidified with glutaraldehyde were always markedly asymmetric due to repulsion, most probably because the glycocalyx, whose thickness has been estimated to be 7.5 nm, prevented close approach of the cell surfaces [40]. We have, however, applied hydrodynamic theory for doublets of rigidly-linked spheres [3] to doublets of sphered red blood cells cross-linked by antibody, and from the measured shear stress at break-up have calculated the force required to separate the cells.

2.3. Normal and shear force acting on spheres of a doublet. We consider a doublet of rigid spheres which rotates exclusively in the x_2x_3-plane of a linear shear field with origin 0 at the centre of the doublet axis, as shown in Fig. 2. Particle coordinates X_i are constructed at 0 such that X_3 is coincident with the doublet axis, X_2 is coplanar with the x_1x_3-plane, and X_1 is perpendicular to the doublet axis.

Rearranging Eq. (2) to yield the force equation gives:

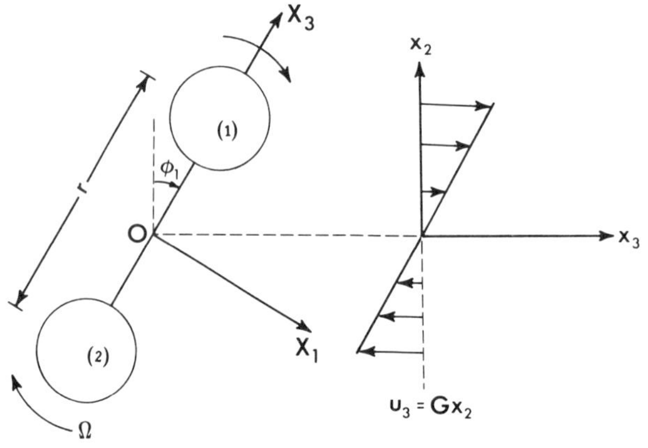

FIGURE 2. Particle coordinates, X_i, and shear field coordinates, x_i, used to describe the rotation of a doublet of rigidly-linked spheres.

$$\frac{3\pi\eta b}{C(r^*)}\,\frac{dr}{dt} = \frac{A(r^*)}{C(r^*)}\,3\pi\eta G b^2 \sin^2\theta_1 \sin 2\phi_1 + F_{int}(h). \tag{8}$$

The term on the left is the hydrodynamic drag resisting approach of the spheres, the first term on the right is the hydrodynamic force, F_3 (referred to particle coordinates) between spheres acting along their line of centres; a maximum, compressive at $\phi_1 - \pi/4$ and tensile at $\phi_1 = \pi/4$. For a rigidly-linked doublet, $dr/dt = 0$, hence at break-up:

$$F_{int}(h) = - F_3 \, . \tag{9}$$

The doublet is also subjected to a shear force, F_1, acting normal to its axis, which is more likely responsible for separation of the spheres. The normal and shear forces may be calculated using the treatment of Arp and Mason [3], as follows:

Under creeping flow conditions, the forces $\mathbf{F}(j)$ and torques $\Gamma(j)$ ($j = 1,2$) acting on the sphere surfaces can be expressed by the general formulation of Brenner and O'Neill [10]:

$$(F) = \begin{pmatrix} \mathbf{F}(1) \\ \mathbf{F}(2) \\ \Gamma(1) \\ \Gamma(2) \end{pmatrix} = - \eta \left\{ (R)(U) + (\Phi)(S) \right\}, \tag{10}$$

where (F) is the force-torque vector, (R) the grand resistance matrix, (Φ)

the shear resistance matrix; $(S) = (S_{11}, S_{22}, S_{33}, S_{23}, S_{13}, S_{12})$ is the shear vector of the rate of strain tensor $\mathbf{S}$, and (U) is the relative velocity spin vector:

$$(U) = \begin{pmatrix} \mathbf{U}(1) - \mathbf{u}(1) \\ \mathbf{U}(2) - \mathbf{u}(2) \\ \Omega(1) - \omega(1) \\ \Omega(2) - \omega(2) \end{pmatrix} \tag{11}$$

where $\mathbf{U}(j) - \mathbf{u}(j)$ and $\Omega(j) - \omega(j)$ represent the respective translational and rotational velocities of sphere j relative to the undisturbed fluid velocity at the centre of each particle. Since the values of (R) and $(\mathbf{\Phi})$ are known, the solution rests on deriving equations for (U) and (S). The spheres move with equal but opposite translational velocities and equal rotational velocities; therefore, consideration of sphere (1) alone suffices to establish the dynamics of the pair. Thus, as the spheres rotate as a rigid dumbbell, the non-zero values of $\Omega(1)$ and $\Omega(2)$ are:

$$\Omega_2(1) = \Omega_2(2) = \Omega, \tag{12}$$

and the non-zero components of $\mathbf{U}(1)$ and $\mathbf{U}(2)$ are:

$$U_1(1) = \tfrac{1}{2}\Omega r, \quad U_1(2) = -\tfrac{1}{2}\Omega r. \tag{13}$$

The components of the velocity field vector $\mathbf{u}$ are related to those of the particle velocity vector $\mathbf{U}$ by:

$$\begin{aligned} U_1 &= u_3\cos\phi_1 = Gx_2\cos\phi_1 = G(X_3\cos^2\phi_1 - X_1\sin\phi_1\cos\phi_1), \\ U_2 &= 0, \\ U_3 &= u_3\sin\phi_1 = Gx_2\sin\phi_1 = G(X_3\sin\phi_1\cos\phi_1 - X_1\sin^2\phi_1). \end{aligned} \tag{14}$$

Whence (U) is given by:

$$(U) = \begin{pmatrix} \tfrac{1}{2}\Omega r - \tfrac{1}{2}Gr\cos^2\phi_1 \\ 0 \\ -\tfrac{1}{2}Gr\sin\phi_1\cos\phi_1 \\ 0 \\ \Omega - \tfrac{1}{2}G \\ 0 \end{pmatrix} \tag{15}$$

The velocity gradient tensor **G**, where $\mathbf{G} = \nabla\mathbf{U_o}$, is given by:

$$\mathbf{G} = \begin{pmatrix} -G\sin\phi_1\cos\phi_1 & 0 & G\cos^2\phi_1 \\ 0 & 0 & 0 \\ -G\sin^2\phi_1 & 0 & G\sin\phi_1\cos\phi_1 \end{pmatrix} \qquad (16)$$

and the rate of strain tensor **S**, where $\mathbf{S} = \frac{1}{2}(\mathbf{G} + \mathbf{G}^\dagger)$ by:

$$\mathbf{S} = \begin{pmatrix} -G\sin\phi_1\cos\phi_1 & 0 & \frac{1}{2}G(\cos^2\phi_1 - \sin^2\phi_1) \\ 0 & 0 & 0 \\ \frac{1}{2}G(\cos^2\phi_1 - \sin^2\phi_1) & 0 & G\sin\phi_1\cos\phi_1 \end{pmatrix} \qquad (17)$$

of which the shear vector $(\mathcal{S})$ is:

$$(\mathcal{S}) = \begin{pmatrix} -G\sin\phi_1\cos\phi_1 \\ 0 \\ G\sin\phi_1\cos\phi_1 \\ 0 \\ \frac{1}{2}G(\cos^2\phi_1 - \sin^2\phi_1) \\ 0 \end{pmatrix} \qquad (18)$$

$(\mathcal{R})$ and $(\boldsymbol{\Phi})$ for sphere (1) are [3]:

$$(\mathcal{R}) = \begin{pmatrix} a & 0 & 0 & 0 & -c & 0 \\ 0 & a & 0 & -c & 0 & 0 \\ 0 & 0 & b^* & 0 & 0 & 0 \\ 0 & -c & 0 & d & 0 & 0 \\ -c & 0 & 0 & 0 & d & 0 \\ 0 & 0 & 0 & 0 & 0 & e \end{pmatrix} \qquad (19)$$

and

$$(\boldsymbol{\Phi}) = \begin{pmatrix} 0 & 0 & 0 & 0 & 2g & 0 \\ 0 & 0 & 0 & 2g & 0 & 0 \\ 0 & 0 & f^*+2g & 0 & 0 & 0 \\ 0 & 0 & 0 & 2h^* & 0 & 0 \\ 0 & 0 & 0 & 0 & -2h^* & 0 \\ 0 & 0 & 0 & 0 & 0 & 0 \end{pmatrix} \qquad (20)$$

where a, b*, c, d, e, f*, g, h* are force and torque coefficients for sphere (1) that are known and tabulated functions of h and of b [3,5].

Solving Eq. (10) for $F_1(1)$, the force acting on sphere (1) along X_1, perpendicular to the doublet axis, yields:

$$F_1(1) = -\eta\ \{a(\tfrac{1}{2}\Omega r - \tfrac{1}{2}Gr\cos^2\phi_1) - c(\Omega - \tfrac{1}{2}G) + gG(\cos^2\phi_1 - \sin^2\phi_1)\}. \quad (21)$$

In order to solve for Ω, advantage is taken of the equality [3]:

$$\Gamma_2^D = rF_1(1) + 2\Gamma_2(1) = 0, \quad (22)$$

where Γ_2^D is the component along X_2 of Γ^D, the torque on a rigid dumbbell about 0; and $\Gamma_2(1)$ is the component along X_2 of $\Gamma(1)$, the torque on sphere (1) about its centre. The solution of Eq.(10) for $\Gamma_2(1)$ is:

$$\Gamma_2(1) = -\eta\ \{-c(\tfrac{1}{2}\Omega r - \tfrac{1}{2}Gr\cos^2\phi_1) + d(\Omega - \tfrac{1}{2}G) - h^*G(\cos^2\phi_1 - \sin^2\phi_1)\}. \quad (23)$$

The solution of Eq. (22) for $\Omega = d\phi_1/dt$, is then:

$$\Omega = \tfrac{1}{2}G(1 - \nu_D\cos 2\phi_1)\ , \quad (24)$$

where ν_D, the angular velocity coefficient = -B(r*), given by [3]:

$$\nu_D = \frac{-\tfrac{1}{2}ar^2 + cr + 2rg - 4h^*}{\tfrac{1}{2}ar^2 - 2rc + 2d}\ . \quad (25)$$

Substituting for Ω in Eq. (21) finally yields:

$$F_1(1) = -\tfrac{1}{2}\eta G\{(-\tfrac{1}{2}ar + 2g) - \nu_D(\tfrac{1}{2}ar - c)\cos 2\phi_1\}. \quad (26)$$

Similarly, solving Eq. (10) for $F_3(1)$, the force acting on sphere (1) along X_3, i.e. along the doublet axis, yields:

$$\begin{aligned} F_3(1) &= -\eta\{-\tfrac{1}{2}Gb^*r\sin\phi_1\cos\phi_1 + (f^* + 2g)G\sin\phi_1\cos\phi_1\}, \\ &= -\tfrac{1}{2}\eta G\{(-b^*r + 2f + 4g)\sin\phi\cos\phi_1\}. \end{aligned} \quad (27)$$

The solutions for the shear and normal forces when doublet rotation is not confined to the x_2x_3-plane, i.e., the polar angle with respect to the x_1-axis, $\theta_1 \neq 90°$ (Fig. 1), are as follows:

$$\text{Shear Force: } (F_1{}^2 + F_2{}^2)^{\frac{1}{2}} = -\tfrac{1}{2}\eta G\,(-\tfrac{1}{2}ar + 2g) + \nu_D(\tfrac{1}{2}ar - c)\} \times \{(\cos 2\theta_2 \cos\phi_2)^2 + (\cos\theta_2 \sin\phi_2)^2\}^{\frac{1}{2}} \quad (28)$$

$$\text{Normal Force: } F_3(1) = -\tfrac{1}{2}\eta G\{(-\tfrac{1}{2}b^*r + f^* + 2g)\}\sin^2\theta_1 \sin 2\phi_1. \quad (29)$$

Here θ_2 and ϕ_2 are the polar and azimuthal angles with x_2 as the polar axis. The above equations may be written in the form:

$$(F_1{}^2 + F_2{}^2)^{\frac{1}{2}} = \beta_1(h)\eta G b^2\{(\cos 2\theta_2 \cos\phi_2)^2 - (\cos\theta_2 \sin\phi_2)^2\}^{\frac{1}{2}} \quad (30)$$

$$F_3 = \beta_3(h)\eta G b^2 \sin^2\theta_1 \sin 2\phi_1, \quad (31)$$

where β_1 and β_3 are force coefficients, functions of h, obtained by factoring out b^2 from the matrix coefficients. Comparison of Eqs. (29) and (8) reveals that $A(r^*)/C(r^*) = -(-\frac{1}{2}b^*r + f^* + 2g)/6\pi b^2$. At h = 20 nm, the probable distance of separation of red cell surfaces [15], $\beta_1 = 7.02$ and $\beta_3 = 19.3$ [63].

2.4. Orthokinetic collision frequency and capture efficiency. From simple geometric arguments assuming rectilinear approach and recession Smoluchowski [57] showed that, in a suspension of N_o spheres per unit volume and in the absence of Brownian diffusion, the flux with which particles collide with a reference sphere - the orthokinetic collision frequency, J_s, - is given by:

$$J_s = \frac{32}{3} N_o G b^3. \quad (32)$$

In the case of macroscopic, neutral spheres suspended in highly viscous liquids, the equation has been confirmed experimentally in Couette [47] and Poiseuille flow [36] despite the fact that the trajectories are not rectilinear [2]. In the above studies, collisions resulted in the spheres spending a short time in close proximity to each other rotating as a doublet according to Eqs. (3) and (4) before separating again. In the present work we also consider the case where attractive inter-particle forces can result in the mutual capture of a pair of spheres leading to the formation of a permanent doublet. The collision capture frequency per reference sphere, J, can then be written:

$$J = \frac{32}{3} \alpha_o N_o G b^3, \quad (33)$$

where $\alpha_o = J/J_s$ is the orthokinetic collision capture efficiency.

Van de Ven and Mason [67] derived an expression for α_o based on an experimentally determined capture cross-section which no longer requires that the colliding spheres follow rectilinear trajectories. They also showed that an average value for the capture efficiency can be implicitly determined from measurements of the number of single spheres and doublets in a suspension flowing past two successive positions in a tube, providing the number of multiplets formed is negligible. Assuming that no break-up of doublets occurs, the combined number of singlets and newly formed doublets N_t at time t is [58]:

$$N_t = N_o e^{-4\alpha_o tGc/\pi}, \quad (34)$$

where N_o is the number of singlets and c their volume fraction at time zero. If S_1 and S_2 are the ratios of singlets to doublets at the first and second positions, respectively, then:

$$\alpha_o = \frac{\pi}{4\overline{tG}c} \ln \frac{S_1(2 + S_2)}{S_1 + S_1S_2 + S_2}, \quad (35)$$

where $\overline{tG}$ is an average determined on any interval of radial distance (R_1,R_2) by:

$$\overline{tG} = \frac{\Delta x_3}{R_2 - R_1} \ln \frac{R_o^2 - R_1^2}{R_o^2 - R_2^2}, \quad (36)$$

Δx_3 being the distance between the measurements of S_1 and S_2. It should be noted, however, that the above theory is limited to doublet formation and cannot be used in situations where appreciable numbers of multiplets form.

3. MEASUREMENT OF FORCE REQUIRED TO BREAK UP DOUBLETS OF RED CELLS

Several investigators have measured fluid shear stresses as an indication of the average strength of aggregation of a cell suspension. However, geometric and fluid mechanical considerations have precluded precise quantitation of applied force [11,53]. Chien, Skalak et al. partly overcame these uncertainties by using the bulk fluid shear stress as a measure of the hydrodynamic force necessary to disaggregate an individual sessile doublet of discoid erythrocytes [17,18]. Their experimental results were at some variance with their computer simulations of adhesion energy as assessed by membrane curvature [56]. Evans et al. have measured the surface affinities of individual cells by manipulating them in micropipettes, bringing them into contact with each other [22,23]. With this technique they have measured the surface affinities of red blood cells that have been agglutinated by plasma and dextrans [13] and the force required to disrupt 2 red cells that have been apposed after exposure to wheat germ agglutinin [24].

3.1. Experimental. We have used a travelling microtube technique [38,64] to observe the flow and break-up of doublets of human red cells of antigenic type A or B, cross-linked by the corresponding antibody [63]. Red cells, obtained from blood washed with phosphate buffer, were simultaneously sphered and swollen in a glycerol solution containing 10^{-4}M sodium dodecyl sulphate, and then fixed in 0.085% glutaraldehyde. A dilute suspension (2.5×10^7 cells/cm^3) was then prepared in aqueous glycerol (viscosity 14-30 mPa s) containing 0.15M NaCl and antiserum at 28-140× dilution. Gentle stirring of the suspension resulted in the formation of doublets, as well as a small number of multiplets.

The doublets were observed through a microscope as the suspension flowed by gravity feed through a 175μm diameter glass tube between two reservoirs. The tube lay on a microscope slide mounted on the vertically positioned stage of a hydraulically-driven microtube apparatus. The doublets were tracked by moving the tube with the velocity, $v_3(R)$, equal and opposite to that of the particles (Fig. 1), and the translational and rotational motions recorded on videotape. The doublets were followed in a constantly accelerating flow, produced by infusing liquid into one of the reservoirs, until break-up, at which point the particle radial position, velocity and orientation were obtained from a frame by frame playback of the videotape (Fig. 3). This enabled G, b, θ_1 and ϕ_1 to be computed, and F_1 and F_3 to be calculated from Eqs. (28) and (29).

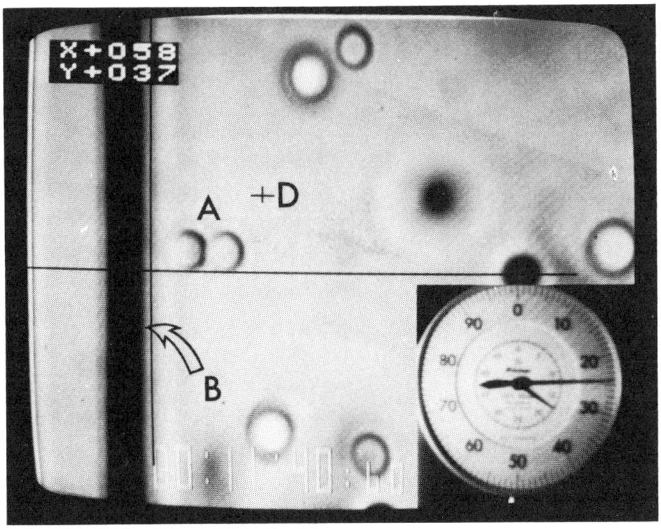

FIGURE 3. Photograph of the TV-monitor showing a doublet being tracked (A), the tube wall (B), the odometer (C) giving axial distance travelled, the cross-hairs (D) and axes of the video-position analyzer used to determine radial position and orientation.

3.2. Results. Table I shows the calculated values of the normal and shear forces of separation as a function of antiserum concentration. The forces are of the order of 10^{-10} - 10^{-11} N and, with the exception of one pair of F_1 values, there was a statistically significant increase of force with increasing antiserum concentration. The values were unaffected by suspending liquid viscosity. It is impossible to determine from the above experiments whether F_1 or F_3 is responsible for doublet separation. On theoretical grounds, for the same energy of adhesion, the shear force required to separate two surfaces is lower than the normal force; the former is integrated over the length of the surface whereas the latter is integrated over the molecular dimensions of bonding. Experimental work has borne out the lower shear forces necessary to separate cells [17].

The antiserum concentrations necessary to produce sufficient numbers of

TABLE I

Effect of Antiserum Concentration on Forces of Separation

[Antiserum] % v/v	n	η mPa s ± s.d.	F_1 nN ± s.d.	F_3 nN ± s.d.
0.733	16	14.4 ± 0.3	0.022 ± 0.010	0.060 ± 0.028
			$p < 0.05$	$p < 0.05$
1.217	17	17.6 ± 0	0.032 ± 0.013	0.083 ± 0.032
			$p < 0.10$	$p < 0.05$
2.404	43	20.0 ± 2.9	0.042 ± 0.020	0.112 ± 0.054
			$p < 0.001$	$p < 0.001$
3.563	28	27.6 ± 0.4	0.072 ± 0.030	0.197 ± 0.083

doublets of sphered cells were appreciably higher than those known to produce significant agglutination of normal biconcave red cells. Most likely, this is due to the rigidity of the sphered cells which, unlike the normal cells are unable to increase the area of contact after the first cross-links between surfaces have been established [25]. The smaller area of contact between the sphered cells will also cause the doublets to be less stable to mechanical disruption. Finally, it was noted that the force estimated to break an antigen-antibody bond of average free energy of binding (8.5 kcal per mole) is $\sim 10^{-10}$ N [8], i.e. of the same order of magnitude as the above values of the shear force F_1 which probably breaks bonds sequentially.

4. PLATELET AGGREGATION IN POISEUILE FLOW

A major concern of modern western society is the prevalence of thromboembolic disorders. Fundamental to the process of thrombus formation is the participation of the blood platelet. When conditions within the blood stream favour the formation of thrombi, platelets adhere to the disrupted or abnormal endothelium to form an initial aggregate. This may grow to occlude the vessel, or it may break away or fragment creating an embolus capable of occluding smaller vessels downstream. Thus, understanding the factors controlling the activation, adhesion, and aggregation of blood platelets is essential to solving the problem of thromboembolic diseases, as well as to designing improved prosthetics and circulatory equipment.

4.1. Measurement of platelet aggregation. The most widely used *in vitro* method of measuring platelet aggregation is the turbidimetric technique known as aggregometry [9]. It measures changes in the amount of light transmitted through 0.5 to 1.0 ml of a stirred suspension of platelets as the cells undergo shape change and/or aggregation in response to an activating agent. In the aggregometer cuvette, however, the shear rate is not well-defined and relatively poorly controlled by the rate of rotation of a metal stir bar. The aggregometer is also insensitive to the presence of microaggregates of fewer than ~ 10 cells which are known to be formed during the first 10 s after addition of an aggregating agent. The advantage of the aggregometer is that the cells and the activator are very rapidly mixed, a condition difficult to achieve in a well-defined flow system.

4.2. Use of a double infusion technique. We have described the design and operation of a microscopic flow system for directly observing platelet aggregation induced by adenosine diphosphate (ADP) under conditions of laminar flow at shear stresses $< 0.1\ Nm^{-2}$, while minimizing the problem of premixing. Aggregation was observed in Poiseuille flow immediately after the introduction of ADP into the bulk of the flowing suspension. This required rapid equilibration of ADP across the tube, and hence small diffusion distances (Diffusion coefficient = $4.8 \times 10^{-10}\ m^2\ s^{-1}$). To this end, a double infusion microtube was constructed, in which, as shown in Fig. 4, ADP was infused continuously from a micropipette tip into plasma containing 3×10^8 platelets per cm^3 flowing through a $100\mu m$ diameter tube with the half time for diffusion equilibrium of ADP < 3 s [6].

4.3. Mechanism of aggregation. In the unactivated state, platelets circulate as smooth, discoid anuclear cells with a mean major diameter of 3.1 μm and particle axis ratio, axis of revolution/diametrical axis = 0.26. In

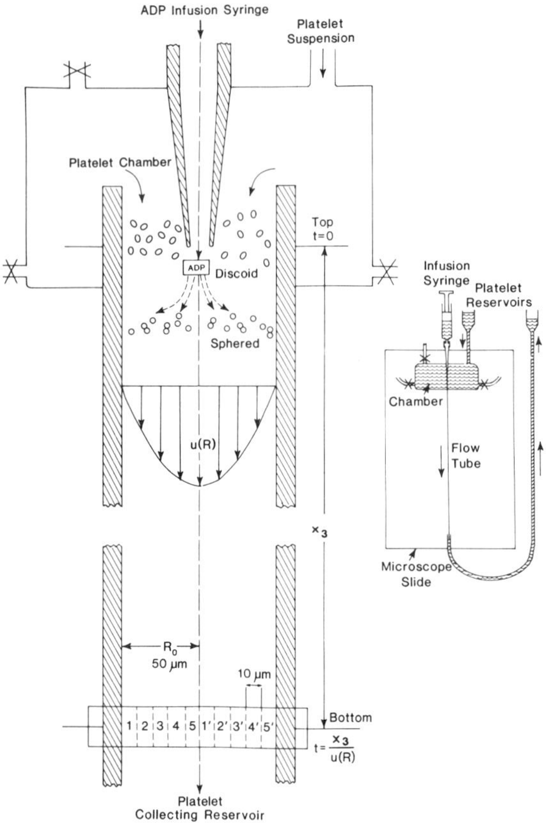

FIGURE 4. The double infusion microtube. Platelet suspension flows between two reservoirs through a chamber and the flow tube. ADP is simultaneously infused via a microsyringe whose tip is concentrically positioned at the entrance of the flow tube. The cells become sphered and form aggregates as a result of shear-induced collisions. At various distances Δx_3 (shown as x_3) their number distribution across the median plane is analyzed by dividing the tube into 5 strips on either side of the axis. The velocity profile $u_3(R)$ of the plasma [shown as u(R)] is assumed equal to that, $v_3(R)$, of the cells and small aggregates. (From [39])

Poiseuille flow, they have been shown to rotate as oblate ellipsoids according to Eq. (4) with a mean $r_e = 0.38$ [28]. Upon activation with ADP at concentrations < 1 μM, used in the experiments, the discoid shape is lost and surface protusions known as pseudopods develop, the overall shape being roughly spherical [29]. Shape change is associated with the exposure of receptor sites on the membrane capable of binding the plasma protein fibrinogen, a molecule which can cross-link the surfaces of adjacent cells. Thus, in shear flow, a certain fraction of collisions results in the formation of doublets, and then higher order aggregates. This process was recorded on cine film at various distances Δx_3 downstream of the ADP infusion site (Fig. 4), and the number distributions of singlets and aggregates measured across the median plane of the tube [6].

4.4. Results

4.4.1. Collision capture efficiency. Aggregation was expressed as the net fraction of platelets in all aggregates, $A' = A - A^o$, where A is the measured fraction of platelets in all aggregates in the median plane of the tube, and A^o is the fraction of cells in aggregates in the control samples in which physiological saline was infused instead of ADP. Experiments were carried out over a range of mean tube shear rates, $\bar{G}$, from 2 - 55 s^{-1}. The results were grouped according to the sex of the donor, since there was a highly significant increase in the mean A' for females over males [7].

Initially, at short distances Δx_3 from the infusion tip, aggregation decreased with increasing $\bar{G}$. Only much further downstream did aggregation at the higher $\bar{G}$ approach and then overtake that at the lower $\bar{G}$. If the two-body collision theory can be applied to the activated, sphered platelets, then in a given tube and for a given suspension, the average number of collisions experienced by a cell in the tube, $\bar{M}$, is independent of the mean linear flow rate, $\bar{u}$, and only a function of Δx_3:

$$\bar{M}(\Delta x_3) = \bar{J}_s \bar{t}, \tag{37}$$

where $\bar{t}$ is the mean transit time = $\Delta x_3/\bar{u}$, $\bar{J}_s = 32N_o\bar{G}b^3/3$, $\bar{G}$ being the mean tube shear rate = $2\bar{u}/R_o$. Hence:

$$\bar{M} = 64N_o b^3 \Delta x_3/3R_o \; . \tag{38}$$

Thus, the results show that, in the initial stages of aggregation when the proportion of triplets and multiplets was small, the collision capture efficiency, α_o, decreased with increasing $\bar{G}$. For example, the values of α_o calculated from Eq. (35) for the female donor in Fig. 5 decreased from 0.27 at $\bar{G} = 7.9$ s^{-1} to 0.04 at $\bar{G} = 53.5$ s^{-1}. Similar results have previously been described in colloidal suspensions of model particles [19,67,72]. This is not unexpected, since Eq. (8) shows that, with increasing $\bar{G}$, both the hydrodynamic drag force and interaction force increase relative to the non-hydrodynamic interaction force, $F_{int}(h)$, and α_o therefore decreases.

In contrast to model particles, platelets exhibit time-dependent changes in response to aggregating agents which will affect α_o. This is shown in Fig. 5 in which the net aggregation, A', has been plotted against the mean

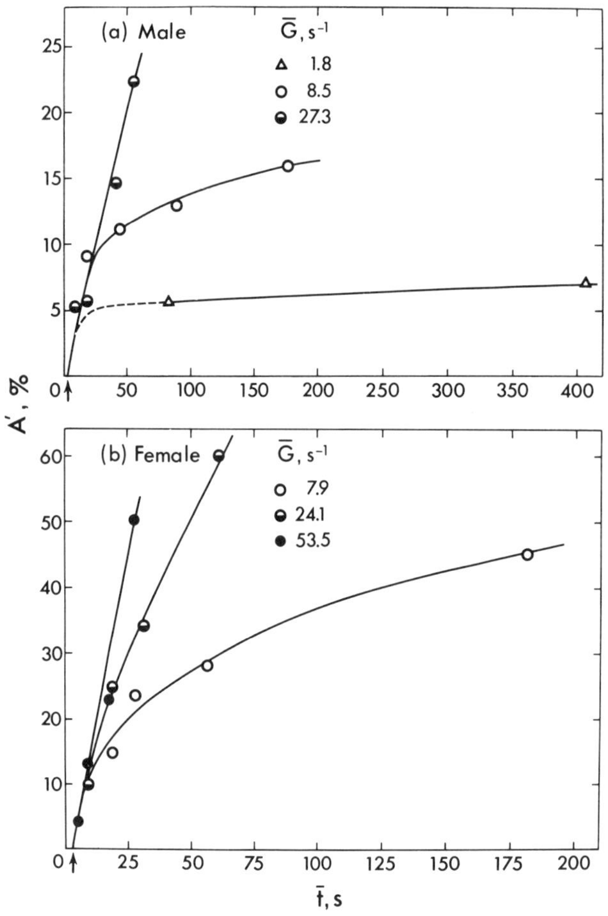

FIGURE 5. Effect of mean tube shear rate, $\bar{G}$, on the time course of aggregation, A', of platelets in plasma from a male and female donor each containing 3×10^8 cells/cm^3. The lines drawn are the best fit by eye extrapolated back to $\bar{t} = 2.6$ s (indicated by the arrows), the half-time for complete diffusion of ADP across the tube. Within experimental error, the rate of aggregation over the first 10 s is equal at all $\bar{G}$. (From [7])

transit time $\bar{t}$. Over the initial 10 s the rate of aggregation, dA'/dt, was independent of shear rate implying that α_o decreased with increasing $\bar{G}$. The subsequent decrease in dA'/dt is believed to be due to an additional drop in α_o as the cells become deactivated past a critical $\bar{t}$, and should apply at all shear rates. Past this critical $\bar{t}$, the rate of aggregation is mainly a function of the collision frequency. At low $\bar{G}$, the collision frequency is too small to counterbalance the effect of platelet deactivation whereas at high $\bar{G}$, it is sufficient to support a high rate of aggregation.

4.4.2. Growth and distribution of aggregates. At each $\bar{G}$, there was a progressive growth in aggregate size with distance from the infusion tip.

Starting at the periphery of the tube, there was a marked increase in the fraction of platelets in aggregatess of 2 to 4 cells. As the aggregates continued to grow in size they migrated toward the tube axis; eventually a large proportion of platelets were found in aggregates of more than 20 cells flowing at radial distance $R < 0.4R_o$. As shown in Fig. 6, aggregate growth followed the pattern predicted by Smoluchowski [57]. Accompanying the fall in the concentration of single platelets were consecutive transient increases in the concentrations of doublets, triplets and then higher-order multiplets finally leading to the appearance of significant concentrations of large aggregates of more than 20 cells. The marked migration of these aggregates toward the tube axis was likely due to a wall exclusion effect since calculations show that inertial effects were small, even at the highest $\bar{u}$ [7,42,55].

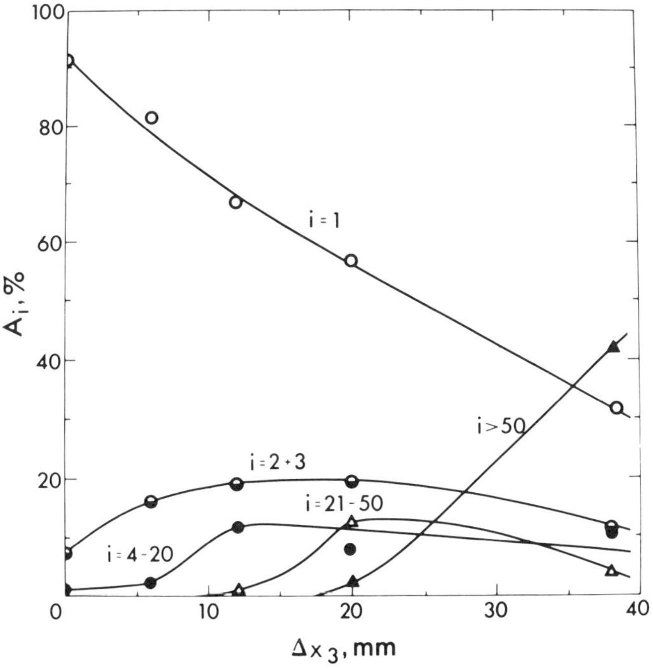

FIGURE 6. Plot of the fraction of platelets in aggregates of size i, (A_i), against Δx_3 for the same donor as in Fig. 5. (From [7])

5. RED CELL AGGREGATION: CONSEQUENCES OF TWO-PHASE FLOW

The main features of the viscometric flow of human and other mammalian blood can be qualitatively accounted for by the ability of the red cell (i) to form linear and branched chain aggregates known as rouleaux whose existence depends mainly on the presence of the protein fibrinogen in plasma, and

(ii) to deform under the influence of fluid stresses in shear flow. Both these properties of the cell result in the non-Newtonian, shear-thinning behaviour of blood. Thus, the apparent viscosity of the suspension decreases with increasing shear rate. This effect has been explained in terms of the progressive break-up of rouleaux at shear rates up to 50 s^{-1} [16,53], followed at higher shear rates by the deformation of the red cells, likened to that of emulsion droplets [20,27,32,52]. The break-up of structures within the suspension upon the imposition of shear and their reformation on standing gives blood at low shear rates properties analogous to those of a pseudoplastic suspension of printing ink [14].

5.1. Two-phase flow in tubes. Here, we are concerned with the consequences of rouleaux formation at low shear rates in tube flow. When observing blood at normal haematocrit in vessels < 200 μm diameter, either *in vivo* or *in vitro*, it is striking to see the change in the flow regime as the flow rate decreases. At high mean linear flow rates, $\bar{u} > 40R_o\ s^{-1}$, the blood appears uniformly dispersed. One cannot distinguish individual red cells except at the wall, where there may be a cell-depleted layer of varying thickness (< 5 μm width) in which individual corpuscles are radially propelled to and from the wall through shear-induced collisions. At low flow rates, $\bar{u} < 10R_o\ s^{-1}$, a two-phase flow develops of a central core of red cells and rouleaux surrounded by a now wider peripheral layer of a very low concentration of rotating single red cells and small rouleaux [31]. When $\bar{u} < 5R_o\ s^{-1}$, the core consists of a network of rouleaux which moves as a plug, the velocity gradient being confined to the periphery. Figure 7 shows photomicrographs of human blood at 20% haematocrit in a 100μm tube at $\bar{u} = 30.8$ and $2.2R_o\ s^{-1}$. Figure 8 gives a plot of the mean relative width, $\bar{R}_c/R_o$, of the red cell and rouleaux core, measured as a function of mean tube shear rate.

5.2. Redistribution of white cells due to red cell aggregation.

5.2.1. Fahraeus effect. The appearance of white cells (leukocytes), notably granulocytes, at the periphery of vessels in the microcirculation is a well-documented phenomenon associated with low blood-flow states such as occur during inflammation. The outward displacement of the white cells from the core of the bloodstream results in their creeping along the vessel wall,

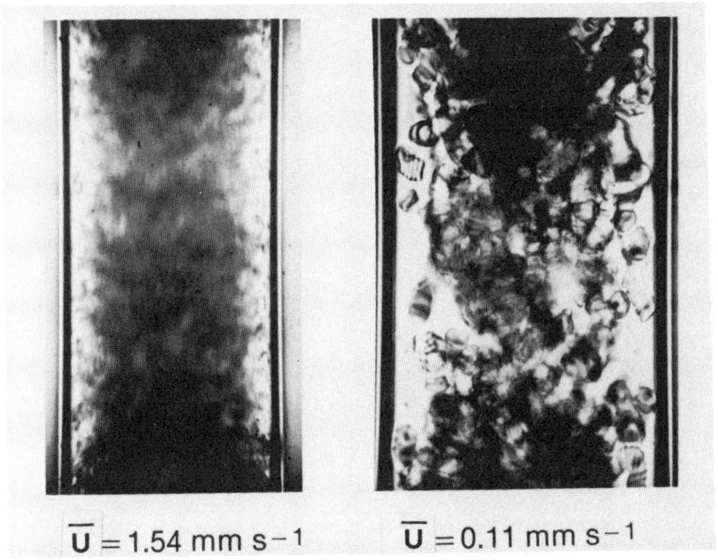

FIGURE 7. Photomicrographs of 20% haematocrit blood flowing at high (left) and low (right) velocities in a 100μm diameter tube. A core of rouleaux of red cells of non-uniform width develops at low ū. At the tube periphery, there are single rouleaux, white cells and platelets.

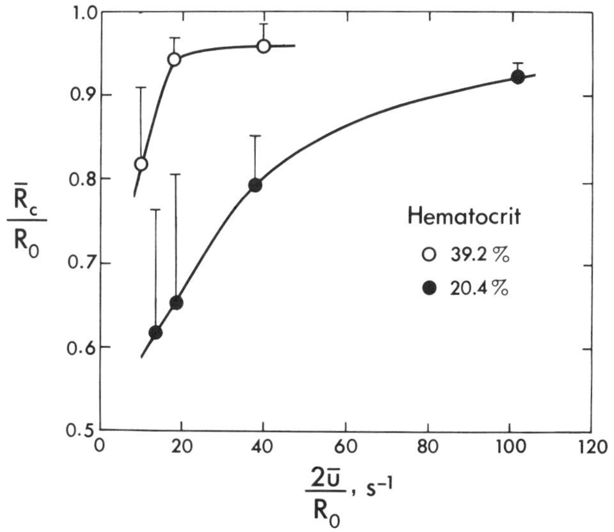

FIGURE 8. Mean values of the radius, R_c, of the red cell core in blood as a function of mean tube shear rate, $2\bar{u}/R_o$ at 20 and 39% haematocrit in a 100μm tube. The points are experimental showing one standard deviation from the mean, and the lines are the best fit drawn by eye. (From [35])

and is referred to as margination. This may be followed by cell-wall adhesion and subsequent emigration into the extravascular space. *In vivo*, Vejlens [68] demonstrated that white cell margination was associated with red cell aggregation, which he induced by intravenous injection of gelatin or fibrinogen in guinea pigs and rabbits, and subsequently examining the fixed vessels under a microscope. More recently, direct measurements were made of the distribution of fluorescent-labelled white cells in blood flowing through capillary tubes of 34-69 μm diameter [50]. It was shown that white cells migrated to the periphery of the tubes when red cell aggregation was induced either by reducing the flow rate or by adding high molecular weight dextrans.

In studies performed in our laboratory, we have quantitated the flow-dependent margination of white cells by measuring blood cell concentrations in the infusing reservoir syringe, n_o, and in 100μm and 150μm tubes, n_t [35]. Providing there is no screening effect of the cells entering the tube from the reservoir (an effect which occurs at $R_o < 15$ μm; [30], at the steady state, mass balance demands that reservoir (or discharge) concentration is equal to the ratio of the mean blood velocity $\bar{u}$, to mean white cell, $\bar{v}_{WBC}$, or red cell velocity $\bar{v}_{RBC}$:

$$\frac{n_t}{n_o} = \frac{\bar{u}}{\bar{v}_{WBC,RBC}} . \tag{40}$$

The classical work of Fahraeus [26] showed that, in the case of red cells, the ratio of tube to discharge haematocrit in a 100μm tube < 1 (the Fahraeus effect), implying that there is a non-uniform distribution of cells in the tube, with a greater axial than peripheral concentration. In the case of white cells, Vejlens [68] reported an experiment in a 100μm tube at a high flow rate ($\bar{u} \sim 140R_o\ s^{-1}$) which gave a value of $n_t/n_o = 0.75 \pm 0.07$ (s.d.), compared to a value of 0.82 for red cells under similar conditions. It was therefore concluded that there was greater inward migration of white cells than red cells.

5.2.2. Results. Blood flowed from a feed reservoir through vertically mounted sets of the 100 or 150μm tubes into a mechanically operated withdrawal syringe at mean velocities $\bar{u}$ from 18 to $280R_o\ s^{-1}$. After suddenly arresting the flow, the red cells in aliquots of the reservoir and of the blood eluted from the tubes were counted using an aperture impedance particle counter.

There was a marked increase in the number concentration of white cells in the tube as the flow rate decreased to $\bar{u} < 40R_o\ s^{-1}$. This is shown in the bar graph of Fig. 9, which gives the values of n_t/n_o at the highest and lowest $\bar{u}$. The effect was more pronounced in the 100μm than in the 150μm tube. Thus, $n_t/n_o > 1.1$ at the lowest flow rate and all haematocrits, implying that $\bar{v}_{WBC} < \bar{u}$. The converse was true at the highest flow rate where $n_t/n_o < 1$ and hence $\bar{v}_{WBC} > \bar{u}$.

In the case of the red cells, there was no such effect, in agreement with previous work [4], n_t/n_o being appreciably < 1 at all flow rates. It was also noted that, even at the high flow rates, there was an enrichment of white cells relative to red cells in the tube. This implies that $\bar{v}_{WBC} < \bar{v}_{RBC}$ and that the red cells had, on average, migrated further toward the axis.

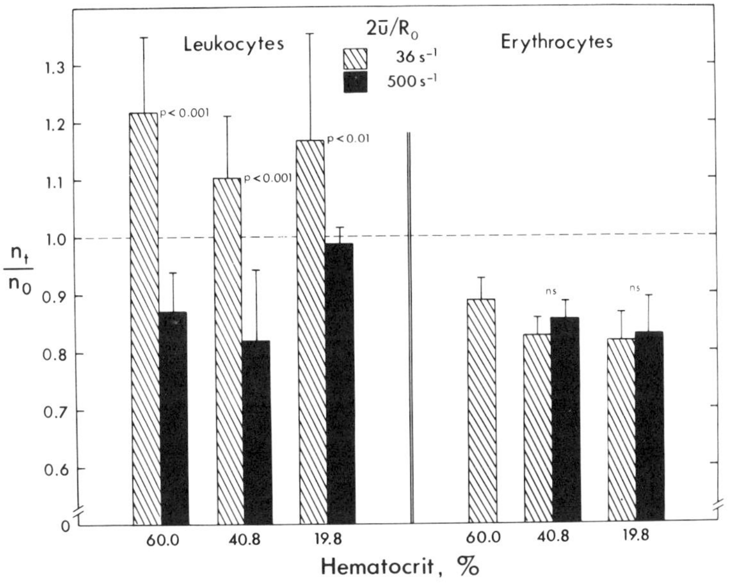

FIGURE 9. Bar graphs of the number concentrations of cells in blood in the 100μm tubes relative ot that in the reservoir, n_t/n_o, at the highest (hatched) and lowest (solid bars) mean linear flow rates, $\bar{u}$, at different reservoir haematocrits. The values of mean tube shear rate $2\bar{u}/R_o$ shown are calculated for Poiseuille flow at the same volume flow rate. (From [35])

The above results for the white cells at low $\bar{u}$ indicate that there was a decrease in the mean cell velocity with decreasing flow rate, and a redistribution of the cells toward the tube periphery. It was strongly suspected that the effect was directly related to red cell aggregation at low shear rate, since, as described above, such aggregation is accompanied by the inward migration of rouleaux (c.f. Figs. 7 and 8). The formation of a core of rouleaux could then displace white cells to the periphery thereby increasing n_o/n_t, as previously postulated by Nobis et al. [50] to explain their results in smaller glass tubes. Indeed, cine films of blood flowing through 100 μm tubes at low flow rates reveal the presence of many white cells as well as platelets in the peripheral red cell-depleted layer.

Proof that red cell aggregation is responsible for the outward displacement of white cells in tube flow was obtained by repeating the experiments with blood cells washed in phosphate-albumin buffer. Here, in the absence of fibrinogen, there is no rouleaux formation, and as can be seen in the bar graph of Fig. 10, the values of n_t/n_o for the white cells were appreciably < 1.0 at all $\bar{u}$. There was now a depletion of white cells in the tube relative to the red cells implying that $\bar{v}_{WBC} > \bar{v}_{RBC}$, and that the white cells had, on average, migrated further toward the axis.

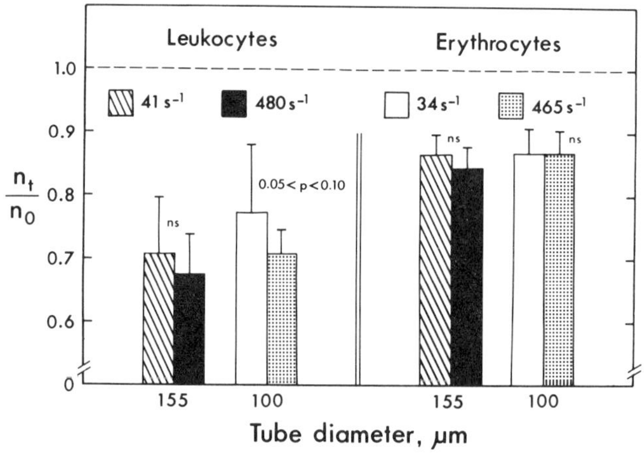

FIGURE 10. Bar graph, as in Fig. 9, of the relative number concentration of cells in 100 and 155 μm tubes in washed blood at 40% haematocrit. In contrast to Fig. 9, n_t/n_o < 0.8 for the white cells, and both at high and low $\bar{u}$ is lower than that for the red cells. The values of n_t/n_o at the high and low mean shear rates (indicated above) are not significantly different. (From [35])

5.3. Pressure drop in two-phase flow.

It is well known that in concentrated suspensions of rigid spheres and discs undergoing tube flow at low Reynolds number the velocity distribution is no longer parabolic as in Poiseuille flow but becomes blunted in the centre of the tube [37]. The local shear rate near the wall is higher, and that near the axis lower than that in Poiseuille flow at the same volume flow rate, resulting in an appreciable increase in apparent viscosity. Providing the distribution of particles in the tube is uniform, the velocity distribution is found to be independent of flow rate, and blunting occurs when the mean interparticle distance is of the same order of magnitude as the particle diameter, and both are not too much smaller than the tube diameter.

However, if there is a redistribution of particles because of inward migration from the wall of the tube, a particle-free zone will develop at the wall resulting in a two-phase flow. Experiments with rigid spheres in steady and oscillatory flow at higher Reynolds number where inertial effects are appreciable have shown that the velocity distribution becomes further blunted as a "plasmatic" zone develops near the wall, accompanied by a corresponding drop in the apparent viscosity [37,42].

In the case of human red blood cells, inward migration in Poiseuille flow has been demonstrated in viscous suspending media at low Reynolds numbers due to cell deformation, and at higher Reynolds number due to inertia of the fluid [32,34]. However, at normal haematocrits, the degree of cell redistribution in a vessel is limited because of particle crowding. The fact that the measured n_t/n_o for red cells in 100μm tubes < 1, is as much due to a wall effect, i.e. the exclusion of cell centres at distances $< \sim 4$ μm from the wall, as to inward migration of the particles. Nevertheless, it does result in an appreciable decrease in apparent viscosity with decreasing tube diameter [4].

As described above, however, the most striking redistribution of cells occurs at the lowest flow rates due to rouleaux formation and the migration of these aggregates into a central core. One would expect, therefore, that the apparent viscosity of blood in tubes of diameters < 300 μm would first increase with decreasing flow rate as rouleaux begin to form at $\bar{G} < 50\ s^{-1}$, and then to decrease as a two-phase flow develops and the width of the peripheral cell-depleted layer increases.

6. NOMENCLATURE

a,b*,c,d,e,f*,g,h*	Force and torque coefficients of a pair of spheres defined in Eqs. (19) and (20)
A; A_i; A^o; A'	Fraction of platelets in all aggregates across the median plane; fraction in aggregates of i cells; fraction of cells in aggregates in control sample; net fraction of cells, = A - A^o
A(r*), C(r*)	Dimensionless functions of r* defined in [5] and in [65]
b	Sphere radius
B(r*)	Angular velocity coefficient defined in Eq. (3)
c	Volume fraction of single spheres
F(j); $F_i(j)$	Force vector acting on sphere j = 1,2; components on sphere j along X_i
$F_{int}(h)$	Non-hydrodynamic forces of interaction as function of h
$F_{attr}(h)$, $F_{rep}(h)$	Attractive and repulsive forces of interaction defined in Eqs. (6) and (7), respectively
G; G(R); $\bar{G}$; **G**	Shear rate; shear rate as function of radial distance R from tube axis; mean value = $2\bar{u}/R_o$; velocity gradient tensor
h	Gap distance between sphere surfaces
J, J_s	Respective collision capture frequency and collision frequency defined in Eqs. (32) and (33)

k	Boltzmann constant
K	Dielectric constant
$\bar{M}(\Delta x_3)$	Average number of collisions per cell in the tube as function of Δx_3
n_t, n_o	Respective number concentrations of blood cells in the tube and infusing reservoir
N_o; N_t	Number concentration of single spheres at $t = 0$; concentration of combined singlets and newly formed doublets at time t
O	Origin of particle-fixed coordinate system X_i at centre of doublet axis
Q	Volumetric flow rate
r; r^*	Centre-to-centre distance of a pair of spheres; r/b
r_e	Equivalent spheroidal axis ratio defined in [37]
R; R_o	Radial distance from the tube axis; tube radius
$\mathbf{S}$, S_{ij}	Rate-of-strain tensor; its components along X_i
t; $\bar{t}$	time; mean transit time in Poiseuille flow
$\mathbf{u}$; u_i	Undisturbed velocity field vector of uniform flow in space-fixed coordinate system; its components along x_i

$u_i(R)$; $v_3(R)$	Component of undisturbed velocity field vector along x_i in Poiseuille flow at radial distance R in tube; velocity of centre of particle in x_3-direction at radial distance R in the tube
$\bar{u}$	Mean linear velocity in the tube
$\mathbf{U}_o$; U_i; $\mathbf{u}(j)$; $u_i(j)$	Undisturbed velocity field vector of uniform shear flow in particle-fixed coordinate system; its components along X_i; at sphere center j; at sphere center j along X_i
$\mathbf{U}_j$; $U_i(j)$	Translational velocity of sphere j; its component along x_i
$\bar{v}_{WBC}$, $\bar{v}_{RBC}$	Respective mean white cell and red cell velocities in the tube
x_i, X_i	Respective space-fixed and particle fixed coordinate systems
Δx_3	Axial distance between measurement positions in the tube

GREEK SYMBOLS

α_o	Collision capture efficiency = J/J_s
$\beta_i(h)$	Coefficient of F_i as a function of h defined in Eqs. (30) and (31)
ε_o	Permittivity of free space
η	Viscosity of suspending medium
κ	Reciprocal Debye length

λ	London wavelength
θ_i, ϕ_i	Polar and azimuthal angles relative to the x_i-axis
ν_D	Angular velocity coefficient of a rigid dumbbell defined in Eq. (25)
$\Gamma(j)$; $\Gamma_i(j)$; Γ^D; Γ_i^D	Torque on sphere j about its centre; its component along X_i; torque on a rigid dumbbell about 0; its component along X_i
Ψ_o	Surface potential
$\omega(j)$; $\omega_i(j)$	Angular velocity of sphere j; its components along X_i
ω_f; $(\omega_f)_i$	Fluid spin vector of the undisturbed flow; its component along X_i
Ω	Angular velocity of a rigid dumbbell

SCRIPT SYMBOLS

$(\mathcal{F})$	Force-torque vector defined in Eq. (10)
$(\mathcal{R})$	Grand resistance matrix defined in Eq. (10); given in Eq. (19)
$(\mathcal{S})$	Shear vector defined in Eq. (10)
$(\mathcal{U})$	Relative velocity-spin vector of a particle system defined in Eq. (10)
(Φ)	Shear resistance matrix defined in Eq. (10); given in Eq. (20)

7. REFERENCES

[1] ADLER, P.M. 1981. Heterocoagulation in shear flow. J. Colloid Interface Sci. **83**: 106-115.

[2] ARP, P.A. and MASON, S.G. 1976. Orthokinetic collisions in simple shear flow. Can. J. Chem. **54**: 769-774.

[3] ARP, P.A. and MASON, S.G. 1977. The kinetics of flowing dispersions. VIII. Doublets of rigid spheres (theoretical). J. Colloid Interface Sci. **61**: 21-43.

[4] BARBEE, J.H. and COKELET, G.R. 1971. The Fahraeus Effect. Microvasc. Res. **3**: 6-16.

[5] BATCHELOR, G.K. and GREEN, J.T. 1972. The hydrodynamic interaction of two small freely moving spheres in a linear flow field. J. Fluid Mech. **56**: 375-400.

[6] BELL, D.N., TEIRLINCK, H.C. and GOLDSMITH, H.L. 1984. Platelet aggregation in Poiseuille flow: I. A double infusion technique. Microvasc. Res. **27**: 297-315.

[7] BELL, D.N. and GOLDSMITH, H.L. 1984. Platelet aggregation in Poiseuille flow. II. Effect of shear rate. Microvasc. Res. **27**: 316-330.

[8] BELL, G.I. 1978. Models for the specific adhesion of cells to cells. Science **200**: 618-627.

[9] BORN, G.V.R. 1962. Aggregation of blood platelets by adenosine diphosphate and its reversal. Nature (London) **194**: 927-929.

[10] BRENNER, H. and O'NEILL, M.E. 1972. On the Stokes resistance of multiparticle systems in a linear shear field. Chem. Eng. Sci. **27**: 1421-1439.

[11] BROOKS, D.E., GOODWIN, J.W. and SEAMAN, G.V.F. 1970. Interactions among erythrocytes under shear. J. Appl. Physiol. **28**: 172-177.

[12] BROOKS, D.E., LEVINE, Y.K., REQUENA, J. and HAYDON, D.A. 1975. van der Waals forces in oil-water systems from the study of thin lipid films. III. Comparison of experimental results with Hamaker constants calculated from Lifshitz theory. Proc. Roy. Soc. **A347**: 179-194.

[13] BUXBAUM, K., EVANS. E.A. and BROOKS, D.E. 1982. Quantitation of surface affinities of red blood cells in Dextran solutions. Biochemistry **21**: 3235-3239.

[14] CASSON, N. 1959. Flow equations for pigment-oil suspensions of the printing ink type. In: "Rheology of Disperse Systems" (Mills, C.C., ed.) Pergamon Press, New York. pp. 84-104.

[15] CHIEN, S. and JAN, K.-M. 1973. Ultrastructural basis of the mechanism of rouleaux formation. Microvasc. Res. **5**: 155-166.

[16] CHIEN, S., USAMI, S., DELLENBACK, R.J., GREGERSON, M.I., NANNINGA, L.B. and GUEST, M.M. 1967. Blood viscosity: influence of erythrocyte aggregation. Science **157**: 829-831.

[17] CHIEN, S., SUNG, L.A., KIM, A., BURKE, A.M. and USAMI, S. 1977. Determination of aggregation force in rouleaux by fluid mechanical technique. Microvasc. Res. **13**: 327-333.

[18] CHIEN, S., SUNG, S.A., SIMCHON, S., LEE, M.L., JAN, K.-M. and SKALAK, R. 1983. Energy balance in red cell interactions. Ann. N.Y. Acad. Sci. **46**: 190-206.

[19] CURTIS, A.S.G. and HOCKING, L.M. 1970. Collision efficiency of equal spherical particles in a shear field. Trans. Faraday Soc. **66**: 1381-1390.

[20] DINTENFASS, L. 1962. Considerations of the internal viscosity of red cell and its effects on the viscosity of whole blood. Angiology **13**: 333-344.
[21] DERJAGUIN, B.V. and LANDAU, L.D. 1941. Acta Physicochim. URSS **14**: 633.
[22] EVANS, E.A. 1980. Minimum energy analysis of membrane deformation applied to pipet aspiration and surface adhesion of red blood cells. Biophys. J. **30**: 265-284.
[23] EVANS, E.A. and BUXBAUM, K. 1981. Affinity of red blood cell membrane for particle surfaces measured by the extent of particle encapsulation. Biophys. J. **34**: 1-12.
[24] EVANS, E.A. and LEUNG, A. 1984. Adhesivity and rigidity of red blood cell membrane in relation to WGA binding. J. Cell Biol. **98**: 1201-1208.
[25] EVANS, E.A. and PARSEGIAN, V.A. 1983. Energetics of membrane deformation and adhesion in cell and vesicle aggregation. Ann. N.Y. Acad. Sci. **416**: 13-33.
[26] FAHRAEUS, R. 1929. The suspension stability of blood. Physiol. Rev. **9**: 241-274.
[27] FISCHER, T.M., STOHR M. and SCHMID-SCHONBEIN, H. 1978. Red blood cell (RBC) microrheology: Comparison of the behavior of single RBC and liquiddroplets in shear flow. A.I.Ch.E. Symp. Ser. **74**: 38-45.
[28] FROJMOVIC, M.M., NEWTON, M. and GOLDSMITH, H.L. 1976. The microrheology of mammalian platelets: Studies of rheo-optical transients and flow in tubes. Microvasc. Res. **11**: 203-215.
[29] FROJMOVIC, M.M. and MILTON, J.G. 1982. Human platelet size, shape and related functions in health and disease. Physiol. Rev. **62**: 185-261.
[30] GAEHTGENS, P., ALBRECHT, K.H. and KREUTZ, F. 1978. Fahraeus effect and cell screening during the flow of blood. I. Effect of variation of flow rate. Biorheology **15**: 147-154.
[31] GOLDSMITH, H.L. 1967. Microscopic flow properties of red cells. Fed. Proc. **26**: 1813-1820.
[32] GOLDSMITH, H.L. and MARLOW, J. 1972. Flow behaviour of erythrocytes. lI. Rotation and deformation in dilute suspensions. Proc. Roy. Soc. (London) **181**: 351-384.
[33] GOLDSMITH, H.L. and MARLOW, J.C. 1979. Flow behavior of erythrocytes. II. Particle motions in concentrated suspensions of ghost cells. J. Colloid Interface Sci. **71**: 383-407.
[34] GOLDSMITH, H.L. and SKALAK, R. 1975. Hemodynamics. Ann. Rev. Fluid Mech. **7**: 213-247.
[35] GOLDSMITH, H.L. and SPAIN, S. 1984. Margination of leukocytes in blood flow through small tubes. Microvasc. Res. **27**: 204-222.
[36] GOLDSMITH, H.L. and MASON, S.G. 1964. The flow of suspensions through tubes. III. Collisions of single uniform spheres. Proc. Roy. Soc. (London) **A282**: 569-591.
[37] GOLDSMITH, H.L. and MASON, S.G. 1967. The Microrheology of Dispersions. In: "Rheology: Theory and Applications", Vol. 4. (F.R. Eirich, ed.) Academic Press, New York. pp. 85-250.
[38] GOLDSMITH, H.L. and MASON, S.G. 1975. Some model experiments in hemodynamics. V. Microrheological techniques. Biorheology **12**:181-192.
[39] GOLDSMITH, H.L., TAKAMURA, K. and BELL, D.N. 1983. Shear-induced collisions between human blood cells. Ann. N.Y. Acad. Sci. **416**: 299-318.

[40] GOLDSMITH, H.L., LICHTARGE, O., TESSSIER-LAVIGNE, M. and SPAIN, S. 1981. Some model experiments in hemodynamics. VI. Two-body collisions between blood cells. Biorheology **18**: 531-555.
[41] HAMAKER, A. 1937. Physica **4**: 1058.
[42] KARNIS, A., GOLDSMITH, H.L. and MASON, S.G. 1966. The flow of suspensions through tubes. V. Inertial effects. Can. J. Chem. Eng. **44**: 181-193.
[43] LEVINE, S., LEVINE, M., SHARP, K.A. and BROOKS, D.E. 1983. Theory of electrokinetic behavior of human erythrocytes. Biophys J. **42**: 127- 135.
[44] LIFSHITZ, E.M. 1961. Soviet Phys. JETP English Transl. **2**: 73.
[45] LIN, C.Y., LEE, K.Y. and SATHER, N.F. 1970. Slow motion of two spheres in a shear field. J. Fluid Mech. **43**: 35-47.
[46] MACDONALD, D.E. 1974. "Blood Flow in Arteries". 2nd Ed., Edward Arnold London, 496 pp.
[47] MANLEY, R. St.J. and MASON, S.G. 1954. Particle motions in sheared suspensions. II. Collisions of uniform spheres. J. Colloid Sci. **7**: 354-369.
[48] NINHAM, B.W. and PARSEGIAN, V.A. 1970. van der Waals forces, special characteristics in lipid-water systems and a general method of calculation based on the Lifshitz theory. Biophys. J. **10**: 646-663.
[49] NINHAM, B.W. and PARSEGIAN, V.A. 1971. Electrostatic potential between surfaces bearing ionizable groups in ionic equilibrium with physiological saline solution. J. Theor. Biol. **31**: 405-428.
[50] NOBIS, U., FRIES, A.R. and GAEHTGENS, P. 1982. Rheological mechanisms contributing to WBC-margination. In "White Blood Cells: Morphology and Rheology as Related to Function" (U. Bagge, G.V.R. Born, and P. Gaehtgens, eds.), Martinus Nijhoff, The Hague/Boston. pp. 57-65.
[51] PARSEGIAN, V.A. and GINGELL, D. 1972. Some features of physical forces between biological cell membranes. J. Adhesion **4**: 283-306.
[52] SCHMID-SCHONBEIN, H. and WELLS, R. 1969. Fluid drop-like transition of erythrocytes under shear. Science **165**: 228-231.
[53] SCHMID-SCHONBEIN, H., GAEHTGENS, P. and HIRSCH, H. 1968. On the shear rate dependence of red cell aggregation in vitro. J. Clin. Invest. **47**: 1447-1454.
[54] SEAMAN, G.V.F. 1975. Electrokinetic behavior of red cells. In: "The Red Blood Cell", Vol. II. (D. MacN. Surgenor, ed.),Academic Press, New York. pp. 1135-1229.
[55] SEGRE, G. and SILBERBERG, A. 1962. Behaviour of macroscopic rigid spheres in Poiseuille flow. II. Experimental results and interpretation. J. Fluid Mech. **14**: 136-157.
[56] SKALAK, R. and CHIEN, S. 1983. Theoretical models of rouleau formation and disaggregation. Ann. N.Y. Acad. Sci. **416**: 138-148.
[57] SMOLUCHOWSKI, M. von. 1917. Versuch einer mathematischen Theorie der Koagulationskinetik kolloider Lösungen. Z. Phys. Chem. **92**: 129-168.
[58] SWIFT, D.L. and FRIEDLANDER, S.K. 1964. The coagulation of hydrosols by Brownian motion and laminar shear flow. J. Colloid Sci. **19**: 621-647.
[59] TAKAMURA, K., GOLDSMITH, H.L. and MASON, S.G. 1979. The microrheology of colloidal dispersions. IX. Effects of simple and polyelectrolytes on rotation of doublets of spheres. J. Colloid Interface Sci. **72**: 385-400.
[60] TAKAMURA, K., GOLDSMITH, H.L. and MASON, S.G. 1981. The microrheology of colloidal dispersions. XII. Trajectories of orthokinetic pair-collisions of latex spheres in a simple electrolyte. J. Colloid Interface Sci. **82**: 175-189.

[61] TAKAMURA, K., GOLDSMITH, H.L. and MASON, S.G. 1981. The microrheology of colloidal dispersions. XIII. Trajectories of orthokinetic pair-collisions of latex spheres in a polyelectrolyte. J. Colloid Interface Sci. **82**: 190-202.
[62] TAKAMURA, K., ADLER, P.M., GOLDSMITH, H.L. and MASON, S.G. 1981. Particle motions in sheared suspensions. XXXI. Rotations of rigid and flexible dumbbells (Experimental). J. Colloid Interface Sci. **83**: 516-530.
[63] THA, S.P., SHUSTER, J. and GOLDSMITH, H.L. Interaction forces between red cells agglutinated by antibody. Submitted for Biophys. J.
[64] VADAS, E.B., GOLDSMITH, H.L. and MASON, 1973. The microrheology of colloidal dispersions. I. The microtube technique. J. Colloid Interface Sci. **43**: 630-648.
[65] VAN DE VEN, T.G.M. and MASON, S.G. 1976. The microrheology of colloidal dispersions. IV. Pairs of interacting spheres. J. Colloid Interface Sci. **57**: 505-516.
[66] VAN DE VEN, T.G.M. and MASON, S.G. 1976. The microrheology of colloidal dispersions. V. Primary and secondary doublets of spheres in shear flow. J. Colloid Interface Sci. **57**: 517-534.
[67] VAN DE VEN, T.G.M. and MASON, S.G. 1977. The microrheology of colloidal dispersions. VII. Orthokinetic doublet formation of spheres. Colloid Polymer Sci. **255**: 468-479.
[68] VEJLENS, G. 1938. The distribution of leukocytes in the vascular system. Acta Path. Microbiol. Scand. **Suppl. 33**: 11-239.
[69] VERWEY, E.G. and OVERBEEK, J.Th.G. 1948. "Theory of the Stability of Lyophobic Colloids", Elsevier Scient. Publ. Co., Amsterdam, 205 pp.
[70] WEISS, L. and GLAVES, D. 1983. Cancer cell damage at the vascular endothelium. Ann. N.Y. Acad Sci. **416**: 681-692.
[71] ZEICHNER, G.R. and SCHOWALTER, W.R. 1977. Use of trajectory analysis to study stability of colloidal dispersions in flow fields. A.I.Ch.E.J. **23**: 243-254.
[72] ZEICHNER, G.R. and SCHOWALTER, W.R. 1979. Effects of hydrodynamic and colloidal forces on the coagulation of dispersions. J. Colloid Interface Sci. **71**: 237-253.

From the McGill University Medical Clinic, The Montreal General Hospital, 1650 Cedar Avenue, Montreal, Quebec, H3G 1A4, Canada.

ACKNOWLEDGMENTS

The work was supported by grant MT-1835 from the Medical Research Council of Canada and by the Quebec Heart Foundation. H.L.G. is a Career Research Investigator, and S.P.T. a Fellow of the Medical Research Council. The authors gratefully acknowledge many helpful discussions with Drs. Raymond Cox, Joseph Shuster, Koichi Takamura and Theodore van de Ven.

R NIEFER & P N KALONI

A cartesian tensor solution of the creeping flow equations of a polar fluid

1. Introduction

Classical fluid mechanics is based upon the stress hypothesis of Cauchy, which states that upon any surface S drawn in a continuum, the action of the material on one side of S upon the other side is given by the distribution of forces over S. The above assumption eventually leads to a symmetric stress tensor. Similarly, in classical fluid mechanics the complete geometric description of the medium is determined by only specifying the location of each particle because the only geometric property of a particle is its position. A simple departure from the classical theory begins with the polar fluid theory. Here, first of all, it is assumed that "across any infinitesimal surface element in a material, the action of the material on one side of the surface upon the material on the other side is equipollent to a force and couple". Secondly, it is also assumed that the particle has not only the geometric properties of position, but also of orientation. These two assumptions finally lead to the introduction of a couple stress tensor and a micro-rotation vector, and also to an asymmetric stress tensor in the theory.

The Cosserat brothers [6] apparently were the first to develop the theory of a polar continuum. Subsequent developments, in some form or the other, particularly relevant to polar fluid theory, have appeared in the works of Born [2], Grad [13], Dahler [8], Aero et al. [1], Condiff and Dahler [5] and Eringen [10]. Review articles by Cowin [7] and Eringen and Kafadar [11] give a comprehensive treatment of the subject.

In the present article we shall develop a method of solution of the creeping motion equation for a polar fluid and then apply the method to solve a few meaningful problems. It is well known that, there are essentially three well-known methods of treating creeping flow equations in a viscous Newtonian fluid [15]. The first is Lamb's general solution, which, though applicable to the widest class of problems, is cumbersome because of its extreme generality. The second is the stream function technique, which is useful for strictly two-dimensional or for those three-dimensional problems which display some form of symmetry. Finally, there is the singularity method, originated by Lorentz [20], which though easy to apply, requires much guess work. In polar fluids, Lamb's solution has recently been extended by Brunn [3] and the stream function technique has been extended by Ramkissoon and Majumdar [24]. The purpose of this chapter is to develop a cartesian tensor solution of the creeping motion equations of the polar fluid theory. Such solutions are basically motivated by different kinds of boundary conditions. After reproducing the basic equations in the next section, the method is presented in section 3. Section 4 then discusses two applications of the method. In the final section, some comments are made about the method as well as some general comments about the theories of polar fluids.

2. Basic Equations

The equations of motion for an incompressible micropolar fluid are [12]:

$$v_{i,i} = 0 \tag{1}$$

$$\rho\dot{v}_i = t_{ji,j} + \rho f_i \tag{2}$$

$$\rho I\dot{\nu}_i = m_{ji,j} + \varepsilon_{ijk}t_{jk} + \rho\ell_i \tag{3}$$

In the above v_i is the velocity vector, ν_i the micro-rotation vector, ρ the mass density, I the micro-inertia, f_i the body force per unit mass, ℓ_i the body couple per unit mass, t_{ij} the stress tensor, m_{ij} the couple stress tensor and ε_{ijk} is the alternating tensor. Also, a superposed dot denotes the material time derivative. The constitutive equations for the stress tensor and the couple stress tensor are:

$$t_{ij} = -p\delta_{ij} + \mu(v_{i,j} + v_{j,i}) + \kappa(v_{j,i} - \varepsilon_{ijk}\,\nu_k) \tag{4}$$

$$m_{ij} = \alpha\nu_{k,k}\delta_{ij} + \beta\,\nu_{i,j} + \gamma\,\nu_{j,i} \tag{5}$$

where p is the thermodynamic pressure and α, β, γ, κ, and μ are constant viscosity coefficients. On substituting (4) and (5) in equations (2) and (3), we get the field equation as:

$$\rho \dot{v}_i = (\mu+\kappa) v_{i,jj} + \kappa \varepsilon_{ijk} \nu_{k,j} - p_{,i} + \rho f_i \tag{6}$$

$$\rho I \dot{\nu}_i = (\alpha+\beta) \nu_{j,ij} + \gamma \nu_{i,jj} + \kappa \varepsilon_{ijk} v_{k,j} - 2\kappa \nu_i + \rho \ell_i \tag{7}$$

The thermodynamic considerations show that the viscosity coefficients must satisfy the following inequalities:

$$\begin{aligned} &(3\lambda + 2\mu + \kappa) \geqslant 0, \qquad (2\mu + \kappa) \geqslant 0,\ \kappa \geqslant 0 \\ &(3\alpha + \beta + \gamma) \geqslant 0, \qquad -\gamma \leqslant \beta \leqslant \gamma,\ \ \gamma \geqslant 0 \end{aligned} \tag{8}$$

The problem of formulating the suitable boundary condition for the micropolar fluid is still unsettled. While for the velocity field, the usual no-slip condition is used; there are at least four different proposals in the literature for the micro-rotation vector. However, for various simplifying reasons, most of the authors employ the adherence boundary condition, in which the micro-rotation vector is taken to be zero on a rigid boundary.

In the situations where the motion is steady, inertial effects, in both equations (6) and (7), are negligible, and there are no body forces nor body couples then the field equations reduce to:

$$p_{,i} = (\mu + \kappa) \nabla^2 u_i + \kappa \varepsilon_{ijk} \nu_{k,i} \tag{9}$$

$$\kappa \varepsilon_{ijk} v_{k,j} = 2\kappa \nu_i - (\alpha + \beta) \nu_{j,ij} - \gamma \nabla^2 \nu_j \tag{10}$$

After several manipulations, it is found that the final form of the equations to be solved is [21]:

$$\nabla^2 p = 0 \tag{11}$$

$$(\nabla^2 - L^2) \nabla^2 v_i = -\frac{2L^2}{\eta} \frac{\partial p}{\partial x_i} \tag{12}$$

$$(\nabla^2 - \frac{2\kappa}{\delta})\overline{\psi} = 0 \tag{13}$$

subject to the requirements that:

$$v_{i,i} = 0 \tag{14}$$

$$\nu_i = \frac{1}{2}\left[1 + \frac{\gamma(\mu+\kappa)}{k^2}\nabla^2 \right]\varepsilon_{ijk}\, v_{k,j} + \frac{\delta}{2\kappa}\frac{\partial\psi}{\partial x_i} \tag{15}$$

Here, ∇^2 is the Laplacian operator and the coefficients L, η and δ are defined as:

$$L^2 = \frac{\kappa(2\mu+\kappa)}{\gamma(\mu+\kappa)}, \quad \delta = (\alpha+\beta+\gamma), \quad \eta = (2\mu+\kappa) \tag{16}$$

3. Cartesian Tensor Solutions

In order to generate solutions of equations (11) to (15), we now write down scalar invariants involving the spatially constant second and third order tensors, a_{ij} and A_{ijk} with the position vector $\underset{\sim}{r}$. The scalar invariants linear in a_{ij} and A_{ijk} are:

(i) a_{ii}, (ii) $\varepsilon_{ijk}a_{kj}X_j$, (iii) $a_{ij}X_iX_j$

(iv) $A_{imm}X_i$, (v) $A_{mim}X_i$, (vi) $A_{mmi}X_i$

(vii) $A_{ijk}X_iX_jX_k$ (17)

In order that (17) be associated with the solutions of equation (11), a general form for $p(\underset{\sim}{r})$ is assumed to be:

$$p(\underset{\sim}{r}) = H^0(r)a_{ii} + H^1(r)\varepsilon_{ijk}a_{kj}X_j$$
$$+ H^2(r)\ A_{imm}X_i + H^3(r)A_{mim}X_i + H^4(r)A_{mmi}X_i$$
$$+ H^5(r)a_{ij}X_iX_j + H^6(r)A_{ijk}X_iX_jX_k \qquad (18)$$

where $r = (X_iX_i)^{1/2}$. Equation (18) will satisfy (11), provided the functions $H^p(r)$ satisfy the equations of the form:

$$\frac{d^2}{dr^2} H^p(r) + \frac{n + (2m-1)}{r} \frac{d}{dr} H^p(r) = G(r) \qquad (19)$$

where n is the dimension of the Euclidean space, m is the order of the coefficient tensor and G(r) is either known or zero. Specific forms for ∇p, $\nabla^2 p$, $v_{\ell,m}$, $v_{\ell,\ell}$, $v_{\ell,mm}$ etc. can be easily computed once the forms for p and v_ℓ have been assumed. In the following, solutions will be given for n=3 and at the end, mention will be made of the special changes necessary for the case n=2. Thus, for the function $p(\underset{\sim}{r})$, it is found that:

$$H^0(r) = -\frac{1}{n} A_1^5\ r^{-n} + A_1^0\ r^{-(n-2)} + A_2^0 - \frac{1}{n} A_2^5\ r^2,$$

$$H^1(r) = A_1^1\ r^{-n} + A_2^1,$$

$$H^2(r) = -\frac{1}{n+2} A_1^6\ r^{-(n+2)} + A_1^2\ r^{-n} + A_2^2 - \frac{1}{(n+2)} A_2^6\ r^2,$$

$$H^3(r) = -\frac{1}{(n+2)} A_1^6\ r^{-(n+2)} + A_1^3\ r^{-n} + A_2^3 - \frac{1}{(n+2)} A_2^6\ r^2,$$

$$H^4(r) = -\frac{1}{(n+2)} A_1^6\ r^{-(n+2)} + A_1^4\ r^{-n} + A_2^4 - \frac{1}{(n+2)} A_2^6\ r^2,$$

$$H^5(r) = A_1^5\ r^{-(n+2)} + A_2^5$$

$$H^6(r) = A_1^6\ r^{-(n+4)} + A_2^6 \qquad (20)$$

where the constants A_q^p $(p,q = 1,2 \ldots\ldots 6)$ are to be determined from the specific boundary conditions. On writing equation (12) as:

$$\nabla^2 u_i = \frac{\partial \bar{p}}{\partial X_i} \quad \text{and} \quad (\nabla^2 - L^2)v_i = u_i \tag{21}$$

where $\bar{p} = -\frac{2L^2}{\eta}p$, we can now write the solutions for equation $(21)_1$ first, and then for $(21)_2$ and (13). Thus, equation $(21)_1$ and the form of $p(r)$, given by (18), suggest that the general form for the velocity u_i in the direction of X_p is given by:

$$\begin{aligned} u_p(\underset{\sim}{r}) &= h_1^0(r)a_{ii}X_p + h_1^1(r)\varepsilon_{ijk}\, a_{kj}X_iX_p + h_1^2(r)\varepsilon_{pjk}a_{kj} \\ &+ h_1^2(r)A_{imm}X_iX_p + h_2^2(r)A_{pmm} + h_1^3(r)A_{mim}X_iX_p \\ &+ h_2^3(r)A_{mpm} + h_1^4(r)A_{mmi}X_iX_p + h_2^4(r)A_{mmp} \\ &+ h_1^5(r)a_{ij}X_iX_jX_p + h_2^5(r)a_{pj}X_j + h_3^5(r)a_{jp}X_j \\ &+ h_1^6(r)A_{ijk}X_iX_jX_kX_p + h_2^6(r)A_{pjk}X_jX_k \\ &+ h_3^6(r)A_{jpk}X_jX_k + h_4^6(r)A_{jkp}X_jX_k \end{aligned} \tag{22}$$

Substitution of (22) and (18) in (21), requires that the functions $h_q^p(r)$ satisfy the following:

$$\text{(i)} \quad \frac{d^2}{dr^2}h_1^p(r) + \frac{n + (2m+1)}{r}\frac{d}{dr}h_1^p(r) = g_1(r) \tag{23}$$

$$\text{(ii)} \quad \frac{d^2}{dr^2}h_q^p(r) + \frac{n + (2m-3)}{r}\frac{d}{dr}h_q^p(r) = g_2(r) \tag{24}$$

where in (ii) $q \neq 1$, and $p \in \{0,1,\ldots\ldots 6\}$ in both (i) and (ii). Also,

$g_1(r)$ and $g_2(r)$ are either known functions or zero. The solutions for (23) and (24), for n=3, are given by:

$$h_1^0(r) = -\frac{1}{(n+2)} A_3^5 r^{-(n+2)} + A_3^0 r^{-n} + \frac{1}{2} A_1^0 r^{(2-n)} + A_4^0 - \frac{(A_2^5 + n A_4^5)}{n(n+2)} r^2$$

$$h_1^1(r) = A_3^1 r^{-(n+2)} + \frac{1}{2} A_1^1 r^{-n} + A_4^1$$

$$h_2^1(r) = -\frac{1}{n} A_3^1 r^{-n} + A_5^1 r^{(2-n)} + A_6^1 + \frac{A_2^1 - 2A_4^1}{2n} r^2$$

$$h_1^2(r) = \frac{-1}{n+4} A_3^6 r^{-(n+4)} + A_3^2 r^{-(n+2)} + \frac{1}{2} A_1^2 r^{-n} + A_4^2 - \frac{(A_2^6+(n+2)A_4^6)}{(n+2)(n+4)} r^2$$

$$h_2^2(r) = \frac{1}{(n+2)(n+4)} A_3^6 r^{-(n+2)} - \frac{(A_1^6 + 2(n+2)[A_3^2 + A_5^6])}{2n(n+2)} r^{-n} + A_5^2 r^{(2-n)} + A_6^2 + \frac{(A_2^2-2[A_4^2+A_6^6])}{2n} r^2 - \frac{(A_2^6-2A_4^6)}{2(n+2)(n+4)} r^4$$

$$h_1^3(r) = \frac{-1}{n+4} A_3^6 r^{-(n+4)} + A_3^3 r^{-(n+2)} + \frac{1}{2} A_1^3 r^{-n} + A_4^3 - \frac{(A_2^6+(n+2)A_4^6)}{(n+2)(n+4)} r^2$$

$$h_2^3(r) = \frac{1}{(n+2)(n+4)} A_3^6 r^{-(n+2)} - \frac{(A_1^6+2(n+2)[A_3^3+A_7^6])}{2n(n+2)} r^{-n} + A_5^3 r^{(2-n)} + A_6^3 + \frac{(A_2^3-2[A_4^3+A_6^6])}{2n} r^2 - \frac{(A_2^6-2A_4^6)}{2(n+2)(n+4)} r^4$$

$$h_1^4(r) = \frac{-1}{(n+4)} A_3^6 r^{-(n+4)} + A_3^4 r^{-(n+2)} + \frac{1}{2} A_1^4 r^{-n} + A_4^4 - \frac{(A_2^6+(n+2)A_4^6)}{(n+2)(n+4)} r^2 \tag{25}$$

$$h_2^4(r) = \frac{1}{(n+2)(n+4)} A_3^6 \, r^{-(n+2)} - \frac{(A_1^6+2(n+2)[A_3^4+A_9^6])}{2n(n+2)} r^{-n}$$

$$+ A_5^4 \, r^{(2-n)} + A_6^4 + \frac{(A_2^4-2[A_4^4+A_{10}^6])}{2n} r^2 - \frac{(A_2^6-2A_4^6)}{2(n+2)(n+4)} r^4$$

$$h_1^5(r) = A_3^5 \, r^{-(n+4)} + \frac{1}{2} A_1^5 \, r^{-(n+2)} + A_4^5$$

$$h_2^5(r) = - \frac{1}{(n+2)} A_3^5 \, r^{-(n+2)} + A_5^5 \, r^{-n} + A_6^5 + \frac{A_2^5-2A_4^5}{2(n+2)} r^2$$

$$h_3^5(r) = \frac{-1}{(n+2)} A_3^5 \, r^{-(n+2)} + A_7^5 \, r^{-n} + A_8^5 + \frac{A_2^5-2A_4^5}{2(n+2)} r^2$$

$$h_1^6(r) = A_3^6 \, r^{-(n+6)} + \frac{1}{2} A_1^6 \, r^{-(n+4)} + A_4^6$$

$$h_2^6(r) = \frac{-1}{(n+4)} A_3^6 \, r^{-(n+4)} + A_5^6 \, r^{-(n+2)} + A_6^6 + \frac{A_2^6-2A_4^6}{2(n+4)} r^2$$

$$h_3^6(r) = \frac{-1}{(n+4)} A_3^6 \, r^{-(n+4)} + A_7^6 \, r^{-(n+2)} + A_8^6 + \frac{A_2^6-2A_4^6}{2(n+4)} r^2$$

$$h_4^6(r) = \frac{-1}{(n+4)} A_3^6 \, r^{-(n+4)} + A_9^6 \, r^{-(n+2)} + A_{10}^6 + \frac{A_2^6-2A_4^6}{2(n+4)} r^2 \qquad (25)$$

On assuming that the functions ψ and v_i, in equations (13) and $(21)_2$, have the same structural form as assumed for p and u_i, we write:

$$\overline{\psi}(\underset{\sim}{r}) = F_0(r)a_{ii} + F_1(r)\varepsilon_{ijk} \, a_{kj} \, X_i + F_2(r)A_{imm}X_i +$$

$$+ F_3(r)A_{mim}X_i + F_4(r)A_{mmi}X_i + F_5(r)a_{ij}X_iX_j +$$

$$+ F_6(r)A_{ijk}X_iX_jX_k \qquad (26)$$

$$v_\ell(\underset{\sim}{r}) = f_1^0(r)a_{ii}X_\ell + f_1^1(r)\varepsilon_{ijk}a_{kj}X_iX_\ell + f_2^1(r)\varepsilon_{\ell jk}a_{kj}$$

$$+ f_1^2(r)A_{imm}X_iX_\ell + f_2^2(r)A_{\ell mm} + f_1^3(r)A_{mim}X_iX_\ell$$

$$+ f_2^3(r)A_{m\ell m} + f_1^4(r)A_{mmi}X_iX_\ell + f_2^4(r)A_{mm\ell}$$

$$+ f_1^5(r)a_{ij}X_iX_jX_\ell + f_2^5(r)a_{\ell j}X_j + f_3^5(r)a_{j\ell}X_j +$$

$$+ f_1^6(r)A_{ijk}X_iX_jX_kX_\ell + f_2^6(r)A_{\ell jk}X_jX_k +$$

$$+ f_3^6(r)A_{j\ell k}X_jX_k + f_4^6(r)A_{jk\ell}X_jX_k \tag{27}$$

The differential equations satisfied by the functions $F_p(r)$ and $f_q^p(r)$ are the homogeneous and inhomogeneous Bessel differential equations:

$$\frac{d^2}{dr^2} F_p(r) + \frac{n+(2m-1)}{r}\frac{d}{dr} F_p(r) - \frac{2\kappa}{\delta} F_p(r) = K_0(r) \tag{28}$$

$$\frac{d^2}{dr^2} f_1^p(r) + \frac{n+(2m+1)}{r}\frac{d}{dr} f_1^p(r) - L^2 f_1^p(r) = K_1(r) \tag{29}$$

$$\frac{d^2}{dr^2} f_q^p(r) + \frac{n+(2m-3)}{r}\frac{d}{dr} f_q^p(r) - L^2 f_q^p(r) = K_q(r) \tag{30}$$

$$(q \neq 1)$$

Here again the functions $K_0(r)$, $K_1(r)$, $K_q(r)$ are either known or zero.

The solutions of the equations (28) to (30) can be carried out with the same level of generality as has been done before for p and u_i. This, however, leads to lengthy and complicated expressions. To illustrate the usefulness of the method we now consider the solutions of the above equations for the functions which involve the coefficient tensor a_{ij} only.

In such a case, the solutions are found to be:

$$F_0(r) = y^{-1/2}[\, D_1^0\, I_{-1/2}(y) + D_1^1 I_{1/2}(y) - \frac{D_1^5}{M^2}\, I_{-5/2}(y) - \frac{D_2^5}{M^2}\, I_{5/2}(y)\,]$$

$$F_1(r) = y^{-3/2}[\, D_1^1\, I_{-3/2}(y) + D_2^1 I_{3/2}(y)\,]$$

$$F_5(r) = y^{-5/2}[\, D_1^5\, I_{-5/2}(y) + D_2^5\, I_{5/2}(y)\,] \qquad (31)$$

where $y = Mr$, $M^2 = 2\kappa/\delta$ and where $I_{p/q}$ is the modified Bessel function of the fractional order. The solutions for the functions $f_q^p(r)$ associated with the tensor a_{ij} are:

$$f_1^0(r) = \frac{1}{5L^2}(A_3^5 + \frac{10}{\eta} A_1^5)r^{-5} - \frac{1}{L^2}(A_3^0 + \frac{2}{\eta} A_1^0)r^{-3} + + \frac{1}{\eta} A_1^0 r^{-1} - \frac{1}{L^2}(A_4^0 + \frac{4L^2}{3\eta} A_2^5) + + \frac{1}{5L^2}(A_4^5 - \frac{2L^2}{3\eta} A_2^5)r^2 + x^{-3/2}[\, B_1^0 I_{-3/2}(x) + + B_2^0 I_{3/2}(x) - \frac{B_1^5}{5L^2} I_{-7/2}(x) - \frac{B_2^5}{5L^2} I_{7/2}(x)\,],$$

$$f_1^1(r) = \frac{-1}{L^2}(A_3^1 + \frac{6}{\eta} A_1^1)r^{-5} + \frac{1}{\eta} A_1^1\, r^{-3} - \frac{1}{L^2} A_4^1 + + x^{-5/2}\, [\, B_1^1 I_{-5/2}(x) + B_2^1 I_{5/2}(x)\,],$$

$$f_2^1(r) = \frac{1}{3L^2}\left(A_3^1 + \frac{6}{\eta} A_1^1\right)r^{-3} - \frac{1}{L^2} A_5^1 r^{-1} +$$

$$+ \frac{1}{L^2}\left(\frac{2}{\eta} A_2^1 - A_6^1\right) + \frac{1}{3L^2}\left(A_4^1 + \frac{L^2}{\eta} A_2^1\right)r^2 +$$

$$+ x^{-1/2}\left[B_3^1 I_{-1/2}(x) + B_4^1 I_{1/2}(x) -\right.$$

$$\left. - \frac{B_1^1}{3L^2} I_{-5/2}(x) - \frac{B_2^1}{3L^2} I_{5/2}(x) \right]$$

$$f_1^5(r) = \frac{-1}{L^2}\left(A_3^5 + \frac{10}{\eta} A_1^5\right)r^{-7} + \frac{1}{\eta} A_1^5 r^{-5} - \frac{1}{L^2} A_4^5 +$$

$$+ x^{-7/2}\left[B_1^5 I_{-7/2}(x) + B_2^5 I_{7/2}(x) \right]$$

$$f_2^5(r) = \frac{1}{5L^2}\left(A_3^5 + \frac{10}{\eta} A_1^5\right)r^{-5} - \frac{1}{L^2} A_5^5 r^{-3} - \frac{1}{L^2}\left(A_6^5 - \frac{2}{\eta} A_2^5\right) +$$

$$+ \frac{1}{5L2}\left(A_4^5 + \frac{L^2}{\eta} A_2^5\right)r^2 + x^{-3/2}\left[B_3^5 I_{-3/2}(x) +\right.$$

$$\left. + B_4^5 I_{3/2}(x) - \frac{B_1^5}{5L^2} I_{-7/2}(x) - \frac{B_2^5}{5L^2} I_{7/2}(x) \right]$$

$$f_3^5(r) = \frac{1}{5L^2}\left(A_3^5 + \frac{10}{\eta} A_1^5\right)r^{-5} - \frac{1}{L^2} A_7^5 r^{-3} - \frac{1}{L^2}\left(A_8^5 - \frac{2}{\eta} A_2^5\right) +$$

$$+ \frac{1}{5L^2}\left(A_4^5 + \frac{L^2}{\eta} A_2^5\right)r^2 + x^{-3/2}\left[B_3^5 I_{-3/2}(x) +\right.$$

$$\left. + B_4^5 I_{3/2}(x) - \frac{B_1^5}{5L^2} I_{-7/2}(x) - \frac{B_2^5}{5L^2} I_{7/2}(x) \right] \qquad (32)$$

where $x = Lr$, $L^2 = \frac{\kappa\eta}{\gamma(\mu+\kappa)} = \frac{\kappa(2\mu+\kappa)}{\gamma(\mu+\kappa)}$

Application of the continuity equation (1) to the functions $f_q^p(r)$ in equation (32) imposes the following restrictions on the coefficients A_j^m, B_j^m,

$$A_1^0 = 0$$

$$A_4^0 = -\frac{1}{3}(A_6^5 + A_8^5)$$

$$\frac{1}{L^2} = A_4^1 = \frac{1}{5\eta} A_2^1$$

$$\frac{1}{L^2} A_5^1 = -\frac{1}{\eta} A_1^1$$

$$\frac{1}{L^2} A_4^5 = \frac{4}{21\eta} A_2^5$$

$$A_7^5 = -A_5^5$$

$$B_1^0 = -\frac{1}{3}(B_3^5 + B_5^5)$$

$$B_2^0 = -\frac{1}{3}(B_4^5 + B_6^5)$$

$$B_1^1 = -\frac{3L^2}{2} B_3^1$$

$$B_2^1 = -\frac{3L^2}{2} B_4^1$$

$$B_1^5 = -\frac{5L^2}{3}(B_3^5 + B_5^5)$$

$$B_2^5 = -\frac{5L^2}{3}(B_3^5 + B_5^5) \qquad (33)$$

Hence, the general solutions for the velocity involving the coefficients a_{ij} in a micropolar fluid flow are:

$$f_1^0(r) = \frac{1}{5L^2}(A_3^5 + \frac{10}{\eta}A_1^5)r^{-5} - \frac{1}{L^2}A_3^0 r^{-3} - \frac{1}{3L^2}(\frac{4}{\eta}A_2^5 - \{A_6^5 + A_8^5\}) -$$

$$- \frac{2}{21\eta}A_2^5 r^2 - \frac{(B_3^5+B_5^5)}{3}x^{-3/2}[\, I_{-3/2}(x) - I_{-7/2}(x)\,] -$$

$$- \frac{(B_4^5+B_6^5)}{3}x^{-3/2}[\, I_{3/2}(x) - I_{7/2}(x)\,]$$

$$f_1^1(r) = \frac{-1}{L^2}(A_3^1 + \frac{6}{\eta}A_1^1)r^{-5} + \frac{1}{\eta}r^{-3} - \frac{1}{5\eta}A_2^1 -$$

$$- \frac{3L^2}{2}x^{-5/2}[\, B_3^1 I_{-5/2}(x) + B_4^1 I_{5/2}(x)\,]$$

$$f_2^1(r) = \frac{1}{3L^2}(A_3^1 + \frac{6}{\eta}A_1^1)r^{-5} + \frac{1}{\eta}A_1^1 r^{-1} + \frac{1}{L^2}(\frac{2}{\eta}A_2^1 - A_6^1) +$$

$$+ \frac{2}{5\eta}A_2^1 r^2 + x^{-1/2}B_3^1\,[I_{-1/2}(x) + 1/2 I_{-5/2}(x)\,] +$$

$$+ x^{-1/2}\,B_4^1[I_{1/2}(x) + 1/2 I_{5/2}(x)\,]$$

$$f_1^5(r) = \frac{-1}{L^2}(A_3^5 + \frac{10}{\eta}A_1^5)r^{-7} + \frac{1}{\eta}A_1^5 r^{-5} - \frac{4}{21\eta}A_2^5 -$$

$$- \frac{5L^2}{3}\,x^{-7/2}\,[(B_3^5+B_5^5)I_{-7/2}(x) + (B_4^5+B_6^5)I_{7/2}(x)]$$

$$f_2^5(r) = \frac{1}{5L^2}(A_3^5 + \frac{10}{\eta}A_1^5)r^{-5} - \frac{1}{L^2}A_5^5 r^{-3} - \frac{1}{L^2}(A_6^5 - \frac{2}{\eta}A_2^5) +$$

$$+ \frac{5}{21\eta}A_2^5 r^2 + x^{-3/2}[B_3^5 I_{-3/2}(x) + \frac{1}{3}(B_3^5+B_5^5)I_{-7/2}(x) +$$

$$+ B_4^5 I_{3/2}(x) + \frac{1}{3}(B_4^5+B_6^5)I_{7/2}(x)\,]$$

$$f_3^5(r) = \frac{1}{5L^2}(A_3^5 + \frac{10}{\eta}A_1^5)r^{-5} + \frac{1}{L^2}A_5^5 r^{-3} - \frac{1}{L^2}(A_8^5 - \frac{2}{\eta}A_2^5) +$$

$$+ \frac{5}{21\eta} A_2^5 r^2 + x^{-3/2}[B_5^5 I_{-3/2}(x) + \frac{1}{3}(B_3^5+B_5^5) I_{-7/2}(x) +$$

$$+ B_6^5 I_{3/2}(x) + \frac{1}{3}(B_4^5+B_6^5) I_{7/2}(x)] \tag{34}$$

Similarly, the general solution for the pressure field associated with the tensor a_{ij} is given by $p(r) = H^0(r)a_{ii} + H^1(r)\varepsilon_{ijk}a_{kj}X_i + H^5(r)a_{ij}X_iX_j$ where $H^0(r)$, $H^1(r)$ and $H^5(r)$ are given by equation (20). Finally, we remark that the above solutions remain valid for n=2 if we change r^{2-n} by $\ln r$ and $\frac{1}{2(n-2)} A_1^m$ by $-\frac{1}{2} A_1^m$ in the above solutions.

In the next section, we shall consider several applications of the above method.

4. Applications

(a) A fluid sphere in a uniform flow field

As a first application of the preceeding method, we consider the problems of a viscous Newtonian fluid past a micropolar fluid drop and the flow of a micropolar fluid past a viscous Newtonian fluid drop. We recall that the problem of a viscous fluid drop in another viscous fluid was first considered by Rybczynski [25] and Hadamard [14]. Corresponding problems in the micropolar fluid were considered by Niefer and Kaloni [23], by using the stream function approach. Here we give, for the first time, the solutions using the method discussed in the previous section.

If we employ the origin of the coordinate system at the centre of the fluid drop, then the boundary conditions for the two problems are:

$$\underset{\sim}{v}_{\infty}^{(e)} = U\underset{\sim}{e}_z, \ \underset{\sim}{\nu}^{(e)} \text{ finite as } r\to\infty$$

$$\underset{\sim}{v}^{(1)}, \underset{\sim}{\nu}^{(1)} \text{ finite at } r=0$$

$$\underset{\sim}{v}^{(e)}.\underset{\sim}{r} = \underset{\sim}{v}^{(1)}.\underset{\sim}{r} = 0 \text{ at } r=a$$

$$\underset{\sim}{v}^{(e)} - (\underset{\sim}{v}^{(e)}.\underset{\sim}{r})\underset{\sim}{r} = \underset{\sim}{v}^{(1)} - (\underset{\sim}{v}^{(1)}.\underset{\sim}{r})\underset{\sim}{r} \quad \text{at } r=a, \tag{35}$$

$$t^{(e)}_{ij} X_j - t^{(e)}_{k\ell} \frac{X_k X_\ell}{r^2} X_i = t^{(i)}_{ij} X_j - t^{(i)}_{k\ell} \frac{X_k X_\ell}{r^2} X_i \quad \text{at } r=a$$

$$\nu_i = \frac{1}{2} S \varepsilon_{ijk} v_{k,j} \quad \text{at } r=a \tag{35}$$

In the above $S \in [0,1]$, and the superscripts (e) and (i) denote the quantities exterior or interior to the drop. In view of the above boundary conditions we take the solutions for $p(\underset{\sim}{r})$, $v_i(\underset{\sim}{r})$ and $\nu_i(\underset{\sim}{r})$ as:

$$p(\underset{\sim}{r}) = (A_1^1 r^{-3} + A_2^1)\varepsilon_{ijk} a_{kj} X_i \tag{36}$$

$$u_\ell(r) = (A_3^1 r^{-5} - \frac{L^2}{\eta} A_1^1 r^{-3} + \frac{L^2}{5\eta} A_2^1)\varepsilon_{ijk} a_{kj} X_i X_\ell$$

$$+ (-A_3^1 r^{-3} - \frac{L^2}{\eta} A_1^1 r^{-1} + A_6^1 - \frac{2L^2}{5\eta} A_2^1 r^2)\varepsilon_{\ell jk} a_{kj} \tag{37}$$

$$v_\ell(\underset{\sim}{r}) = [- \frac{1}{L^2}(A_3^1 + \frac{6}{\eta} A_1^1) r^{-5} + \frac{1}{\eta} A_1^1 r^{-3} - \frac{1}{5\eta} A_2^1$$

$$- \frac{3L^2}{2} C_3^1 d_7(\psi) e^{\psi} + \frac{3L^2}{2} C_4^1 d_8(\psi) e^{-\psi}]\varepsilon_{ijk} a_{kj} X_i X_\ell$$

$$+ [\frac{1}{3L^2} (A_3^1 + \frac{6}{\eta} A_1^1) r^{-3} + \frac{1}{\eta} A_1^1 r^{-1} + \frac{1}{L^2}(\frac{2}{\eta} A_2^1 - A_6^1)$$

$$+ \frac{2}{5\eta} A_2^1 r^2 + C_3^1(\frac{\psi^2}{2} d_7(\psi) + d_5(\psi)) e^{\psi}$$

$$- C_4^1(\frac{\psi^2}{2} d_8(\psi) + d_6(\psi) e^{-\psi}] \varepsilon_{\ell jk} a_{kj} \tag{38}$$

$$\nu_\ell(\underset{\sim}{r}) = [\frac{1}{\eta} A_1^1 r^{-3} - \frac{1}{2\eta} A_2^1 - \frac{3\eta}{2\gamma} C_3^1 (\frac{d_5^1 + d_5}{\psi}) e^{\psi}$$

$$+ \frac{3\eta}{2\gamma} (\frac{d_6^1 - d_6}{\psi}) e^{-\psi}](a_{\ell q} - a_{q\ell}) x_q \tag{39}$$

and find the other useful expression as:

$$t_{\ell m}\frac{X_\ell X_m}{r^2} = -\frac{\eta}{2}[-\frac{4}{L^2}(A_3^1 + \frac{6}{\eta}A_1^1)r^{-5} + \frac{6}{\eta}A_1^1 r^{-3}$$

$$+ \frac{6}{5\eta}A_2^1 - 6L^2C_3^1 d_7(\psi)e^{\psi} + 6L^2C_4^1 d_8(\psi)e^{-\psi}]\varepsilon_{ijk}a_{kj}X_i \tag{40}$$

$$t_{\ell m}\frac{X_\ell}{r} - t_{pq}\frac{X_p X_q}{r^2}\frac{X_m}{r} = -\frac{\eta}{2}[-\frac{2}{L^2}(A_3^1 + \frac{6}{\eta}A_1^1)r^{-6}$$

$$+ \frac{3}{5\eta}A_2^1 r^{-1} - 3L^3\ C_3^1\frac{d_7(\psi)}{\psi}e^{\psi} + 3L^3\ C_4^1 d_8(\psi)e^{-\psi}]$$

$$\times\ \varepsilon_{mjk}(a_{jq} - a_{qj})X_q X_k \tag{41}$$

In the above, we note that if the viscous fluid is outside of the sphere, then,

$$A_2^1 = A_6^1 = 0$$

and if the viscous fluid is inside of the sphere, then:

$$A_1^1 = A_3^1 = 0$$

Similarly, if the micropolar fluid is outside of the fluid sphere then:

$$A_2^1 = 0,\quad A_6^1 = -L^2,\quad C_3^1 = 0;$$

and if it is inside of the sphere, then:

$$A_1^1 = A_3^1 = 0,\quad C_3^1 = C_4^1$$

On employing the boundary conditions (35) in the above solution, and keeping the preceding observations in mind, we obtain a system of equations which, for a micropolar fluid past a viscous Newtonian sphere, becomes:

$$- \frac{2}{3L^2} (A_3^1 + \frac{6}{\eta^{(e)}} A_1^1) a^{-3} + \frac{2}{\eta} A_1^1 a^{-1} + 1$$

$$+ [L^2 a^2 d_8(La) - d_6(La)] e^{-La} C_4^1 = 0,$$

$$A_6^1 + \frac{1}{5\eta} A_2^1 a^2 = 0$$

$$\frac{1}{3L^2} (A_3^1 + \frac{6}{\eta} A_1^1) a^{-3} + \frac{1}{\eta} A_1^1 a^{-1} + 1 - [\frac{L^2 a^2}{2} d_8(La) + d_6(La)] e^{-La} C_4^1$$

$$= A_6^1 + \frac{2}{5\eta} A_2^1 a^2, \tag{42}$$

$$\eta^{(e)} [- \frac{2}{L^2} (A_3^1 + \frac{6}{\eta} A_1^1) a^{-5} + 3L^2 d_8(La) e^{-La} C_4^1] = \eta^{(i)} \frac{3}{5\eta} A_2^1,$$

$$\frac{1}{\eta} A_1^1 a^{-3} + \frac{3\eta}{2\gamma} (\frac{d_8(La) - d_6(La)}{La}) e^{-La} C_4^1 = \frac{-\delta}{2\eta} A_2^1$$

The solution of the above system, with $\sigma = \frac{\eta^{(e)}}{\eta^{(i)}} = \frac{(2\mu+\kappa)^{(e)}}{2\mu^{(i)}}$ is:

$$\frac{1}{10\eta} A_2^1 a^2 = \frac{\sigma}{4(1+\sigma)} - \frac{\sigma}{4(1+\sigma)} d_6(La) e^{-La} C_4^1,$$

$$\frac{1}{2} A_6^1 = \frac{-\sigma}{4(1+\sigma)} + \frac{\sigma}{4(1+\sigma)} d_6(La) e^{-La} C_4^1,$$

$$\frac{1}{\eta} A_1^1 a^{-1} = \frac{-(2\sigma+3)}{4(1+\sigma)} + \frac{2\sigma+3}{4(1+\sigma)} d_6(La) e^{-La} C_4^1,$$

$$- \frac{1}{3L^2} (A_3^1 + \frac{6}{\eta} A_1^1) a^{-3} = \frac{1}{4(1+\sigma)} - \frac{1}{4(1+\sigma)} [d_6(La)$$

$$+ 2(1+\sigma) L^2 a^2 d_8(La)] e^{-La} C_4^1 \tag{43}$$

$$e^{-La}C_4^1 = \frac{\kappa^{(e)}\{3 + (2-5s)\sigma\}La}{\kappa^{(e)}\ 3+(2-5s)\sigma\} - 6(\mu+\kappa)^{(e)}(1+\sigma)(1+La)}$$

With the constants known, the solutions for the velocity, micro-rotation vector and the pressure field are complete. To compute the drag on the sphere we recall the formula:

$$D = 2\pi a^2 \int_o^{\pi} (t_{rr} \cos\theta - t_{rr} \sin\theta)\Big|_{r=a} \sin\theta \, d\theta$$

On making the appropriate calculations for t_{rr} and then substituting in the above expression we find:

$$D = \frac{-\ 6\Pi(\mu + \frac{\kappa}{2})^{(e)}(1+\frac{2}{3}\sigma)Ua}{(1+\sigma)}$$

$$\times \left[\frac{6(1+\sigma)(\mu^{(e)}+\kappa^{(e)})(1+La)}{6(1+\sigma_2)(\mu^{(e)}+\kappa^{(e)})(1+La)-\kappa^{(e)}\{3+(2-5s)\sigma\}} \right] \qquad (44)$$

which is exactly the same as obtained by Niefer and Kaloni [22] by using the stream function method. For further discussion about the above result, we, therefore, refer to this paper.

For a micropolar fluid drop in a viscous Newtonian fluid, and employing the appropriate boundary conditions (35) in solutions (36) to (41) we find:

$$\frac{2}{3} A_3^1 a^{-3} + \frac{2}{\eta} A_1^1 a^{-1} + 1 = 0$$

$$\frac{1}{L^2}(\frac{2}{\eta} A_2^1 - A_6^1) + \frac{1}{5\eta} A_2^1 a^2 + C_4^1[- \{L^2a^2d_7(La) - d_5(La)\}e^{La}$$

$$+ \{L^2a^2d_8(La) - d_6(La)\}e^{-La}] = 0$$

$$\frac{1}{L^2}\left(\frac{2}{\eta} A_2^1 - A_6^1\right) + \frac{2}{5\eta} A_2^1 a^2 + C_4^1 [\{ \frac{L^2 a^2}{2} d_7(La) + d_5(La) \} e^{La}$$

$$- \{ \frac{L^2 a^2}{2} d_8(La) + d_6(La) \} e^{-La}] = - \frac{1}{3} A_3^1 a^{-3} + \frac{1}{\eta} A_1^1 a^{-1} + 1,$$

$$\eta^{(i)} [\frac{3}{5\eta} A_2^1 - 3L^2 \{ d_7(La) e^{La} - d_8(La) e^{-La} \} C_4^1] = \eta^{(e)} 2A_3^1 a^{-5},$$

$$- \frac{1}{2\eta} A_2^1 - \frac{3\eta}{2\gamma} [\frac{d_5^1(La) + d_5(La)}{La} e^{La} - \frac{d_6^1(La) - d_6(La)}{La} e^{-La}] C_4^1$$

$$= \frac{s}{\eta} A_1^1 a^{-3} \qquad (45)$$

The above system of equations, with $\sigma = \frac{\eta^{(e)}}{\eta^{(i)}} = \frac{2\mu^{(e)}}{(2\mu+\kappa)^{(i)}}$, has the solution:

$$\frac{1}{10\eta} A_2^1 a^2 = \frac{\sigma}{4(1+\sigma)} + \frac{2-3\sigma}{4(1+\sigma)} [L^2 a^2 d_7(La) e^{La} - L^2 a^2 d_8(La) e^{-La}] C_4^1,$$

$$\frac{1}{2L^2}\left(\frac{2}{\eta} A_2^1 - A_6^1\right) = \frac{-\sigma}{4(1+\sigma)} + \frac{5}{4(1+\sigma)} [L^2 a^2 d_7(La) e^{La}$$

$$- L^2 a^2 d_8(La) e^{-La}] C_4^1 - \frac{1}{2} [d_5(La) e^{La} - d_6(La) e^{-La}] C_4^1$$

$$\frac{1}{\eta} A_1^1 a^{-1} = \frac{(2\sigma+3)}{4(1+\sigma)} + \frac{5C_4^1}{4(1+\sigma)} [L^2 a^2 d_7(La) e^{-La} - L^2 a^2 d_8(La) e^{-La}]$$

$$\frac{1}{3} A_3^1 a^{-3} = \frac{1}{4(1+\sigma)} - \frac{5}{4(1+\sigma)} [L^2 a^2 d_7(La) e^{La} - L^2 a^2 d_8(La) e^{-La}] C_4^1,$$

$$C_4^1 = k^{(i)}\{3s+(2s-5)\sigma\} \div 5k^{(i)} \ [\ (s+2)-3\sigma\}\{L^2a^2d_7(La)e^{La}$$

$$-L^2a^2d_8(La)e^{-La}\} + 6(\mu+\kappa)^{(i)}(1+\sigma)\ La(d'^5(La)+d^5(La))e^{La}$$

$$- La(d'^4(La)-d_4(La))e^{-La}\ \} \tag{46}$$

Here again, by substituting the values of the above constants in the original solutions we obtain the required solution. The drag force, in the present case, turns out to be:

$$D_1 = 4\pi\ 2\mu^{(e)}\ [\ \frac{-(3+2\sigma)Ua}{4(1+\sigma)} - \frac{5}{2(1+\sigma)}\ \{\ \overline{M}-\overline{N}- \frac{L^2a^2}{3} N\}\ \frac{C_4^1}{3}\ ] \tag{47}$$

where C_4^1 is given by (46) and where:

$$\overline{M} = a \cosh\ (La), \qquad \overline{N} = \frac{\sinh\ (La)}{L}$$

Again, we point out that this result is in complete agreement with the result of Niefer and Kaloni [22] obtained by the stream function method.

(b) <u>A Fluid Sphere in a Linear Shear Field</u>

In this section we consider another application of the method by treating the problem of a micropolar fluid sphere in a viscous Newtonian fluid. We recall that for a solid sphere this problem was treated by Einstein [9] and for a viscous fluid sphere by Taylor (26]. In each of the above cases, the expressions for the effective viscosity were obtained. In this section we extend Taylor's [26] results by considering a micropolar fluid drop suspended in a viscous fluid in which the latter is undergoing a shear flow. Following Taylor we shall also assume that the distortions remain small and that the shape of the drop remains nearly spherical.

For any linear shearing flow the upstream boundary condition $\underset{\sim}{u}_{\infty} = \underset{\sim}{a}\cdot\underset{\sim}{r}$ indicates that the appropriate choices for p, v_p, ψ and ν_p are:

$$p^{(i)} = (A_1^5 r^{-5} + A_2^5) a_{ij} X_i X_j \qquad (48)$$

$$v_p^{(i)} = [- \frac{1}{L^2} (A_3^5 + \frac{10}{\eta} A_1^5) r^{-7} + \frac{1}{\eta} A_1^5 r^{-5} - \frac{1}{L^2} A_4^5$$

$$+ C_1^5 \, d_1(Lr) e^{Lr} - C_2^5 \, d_2(Lr) e^{-Lr}] a_{ij} X_i X_j X_p$$

$$+ [\frac{1}{5L^2} (A_3^5 + \frac{10}{\eta} A_1^5) r^{-5} - \frac{1}{L^2} A_5^5 r^{-3} + \frac{1}{L^2} (\frac{2}{\eta} A_2^5 - A_6^5)$$

$$+ \frac{1}{5L^2} (A_4^5 + \frac{L^2}{\eta} A_2^5) r^2 - \frac{C_1^5}{5L^2} (Lr)^2 d_1(Lr) e^{Lr} + \frac{C_2^5}{5L^2} (Lr)^2 d_2(Lr) e^{-Lr}$$

$$+ C_3^5 \, d_3(Lr) e^{Lr} - C_4^5 \, d_4(Lr) e^{-Lr}] a_{pj} X_j + [\frac{1}{5L^2} (A_3^5 + \frac{10}{\eta} A_1^5) r^{-5}$$

$$- \frac{1}{L^2} A_7^5 \, r^{-3} + \frac{1}{L^2} (\frac{2}{\eta} A_2^5 - A_8^5) + \frac{1}{5L^2} (A_4^5 + \frac{L^2}{\eta} A_2^5) r^2$$

$$- \frac{1}{5L^2} C_1^5 (Lr)^2 d_1(Lr) e^{Lr} + \frac{1}{5L^2} C_2^5 (Lr)^2 d_2(Lr) e^{-Lr}$$

$$+ C_5^5 \, d_3(Lr) e^{Lr} - C_6^5 \, d_4(Lr) e^{-Lr}] a_{jp} X_j \qquad (49)$$

$$\psi^{(i)} = [C_7^5 \, d_3(Mr) e^{Mr} - C_8^5 \, d_4(Mr) e^{-Mr}] \varepsilon_{ijk} a_{kj} X_i$$

$$\nu_p^{(i)} = [\frac{1}{2}(\frac{A_1^5}{\eta} - \frac{3A_5^5}{L^2})r^{-5} - \frac{A_2^5}{3\eta} - \frac{\eta}{3\gamma}(4C_3^5+C_5^5)[\frac{d_3'(Lr)+d_3(Lr)}{Lr}]e^{Lr}$$

$$+ \frac{\eta}{3\gamma}(4C_4^5+C_6^5)[\frac{d_4'(Lr)-d_4(Lr)}{Lr}]e^{-Lr}$$

$$+ \frac{\kappa}{\mu+\kappa} C_7^5 [\frac{d_3'(Mr)+d_3(Mr)}{Mr}]e^{Mr}$$

$$- \frac{\kappa}{\mu+\kappa} C_8^5[\frac{d_4'(Mr)-d_4(Mr)}{Mr}]e^{-Mr}]\ \varepsilon_{p\ell m}a_{\ell j}X_j X_m$$

$$+ [\frac{1}{2}(\frac{A_1^5}{\eta} + \frac{3A_5^5}{L^2})r^{-5} - \frac{A_2^5}{3\eta} - \frac{\eta}{3\gamma}(C_3^5+4C_5^5)[\frac{d_3'(Lr)+d_3(Lr)}{Lr}]e^{Lr}$$

$$+ \frac{\eta}{3\gamma}(C_4^5+4C_6^5)[\frac{d_4'(Lr)-d_4(Lr)}{Lr}]e^{-Lr}$$

$$- \frac{\kappa}{\mu+\kappa} C_7^5[\frac{d_3'(Mr)+d_3(Mr)}{Mr}]e^{Mr}$$

$$+ \frac{\kappa}{\mu+\kappa} C_8^5 [\frac{d_4'(Mr)-d_4(Mr)}{Mr}]e^{-Mr}]\varepsilon_{p\ell m}a_{j\ell}X_j X_m$$

$$+ [\frac{-A_5^5}{L^2} r^{-3} - \frac{(A_6^5-A_8^5)}{2L^2} + \frac{\mu+\kappa}{\kappa}(C_3^5-C_5^5)d_3(Lr)e^{Lr}$$

$$- \frac{\mu+\kappa}{\kappa}(C_4^5-C_6^5)d_4(Lr)e^{-Lr}$$

$$+ \frac{\delta}{2\kappa} C_7^5(d_3(Mr)+(Mr)[d_3'(Mr)+d_3(Mr)])e^{Mr}$$

$$- \frac{\delta}{2\kappa} C_8^5(d_4(Mr)+(Mr)[d_4'(Mr)-d_4(Mr)])e^{-Mr}]\varepsilon_{pmn}a_{nm} \qquad (50)$$

The above is the solution for the micropolar fluid inside the droplet. For the viscous fluid outside the sphere, $p^{(e)}$ has a similar structure as above but $v_\ell^{(e)}$ is given by:

$$v_\ell^{(e)} = (A_3^5 r^{-5} + \frac{1}{2\mu} A_1^5 r^{-5} - \frac{2}{21\mu} A_2^5) a_{ij} X_i X_j X_\ell$$

$$+ (- \frac{1}{5} A_3^5 r^{-5} + A_5^5 r^{-3} + A_6^5 + \frac{5}{42\mu} A_2^5 r^2) a_{\ell j} X_j$$

$$+ (- \frac{1}{5} A_3^5 r^{-5} - A_5^5 r^{-3} + A_8^5 + \frac{5}{42\mu} A_2^5 r^{-2}) a_{j\ell} X_j \qquad (51)$$

On applying the following boundary conditions:

$$p^{(e)} \to 0 \quad \text{and} \quad v_\ell^{(e)} \to a_{\ell j} X_j \qquad \text{as } r \to \infty$$

$$v_\ell^{(i)} \text{ is finite and } \nu_\ell^{(i)} \text{ is finite at } r = 0$$

$$v_\ell^{(e)} X_\ell = v_\ell^{(i)} X_\ell = 0 \qquad \text{at } r = a \qquad (52)$$

$$v_\ell^{(e)} - v_p^{(e)} \frac{X_p X_\ell}{r^2} = v_\ell^{(i)} - v_p^{(i)} \frac{X_p X_\ell}{r^2} \quad \text{at } r = a$$

$$t_{ij}^{(e)} X_j - t_{mn}^{(e)} \frac{X_m X_n}{r^2} X_i = t_{ij}^{(i)} X_j - t_{mn}^{(i)} \frac{X_m X_n}{r^2} X_i \quad \text{at } r = a$$

$$\nu_\ell^{(i)} = \frac{s}{2} \varepsilon_{ijk} v_{k,j}^{(e)} \qquad 0 \leqslant s \leqslant 1, \quad \text{at } r = a$$

in the above solutions we obtain the following system of linear algebraic equations for the determination of the coefficients:

$$\frac{3}{5} A_3^5 a^{-5} + \frac{1}{\eta^e} A_1^5 a^{-3} + 1 = 0$$

$$\frac{1}{L^2} \left(\frac{4}{\eta^i} A_2^5 - (A_6^5 + A_8^5)\right) + \frac{2}{7\eta^i} A_2^5 a^2 + (C_4^5 + C_6^5)[(L^2 a^2 d_1(La) - d_3(La))e^{La}$$

$$+ (L^2 a^2 d_2(La) - d_4(La))e^{-La}] = 0$$

$$-\frac{1}{5} A_3^5 a^{-5} + A_5^5 a^{-3} + 1 = \frac{1}{L^2} \left(\frac{2}{\eta^i} A_2^5 - A_6^5\right) + \frac{5}{21\eta^i} A_2^5 a^2$$

$$-(C_4^5 + C_6^5)\left[\frac{(L^2 a^2)}{3} (d_1(La)e^{La} + d_2(La)e^{La})\right]$$

$$- C_4^5 [d_3(La)e^{La} + d_4(La)e^{-La}]$$

$$-\frac{1}{5} A_3^5 a^{-5} - A_5^5 a^{-3} = \frac{1}{L^2} \left(\frac{2}{\eta^i} A_2^5 - A_8^5\right) + \frac{5}{21\eta^i} A_2^5 a^2$$

$$-(C_4^5 + C_6^5)\left[\frac{(L^2 a^2)}{3} (d_1(La)e^{La} + d_2(La)e^{-La})\right]$$

$$- C_6^5 [d_3(La)e^{La} + d_4(La)e^{-La}]$$

$$\frac{\eta^{(e)}}{2} \left[\frac{8}{5} A_3^5 a^{-5} + \frac{1}{\eta^e} A_1^5 a^{-3} - 3A_5^5 a^{-3} + 1\right] = \frac{\eta^{(i)}}{2} \left\{\frac{1}{L^2} \left(\frac{4}{\eta^i} A_2^5 - (A_6^5 + A_8^5)\right)\right.$$

$$+ \frac{16}{21\eta^i} A_2^5 a^2 - \frac{2(C_4^5 + C_6^5) L^2 a^2}{3} [(Lad_1'(La) + 3d_1(La) + Lad_1(La))e^{La}$$

$$+ (Lad_2'(La) + d_2(La) - Lad_2(La))e^{-La}]$$

$$-2C_4^5 [(Lad_3'(1a) + d_3(La) + Lad_3(La))e^{La}$$

$$+(Lad_4'(La)+d_4(La)-Lad_4(La))e^{-La}]$$

$$-\frac{\delta C_8^5}{\eta}\left(d_3(Ma)e^{Ma} + d_4(Ma)e^{-Ma}\right)\}$$

$$\frac{\eta^{(e)}}{2}\left[-\frac{16}{5} A_3^5 a^{-7} - \frac{2}{\eta^e} A_1^5 a^{-5} - \frac{2}{a^2}\right] = \frac{\eta^{(i)}}{2}\{\frac{-2}{L^2a^2}\left(\frac{4}{\eta^i} A_2^5-(A_6^5+A_8^5)\right)$$

$$-\frac{32}{21\eta^i} A_2^5 + \frac{4L^2}{3}(C_4^5+C_6^5)[(Lad_1'(La)+3d_1(La)+Lad_1(La))e^{La}$$

$$+ (Lad_2'(La)+3d_2(La)-Lad_2(La))e^{-La}]$$

$$+ 2L^2(C_4^5+C_6^5)[\left(\frac{Lad_3'(La)+d_3(La)+Lad_3(La)}{L^2a^2}\right)e^{La}$$

$$+ \left(\frac{Lad_4(La)+d_4(La)-Lad_4(La)}{L^2a^2}\right)e^{-La}]\}$$

$$\frac{-A_2^5}{3\eta^i} + \frac{\eta^i}{3\gamma}(4C_4^5+C_6^5)\left(\frac{d_3'(La)+d_3(La)}{La} e^{La} + \frac{d_4'(La)-d_4(La)}{La} e^{-La}\right)$$

$$- C_8^5\left(\frac{d_3'(Ma)+d_3(Ma)}{Ma} e^{Ma} + \frac{d_4'(Ma)-d_4(Ma)}{Ma} e^{-Ma}\right)$$

$$= \frac{S}{2}\left(\frac{1}{\eta^e} A_1^5 + 3A_5^5\right)a^{-5} \tag{53}$$

$$\frac{-A_2^5}{3\eta^i} + \frac{\eta^i}{3\gamma}(C_4^5+4C_6^5)\left(\frac{d_3'(La)+d_3(La)}{La} e^{La} + \frac{d_4'(La)-d_4(La)}{La} e^{-La}\right)$$

$$+ C_8^5\left(\frac{d_3'(Ma)+d_3(Ma)}{Ma} e^{Ma} + \frac{d_4'(Ma)-d_4(Ma)}{Ma} e^{-Ma}\right) = \frac{S}{2}\left(\frac{1}{\eta^e}A_1^5-3A_5^5\right)a^{-5}$$

$$\frac{-(A_6^5-A_8^5)}{2L^2} - \frac{\mu+\kappa}{\kappa}(C_4^5-C_6^5)(d_3(La)e^{La}+d_4(La)e^{-La})$$

$$- \frac{\delta}{2\kappa} C_8^5[(Mad_3'(Ma)+d_3(Ma)+Mad_3(Ma))e^{Ma}$$

$$+ (Mad_4'(Ma)+d_4(Ma)-Mad_4(Ma))e^{-Ma}] = \frac{S}{2}(2A_5^5a^{-3}+1)$$

The solution of the above system of equations is given, with $\sigma = \eta^{(i)}/\eta^{(e)}$, by:

$$A_3^5\mathbf{a}^{-5} = \frac{5\sigma}{2(1+\sigma)} + \frac{5\sigma}{2(1+\sigma)} [(\frac{7L^2a^2d_1(La)-2La(d_3'(La)+d_3(La))}{3} e^{La})$$

$$+ (\frac{7L^2a^2d_2(La)-2La(d_4'(La)-d_4(La))}{3} e^{-La})] (C_4^5+C_6^5)$$

$$\frac{A_1^5}{\eta^e a^3} = \frac{-(5\sigma+2)}{2(1+\sigma)} - \frac{\sigma}{2(1+\sigma)} [[7L^2a^2d_1(La)-2La(d_3'(La)+d_3(La))]e^{La}$$

$$+ [7L^2a^2d_2(La)-2La(d_4'(La)-d_4(La))]e^{-La}] (C_4^5+C_6^5)$$

$$\frac{1}{L^2} (\frac{2}{\eta^i} A_2^5-A_6^5) = \frac{2\sigma-1}{4(1+\sigma)} - \frac{(C_4^5+C_6^5)}{4(1+\sigma)} [[7L^2a^2d_1(La)+2La(d_3'(La)+d_3(La))$$

$$-(2\sigma+2)d_3(La)]e^{La} + [7L^2a^2d_2(La)+2La(d_4'(La)-d_4(La))$$

$$-(2\sigma+2)d_4(La)]e^{-La}] + \frac{1}{6} [[2\sigma La(d_3'(La)+d_3(La))$$

$$+(2\sigma+3)d_3(La)]e^{La} + [2\sigma La(d_4'(La)-d_4(La))$$

$$+(2\sigma+3)d_4(La)]e^{-La}] (C_4^5-C_6^5) +$$

$$+ \frac{\delta\sigma}{3\eta^{i}} [\ d_3(Ma)e^{Ma}+d_4(Ma)e^{-Ma}\ ]\ C_8^5$$

$$\frac{1}{L^2}\left(\frac{2}{\eta^{i}} A_2^5-A_8^5\right) = \frac{-(2\sigma+5)}{4(1+\sigma)} - \frac{(C_4^5+C_6^5)}{4(1+\sigma)} \{\ [\ 7L^2a^2d_1(La)+2La(d_3'(La)$$

$$+ d_3(La))-(2\sigma+2)d_3(La)\ ]e^{La} + [\ 7L^2a^2d_2(La)+2La(d_4'(La)$$

$$- d_4(La))-(2\sigma+2)d_4(La)\ ]e^{-La}\} - \frac{1}{6} \{[\ 2\sigma La(d_3'(La)+d_3(La))$$

$$+(2\sigma+3)d_3(La)\ ]e^{La} + [\ 2\sigma La(d_4'(La)-d_4(La)+(2\sigma+3)d_4(La)\ ]e^{-La}\ \}$$

$$(C_4^5-C_6^5) - \frac{\delta\sigma}{3\eta^{i}} [\ d_3(Ma)e^{Ma}+d_4(Ma)e^{-Ma}\ ]C_8^5 \qquad (54)$$

$$\frac{4a^2}{21\eta^{i}} A_2^5 = \frac{1}{1+\sigma} + \frac{1}{3(1+\sigma)} \{\ [\ 2\sigma La(d_3'(La)+d_3(La))$$

$$-(2\sigma-5)L^2a^2d_1(La)\ ]e^{La} + [\ 2\sigma La(d_4'(La)-d_4(La))$$

$$-(2\sigma-5)L^2a^2d_2(La)\ ]e^{-La}\ \}\ (C_4^5+C_6^5)$$

$$\frac{A_5^5}{a^3} = \frac{\sigma}{3} \{\ [\ La(d_3'(La)+d_3(La))+d_3(La)\ ]e^{La}$$

$$+ [\ La(d_4'(La)-d_4(La))+d_4(La)\ ]e^{-La}\ \}\ (C_4^5-C_6^5)$$

$$+ \frac{\delta\sigma}{3\eta^{i}} [\ d_3(Ma)e^{Ma}+d_4(Ma)e^{-Ma}\ ]\ C_8^5$$

$$(C_4^5+C_6^5) = 3\kappa[5S\sigma+(2S-7)] \div [6\kappa S\sigma^2+(6\kappa-8\mu)\sigma-8(\mu+\kappa)]$$

$$\{[La(d_3'(La)+d_3(La))]e^{La} + [La(d_4'(La)-d_4(La))]e^{-La}\}$$

$$-7\kappa[(2+3S)\sigma-5]\{L^2a^2d_1(La)e^{La}+L^2a^2d_2(La)e^{-La}\}$$

$$\{\frac{\mu^i+\kappa^i-S\kappa^i\sigma}{\kappa^i}[\, La(d_3'(La)+d_3(La))e^{La} + La(d_4'(La)-d_4(La))e^{-La}]$$

$$-S\sigma[d_3(La)e^{La}+d_4(La)e^{-La}]\}\ (C_4^5-C_6^5)$$

$$-\frac{\delta^i}{\eta^i}\{\frac{\gamma^i L^2}{\kappa^i}[Ma(d_3'(Ma)+d_3(Ma))e^{Ma}+Ma(d_4'(Ma)-d_4(Ma))e^{-Ma}]$$

$$+S\sigma[d_3(Ma)e^{Ma}+d_4(Ma)e^{-Ma}]\}C_8^5 = 0 \qquad (55)$$

$$\{\frac{(S-1)\sigma}{3}[La(d_3'(La)+d_3(La))e^{La}+La(d_4'(La)-d_4(La))e^{-La}]$$

$$+\left(\frac{(S-1)\sigma}{3}+\frac{\eta^i}{2\kappa^i}\right)[\, d_3(La)e^{La}+d_4(La)e^{-La}\,]\}(C_4^5-C_6^5)$$

$$+\frac{\delta^i}{\eta^i}\{\frac{\eta^i}{2\kappa^i}[\, Ma(d_3'(Ma)+d_3(Ma))e^{Ma}+Ma(d_4'(Ma)-d_4(Ma))e^{-Ma}\,]$$

$$+\left(\frac{(S-1)\sigma}{3}+\frac{\eta^i}{2\kappa^i}\right)[\, d_3(Ma)e^{Ma}+d_4(Ma)e^{-Ma}\,]\}C_8^5 = \frac{1-S}{2}$$

It is of some interest to calculate the effective viscosity of the suspension. Following Taylor's approach in detail, we find that the effective viscosity η^* satisfies:

$$\eta^* = \eta - \frac{4\pi}{3V_1}\Sigma A_1^5 \qquad (56)$$

where η is the viscosity of the ambient Newtonian fluid, V_1 is the volume under consideration and ΣA_1^5 is the sum of the values A_1^5 for all particles involved. For a single particle, on using the expression for A_1^5 from $(54)_2$ and defining $\phi = \frac{4\pi a^3}{3V_1}$, the volume fraction, we obtain:

$$\frac{\eta^*}{\eta^{(e)}} = 1 + \frac{5\phi}{2}\left(\frac{\sigma + \frac{2}{5}}{\sigma + 1}\right)\left[1 + \frac{\sigma}{5\sigma+2}\{[7L^2a^2d_1(La)-2La(d_3'(La) + d_3(La))]e^{La} + [7L^2a^2d_2(La)-2\sigma La(d_4'(La) + d_4(La))]e^{-La}\}(C_4^5+C_6^5)\right] \tag{57}$$

where

$$(C_4^5+C_6^5) = 3\kappa[5S\sigma+(2S-7)] \div [6\kappa 5\sigma^2+(6\kappa-8\mu)\sigma-8(\mu+\kappa)]\{[La(d_3'(La) + d_3(La))]e^{La} + [La(d_4'(La)-d_4(La))]e^{-La}\} - 7\kappa[(2+3S)\sigma-5]\{L^2a^2d_1(La)e^{La}+L^2a^2d_2(La)e^{-La}\} \tag{58}$$

Inspection of equation (57) shows that it reduces to the expression obtained by Taylor [26], for the effective viscosity of an emulsion, when κ approaches zero. In the absence of the explicit nature of the various constants involved, it is difficult to make further comments. One fact, however, is clearly evident; the effective viscosity depends strongly upon 'S', i.e., upon the nature of the boundary condition employed for the microrotation vector $\underset{\sim}{\nu}$.

5. Concluding Remarks

In this paper we have proposed a method of solution of creeping flow equations in polar fluid theory and we have given two applications. Further applications of the method, in its direct or indirect form, have been considered by Niefer and Kaloni [23] and Kaloni [16,17]. It is clear that the method, though easily applicable to a certain class of problems, is less general than the method proposed by Brunn [3]. In comparison to the stream function method, we note that while in the present approach we easily determine velocities, pressure, etc. directly from the main solution, much work still needs to be done, in the stream function method in determining the above quantities, particularly the pressure. Furthermore, the stream function method is applicable to two-dimensional or axisymmetric problems only. It is also possible that the present method can be made applicable to quasi-steady creeping flow equations of a polar fluid when the time dependence is easily separable. Finally, we wish to emphasize that all solutions in polar fluid theory are strongly dependent upon the initial and boundary conditions. In finding the drag force on the sphere and the effective viscosity of the suspension, in the earlier sections, we have noted that these quantities not only depend upon the nature of the constitutive coefficients but also upon the parameter S. If the theory is viewed from the molecular approach then the boundary conditions could be altogether different. In both his papers, Brunn [3,4] elaborates these points and shows how the results change drastically by introducing slight changes in the boundary conditions.

Inspite of the many papers that have been written on polar fluid theory, it appears that the general appeal of the theory has been far less convincing than it was originally thought. One basic reason, for such a nonacceptance, is that we still have not been able to identify it, in a clear cut manner, with some real materials. While there are always some statements in the literature about the application of the theory to colloidal suspensions, liquid crystals, animal blood, etc., we have found no clear evidence of such proposals. It seems likely that more complicated and generalized forms of the theory are needed to describe real materials. On the other hand, recent papers by Leslie [18,19] put forth some hope in this direction. By considering linear constitutive equations, as in the polar fluid theory, but allowing them to be hemitropic and not isotropic, Leslie finds some surprising predictions. We, however, have to wait for a few more results before commenting further on these new forms of equations of Leslie [18].

Acknowledgement

The authors acknowledge the support from NSERC through Grant A7728.

Nomenclature

a	=	radius of undeformed sphere
a_{ij}	=	spatially constant second order tensor
A_{ijk}	=	spatially constant third order tensor
A_g^p, B_n^m, C_s^r	=	arbitrary constants
$d_1(x)$	=	e^x, $d_2(x) = e^{-x}$, $d_3(x) = (\frac{1}{x^2} - \frac{1}{x^3})$
$d_4(x)$	=	$(\frac{1}{x^2} + \frac{1}{x^3})$, $d_5(x) = (\frac{1}{x^3} - \frac{3}{x^4} + \frac{3}{x^4})$
$d_6(x)$	=	$(\frac{1}{x^3} + \frac{3}{x^4} + \frac{3}{x^5})$, $d_7(x) = (\frac{1}{x^4} - \frac{6}{x^5} + \frac{15}{x^6} - \frac{15}{x^7})$
$d_8(x)$	=	$(\frac{1}{x^4} + \frac{6}{x^5} + \frac{15}{x^6} + \frac{15}{x^7})$
(e), (i)	=	superscripts (e) and (i) denote the quantities exterior or interior to the fluid drop, respectively
f_i	=	body force per unit mass
I	=	micro inertia moment of the particle
$I_{p/a}$	=	modified Bessel function of first kind
ℓ_i	=	body couple per unit mass
L	=	combination of material constants defined by Equation (16)
m_{ij}	=	couple stress tensor
p	=	thermodynamic pressure
S	=	a constant parameter lying in [0,1]
t_{ij}	=	Cauchy stress tensor
u_i	=	a vector variable defined in Equation (21)
v_i	=	velocity vector
ω_i	=	vorticity vector
ε_{ijk}	=	alternating tensor
ρ	=	mass density
ν_i	=	micro-rotation vector
$\alpha,\beta,\gamma,\kappa,\mu$	=	viscosity coefficients
δ, η	=	combination of viscosity coefficients defined by Equation (16)
ψ	=	Lr, first appeared in Equation (40)
$\bar{\psi}$	=	scalar variable defined by Equation (13)

References

1. Aero, E.L., Bulygin, A.N. and Kuvshinskii, E.V., Prikl. Mat. Mekh., 29, 297-308 (1963).
2. Born, M., Z. Phys., 1, 221-249 (1920).
3. Brunn, P.O., Int. J. Engng. Sci., 20, 575-585 (1982).
4. Brunn, P., Rheol. Acta, 14, 1039-1054 (1975).
5. Condiff, D.W. and Dahler, J.S., Phys. Fluids, 7, 842-854 (1964).
6. Cosserat, E. and Cosserat, F., "Theorie des corps deformables", Hermann Paris (1909).
7. Cowin, S.C., Adv. Appl. Mech., 14, 279-347 (1974).
8. Dahler, J.S., J. Chem. Phys., 30, 1447-1475 (1959).
9. Einstein, A., Ann. Phys., 34, 591 (1911).
10. Eringen, A.C., Int. J. Eng. Sci., 2, 205-217 (1964).
11. Eringen, A.C. and Kafadar, C.B., Continuum Physics IV, 1-73 (1976).
12. Eringen, A.C., J. Math. Mech., 16, 1-18 (1966).
13. Grad, H., Commun. Pure Appl. Math., 5, 455-494 (1952).
14. Hadamard, J.S., Rev. Acad. Sci. (Paris), 152, 1735-1738 (1911).
15. Happel, J. and Brenner, H., Low Reynolds Number Hydrodynamics, Noordhoff, Leyden (1973).
16. Kaloni, P.N., Lett. Appl. Engng. Sci., 21, 1001-1008 (1983).
17. Kaloni, P.N., Int. J. Engng. Sci. (In Press) (1986).
18. Leslie, F.M., Arch. Rat. Mech. Anal., 70, 189-202 (1979).
19. Leslie, F.M., J. Non-Newtonian Fluid Mech., 14, 161-172 (1984).
20. Lorentz, H.A., Verlag Akad. Wet., Amsterdam, Vol. 5 (1887).
21. Niefer, R., "Boundary Value Problems in Continuum Mechanics", Dissertation, University of Windsor (1980).
22. Niefer, R. and Kaloni, P.N., J. Engng. Math., 14, 107-116 (1980).
23. Niefer, R. and Kaloni, P.N., Int. J. Engng. Sci, 19, 959-966 (1981).
24. Ramkisson, H. and Majumdar, S.R., Phys. Fluids, 19, 703-712 (1976).
25. Rybczynski, W., Bull. Acad. Sci., Cracoire (A), 40-46 (1911).
26. Taylor, G.I., Proc. Roy. Soc., London (A), 146, 501 (1934).

Author index

Subject index